On the Frontiers of the Indian Ocean World

This is the first interdisciplinary history of Lake Tanganyika and of eastern Africa's relationship with the wider Indian Ocean World during the nineteenth century. Philip Gooding deploys diverse source materials, including oral, climatological, anthropological, and archaeological sources, to ground interpretations of the better-known, European-authored archive in local epistemologies and understandings of the past. Gooding shows that Lake Tanganyika's shape, location, and distinctive lacustrine environment contributed to phenomena traditionally associated with the history of the wider Indian Ocean World being negotiated, contested, and reimagined in particularly robust ways. He adds novel contributions to African and Indian Ocean histories of urbanism, the environment, spirituality, kinship, commerce, consumption, material culture, bondage, slavery, Islam, and capitalism. African peoples and environments are positioned as central to the histories of global economies, religions, and cultures.

Philip Gooding is a postdoctoral fellow at the Indian Ocean World Centre, McGill University.

Cambridge Oceanic Histories

Edited by

David Armitage
Alison Bashford
Sujit Sivasundaram

Across the world, historians have taken an oceanic turn. New maritime histories offer fresh approaches to the study of global regions, and to long-distance and long-term connections. Cambridge Oceanic Histories includes studies across whole oceans (the Pacific, the Indian, the Atlantic) and particular seas (among them, the Mediterranean, the Caribbean, the North Sea, the Black Sea). The series is global in geography, ecumenical in historical method, and wide in temporal coverage, intended as a key repository for the most innovative transnational and world histories over the longue durée. It brings maritime history into productive conversation with other strands of historical research, including environmental history, legal history, intellectual history, labour history, cultural history, economic history and the history of science and technology. The editors invite studies that analyse the human and natural history of the world's oceans and seas from anywhere on the globe and from any and all historical periods.

On the Frontiers of the Indian Ocean World

Ocean World

A History of Lake Tanganyika, c.1830–1890

Philip Gooding

McGill University

CAMBRIDGE
UNIVERSITY PRESS

CAMBRIDGE
UNIVERSITY PRESS

University Printing House, Cambridge CB2 8BS, United Kingdom

One Liberty Plaza, 20th Floor, New York, NY 10006, USA

477 Williamstown Road, Port Melbourne, VIC 3207, Australia

314–321, 3rd Floor, Plot 3, Splendor Forum, Jasola District Centre, New Delhi – 110025, India

103 Penang Road, #05–06/07, Visioncrest Commercial, Singapore 238467

Cambridge University Press is part of the University of Cambridge.

It furthers the University's mission by disseminating knowledge in the pursuit of education, learning, and research at the highest international levels of excellence.

www.cambridge.org
Information on this title: www.cambridge.org/9781009100748
DOI: 10.1017/9781009122023

© Philip Gooding 2022

First published 2022

A catalogue record for this publication is available from the British Library.

Library of Congress Cataloging-in-Publication Data
Names: Gooding, Philip, 1988– author.
Title: On the frontiers of the Indian Ocean world: a history of Lake Tanganyika, 1830–1890 / Philip Gooding, McGill University, Montréal.
Other titles: Cambridge oceanic histories.
Description: Cambridge, United Kingdom ; New York, NY: Cambridge University Press, 2022. | Series: Cambridge oceanic histories | Includes bibliographical references and index.
Identifiers: LCCN 2022010295 (print) | LCCN 2022010296 (ebook) | ISBN 9781009100748 (hardback) | ISBN 9781009114189 (paperback) | ISBN 9781009122023 (epub)
Subjects: LCSH: Tanganyika, Lake–History–19th century. | Africa, Eastern–History–19th century. | Africa, Eastern–Commerce–History. | Indian Ocean Region–History–19th century. | Indian Ocean Region–Commerce–History.
Classification: LCC DT365.7 .G66 2022 (print) | LCC DT365.7 (ebook) | DDC 967.8/28–dc23/eng/20220407
LC record available at https://lccn.loc.gov/2022010295
LC ebook record available at https://lccn.loc.gov/2022010296

ISBN 978-1-009-10074-8 Hardback

For Émilie, Adèle, and Mathis. I love you all.

Contents

Figures

Acknowledgements

Monographs by first-time authors have a reputation for long acknowledgements sections, in which everybody but nobody who has had anything to do with the project is thanked. This section will hardly buck the trend (although I'll try not to go overboard), but before I get to thanking everybody, there are two other things I would like to acknowledge first.

The first of these is my privilege. As an able-bodied, white, cis-het male brought up in the UK and now living in Canada, I have benefited from several explicit and implicit institutional advantages. All these advantages have played a role in me writing this book. They have opened doors for me that would otherwise have remained closed, and they have provided me with research environments that have been geared to the success of people like me. I write at a time now, however, when the institutional imbalances that such privileges foster are being vociferously challenged. I strongly support these challenges. I hope that the environments that researchers work in can be reformed or revolutionised in ways that benefit the entire scholarly community, and to be an ally in making such changes come to fruition.

The second 'acknowledgement' to make is of my mental health and that of many of my peers. This project, at times, made me miserable, particularly when I was writing it up for my PhD. I often felt isolated; I felt guilty when I took breaks; my social life disappeared. I've often expressed to graduate students the importance of a life outside academia to get through a doctoral programme. If only I followed my own advice. Things did get better for me, especially after I relocated to Montreal. I also had strong familial support, especially from my wife. But I know that many graduate students and early career scholars don't have access to this kind of familial support, and most don't have the opportunities to migrate that I did. I thus hope that more robust institutional support, especially for graduate students, can be developed to make 'struggling' a lesser feature of research and writing in the future. The Covid crisis in the last two years has made the need for more support of this kind even more apparent.

Now to the thank yous: I will be forever thankful to the elders who I met and interviewed on the shores of Lake Tanganyika, who divulged their communities' histories to me, and who challenged me to rethink the ways in which I approached the documentary record. I hope I have done their accounts justice. Any and all shortcomings are my own, and I apologise for them in advance.

Two scholars in particular have had a major influence on this book, as is evident from its title. The 'frontier' stems directly from the work of my primary BA, MA, and PhD supervisor, Professor Richard Reid; the 'Indian Ocean World' stems from the work of my postdoctoral supervisor, Professor Gwyn Campbell. Thank you both for your inspiration and guidance over several years. To Richard – thank you for your patience and support, not least when I decided that I wanted to move away from London at a crucial stage in my doctoral programme. To Gwyn – thank you for welcoming me into the community at the Indian Ocean World Centre (IOWC) and for providing me with the space in which to continue my doctoral and postdoctoral studies.

There are, moreover, several scholars who have provided large and small pieces of advice and guidance throughout my academic career. To William Clarence-Smith, John Parker, Giacomo Macola, Peter Hynd, Geert Castryck, Stephen Rockel, Karin Pallaver, Hannah Whittaker, Ben Kirby, Zozan Pehlivan, Tyler Yank, Jonathan Walz, Andy Ivaska, and Alastair McClure – your contributions to this book have been diverse and changing over a long time. Please know that they are very appreciated. I regret that I have somewhat lost contact with some of you in recent years. Time and distance have been cruel. I hope we get to talk, meet, or even just email or tweet each other again soon.

Further thanks go to Fabrice Munezero and Hamisi Hababi. You were kinder and better research assistants in respectively Burundi and Tanzania than I can ever have reasonably hoped for when I met you. I hope we meet again. Additionally, thank you to Ivy Gathambo and Désiré Kathihabwa for your translation efforts and to several archivists for assisting my research: Fritz Stenger and François Richard at the White Fathers' archive in Rome; Mathilde Leduc-Grimaldi and Tom Morren at the Royal Museum for Central Africa in Tervuren; and everyone at the SOAS Special Collections, Zanzibar National Archives, and Royal Geographical Society.

There are several others I could list to thank for little tit-bits of information here and there – on research assistants, publishing, archives, and much more. Some are impossible to name, such as the two anonymous peer reviewers who offered wonderful insights on how to develop the manuscript into a book. But to attempt to name everyone I *could* name who has had some influence would almost inevitably result in leaving more than one of you out. So, in a clear cop-out, here is just a thank you to everyone else who I've had contact with over the last several years who has helped to turn this book into what it is. I hope you know who you are. Thank you.

Thanks also to the Wolfson Foundation for funding my PhD research, on which this book is based, and the Social Sciences and Humanities Research Council of Canada for funding my postdoctoral fellowship at the IOWC, during which I wrote it up. Thanks also to the editors of *Slavery and Abolition* and *The Journal of African History* for allowing me to revise and reprint articles in respectively Chapters 6 and 7 of this book. And special thanks to those who I have worked with at Cambridge University Press in the last months, principally Lucy Rhymer, Rachel Blaifeder, Emily Plater, Natasha Whelan, Niranjana Harikrishnan, and Michael Watson, as well as to Dan Harding for his copyediting efforts.

Finally, and most importantly – thank you to my family. Mum, Dad, Ruth, Mike, Granny, Grandma, Grandad and Grandad – thank you. And to Émilie, Adèle, and Mathis – this book is dedicated to you. I met you, Émilie, in the summer before I started my doctoral programme. You have barely known me while this project has not been dominating my work life. I made the following observation in the acknowledgements section of my PhD thesis, but it bears repeating: you often said that it was not just me doing this project, but both of us, given how it impacted our lives. This was, of course, very true throughout. Thank you for keeping me grounded; thank you for showing me the value of breaks; thank you for everything. And to Adèle and Mathis – you're a little young to read even this acknowledgements section right now. Maybe you'll give the whole book a try when you're older; maybe you won't. Either way, it doesn't matter – just know that your arrival in 2017 and 2019 was an integral part of the process that led to this book's creation.

Note on the Text

In line with recent trends in histories of the East African interior, this book drops Bantu language group prefixes from translated words. For example, it is now usual in academic writing to write 'the Nyamwezi' rather than 'the Wanyamwezi' for the people of Unyamwezi and 'the Ganda' rather than 'the Baganda' for the people of Buganda. This is because, in the latter translations, the Bantu-language prefix (Wa- or Ba-) repeats the article; that is, 'the Wanyamwezi' literally translates as 'the the Nyamwezi' and 'the Baganda' literally translates as 'the the Ganda'. For unknown reasons, however, it has not been customary in histories of the East African coast and islands to drop such prefixes from translations of Swahili words. Historians still refer to 'the *waungwana*' (literally: 'the the gentlemen') and 'the *washenzi*' ('the the barbarians'). Given the convoluted nature of such translations and the fact that this is a history of an interior region of East Africa, it is thought prudent to break with this pattern when using Swahili words. Thus, 'the *waungwana*' becomes 'the *ngwana*' and 'the *washenzi*' becomes 'the *shenzi*'.

Throughout the text, Lake Tanganyika is referred to as being 'in East Africa'. The author acknowledges that this is a somewhat problematic geographic representation. 'East Africa', as describing the region covered by the nation-states of Kenya, Tanzania, Uganda, Rwanda, and Burundi, as well as parts of the eastern Democratic of the Congo, is a colonial and post-colonial invention, and one of the aims of this book is to challenge such Eurocentric spatial frames. But 'East Africa' remains in some ways useful. Much of the book focuses on regions within the bounds of those aforementioned nation-states. 'East Africa' is also more geographically specific than 'eastern Africa', which can refer to regions as far south as the eastern Cape and as far north as Egypt, and is especially applicable to Ethiopia and the Horn. A more appropriate term might be 'equatorial eastern Africa', but this is unnecessarily long and hinders readability, especially when describing someone or something as 'equatorial eastern African'. Thus, despite their problems, in this book, 'East Africa' and 'East African' are used, although the reader is invited to substitute 'equatorial eastern Africa(n)' if it aids their understanding to do so.

Abbreviations

A.G.M.Afr	Archivio Generale dei Missionari d'Africa (General Archive of Missionaries of Africa)
AIA	Association Internationale Africaine (International African Association)
CMS	Church Missionary Society
CWM	Council for World Missions
DRC	Democratic Republic of the Congo
ENSO	El Niño Southern Oscillation
IOD	Indian Ocean Dipole
IOW	Indian Ocean World
LIA	Little Ice Age
LMS	London Missionary Society
NA RGS	National Archives held at the Royal Geographical Society
RMCA ESA	Royal Museum for Central Africa, Emile Storms Archive
RMCA HMSA	Royal Museum for Central Africa, Henry Morton Stanley Archive
ZNA	Zanzibar National Archives

Introduction
Lakes, Oceans, and Littorals in History

Mohammed bin Khalfan el-Barwani arrived on the shores of Lake Tanganyika sometime between the end of 1876 and early 1879. He was born in c.1855 in Lindi on the East African coast into a family with kinship ties to Oman. He was educated in Zanzibar, he was a member of the Qadiriyya Brotherhood, and he was soon to negotiate his entry into the most influential commercial network in nineteenth-century East Africa. This commercial network was funded by a Kachchhi firm, the most prominent representative of which in eastern Africa was a member of the Omani sultan of Zanzibar's court. As Mohammed's prominence grew on the shores of Lake Tanganyika, he earned the nickname Rumaliza, which translates as 'The Terminator' or 'The Finisher'.[1] His rise is synonymous with several well-known phenomena in nineteenth-century East African history, including increasing levels of militarism in politics; increasing influence of traders emanating from East Africa's coast and islands (coastal traders) over interior regions' affairs; and East Africa's Great Lakes region's integration with the world economy.[2] Yet, a deeper reflection on Rumaliza's commercial, religious, and kinship associations reveals a history with additional layers and contexts. Rumaliza's arrival on the shores of Lake Tanganyika at the end of the 1870s was part of a broader trend that began in the early part of the nineteenth century in which phenomena traditionally associated with littoral regions of the wider Indian Ocean World (IOW) entered East Africa's Great Lakes region for the first time.

---

[1] For a fuller version of Rumaliza's biography, see: B. G. Martin, 'Muslim politics and resistance to colonial rule: Shaykh Uways B. Muhammad Al-Barawi and the Qadiriya Brotherhood in East Africa', *The Journal of African History*, 10, 3 (1969), 471–86.
[2] Richard J. Reid, *War in Pre-colonial Eastern Africa: The patterns and meanings of state-level conflict in the nineteenth century* (Athens, OH: Ohio University Press, 2007), 112–13; Philip Gooding, 'History, politics, and culture in Central Tanzania', *Oxford Research Encyclopedia of African History* (2019), 7–9.

At the time of Rumaliza's arrival on Lake Tanganyika's shores, 'a great ... immigration' in the opposite direction was taking place.[3] This was a migration of populations referred to as 'Manyema', a heterogeneous body of people from the present-day eastern Democratic Republic of the Congo (DRC). It began sometime during the 1860s but had historical precedent in migrations that traversed Lake Tanganyika in a west–east direction in the deeper past.[4] Some nineteenth-century immigrant Manyema arrived as traders, but most were forced to migrate either in captivity or because their villages and fields had been destroyed by predatory raiders and elephant hunters.[5] As they arrived in what is now mainland Tanzania, many were ostracised for being *shenzi* (Swahili: barbarians, savages; sing. *mshenzi*; pl. *washenzi*), and they were frequently accused of being cannibals.[6] Some made a living through waged porterage; others did so through bondage to prominent traders, including Rumaliza.[7] Both these paths had the potential to enhance their status and to acquire them kinship, knowledge of Islam, and access to credit networks that stretched across the western IOW. As traders such as Rumaliza brought phenomena native to littoral regions of the IOW to East Africa's Great Lakes region, Manyema and other inland populations entered structures associated with the wider IOW from the opposite direction.

[3] Zanzibar National Archives (hereafter ZNA) AA2-29 Hore to Kirk, 25 Feb. 1880.

[4] Beverly Bolser-Brown, 'Ujiji: The history of a lakeside town, c.1800–1914' (unpublished PhD diss., Boston University, 1973), 36–7; Michele Wagner, 'Trade and commercial attitudes in Burundi before the nineteenth century', *International Journal of African Historical Studies*, 26, 1 (1993), 155; Shun'ya Hino, 'Neighbourhood groups in African urban society: Social relations and consciousness of Swahili people of Ujiji, a small town of Tanzania, East Africa', *Kyoto University African Studies*, 6 (1971), 2; Jan Vansina, 'Notes sur l'histoire du Burundi', *Aequatoria*, 24, 1 (1961), 4–5; Mgr. Lechaptois, *Aux rives du Tanganika: Étude ethnographique couronée par la Société de géographie de Paris* (Algiers: Missionaires d'Afrique, 1913), 29–30; Robert Schmitz and Cyrille van Overbergh, *Les Baholoholo* (Brussels: A. Dewit, 1912), 273.

[5] David Northrup, *Beyond the Bend in the River: African labor in eastern Zaire* (Athens, OH: Ohio University Center for African Studies, 1988), 27; Katharina Zöller, 'Crossing multiple borders: "The Manyema" in colonial East Central Africa', *History in Africa*, 46 (2019), 303; Sheryl McCurdy, 'Transforming associations: Fertility, therapy, and the Manyema diaspora in Urban Kigoma, Tanganyika, c.1850–1993' (unpublished PhD diss., Columbia University, 2000), 74–8.

[6] Reid, *War in Pre-colonial Eastern Africa*, 219; Jonathon Glassman, *Feasts and Riot: Revelry, rebellion, and popular consciousness on the Swahili coast, 1856–1888* (Portsmouth, NH: Heinemann, 1994), 2; McCurdy, 'Transforming associations', 59–78.

[7] Stephen J. Rockel, *Carriers of Culture: Labor on the road in nineteenth-century East Africa* (Portsmouth, NH: Heinemann, 2006), 18; Zöller, 'Crossing multiple borders', 306; Geert Castryck, 'Bordering the lake: Transcending spatial orders in Kigoma-Ujiji', *International Journal of African Historical Studies*, 52, 1 (2019), 119–20.

The IOW is defined here as a macro-region spanning eastern Africa, the Middle East and South, Southeast, and East Asia. The idea of the regions around the Indian Ocean comprising a distinct 'world' has grown in popularity since the 1980s, most notably in more recent years through the works of Michael Pearson and Gwyn Campbell. This work, inspired by that of Fernand Braudel on the 'Mediterranean world', argues that the regions around the IOW were bound by a 'deep structure', which has underpinned historical contexts, continuities, and changes over the *longue durée*.[8] For these IOW scholars, this 'deep structure' is the Indian Ocean monsoon system, which is the basis for agriculture and, until the coming of steam in the mid-nineteenth century, travel around the IOW. Thus, the productive bases and the physical lines of trade around the ocean were indelibly shaped by the monsoon system. Moreover, trade begat exchanges of cultures over time, and thus historians have also discussed cultural connections that pervade the IOW, such as through histories of Islam, urban cosmopolitanism, and patterns of bondage.[9] Lake Tanganyika lies towards the western edge of this system. The agricultural base in the regions around it is dependent on monsoon rains, and seasonal changes in the direction of wind affect sail-powered travel across it. The nineteenth century represents the first time that the physical lines of connection expressed in trade and culture reached there directly, too. This book is about how these physical lines of connection developed and the roles that littoral and inland populations around Lake Tanganyika had in shaping them.

The Ivory Trade in IOW and Global Contexts

The core historical development leading to the encounter between traders such as Rumaliza and populations such as the Manyema was the expansion of the global ivory trade. The ivory trade emanating from

---

[8] See, for example: Michael N. Pearson, *The Indian Ocean* (London: Routledge, 2003), 13–27; Gwyn Campbell, *Africa and the Indian Ocean World from Early Times to circa 1900* (Cambridge: Cambridge University Press, 2019), 1–21; Fernand Braudel, *The Mediterranean and the Mediterranean World in the Age of Philip II*, Vol. I, trans. Siân Reynolds (Berkeley: University of California Press, 1995). For summaries and critiques of this perspective, see: Sujit Sivasundaram, 'The Indian Ocean', in *Oceanic Histories*, eds. David Armitage, Alison Bashford, and Sujit Sivasundaram (Cambridge: Cambridge University Press, 2017), 46–54; Geert Castryck, 'Indian Ocean Worlds', in *The Routledge Handbook of Transregional Studies*, ed. Matthias Middel (New York: Routledge, 2019), 102–9.

[9] Edward A. Alpers, *The Indian Ocean in World History* (Oxford: Oxford University Press, 2014), 40–68; Prita Meier, *Swahili Port Cities: The architecture of elsewhere* (Bloomington: Indiana University Press, 2016), 1–25; Gwyn Campbell, ed. *Bondage and the Environment in the Indian Ocean World* (Cham: Palgrave Macmillan, 2018).

East Africa is an ancient one. The earliest known text that refers to equatorial regions, dated sometime around the middle of the first century CE, identified the region as an ivory exporter.[10] Even so, East Africa was probably peripheral to the oceanic ivory trading during these times, as carvers in South Asia, in the Middle East, and around the Mediterranean preferred the harder ivory of Asian elephants.[11] Demand for the softer East African ivory fluctuated thereafter, but consistent demand outside East Africa probably developed from the sixteenth century onwards, when bangles made out of the cross-section of an elephant's tusk became fashionable in marriage ceremonies among South Asian women.[12] The tusks of African elephants were preferred to those of Asian elephants for this purpose as, being generally larger, their cross sections could more reliably be carved into adequate bangles. By the nineteenth century, South Asians were carving East African ivory into a range of everyday objects, including toys, models, chess and draughts pieces, puppets, and boxes.[13] The economies of whole towns in present-day north-western India, most notably Surat, were built on the working of East African ivory.[14] Consequently, during the nineteenth century, Gujaratis and Kachchhis, mediated through business connections in Oman, Zanzibar, and mainland coastal East Africa, became the principal financiers of ivory caravans heading into East Africa's deep interior (see Figure I.1).

Nineteenth-century South Asians, though, were not merely responding to demand for East African ivory in India. Indeed, they were principally supplying demand in industrialising Europe and North America. The first American patent for an industrial ivory-working machine was signed in 1799. Several more followed – for the manufacture of piano keys, billiard balls, combs, and cutlery and cane handles, among other

[10] Lionel Casson, *The Periplus Maris Erythraei: Text with introduction, translation, and commentary* (Princeton: Princeton University Press, 2012), 61.

[11] Campbell, *Africa and the Indian Ocean World*, 62.

[12] Abdul Sheriff, *Slaves, Spices and Ivory in Zanzibar: Integration of an East African commercial empire into the world economy, 1770–1873* (Woodbridge: James Currey, 1987), 78; Pedro Machado, *Ocean of Trade: South Asian merchants, Africa and the Indian Ocean, 1750–1850* (Cambridge: Cambridge University Press, 2014), 170–1. For more on the links between India and East Africa in the 'early modern' period, see: Sanjay Subrahmanyam, 'Between eastern Africa and western India, 1500–1650: Slavery, commerce, and elite formation', *Comparative Studies in Society and History*, 61, 4 (2019), 805–34.

[13] R. W. Beachey, 'The East African ivory trade in the nineteenth century', *The Journal of African History*, 8, 2 (1967), 288; Martha Chaiklin, 'Ivory in world history: Early modern trade in context', *History Compass*, 8, 6 (2010), 530–42.

[14] Martha Chaiklin, 'Surat and Bombay: Ivory and commercial networks in western India', in *The Dutch and English East India Companies: Diplomacy, trade and violence in early modern Asia*, eds. Adam Clulow and Tristan Mostert (Amsterdam: Amsterdam University Press, 2018), 101–24.

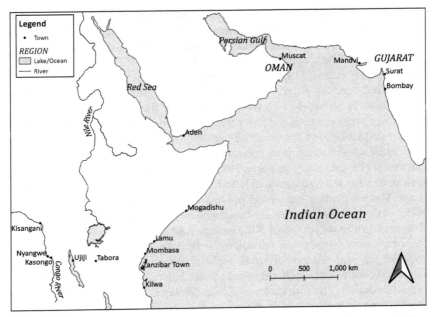

Figure I.1 Map of the major ivory trading centres in the western Indian Ocean World. Drawn by the author.

products. Just as in north-western India, whole towns emerged that were dependent on ivory working, most notably Ivoryton, Connecticut and others in New England.[15] Again, the softer, larger East African ivory was demanded more than South Asian ivory in this context. It was less liable to splitting during the industrial process, and larger tusks were especially needed for the manufacture of billiard balls, which were cut from the tusks' core. Growing demand in the industrialising West inflated the price of East African ivory on the world market. Its value in Zanzibar increased by a factor of around 4.5 between 1820 and 1870.[16] Representatives of American firms attempted to take control of the trade from Zanzibar, but Gujarati and Kachchhi businessmen and their Omani

---

[15] John Frederick Walker, *Ivory's Ghosts: The white gold of history and the fate of elephants* (New York: Atlantic Monthly Press, 2009), 85–6; Alexandra Celia Kelly, *Consuming Ivory: Mercantile legacies of East Africa and New England* (Seattle: University of Washington Press, 2021), 58–66.

[16] Sheriff, *Slaves, Spices and Ivory*, 88.

political allies largely thwarted them.[17] The British, meanwhile, found it more efficient for most of the nineteenth century to buy the majority of their East African ivory from colonial centres in India, especially Bombay (Mumbai).[18] They sought to harness and shape IOW networks rather than replace them. Thus, the growing global capitalist economy of the nineteenth century entered the interior of East Africa through the mediation of IOW networks and not directly from the North Atlantic.

The growing value of the ivory trade enabled South Asian firms to fund ever more ambitious commercial expeditions into the East African interior. They were aided in this context by the Omani sultan, who moved his capital to Zanzibar in the early 1830s (Zanzibar and Oman had distinct sultanates from 1856 onwards). Subsequently, Omani and other coastal East African traders expanded pre-existing caravan routes heading from the coast into the interior. A 'northern route' departing Mombasa and Pangani in the direction of Kilimanjaro and thence to the Serengeti was an important ivory route throughout the nineteenth century, though it was largely the reserve of small-scale trading parties.[19] Additionally, a southern route departed the coast from Kilwa and surrounding towns and headed in the direction of Lake Malawi. Kilwa's long history of maritime connections with the wider IOW may have contributed to the prominence of this route in the early nineteenth century. However, the proportion of ivory being shipped to Zanzibar from Kilwa decreased markedly as the century wore on, and its key export from the deep interior later became people for enslavement.[20] Instead, the 'core' commercial routes that exported ivory came to be those that departed the coast at Saadani, Mbwamaji, and especially Bagamoyo.[21] Having departed from these towns, Omani and other coastal East African traders established themselves in towns across mainland East Africa, including around Lake Tanganyika. The most prominent towns in the wider region were Tabora (where coastal traders settled in c.1850), Rubaga (Buganda, in present-day Kampala; c.1855), Ujiji (c.1860), Nyangwe (c.1865), Kasongo (c.1865), and Kisangani (known to Europeans at the time as

---

[17] Chhaya Goswami, *The Call of the Sea: Kachchhi traders in Muscat and Zanzibar, c.1800–1880* (New Delhi: Orient Blackswan, 2011).

[18] Sheriff, *Slaves, Spices and Ivory*, 85–6; Thomas Metcalf, *Imperial Connections: India in the Indian Ocean arena, 1860–1920* (Berkeley: University of California Press, 2007), 166–8.

[19] Sheriff, *Slaves, Spices and Ivory*, 174; Jonathan Walz, 'Route to a regional past: An archaeology of the lower Pangani (Ruvu) Basin, Tanzania, 500–1900 C.E.' (unpublished PhD diss., University of Florida, 2010), 48–50.

[20] Sheriff, *Slaves, Spices and Ivory*, 158–64.

[21] Sheriff, *Slaves, Spices and Ivory*, 174–83. Mbwamaji is often forgotten in this context. See: Stephen J. Rockel, 'Forgotten caravan towns in 19th century Tanzania: Mbwamaji and Mpwapwa', *Azania: Archaeological Research in Africa*, 41, 1 (2006), 1–25.

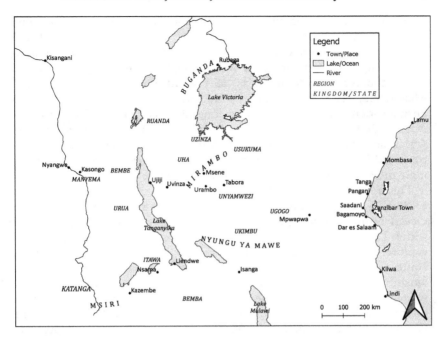

Figure I.2 Map of the major East African commercial centres and regions in the nineteenth century. Drawn by the author.

Stanley Falls; c.1885) – the last of these being on the northern bend of the Congo River, over 2,000 kilometres from the East African coast (see Figure I.2).

The expansion of the global ivory trade brought many inland East Africans into direct and sustained contact with trans-IOW commercial networks and the broader world economy for the first time. Many among them became crucial to how the ivory trade functioned. For much of the nineteenth century, traders who came to be known as 'Nyamwezi', from present-day west-central Tanzania, were the principal traders bringing ivory to the East African coast and islands.[22] They and other inland East Africans were also the principal porters, elephant hunters, and suppliers

---

[22] Andrew Roberts, 'Nyamwezi trade', in *Pre-Colonial African Trade: Essays on trade in central and eastern Africa before 1900*, eds. Richard Gray and David Birmingham (Oxford: Oxford University Press, 1970), 49–50; Sheriff, *Slaves, Spices and Ivory*, 175; Rockel, *Carriers of Culture*, 35; Ralph A. Austen, 'Patterns of development in nineteenth-century East Africa', in *African Historical Studies*, 4, 3 (1971), 647; Karin Pallaver, 'New modes of production, urbanization and the development of Islam in nineteenth-century

of provisions to passing caravans throughout the century. Additionally, the ivory trade acted as a stimulant for a 'revolution' in political and military affairs.[23] New states emerged under the leadership of Mirambo and Nyungu ya Mawe, both of whom sought to militarily control and direct the ivory trade in parts of present-day western Tanzania.[24] Meanwhile, older states, such as Buganda, reformed themselves and became increasingly interested in long-distance trade.[25] In short, the ivory trade became a key feature of political and economic life in East Africa and connected inland East Africans to broader structures that traversed the western IOW, which themselves were becoming increasingly integrated with the growing global capitalist economy.

This represents the context for this history of Lake Tanganyika in c.1830–90. This book is an investigation of how people from the Indian Ocean littoral and East Africa's deep interior encountered each other within Lake Tanganyika's distinctive lacustrine environment. It seeks to explore the answers to several questions: how did Rumaliza and his contemporaries, with their Islamic beliefs, their urban cultures, and their kinship and commercial connections across maritime regions of the western IOW, perceive the people they encountered in the East African interior? At the same time, how did inland East Africans from around the Great Lakes region, such as the Manyema, who were primarily rural and had local belief systems and networks, perceive the new arrivals from the Indian Ocean littoral? Moreover, how did the encounters between these ostensibly distinct peoples affect their respective belief systems, commercial networks, material cultures, and institutions? The Lake Tanganyika case study and the IOW context add additional layers to these questions: how did the lacustrine environment affect encounters between diverse populations in East Africa's interior? And how did nineteenth-century encounters in East Africa's deep interior affect structures whose origins lay in littoral regions of the IOW? What emerges from these discussions is

Tanzania', in *Themes in Modern African History and Culture*, eds. Lars Berge and Irma Taddia (Padova: Libreria Universitaria, 2013), 34, 36.

[23] Richard J. Reid, *Warfare in African History* (Cambridge: Cambridge University Press, 2012), ch. 5; Andrew Roberts, 'Political change in the nineteenth century', in *A History of Tanzania*, eds. I. N. Kimambo and A. J. Temu (Nairobi: East African Publishing House, 1969); Steven Feierman, *The Shambaa Kingdom: A history* (Madison: University of Wisconsin Press, 1974), 171.

[24] Norman R. Bennett, *Mirambo of Tanzania 1840?–1884* (New York: Oxford University Press, 1971); Aylward Shorter, 'Nyungu-ya-Mawe and the "Empire of the Ruga-Rugas"', *The Journal of African History*, 9, 2 (1968), 235–59; Michelle R. Moyd, *Violent Intermediaries: African soldiers, conquest, and everyday colonialism in German East Africa* (Athens, OH: Ohio University Press, 2014), 73–82.

[25] Richard J. Reid, 'The Ganda on Lake Victoria: A nineteenth-century East African imperialism', *The Journal of African History*, 39, 3 (1998), 349–63.

a history of cultural exchange and interaction, processes which were particularly robust within Lake Tanganyika's distinct environmental context. Cultural forms emanating from the wider IOW and East Africa's Great Lakes region took on new forms and influences as peoples from these regions encountered each other in large numbers for the first time. As will be seen, this had significant consequences for the history of the wider IOW.

Lake Tanganyika as 'Meeting Place'

Lake Tanganyika lies almost at the centre of the African continent, about 1,000 kilometres west of the Indian Ocean at its closest point. It is Africa's deepest and most voluminous lake, and it is second in the world in both categories only to Lake Baikal in Russia. Early nineteenth-century populations living on its western and eastern shores looking north and south viewed it as 'endless', in the manner of someone looking over an ocean.[26] However, despite its size and oceanic connotations, it has received little historical attention, at least compared to Lakes Victoria and Malawi, and especially compared to surrounding terrestrial zones.[27] In this sense, Lake Tanganyika has yet to be 'written into' history.[28] This belies its importance during the nineteenth century as a distinctive environmental and commercial zone that linked the furthest reaches of ivory trading networks.[29] Nineteenth-century Europeans, meanwhile, saw Lake Tanganyika as so important that they considered it a potential

---

[26] Allen F. Roberts, 'Heroic beasts and beastly heroes: Principals of cosmology and chiefship among the lakeside Batabwa of Zaire' (unpublished PhD diss., University of Chicago, 1981), 89.

[27] For histories related to Lakes Victoria and Malawi, see, for example: Richard J. Reid, *Political Power in Pre-colonial Buganda: Economy, society and warfare in the nineteenth century* (Oxford: James Currey, 2002), 227–48; Edward A. Alpers, 'Trade, state, and society among the Yao in the nineteenth century', *The Journal of African History*, 10, 3 (1969), 405–20.

[28] The idea of 'writing in' a geographical feature into a broader history is explored in: Debjani Bhattacharyya, *Empire and Ecology in the Bengal Delta: The making of Calcutta* (Cambridge: Cambridge University Press, 2018), 3. Oceanic scholars may regard historical writing on the East African Great Lakes as 'terracentric'. See: Sujit Sivasundaram, Alison Bashford, and David Armitage, 'Introduction: Writing world oceanic histories', in *Oceanic Histories*, eds. Armitage, Bashford, and Sivasundaram, 4; Rila Mukherjee, 'Escape from terracentrism: Writing a water history', *Indian Historical Review*, 41 (2014), 87–101.

[29] Beverly Bolser-Brown, 'Muslim influence on trade and politics in the Lake Tanganyika region', *African Historical Studies*, 4, 3 (1971), 617–29; Brown, 'Ujiji'; Allen F. Roberts, *A Dance of Assassins: Performing early colonial hegemony in the Congo* (Bloomington: Indiana University Press, 2013); McCurdy, 'Transforming associations'; Castryck, 'Bordering the lake', 109–32.

source of the Nile – a Victorian-era obsession. One such 'explorer', Richard Burton, who arrived at the lake in 1858, translated the word, 'Tanganyika', as 'meeting-place'.[30] While the accuracy of this translation is dubious, it encapsulates much about Lake Tanganyika's nineteenth-century history and its connections with the wider IOW.[31] The lacustrine environment, Lake Tanganyika's distinctive shape, and its position in relation to ivory networks attracted traders, caravan workers, refugees, and religious entrepreneurs to the lakeshore, where they encountered an established mix of farmers, fishermen, and other traders. Thus, the lakeshore was a 'meeting place' for a wide variety of actors.

The idea of Lake Tanganyika as a 'meeting place' builds on broader understandings of large lakes, seas, and oceans in history. A significant contribution in this context comes from Fernand Braudel, his peers in the 'second generation' of the *Annales* movement, and several scholars of Mediterranean history who have been inspired by their perspectives.[32] Braudel argued that people living in coastal regions experienced different 'rhythms' of life to those inhabiting terrestrial regions.[33] In J. R. McNeill's terms, the shoreline environment represents an 'ecological niche' that has provoked distinct forms of individual and cultural adaptation.[34] Thus, while the sea may divide terrestrial zones, its shoreline links its peoples, expressed in shared cultures and in physical lines of connection made through commerce and kinship.[35] Nevertheless, such zones have also been noted for their diversity. They have rarely been governed by one ruler (Ancient Rome's hold over much of the Mediterranean is largely an aberration) and they have experienced a range of different influences from their hinterlands. Port towns have often been observed as the locations in which such influences meet. They have attracted people to facilitate others' crossings to opposite

---

[30] Richard F. Burton, *The Lake Regions of Central Africa: A picture of exploration* (New York: Harper & Brothers, 1860), 367.

[31] For more analysis of the meaning of 'Tanganyika', see: Roberts, 'Heroic beasts', 132.

[32] See, for example: Braudel, *The Mediterranean*; Peter Burke, *The French Historical Revolution: the Annales school*, 2nd ed. (Cambridge: Polity, 2014), 36–72; J. R. McNeill, *The Mountains of the Mediterranean World: An environmental history* (Cambridge: Cambridge University Press, 1992); Peregrine Horden and Nicholas Purcell, *The Corrupting Sea: A study in Mediterranean History* (Oxford: Oxford University Press, 2000).

[33] Braudel, *The Mediterranean*, I, 14.   [34] McNeill, *Mountains of the Mediterranean*, 3.

[35] Horden and Purcell, *The Corrupting Sea*; Christopher Gratien, 'The mountains are ours: Ecology and settlement in late Ottoman and early republican Cilicia, 1856–1956' (unpublished PhD diss., Georgetown University, 2015), 5–6. For examples from the IOW, see: Michael N. Pearson, 'Littoral society: The concept and the problems', *Journal of World History*, 17, 4 (2006), 353–73; Michael N. Pearson, 'Littoral society: The case for the coast', *The Great Circle*, 8, 1 (1985), 1–8.

shores, which has given rise to market centres and sites of cultural exchange.[36] Understandings of littoral spaces have thus often attempted to balance emphasis on 'diversity' and 'connectivity'.[37] Regardless, histories of the regions around large bodies of water stress the distinctive ways of life that littoral populations have contributed to.[38] They are the 'meeting places' of a range of influences.

There is significant evidence for Lake Tanganyika's place in these broader oceanic histories over the *longue durée*. As far as is known, no singular political power has ever established sovereign governance over all of Lake Tanganyika's shores. Presently, it is divided between four nation states – Burundi, Tanzania, Zambia, and the DRC – and in the nineteenth century, it was loosely divided between 10–15 interconnected 'peoples' (see Figure I.3).[39] Some of these peoples, such as the Rundi, Jiji, and Fipa, had dynastic chiefs based in the lake's surrounds. Some also had political and cultural links to broader structures in East Africa's terrestrial zones: the south-western and north-western shores were respectively tied to broader Luba and Bembe complexes from the mid to late eighteenth century, and much of the eastern shore was affected firstly by Ngoni raiders from the south in the 1840s to 1850s, and then also by the presence of Mirambo in the 1870s to 1880s.[40] However, neither the dynastic chiefs nor these complexes claimed jurisdiction beyond the shoreline closest to them, and almost all everyday matters on the lakeshore were presided over by village or district chiefs, whose territorial bases rarely stretched beyond a few square kilometres. The peoples of these villages and districts had their own ways of life and traditions of origin, and some of the latter traversed the lake. Rundi, Jiji, and Bende chiefs on the lake's eastern shore trace their origin to migrants from the lake's western shore, for example – in contrast to the traditions of origin of peoples living just a few kilometres inland, who

---

[36] Horden and Purcell, *The Corrupting Sea*, 89–122.

[37] Horden and Purcell, *The Corrupting Sea*, 22–5, 123–72.

[38] Johannes Preiser-Kapeller, 'Liquid frontiers: A relational analysis of maritime Asia Minor as a religious contact zone in the thirteenth-fifteenth centuries', in *Islam and Christianity in Medieval Anatolia*, eds. A. C. S. Peacock, Bruno de Nicola, and Sara Nur Yildiz (Burlington: Ashgate, 2015), 117; Braudel, *The Mediterranean*, I, 222.

[39] Edward C. Hore, 'On the twelve tribes of Tanganyika', *Proceedings of the Anthropological Institute of Great Britain and Ireland*, 12 (1883), 2–21.

[40] Thomas Q. Reefe, *Rainbow and the Kings: A history of the Luba Empire to 1891* (Berkeley: University of California Press, 1981); Reuben A. Loffman, *Church, State, and Colonialism in Southeastern Congo, 1890–1962* (Cham: Palgrave Macmillan, 2019), 37; Reid, *War in Pre-colonial Eastern Africa*, 117; Thomas T. Spear, *Zwangendaba's Ngoni 1821–1890: A political and social history of a migration* (Madison: African Studies Program, University of Wisconsin, 1972), 1–43.

Figure I.3 Map of major centres, missionary stations, nature spirits, and regions surrounding Lake Tanganyika in the nineteenth century. Drawn by the author.

trace their heritage to the north.[41] Lake Tanganyika divided East Africa's larger polities, states, and complexes while also linking its littoral peoples.

Certain aspects of the lakeshore's environment probably contributed to it becoming a particularly prominent 'meeting place' for lakeshore and other populations. The lake is surrounded by mountains, except around its south-eastern shores, which are plains. This mountainous environment represents a wall around the lake's shoreline that, to a certain degree, has discouraged direct outside interference in the lakeshore's affairs.[42] On most of the western shore, the mountains descend directly into the lake. The steepness of the terrain and the rockiness of the soil in these regions has hindered the establishment of large population centres, except in a few isolated locales, such as around the Lukuga and Lufuko Rivers, and at present-day Uvira and Baraka. Given the nature of the physical environment around them, it has been natural for people in these locations to look around and across the lake for regional interaction, rather than towards mountainous, terrestrial zones.[43] Lake Tanganyika's eastern littoral, meanwhile, is known for its fertility, both on land and in the lake itself. North-eastern parts of the lake are particularly notable fishing regions – the small whitebait-like *dagaa* are synonymous with the region.[44] This part of the lakeshore is also unusual for the Great Lakes in that palm trees grow wild there. These features allowed lakeshore populations in this region to develop somewhat distinct productive bases.[45] They also attracted inland traders to the region,

---

[41] Brown, 'Ujiji', 36–7; Wagner, 'Trade and commercial attitudes', 155; Hino, 'Neighbourhood groups', 2; Vansina, 'Notes sur l'histoire', 4–5; Lechaptois, *Aux rives du Tanganyika*, 29–30; Schmitz and Overbergh, *Les Baholoholo*, 273; Archivio Generale dei Missionari d'Africa (hereafter: A.G.M.Afr.) C.16-7. Journal du P. Deniaud, 21 Feb. 1880; Interview with Daniel Rucintingo, 7 Nov. 2013; Interview with Rashidi Hamisi bin Kasa, 12 Nov. 2013; Interview with Hamisi Feuse Kabwe Katanga, 14 Nov. 2013; Interview with Zuberi Shabani Aburula, 12 Nov. 2013; Interview with Branbati Ali Kiola and Isa Pama Kiola, 12 Nov. 2013; Interview with Selimani Kadudu Musa, 13 Nov. 2013; Interview with Musa Isa Rubinga, 14 Nov. 2013.

[42] For a further reflection on the role of mountains around maritime space, see: McNeill, *Mountains of the Mediterranean*, 12–14.

[43] Horden and Purcell, *The Corrupting Sea*, 123–72.

[44] Brown, 'Ujiji', 41; McCurdy, 'Transforming associations', 70, 76.

[45] David S. Newbury, *Land beyond the Mists: Essays on identity and authority in precolonial Congo and Rwanda* (Athens, OH: Ohio University Press, 2009), 287; Jean-Pierre Chrétien, *L'Afrique des grands lacs: Deux milles ans d'histoire* (Paris: Flammarion, 2000), 188. Similar patterns are observable from evidence of iron-working around Lake Tanganyika's south-eastern shores. See: Bertram B. B. Mapunda, 'Fipa iron technologies and the implied social history', in *East African Archaeology: Foragers, potters, smiths, and traders*, eds. Chapurukha M. Kusimba and Sibel B. Kusimba (Philadelphia: University of Pennsylvania Press, 2010), 74–8.

who sought fish and palm oil in exchange for iron goods and salt.[46] The lake and its mountainous surrounds promoted lake-focused ways of living for littoral populations, limited the extent of outside interference, and attracted regional traders.

The direction and conduct of the nineteenth-century global ivory trade enhanced the scope and intensity of interaction around and across Lake Tanganyika's shores. Coastal traders started visiting Ujiji's lakeshore region in c.1830. Up to c.1860, most did so in 'flying caravans' that returned to Tabora in Unyamwezi once traders had finished their business in lakeshore markets, although a small few among them crossed the lake and headed into the eastern Congo rainforests.[47] Until the mid-nineteenth century, therefore, the lake was somewhat a barrier to sustained commercial expansion from the Indian Ocean littoral. No doubt, Lake Tanganyika's north–south trajectory versus the coastal traders' east–west direction of travel contributed to this feature. However, once news reached regions further east that the Manyema region had abundant, cheap, and high-quality ivory, coastal traders reimagined Lake Tanganyika's role in their commercial networks.[48] It became increasingly urgent that they traverse the lake, which only spans eighty-two kilometres at its widest point and is significantly thinner than that at all of the frequently used nineteenth-century crossings. This necessitated coastal traders' use and development of boating infrastructure to cross the lake, as well as the growth of market-oriented port towns that were capable of housing, feeding, and organising caravans for onward travel. These port towns attracted a range of peoples – traders, workers, and refugees to name a few. They became the 'meeting places' for peoples and influences from the lakeshore, the eastern Congo rainforests, other parts of the Great Lakes region, and East Africa's Indian Ocean littoral.

The influence of peoples from the Indian Ocean littoral on the shores of Lake Tanganyika represents an encounter between two water-facing, oceanic cultures. The history of the IOW since the first millennium BCE has been intimately linked with maritime commercial and cultural exchange.[49] Port towns as cosmopolitan centres and 'meeting places'

---

[46] J. E. G. Sutton and Andrew Roberts, 'Uvinza and its salt industry', *Azania: Archaeological Research in Africa*, 3, 1 (1968), 45–86; Jean-Pierre Chrétien, 'Le commerce du sel de l'Uvinza an XIXe siècle: De la cueillette au monopole capitaliste', *Revue française d'histoire d'outre-mers*, 65, 240 (1978), 401–22; Roberts, 'Nyamwezi trade', 44–5; Newbury, *Land beyond the Mists*, 307.

[47] Burton, *Lake Regions*, 316.   [48] Sheriff, *Slaves, Spices and Ivory*, 172–90.

[49] See, for example: K. N. Chaudhuri, *Trade and Civilisation in the Indian Ocean: An economic history from the rise of Islam to 1750* (Cambridge: Cambridge University Press, 1985); Janet L. Abu-Lughod, *Before European Hegemony: The world system A.D. 1250–1350* (Oxford: Oxford University Press, 1989); Gwyn Campbell (ed.), *Early*

have been a central feature of this history.[50] Although sometimes over-looked by IOW historians, East Africa was an integrated part of the IOW's networks since antiquity, most notably via Rhapta – a town that was probably located on the coast of present-day south-eastern Tanzania.[51] However, before the nineteenth century, few, if any, people who originated in littoral regions of the IOW entered East Africa's deep interior. Inhabitants of the coast instead relied on interior populations to supply them with various goods, including ivory, for resale into the wider IOW economy. In this context, conditions in the interior have often been construed as incompatible with coastal populations' maritime-facing sensibilities.[52] However, shared themes and landscapes between the histories of Lake Tanganyika and the IOW over the *longue durée* show that historical trajectories of coast and interior were far from dichotomous. Meanwhile, increased levels of migration to, from, and across Lake Tanganyika and East Africa's Indian Ocean littoral region during the nineteenth century served to enhance the physical connections between the lakeshore and the wider IOW.

Locating the IOW in Lake Tanganyika's Nineteenth-Century History

This book proposes the 'frontier' to conceptualise Lake Tanganyika's position within the wider IOW. Referring to the idea of the frontier necessarily invokes the classic works of Frederick Jackson Turner, Dietrich Gerhard, and Igor Kopytoff, who respectively wrote on frontiers in American, comparative, and African history.[53] The intention is not to

---

Exchange between Africa and the Wider Indian Ocean World (Cham: Palgrave Macmillan, 2016).

[50] These ports have often been referred to as 'emporia'. See: Chapter 1; Chaudhuri, *Trade and Civilisation*, 99–100; Pearson, *Indian Ocean*, 31; Alpers, *The Indian Ocean*, 48; Stephanie Wynne-Jones and Adria LaViolette (eds.), *The Swahili World* (London: Routledge, 2017), 133–81.

[51] Carl Hughes and Ruben Post, 'A GIS Approach to finding the metropolis of Rhapta', in *Early Exchange*, ed. Campbell, 135–55; Casson, *Periplus*, 61.

[52] For a recent critique of this perspective, see: Chapurukha M. Kusimba and Jonathan R. Walz, 'When did the Swahili become maritime? A reply to Fleisher et al. (2015), and to the resurgence of maritime myopia in the archaeology of the East African coast', *American Anthropologist*, 120, 3 (2018), 429–43. This builds on archaeological work referring to the deeper past that construes the East African interior as integral to understandings of the coast. See, for example: Felix Chami, 'Graeco-Roman trade link and the Bantu migration theory', *Anthropos*, 94 (1999), 205–15.

[53] Frederick Jackson Turner, 'The significance of the frontier in American history', *Report of the American Historical Society* (1893), 199–227; Dietrich Gerhard, 'The frontier in comparative view', *Comparative Studies in Society and History*, 1, 3 (1959), 205–29; Igor Kopytoff, 'The internal African frontier: The making of an African political culture', in

redefine what 'the frontier' means here; rather, it is to build on some of the key themes and perspectives associated with the term, as discussed by such scholars. Socio-political instability, economic opportunity, and heightened levels of cultural exchange pervade understandings of frontiers, and they pervade this book.[54] The prominence of these themes may partly be explained by the role of frontiers in history. Just like many large bodies of water, they have performed the function of 'meeting places'. In the aforementioned classic texts, the frontier represented the line of furthest migration of pioneers entering what was for them *terra incognita*. With few exceptions, such migrants have rarely entered 'virgin' ground, and instead have encountered pre-existing settlers, often provoking competition, violence, and/or interaction. Yet, given this role as 'meeting place', it may hardly be surprising that some frontiers have been seen to be 'fixed' around certain ecological features, such as large bodies of water. Ralph W. Brauer referred to 'sea frontiers' in the history of medieval Islam, and Johannes Preiser-Kapella referred to the 'liquid frontiers' of maritime medieval Anatolia.[55] These maritime regions were the edges of empires and cultural contact zones. The concept of the frontier emphasises the robustness of the encounters on Lake Tanganyika's shores during the nineteenth century.

This is not the first time that the idea of the frontier has been applied to East African history. Kopytoff's work on the 'African frontier' was probably more inspired by eastern and southern Africa than it was western and northern, for example.[56] Also, older analyses of East Africa's nineteenth-century history featured analysis of the 'ivory frontier' – the westward movement of ivory traders from the coast, who depopulated the regions they inhabited of elephants.[57] This has recently been

---

The African Frontier: The reproduction of traditional African societies, ed. Igor Kopytoff (Bloomington: Indiana University Press, 1987), 3–87.

[54] For case studies on frontiers in other regions in which such themes have been prevalent, see, for example: Alan V. Murray (ed.), *The Clash of Cultures on the Medieval Baltic Frontier* (Farnham: Ashgate, 2009); Muzaffar Alam and Sanjay Subrahmanyam, 'The Deccan frontier and Mughal expansion, ca.1600: Contemporary perspectives', *Journal of the Economic and Social History of the Orient,* 47, 3 (2004), 357–89; A. C. S. Peacock (ed.), *The Frontiers of the Ottoman World* (Oxford: Oxford University Press, 2009); Richard J. Reid, *Frontiers of Violence in North-East Africa: Genealogies of conflict since c.1800* (Oxford: Oxford University Press, 2011), 9–23.

[55] Ralph W. Brauer, 'Boundaries and frontiers in medieval Muslim geography', *Transactions of the American Philosophical Society,* 86, 6 (1995), 36; Preiser-Kapeller, 'Liquid frontiers', 117–46.

[56] James McDougall, 'Frontiers, borderlands and Saharan/World history', in *Saharan Frontiers: Space and mobility in northwest Africa,* eds. James McDougall and Judith Scheele (Bloomington: Indian University Press, 2012), 73–90.

[57] Beachey, 'The East African ivory trade', 269–90; Sheriff, *Slaves, Spices and Ivory,* 183–90.

challenged through analysis that shows that elephants were hunted in the deep interior for the purposes of ivory trading since before the arrival of coastal traders, and that elephants continued to inhabit the regions east of coastal trader settlements throughout the nineteenth century.[58] The 'frontier' referred to here, then, is not an 'ivory frontier'. More recently, Fahad Ahmad Bishara used the term 'frontier' to describe the movement of Omani traders during the nineteenth century to 'Zanzibar' – 'a metonym for the islands and ports of East Africa' – and then inland laden with north-west Indian credit.[59] In this sense, he conceived East Africa in its entirety as a frontier zone for Omani and Indian business interests. Absent from Bishara's discussion, though, are the African peoples and subregions that Omanis encountered as they entered this zone. In the classic works on frontiers, such peoples would have been integral to the analysis; the conception of 'sea' and 'liquid' frontiers, meanwhile, suggests that encounters would have been particularly robust on the shores of large lakes such as Lake Tanganyika. Closer engagement with the idea of the 'frontier' necessitates inserting African peoples and landscapes into the histories of Omani traders and Indian credit in the western IOW.

The concept of the frontier also suggests a geographical edge. This may be linked to the French definition of *frontière*, which also translates as 'border', a term usually used in African studies to describe the boundaries of colonial and post-colonial states. Extrapolating this definition to nineteenth-century East Africa is somewhat problematic given the often fluid nature of geographical boundaries in pre-colonial eras. However, it is still arguable that Lake Tanganyika and the Great Lakes more broadly were on the western geographical edge of the IOW. In environmental terms, the Great Lakes region is near the intersection of the Indian Ocean and Atlantic climatic systems. Additionally, for most of the nineteenth century, it represents the western limit of coastal trader expansion. Even present-day Kisangani on the northern bend of the Congo River, the coastal traders' westernmost settlement established during the 1880s, has significant environmental ties to the Indian Ocean as, up to this point, the Congo River is fed by many tributaries whose water comes via the Indian Ocean monsoon system. This pattern stops with the joining of the Lomani River, about 130 kilometres to Kisangani's west,

---

[58] Bernhard Gissibl, *The Nature of German Imperialism: Conservation and the politics of wildlife in colonial East Africa* (New York: Berghahn Books, 2016), 36–40; Ashley N. Coutu, Julia Lee-Thorp, Matthew J. Collins, and Paul J. Lane, 'Mapping the elephants of the 19th century East African ivory trade with a multi-isotope approach', *PLoS ONE*, 11, 10 (2016), 1–23.

[59] Fahad Ahmad Bishara, *A Sea of Debt: Law and economic life in the western Indian Ocean, 1780–1950* (Cambridge: Cambridge University Press, 2017), 33, 39.

which is fed primarily by an Atlantic system. Heterogeneous Manyema populations, meanwhile, who originated in the space between Lake Tanganyika and present-day Kisangani, became prominent migrant populations across what is now Tanzania, including its coastal and island regions.[60] Thus, both environmental and human factors point to East Africa's Great Lakes region as a western frontier of the IOW.

Invoking the frontier here builds on recent East Africanist historical scholarship on translocalism. Pioneered largely by German and German-based scholars who mostly focus on the twentieth century, translocalism depicts fluid territorialities and cultural connections across ostensible boundaries.[61] Thus, people inhabiting one locality might have a cultural affinity and connection to another apparently distinct locality. In this context, Julia Verne argued that certain people born or descended from East Africa's Indian Ocean littoral who now inhabit Sumbawanga in present-day south-western Tanzania 'feel a connection to the Indian Ocean and try their best to intensify it'.[62] In this way, she argued that aspects of East Africa's Indian Ocean littoral pervade understandings of 'being' in the deeper interior, and in so doing, she asked where the ends of the Indian Ocean are actually located.[63] Given the above analysis, it is reasonable to suggest that they extend well into the Great Lakes region and as far as the eastern Congo rainforests, at least since the nineteenth century.[64] Speaking more broadly, Ulrike Freitag and Achim von Oppen

---

[60] Zöller, 'Crossing multiple borders', 299–326; Castryck, 'Bordering the lake', 119–20; McCurdy, 'Transforming associations', 59–78.

[61] Achim Von Oppen, 'The making and unmaking of boundaries in the Islamic world: Introduction', *Die Welt des Islams*, New Series, 41, 3 (2001), 284–5; Geert Castryck, 'Living Islam in colonial Bujumbura: The historical translocality of Muslim life between East and Central Africa', *History in Africa*, 46 (2019), 263–98; Geert Castryck, Achim Von Oppen, and Katharina Zöller, 'Introduction: Bridging histories of East and Central Africa', *History in Africa*, 46 (2019), 1–22; Ulrike Freitag and Achim Von Oppen (eds.), *Translocality: The study of globalising processes from a southern perspective* (Leiden: Brill, 2010); Julia Verne, 'The ends of the Indian Ocean: Tracing coastlines in the Tanzanian "hinterland"', *History in Africa*, 46 (2019), 359–83; Zöller, 'Crossing multiple borders', 299–326; Julia Verne, *Living Translocality: Space, culture and economy in contemporary Swahili trade* (Stuttgart: Franz Steiner Verlag, 2012); Stephen J. Rockel, 'From shore to shore: People, places, and objects between the Swahili coast and Lake Tanganyika', in *World on the Horizon: Swahili arts across the Indian Ocean*, eds. Prita Meier and Allyson Purpura (Champaign, IL: Krannert Art Museum and Kinkead Pavilion, 2018), 71–88.

[62] Verne, 'The ends of the Indian Ocean', 373.

[63] Verne, 'The ends of the Indian Ocean', 369–73.

[64] See also: Armand Abel, *Les Musulmans Noirs du Maniema* (Brussels: Publications du centre pour l'étude des problèmes du monde musulman contemporain, 1960); S. Bimangu and Tshishiku Tshibangu, 'Contribution à l'histoire de l'implantation de l'islam au Zaïre', *Paideuma*, 24 (1978), 225–30; Jean-Pierre Chrétien, *L'Invention de l'Afrique des grands lacs: Une histoire du XXᵉ siècle* (Paris: Karthala, 2010).

argue that 'frontiers … often provide privileged spaces for the manifest-ation of translocality'.[65] Frontiers are often sites of mobility, migration, and cultural encounters, which can lead to the creation of communities, cultures, and ideas that transcend ostensible boundaries, à la the German school of 'translocality'.[66] Such ties were particularly strong on the shores of Lake Tanganyika. The combination of high levels of migration to, from, and across the lake, the lacustrine environment as a 'meeting place', and the growth of cosmopolitan port towns encouraged the development of translocal ties from the lakeshore to other regions in East Africa, including to the Indian Ocean littoral.

Analysing the history of Lake Tanganyika as a frontier of the IOW has several repercussions for East Africanist and IOW scholarship. First, it breaks with trends that analyse littoral and interior regions of East Africa separately. The reasons that underpin this historiographical division are numerous, and some of them validly remain in place.[67] One cannot explore a nineteenth-century history of Sufi scholars in the interior as on the littoral, for example, and likewise, the history of state-level vio-lence during the same period is the reserve of the interior.[68] However, there are uncomfortable colonial roots to the division that need to be addressed. Owing to partly perceptions of its more 'advanced' architec-ture, Victorian-era Europeans saw the East African coast as an 'Arab' civilisation, while the interior was distinctly 'African' and thus also (in their eyes) inferior.[69] While historians have done much to obliviate this heavily racialised thinking from current discourse, the ongoing division between histories of the coast and interior can nevertheless be seen partly as a colonial legacy.[70] Thus, archaeologists such as Chapurukha Kusimba and Jonathan Walz have recently railed against a recent

[65] Ulrike Freitag and Achim Von Oppen, 'Introduction: "Translocality" – an approach to connection and transfer in area studies', in *Translocality*, eds. Freitag and Von Oppen, 10.

[66] Freitag and Von Oppen, 'Introduction', 1–21; McDougall, 'Frontiers, borderlands', 73–90.

[67] See: Felicitas Becker and Joel Cabrita, 'Introduction: Performing citizenship and enacting exclusion on Africa's Indian Ocean littoral', *The Journal of African History*, 55, 2 (2014), 161–71; Abdul Sheriff, 'The Swahili in the African and Indian Ocean worlds to c.1500', *Oxford Research Encyclopedia of African History* (2017), 1–32.

[68] Anne K. Bang, *Islamic Sufi Networks in the western Indian Ocean (c. 1880–1940): Ripples of reform* (Leiden: Brill, 2014); Reid, *War in Pre-colonial Eastern Africa*.

[69] For a summary deconstruction of this dated paradigm, see, for example: Graham Connah, *African Civilizations: An archaeological perspective*, 3rd ed. (Cambridge: Cambridge University Press, 2015), 234–6.

[70] See also: Michelle Decker, 'The "autobiography" of Tippu Tip', *Interventions*, 17, 5 (2015), 746–7.

resurgence of what they call 'maritime myopia' in coastal archaeology.[71] They argue that current archaeologists should show a deeper appreciation of connections over terrestrial spaces to understand the coast's past, contrary to colonial paradigms and against recent archaeological trends that have increasingly looked towards the ocean.[72] This book argues likewise for the nineteenth century. Oceanic histories should consider inland connections more deeply, while inland histories should have a deeper appreciation for maritime influences.

Second, inserting the IOW into the history of the East African interior necessitates analysis of themes that are frequently overlooked in the latter region's historiography. Most histories of nineteenth-century East Africa were written during the 1960s and 1970s. These works have, perhaps unfairly, been labelled as 'nationalist writing', a term that stresses the influence of mid-twentieth-century nationalist movements on how historians of that era thought about the pre-colonial past. Although many of these texts remain vital, it is arguable that much of what was written had understanding trends in Africa's newly independent nation states in mind.[73] This often meant a preoccupation with politics and economics, at the expense of social and cultural histories. Indeed, the former themes remain prevalent in several more recent works on 'pre-colonial' East Africa.[74] Lake Tanganyika's absence from most of these histories may partly be attributed to it not fitting within these themes: unlike around other Great Lakes, trends towards centralisation and statehood did not emerge on Lake Tanganyika's shores during the nineteenth century. However, an IOW perspective necessitates incorporating more social and cultural elements. Islam, urbanism, bondage, human–environment interaction, and cultural associations with *riziculture* are all prominent features of IOW histories, but they have yet to receive their due attention

---

[71] Kusimba and Walz, 'When did the Swahili become maritime?', 429–43. For context in support of their argument, see, for example: Jonathan Walz, 'Inland connectivity in ancient Tanzania', *Islamic Africa*, 8 (2017), 217–17; Jonathan Walz, 'Routes to history: Archaeology and being articulate in eastern Africa', in *The Death of Prehistory*, eds. Peter R. Schmidt and Stephen A. Mrozowski (Oxford: Oxford University Press, 2013), 69–91; Walz, 'Route to a regional past', 345–9.

[72] Jeffrey Fleisher, Paul Lane, Adria LaViolet, Mark Horton, Edward Pollard, Eréndira Quintana Morales, Thomas Vernet, Annalisa Christie, and Stephanie Wynne-Jones, 'When did the Swahili become maritime?', *American Anthropologist*, 117, 1 (2015), 100–15.

[73] Gooding, 'History, politics, and culture', 19–20.

[74] Scholarship on Buganda since c.2000 is particularly notable in this context. See, for example: Reid, *Political Power*; Holly Elisabeth Hanson, *Landed Obligation: The practice of power in Buganda* (Portsmouth, NH: Heinemann, 2003); Henri Médard, *Le royaume du Buganda au XIXᵉ siècle: Mutations politiques et religieuses d'un ancien état d'Afrique de l'est* (Paris: Karthala, 2007).

in Great Lakes East Africanist circles.[75] Limited exceptions in this context include Stephen Rockel's work on labour culture among Nyamwezi porters, as well as various studies on slave trades, slavery, and urbanism.[76] Yet, despite their thematic cogency with some features of wider IOW history, as Rockel recently pointed out, East Africanists have yet to fully investigate the ways in which interior East African and wider IOW trajectories might be related.[77] The IOW perspective inserts overlooked themes and wider perspectives into understandings of East Africa's history.

Finally, inserting the interior of East Africa into the history of the wider IOW builds on recent works on IOW history that have gone beyond analysis of littoral regions. Histories of littoral regions still dominate conceptions of the IOW, but some IOW scholars have also been drawn further inland. This may partly be attributed to recent interest in 'human–environment interaction', which stresses the importance of climatic and environmental factors in human history. In the IOW, this has led to studies that define the macro-region as the area whose agricultural regimes are dependent on rains brought via the Indian Ocean monsoon system, rather than limiting themselves to those who were engaged in maritime trade using the monsoon winds.[78] The region directly affected by monsoon rains stretches as far as, for example, northern China and Egypt, the latter of which's agricultural regime is dependent on rain falling in highland Ethiopia, which feeds the annual Nile floods. Building on this, scholars have also begun to explore how such regions have also interacted with other prevailing themes in IOW history, namely commercial and cultural exchange. Core regions of the Mongol and

---

[75] Chaudhuri, *Trade and Civilisation*; Abu-Lughod, *Before European Hegemony*; Kenneth McPherson, *The Indian Ocean: A history of people and the sea* (New York: Oxford University Press, 1993); Pearson, *The Indian Ocean*; Abdul Sheriff, *Dhow Cultures of the Indian Ocean: Cosmopolitanism, commerce, and Islam* (London: Hurst, 2010); Alpers, *The Indian Ocean*. For cultural associations of rice and *riziculture*, see, for example: Sarah C. Walshaw, 'Converting to rice: Urbanization, Islamization and crops of Pemba Island, Tanzania, AD 700–1500', *World Archaeology*, 42, 1 (2010), 137–54.

[76] Rockel, *Carriers of Culture*; Henri Médard and Shane Doyle (eds.), *Slavery in the Great Lakes Region of East Africa* (Oxford: James Currey, 2006); Jan-Georg Deutsch, *Emancipation without Abolition in German East Africa, c.1884–1914* (Athens, OH: Ohio University Press, 2006); Henri Médard, Marie-Laure Derat, Thomas Vernet, and Marie-Pierre Ballarin (eds.), *Traites et esclavages en Afrique orientale et dans l'Ocean Indien* (Paris: Karthala, 2013); Andrew Burton, 'Urbanisation in Eastern Africa: An historical overview, c.1750–2000', *Azania: Archaeological Research in Africa*, 36–7, 1 (2001), 1–28.

[77] Rockel, 'From shore to shore', 71–88.

[78] Indian Ocean World Centre, 'Appraising risk, past and present: Interrogating historical data to enhance understanding of environmental crises in the Indian Ocean World': www.appraisingrisk.com/about-us-2/ (accessed 10 June 2020).

Mughal empires have recently been analysed in terms of their relationship to the wider IOW in these terms.[79] Interestingly, Pius Malekandathil identified riverine areas in interior South Asia as important sites of cultural production associated with monetary flows from the IOW, thus further suggesting the importance of water-facing areas for linking littoral and inland regions of the IOW.[80] The absence of comparable studies for nineteenth-century East Africa, a time during which links between the deep interior and the IOW littoral were particularly intense, is in part the raison d'être for this book.

Moreover, centring a history of the IOW on an interior region builds on 'Braudelian' perspectives of space. Braudel most famously wrote a history of the Mediterranean world in the context of the *longue durée* that stressed the importance of the environment.[81] His perspectives have influenced much about IOW history since the 1980s, leading most IOW historians to privilege maritime connections across the Indian Ocean over analysis of connections between inland and littoral regions (notwithstanding the aforementioned recent additions to IOW historiography).[82] The focus on littoral regions and maritime connections, however, represents only one reading of Braudel's core arguments. This is because Braudel did not start his seminal text with the Mediterranean coast. Rather, he began with an analysis of mountains, plateaux, hills, foothills, and plains.[83] He asked rhetorically, 'how can one ignore these conspicuous actors, the half-wind mountains, where man has taken root like a hardy plant?'[84] Moreover, he stressed the importance of 'pressures', 'rhythms', and 'influences' from more distant regions – the Sahara, the Atlantic and northern Europe – on Mediterranean history.[85] These surrounding hinterlands were crucial to his conception of the Mediterranean world, and they provided the context for his more well-known discussions of the coastline 'core' of the region. In a similar vein, this book takes the position that inland regions of the wider IOW were an

---

[79] Pius Malekandathil (ed.), *The Indian Ocean in the Making of Early Modern India* (London: Routledge, 2017); Morris Rossabi, 'Mongol Empire and its impact on Chinese porcelains', in *Early Global Interconnectivity across the Indian Ocean World*, Vol. II, *Exchange of Ideas, Religions, and Technologies*, ed. Angela Schottenhammer (Cham: Palgrave Macmillan, 2019), 251–9.

[80] Pius Malekandathil, 'Introduction', in *The Indian Ocean*, ed. Malekandathil, 23–4. Recent work on Islam in the IOW is similarly notable for identifying this trend. See: Sugata Bose and Ayesha Jalal (eds.), *Oceanic Islam: Muslim universalism and European imperialism* (New Delhi: Bloomsbury, 2020).

[81] Braudel, *The Mediterranean*, I.

[82] See, for example: Pearson, *The Indian Ocean*, 4–12.

[83] For the Mediterranean, this approach has been built upon most significantly in: McNeill, *Mountains of the Mediterranean*.

[84] Braudel, *The Mediterranean*, I, 29.   [85] Braudel, *The Mediterranean*, I, 177, 222, 225.

integral feature of its history. In East Africa, these inland regions grew in importance during the nineteenth century, as travel between the Indian Ocean littoral and the Great Lakes became commonplace. Like Braudel's impressions of the mountains in Mediterranean history, East Africa's Great Lakes cannot be 'ignored' in understandings of the IOW. Moreover, if coastlines and littoral regions represent the IOW's 'core' in a Braudelian sense, then inland regions can be conceived as these regions' frontiers.

Sources and Methods

This book draws primarily on European-authored sources written during the nineteenth century, which are supplemented mostly by my own oral sources. The documentary material includes texts written by 'explorers', such as Richard Burton and Henry Morton Stanley, and archival materials from the London Missionary Society (LMS), the White Fathers (Les Pères Blancs), and the International African Association (Association Internationale Africaine, AIA), who inhabited lakeshore regions from the late 1870s (the AIA departed in 1885). These sources are moreover supplemented by materials in the UK National Archives held at the Royal Geographical Society, the Zanzibar National Archives (ZNA), and the Church Missionary Society Archives. Thus, the source material for this book resembles more closely the histories of 'pre-colonial' East Africa that were written in the 1960s and 1970s than that recently used by, for example, Fahad Ahmad Bishara and Thomas F. McDow for the history of the western IOW. Bishara and McDow based their studies on legal documents written in Arabic, which are housed at the ZNA and in Oman.[86] Rather than trying to replicate Bishara's and McDow's methodological approaches, this book seeks to use the more widely known material from 'explorer' publications and missionary archives to answer questions that emerge from analysing their works. Their core contributions have been to chart networks of credit, debt, kinship, and mobility across the western Indian Ocean and into the East African interior. While pioneering, their works now necessitate rereading the better-known archives to examine how Africans encountered, interacted with, and affected these networks. The Arabic sources do not refer to these themes and historians have yet to pick up this thread. Up to now, the trend has been to see East Africans' histories of the period as somewhat distinct from, in conflict with, or enslaved by those emanating from the Indian Ocean

---

[86] Bishara, *A Sea of Debt*, 19–23; Thomas F. McDow, *Buying Time: Debt and mobility in the western Indian Ocean* (Athens, OH: Ohio University Press, 2018), 41–5.

littoral.[87] Closer analysis of the better-known source material shows these perspectives to be unsatisfactory.

Rereading the archive to make ostensibly 'new' pre-colonial East African histories is not an entirely original pursuit. Rockel's seminal text on Nyamwezi *pagazi* (Swahili: porters; sing. *mpagazi*; pl: *wapagazi*) was built on the same idea. He contested 'along the grain' readings of the sources that regarded Nyamwezi *pagazi* as slaves, and argued that such notions were partially attributable to nineteenth-century Europeans not understanding the systems of labour they encountered, as well as their preconceived interest in stopping a 'slave trade'.[88] In so doing, he convincingly argued for the existence of a pervasive labour culture among Nyamwezi and other porters, while also displaying on full view the problematic nature of the source material. Of course, many of the problems of nineteenth-century European-authored sources written in Africa are well known. The extent to which they reflect more the values of nineteenth-century Europe than the peoples and cultures the authors wrote about is an ongoing debate, even if it is now generally accepted that they usually reflect more the encounter between the two than one or the other.[89] Even so, for a variety of reasons, they are often especially limited for providing details for histories with a distinctly cultural focus. It has been argued that the sources are 'simply not available' for histories of pre-colonial Africa 'from below', making them 'extremely difficult, if not impossible'.[90] With this difficulty acknowledged (though the

---

[87] From an Africanist perspective, this trend may be seen to have begun with Roberts' edited volume, *Tanzania before 1900* (Andrew Roberts (ed.), *Tanzania before 1900* (Nairobi: East African Publishing House, 1968)). In the introduction, Roberts wrote: 'When the idea of compiling a book such as this was first suggested, someone observed that it would "strike a blow against the long tyranny of the coast"' (p. 5). While this was more a throwaway comment than a point of analysis, this immediately set the history of the interior up as in opposition to the history of the coast, which had up to that point received significantly more attention. For similarly themed work, see: Norman R. Bennett, *Arab versus European: Diplomacy and war in nineteenth-century East Central Africa* (New York: Africana Pub. Co., 1986); Bennett, *Mirambo of Tanzania*. The centrality of slavery to the relationship between coastal and interior populations has been perpetuated by recent work focusing on the western IOW. See, for example: Bishara, *A Sea of Debt*, 75–8.

[88] Rockel, *Carriers of Culture*, 3–33; Ann Laura Stoler, *Along the Archival Grain: Epistemic anxieties and colonial common sense* (Princeton: Princeton University Press, 2009). See also: Karin Pallaver, 'Nyamwezi participation in nineteenth-century East African long-distance trade: Some evidence from missionary sources', *Africa: Rivista trimestrale di studi e documentazione dell'Istituto italiana per l'Africa e l'Oriente*, 6, 3 (2006), 513–31.

[89] T. C. McCaskie, 'Cultural encounters: Britain and Africa in the nineteenth century', in *The Oxford History of the British Empire*, Vol. III, *The Nineteenth Century*, ed. Andrew Porter (Oxford: Oxford University Press, 1999), 665–90.

[90] Richard J. Reid, 'Past and presentism: The "precolonial" and the foreshortening of African history', *The Journal of African History*, 52, 2 (2011), 137.

impossibility contested), it is perhaps appropriate to state at the outset that often the source material for this book is more suggestive than definitive, even if it is the opinion of this author that the extracts referred to are invariably significant. Rockel's pioneering scholarship has already shown this to be the case with similarly themed work.

Cultural interaction is particularly difficult to pick out of the archive because nineteenth-century Europeans were predisposed to condemn any that took place. They saw Africans, especially those from the interior, as distinctly 'tribal', and thus classifiable into homogenous groups.[91] They frequently referred in insulting terms to those who they saw as contravening these heavily racialised assumptions by adopting and adapting ostensibly 'foreign' cultural phenomena.[92] By contrast, they regarded some Muslims on the coast, who they usually referred to as Arabs, as somewhat 'respectable' and thus not intrinsically 'tribal'. This was in line with the broader European discourse of that era that regarded Muslims as 'semi-civilised' – as occupying a space between the 'civilised' European and the 'tribal' African. Thus, encounters between 'semi-civilised Muslims' and 'tribal Africans' in the interior of East Africa were particularly galling to nineteenth-century Europeans. They saw them as demeaning to coastal Muslims and based on mimicry from the perspective of interior Africans. They reserved special resentment for the 'Swahili', who were usually of African, coastal origin, and who Victorian-era Europeans frequently referred to as 'half-caste' – a heavily racialised term implying impurity. Such prejudices were also contradictory. They sometimes referred people they described as slaves as *ngwana*, a term usually used to describe respected, freeborn Muslims (Swahili: sing. *muungwana*; pl. *waungwana*). These contradictions leave open questions of agency, social status, labour conditions, and kinship relations – themes that are analysed in more depth later in this book. Nevertheless, these blurred distinctions in the archive make sure interpretations hard to come by.

Oral sources help considerably in tearing Victorian-era European prejudices away from discussions about cultural exchanges. In 2013, I conducted twenty-seven semi-structured interviews with elders over a three-month period along the eastern shore of Lake Tanganyika, from Bujumbura in the north to Mpulungu in the south. Those made in Burundi were conducted in a mixture of Kirundi, French, and English; those in Tanzania were conducted in a mixture of Swahili and English.

---

[91] V. Y. Mudimbe, *The Invention of Africa: Gnosis, philosophy, and the order of knowledge* (Bloomington: Indiana University Press, 1988), 1–23.
[92] See especially Chapters 6 and 7.

All were conducted with the help of local research assistants, most notably Fabrice Munezero in Burundi and Hamisi Ali Juma al-Hey (who everyone knows as Hababi) in Kigoma, Ujiji, and their environs. Direct quotations from oral sources in the following paragraphs and chapters are direct translations of elders' responses made by native Kirundi and Swahili speakers who listened to the recordings. Questions were prepared in advance. They covered most of the key themes of nineteenth-century Great Lakes historiography, such as migration, commerce, lacustrine travel, warfare, slavery, and political change. However, they were also kept broad, in an attempt to not restrict informants' own understandings of the past.[93] The resultant answers thus went in a variety of directions, leading to follow-up questions on a range of subjects. Frequently, informants expanded on themes that have received little historical analysis in the Great Lakes context, but which are prominent in understandings of the western IOW. These included Islam, kinship connections to peoples in the wider IOW, and contestations over the extent and meaning of slavery and slave trading. Informants' ideas on these topics 'illuminated' the archive in new ways, allowing for more locally grounded interpretations therein.[94]

Many of the challenges and opportunities of using oral sources in African history are well known. Phrases and meanings that may have been lost in translation and across cultures must be accounted for, as does the nature of the encounter between the interviewer and interviewee.[95] My outsider status almost certainly limited what some informants were willing to discuss. Additionally, interviewees often began by asking me questions – about my age, marital status, and whether I had children. The fact that I married before my oral research probably increased the amount that interviewees were willing to tell me; the fact that I did not yet have children was probably taken as a sign of my youth, and probably did the opposite. Nevertheless, the histories as relayed to

---

[93] This is inspired by methodologies of 'life histories'. See: Jamie Monson, '*Maisha:* Life history and the history of livelihood along the TAZARA railway in Tanzania', in *Sources and Methods in African History: Spoken, written, unearthed*, eds. Toyin Falola and Christian Jennings (Rochester, NY: University of Rochester Press, 2003), 312–30.

[94] Corinna M. Peniston-Bird, 'Oral history: The sound of memory', in *History Beyond the Text: A student's guide to approaching alternative sources*, eds. Sarah Barber and Corinna M. Peniston-Bird (Abingdon: Routledge, 2009), 107; John Tosh and Sean Lang, *The Pursuit of History: Aims, methods and new directions in the study of modern history*, 4th ed. (Edinburgh: Pearson Education, 2006), 316.

[95] Susan K. Burton, 'Issues on cross-cultural interviewing: Japanese women in England', in *The Oral History Reader*, 2nd ed., eds. Robert Perks and Alistair Thomson (Abingdon: Routledge, 2006), 166–74; Francis Good, 'Voice, ear, and text: Words, meaning, and transcription', in *The Oral History Reader*, eds. Perks and Thomson, 362–3.

me by my informants, especially in Ujiji, Bujumbura, and south-western Burundi, are integral to this book, particularly in later chapters. Ujiji and its environs have what might be regarded as its own bottom-up intellectual history, such as described in Steven Feierman's *Peasant Intellectuals*, which contests prevailing historical narratives about its community.[96] This is related to the prominent centres of Islamic education in town, frustration with Tanzania's central government, and opposition to the town's history as displayed in the Livingstone Memorial Museum. The latter is a prominent tourist attraction near to Ujiji's lakeshore. Among other things, the exhibits stress the importance of the slave trade in Ujiji's nineteenth-century history – a history of brutality that Ujiji's intellectual history contests.[97] Oral histories in Burundi, meanwhile, were indelibly shaped by collective memories of the period before ethnic conflict and of the time before the European arrival. In both locations, current and recent circumstances strengthened local impressions of the deeper past.

The importance of current and recent circumstances to the oral histories referred to means that a problem of 'presentism' is necessarily encountered. It is somewhat difficult to gauge the extent to which my oral materials tell accurate descriptions of the past, or if they were relayed to me in ways that helped interviewees to understand the present.[98] This problem is all the starker in Ujiji, where admitting to a past in slavery could bring into question the current town's Islamic character. It is arguable that informants' denial of aspects of slave history as told in most interpretations of the archive are similar to denials of similar phenomena in other regions, where the history of slavery has been minimised to not bring shame or disrepute on the community.[99] However, as is explored in greater depth in Chapters 6 and 7, informants did not deny the extent

[96] Stephen Feierman, *Peasant Intellectuals: Anthropology and history in Tanzania* (Madison: University of Wisconsin Press, 1990); Jonathon L. Earle, 'African intellectual history and historiography', *Oxford Research Encyclopedia of African History* (2018), 1–34.

[97] See especially Chapters 6 and 7.

[98] Eric Hobsbawm and Terence Ranger (eds.), *The Invention of Tradition* (New York: Cambridge University Press, 2012); Terence Ranger, 'The invention of tradition revisited: The case of colonial Africa', in *Legitimacy and the State in Twentieth-Century Africa: Essays in honour of A.H.M. Kirk-Greene*, eds. Terence Ranger and Olufemi Vaughan (Oxford: St Antony's/Macmillan Series, 1993), 62–111; Wyatt MacGaffey, 'Changing representations in Central African history', *The Journal of African History*, 46, 2 (2005), 189–207.

[99] See, for example: Andrew F. Clark, 'The challenges of cross-cultural oral history: Collecting and presenting Pulaar traditions on slavery from Bundu, Senegambia (West Africa)', *The Oral History Review*, 20, 1–2 (1992), 4; Sandra L. Richards, 'What is to be remembered? Tourism to Ghana's slave castle-dungeons', *Theatre Journal*, 57, 4 (2005), 629–30; Bayo Holsey, 'Slavery tourism: Representing a difficult history in Ghana', in *The Oxford Handbook of Public History*, eds. Paula Hamilton and James B. Gardner (Oxford: Oxford University Press, 2017), 483–4.

of slave trading or slavery in ways that are irreconcilable with the archive. Rather, they did so in ways that are cogent with themes in recent studies of bondage and Islam in the IOW. Such histories discuss the multiplicity of the bonded experience, the variety of Islamic contexts that such experiences took place in, and the heterodox nature of Islamic practice in frontier regions.[100] Moreover, as the remainder of this book elucidates, hints towards these kinds of histories exist in the archive, even if they are yet to be explored. With this in mind, the point here is not to disregard the archive in light of oral evidence; it is to state that the oral record allows for interpretations of the archive to be recontextualised with local perspectives at the core.

Finally, parts of this book are also informed by sources that are neither archival nor oral in nature. Anthropological sources are prominent in a chapter on lacustrine cosmologies (Chapter 3), and archaeological sources feature in chapters on urbanism (Chapter 1) and material culture (Chapter 5). In the case of Chapter 5, these sources add to existing understandings of material exchanges between Indian Ocean littoral and interior populations, as described most notably by Pedro Machado and Jeremy Prestholdt through the use of archival sources.[101] Additionally, climatological sources are central to Chapter 2, which focuses on the theme of human–environment interaction. These kinds of sources have grown significantly in number and quality since the 1990s.[102] This may partly be explained by increasing concern with the present and future effects of global warming. Using historical climatological data and understanding the effects of long- and short-term climatic fluctuations in the past is seen by some as integral to combatting and mitigating the effects of the current climate crisis.[103] For historians, this means that climatologists have provided the materials to give their readings of the archive a deeper appreciation of their climatic and environmental contexts. These have the capacity to further understandings of,

---

[100] See, for example: Gwyn Campbell, 'Introduction: Slavery and other forms of unfree labour in the Indian Ocean world', *Slavery and Abolition*, 24, 2 (2003), ix–xxxi; William G. Clarence-Smith, *Islam and the Abolition of Slavery* (London: C. Hurst & Co., 1988); Sebastian Prange, *Monsoon Islam: Trade and faith on the medieval Malabar Coast* (New York: Cambridge University Press, 2018), 1–24.

[101] Machado, *Ocean of Trade*, 120–67; Jeremy Prestholdt, *Domesticating the World: African consumerism and the genealogies of globalization* (Berkeley: University of California Press, 2008). See also: William G. Clarence-Smith, 'The textile industry in eastern Africa', in *Africa's Development in Historical Perspective*, eds. Emmanuel Kwaku Akyeampong, Robert H. Bates, Nathan Nunn, and James A. Robinson (New York: Cambridge University Press, 2014), 264–94.

[102] Sharon E. Nicholson, 'Climatology: Methods', *Oxford Research Encyclopedia of African History* (2017), 1–38.

[103] Indian Ocean World Centre, 'Appraising Risk'.

for example, the transmission of disease, migration, and political instability, all of which have been linked in different ways to climatic fluctuations.[104] Crucially, in East Africa's Great Lakes region, climatic fluctuations are primarily associated with phenomena that are intrinsically tied to the Indian Ocean monsoon system.[105] Thus, a deeper appreciation of climatic and environmental factors in the history of the Great Lakes necessitates a deeper appreciation of the region's connections to the wider IOW.

Structure

The following chapters are divided into two parts. Part I, entitled, 'Demarcations of Space', comprises Chapters 1 through 3. It details changes to Lake Tanganyika's environment during the nineteenth century, as well as changes to how people perceived and understood that environment. Chapter 1 explores the emergence of port towns on Lake Tanganyika's shores. It uses archival and archaeological sources to situate this history within the broader contexts of 'emporia' and architectural change on East Africa's Indian Ocean littoral and the wider IOW over the *longue durée*. Chapter 2 examines changing land use in rural areas around Lake Tanganyika's emporia. It uses climatological sources to contextualise how changes to the principal crops grown affected yields, and thus also food abundance/scarcity and competition for resources at different times. This history runs in parallel to histories of agricultural and economic production in the wider IOW that are intrinsically tied to fluctuations in the Indian Ocean monsoon system. Chapter 3 examines human encounters with the lake itself, detailing how the lake was integral to daily life. How the lake was perceived, moreover, was shaped by fluctuations in its level and to cultural encounters between Great Lakes and Indian Ocean littoral populations. In sum, this section examines how human- and climate-inspired changes to the lakeshore environment affected how peoples of different regional and cultural backgrounds encountered each other at different times.

Part II, comprising four chapters, is called 'Interactions'. It focuses on the themes through which people encountered each other on the lakeshore, starting with, in Chapter 4, interactions among coastal traders.

---

[104] Nicholson, 'Climatology: Methods', 1–38; Philip Gooding, 'Tsetse flies, ENSO, and murder: The Church Missionary Society's failed ox-cart experiment of 1876–78', *Africa: Rivista semestrale di studi e ricerche*, 1, 2 (2019), 21–36.

[105] Campbell, *Africa and the Indian Ocean World*; Sharon E. Nicholson, 'Climate and climatic variability of rainfall over eastern Africa', *Reviews of Geophysics*, 55, 3 (2017), 590–635.

This chapter contests older works that approach the coastal traders as a homogenous group and shows how rivalry and competition between different kinship groups informed – and was informed by – encounters on East Africa's Indian Ocean littoral. Chapter 5 examines exchanges of material cultures. It shows the different ways populations on the lakeshore incorporated global commodities, such as glass beads, cotton cloths, and guns into their everyday lives, while accounting for coastal traders' cultural influence in this context. Chapter 6 analyses structures of bondage on the lakeshore. It builds on recent works in IOW history that have blurred the distinctions between 'slavery' and 'freedom', and notes the importance of enslavers, the enslaved, and the formerly enslaved in shaping this aspect of Lake Tanganyika's history.[106] Chapter 7 examines Islam on Lake Tanganyika's shores. It explores the ways in which coastal traders adapted their religious practices to the lakeshore environment and how new converts acculturated their new religion to their pre-existing knowledge of the spiritual world. Collectively, these four chapters show how interactions between and among Indian Ocean littoral and Great Lakes populations on the shores of Lake Tanganyika led to the development of distinct cultural forms.

The book finishes with an Epilogue that shows how examining encounters in East Africa's deep interior helps to further contextualise one of the most well-known episodes in nineteenth-century coastal history, namely the riots of 1888 and the subsequent outbreak of Abushiri Rebellion (1888–90). Far from being an unimportant periphery, Lake Tanganyika was a key frontier zone of the IOW during the nineteenth century. Encounters in that frontier zone affected the broader trajectory of history in parts of the littoral 'core' of the macro-region.

---

[106] See, for example: Campbell, 'Slavery and other forms of unfree labour', ix–xxxi.

Part I

Demarcations of Space

1   The Growth of 'Emporia'

By the 1880s, numerous towns dotted Lake Tanganyika's shoreline. For many people, a town's primary function was its port, which facilitated commerce to, from, and across the lake. Regional products in trades that predated the arrival of coastal traders were important here, such as salt from Uvinza, palm oil from the north-eastern lakeshore, and iron from the interior of Urundi. Over the course of the nineteenth century, though, the towns linking these regional trades became increasingly tied to the ivory trade, stretching from the deep East African interior to the wider IOW and beyond. These trades attracted peoples from diverse regions – including the Indian Ocean littoral, Unyamwezi, Lake Tanganyika's hinterland, and Manyema – to emergent lakeshore towns as traders and labourers. Additionally, they attracted the daily coming and going of farmers who sold their surplus produce to townspeople and passing caravans. The towns' size and prominence additionally gave them further roles in their regional contexts. Increasingly, they became goals for refugees – their size giving them an intrinsically protective character versus the violence of surrounding rural areas, such as that which was associated with the growth of Mirambo's state. They also served administrative and religious purposes, as people inhabiting lakeshore towns sought to influence their surrounds and as people of diverse belief systems encountered each other.[1] In short, these port towns were the core commercial and cultural 'meeting places' on the lakeshore.

Ujiji was the largest of these towns. Presently, Ujiji refers only to a district in the Kigoma urban space, but at the end of the nineteenth century, it was a conglomeration of districts that included what is now the centre of Kigoma.[2] Geert Castryck has recently referred to 'Kigoma-Ujiji' as a town that encapsulates the whole urban space since the

---

[1] Richard J. Reid, 'Warfare and urbanisation: The relationship between town and conflict in pre-colonial eastern Africa', *Azania: Archaeological Research in Africa*, 36–7 (2001), 46.
[2] Interview with Saidi Hamisi Kunga, 11 Nov. 2013.

mid-nineteenth century.[3] Nevertheless, Kigoma is usually referred to as a town of colonial origin, and its roots are usually traced to migrations during that period and to the construction of the German-built Central Railway and harbour.[4] Population estimates for pre-colonial Ujiji vary. In 1876, one 'explorer' estimated that 3,000 people lived in Ujiji; in 1883, a missionary estimated that there were closer to 5,000.[5] This probably represents a period of demographic growth, but both estimates are probably low. Subsequent analysis in this chapter suggests that Ujiji's population, a figure which should include Kigoma as part of a broader urban conglomeration, was closer to 10,000 in the 1880s. Some other towns on the lakeshore, including missionary stations and other commercial centres, had populations in the low thousands by 1890, though passing caravans could significantly increase that number for short periods of time. This is significant because up to around mid-century, all of Lake Tanganyika's shoreline settlements were small fishing villages, the largest of which had populations in the low hundreds. In the second half of the nineteenth century, Lake Tanganyika's shores were urbanising.

The growth of towns around Lake Tanganyika aligned its history with broader histories of 'emporia' in the IOW. The association between the idea of 'emporia', literally meaning 'centres of commerce', and the IOW began in antiquity. *The Periplus of the Erythraean Sea*, a first-century travel document, described different types of emporia in the western IOW, each with different governance structures and purposes.[6] Since then, historians have used the term to centre commerce and the marketplace in understandings of port towns in the IOW.[7] Additionally, pre-colonial histories of, for example, Aden, Bombay (Mumbai), and Batavia (Jakarta) – three prominent emporia in IOW history – highlight 'their cosmopolitanism ... and [point] to the rich interregional convergences

[3] Castryck, 'Bordering the lake', 109–32.
[4] Castryck, 'Bordering the lake', 112; McCurdy, 'Transforming associations', 2; Juhani Koponen, *Development for Exploitation: German colonial policies in mainland Tanzania, 1884–1914* (Hamburg: Lit Verlag, 1994), 622–5.
[5] Henry Morton Stanley, *Through the Dark Continent or the Sources of the Nile around the Great Lakes of Equatorial Africa and down the Livingstone River to the Atlantic Ocean*, Vol. II (London: Sampson Low, Marston, Searle & Irvington, 1878), 6; Ameet Vyncke, *Brieven van een vlaamschen missionaries in Midden-Afrika*, Vol. II (Rousselare: J. de Meester, 1898), 228; Beverly Bolser-Brown and Walter Brown, 'East African trade towns: A shared growth', in *A Century of Change in Eastern Africa*, ed. W. Arens (The Hague: Morton Publishers, 1976), 197.
[6] Casson, *Periplus*, 271–6.
[7] Chaudhuri, *Trade and Civilisation*, 98–118; Pearson, *The Indian Ocean*, 31; Alpers, *The Indian Ocean*, 48; Wynne-Jones and LaViolette, *The Swahili World*, 133.

that appeared at these coastal nodes'.[8] These towns were sites of cultural exchange and innovation, as well as commerce. Nevertheless, as these examples suggest, most IOW histories of emporia have focused on towns in littoral regions. In K. N. Chaudhuri's terms, the IOW's emporia were 'great port-towns' whose peoples were directly engaged in maritime commerce.[9] Towns as 'emporia' have been central to understandings of commercial and cosmopolitan connections across oceanic space in the IOW over the *longue durée*.

The extension of these patterns to inland regions of East Africa occurred during the nineteenth century.[10] This was also a time of transition for many towns in the western IOW. Bombay (Mumbai), Mandvi, Muscat, and Zanzibar grew significantly in size and/or importance during this time period, a pattern for each that can at least partially be attributed to their connections to trans-IOW commercial networks.[11] The growth of towns, such as Bagamoyo, Tabora, and Ujiji on the East African mainland thus partly reflects the entrance of these networks into these towns' respective vicinities.[12] In making this point, this chapter builds on the 1970s work of Beverly and Walter Brown, which argued for the existence of 'numerous and complex' 'similarities' in Bagamoyo's, Tabora's, and Ujiji's 'historical experience' during the nineteenth century.[13] The point here is to situate these linkages within a broader regional and temporal context. Reference to the wider IOW shows that the 'similarities of ... historical experience' were not limited to the three 'trade towns' that Brown and Brown analysed on East Africa's mainland. Rather, the 'complexities' that they identified transcended many towns in the western IOW. Moreover, linking interior towns' histories to the

---

[8] Nancy Um, *The Merchant Houses of Mocha: Trade and architecture in an Indian Ocean port* (Seattle: University of Washington Press, 2009), 8–9.

[9] Chaudhuri, *Trade and Civilisation*, 98–118. For East Africa, see: Paul Sinclair, 'Urbanism', in *The Swahili World*, eds. Wynne-Jones and LaViolet, 185.

[10] Andrew Burton, 'Urbanization in East Africa, circa 900–2010', *Oxford Research Encyclopedia of African* History (2017), 9–10; Jonathan Walz, 'Early inland entanglement in the Swahili world', in *The Swahili World*, eds. Wynne-Jones and LaViolet, 391–2; Chapurukha M. Kusimba, Sibel B. Kusimba, and Laure Dussubieux, 'Beyond the coastalscapes: Preindustrial social and political networks in East Africa', *The African Archaeological Review*, 30, 4 (2013), 399–426.

[11] Sheriff, *Slaves, Spices and Ivory*, 85–6; McDow, *Buying Time*, 26–8; Bishara, *A Sea of Debt*, 24–5; M. Reda Bhacker, *Trade and Empire in Muscat and Zanzibar: Roots of British domination* (London: Routledge, 1992), 15–30; Beatrice Nicolini, 'Re-reading the role of Oman within its international trade relations from 16th to the 19th centuries', in *Regionalizing Oman: Political, economic and social dynamics*, ed. S. Wippel (Dordrecht: Springer Science, 2013), 152; Chhaya Goswami, *Globalization before Its Time: The Gujarati merchants from Kachchh* (Delhi: Penguin, 2016), 29–33, 159–69.

[12] Burton, 'Urbanisation in eastern Africa', 13.

[13] Brown and Brown, 'East African trade towns', 183.

longue durée history of emporia in the IOW adds further temporal dynamics. It is argued here that some features of Lake Tanganyika's nineteenth-century urban emporia had antecedents in the wider IOW's deeper past, especially from the East African coast.

Towns on Lake Tanganyika's shores and elsewhere in East Africa nevertheless had some distinctive characteristics. For example, in contrast to Chaudhuri's conception of IOW emporia, which 'prospered and declined in a pendulum motion of long-term cycles', the rise and decline of many nineteenth-century towns in mainland East Africa occurred at a much more rapid pace.[14] This can partly be attributed to many East African towns' lack of time-depth and their relatively small size compared to many of their contemporaries in the western IOW. For the East African interior, this was necessarily a symptom of being on the frontiers of trans-IOW commercial networks, but for all of East Africa, the redirection of trade routes, the arrival of predatory raiders, and environmental and political changes could have catastrophic effects on burgeoning towns, while also contributing to the growth of others elsewhere.[15] The declines of Bagamoyo and Ujiji versus the rise of Dar es Salaam and Kigoma in the early colonial period are testament to the last two phenomena. Bagamoyo's decline is attributable largely to political changes instituted in 1890, when the German colonial government replaced it with Dar es Salaam as the capital of German East Africa; Ujiji's decline is attributable to the German preference for Kigoma as the location of a harbour, which itself was attributable to political and environmental concerns.[16] Rapid historical change begat rapid rises and declines in East Africa's nineteenth-century emergent emporia.

Even so, trends towards urbanisation on Lake Tanganyika's shores were particularly strong compared to other interior East African regions. Traders travelling between the Congo rainforests and the Indian Ocean littoral increasingly required passage across Lake Tanganyika from just after mid-century onwards, which necessitated the existence of port towns. Thus, declining or abandoned lakeshore towns were often replaced by other emergent ones that served similar port functions, and formerly declining towns had the capacity to re-emerge at later dates. Ujiji, for example, was reported as a 'relic' in

---

[14] Chaudhuri, *Trade and Civilisation*, 99.
[15] Reid, 'Warfare and urbanisation', 46; Reid, *War in Pre-colonial Eastern Africa*, 161–72.
[16] Castryck, 'Bordering the lake', 121; Gooding, 'History, politics, and culture', 11; Pallaver, 'New modes of production', 40–1.

1858, before experiencing a boom akin to the California gold rush in the 1860s and 1870s, but was then described 'deserted and decayed' in the mid-1880s.[17] Similarly, a town on the lake's south-western shore referred to either as Pamlilo or Akalunga went from being 'one of the largest villages' that 'explorer' Verney Lovett Cameron had seen in Africa in 1874, to a 'third or fourth-rate village' whose 'glory must have departed it' in 1879.[18] Meanwhile, Pamlilo's decline occurred as Liendwe, a town on the other side of a bay, was growing in importance as a commercial centre. These patterns stand in contrast to some towns in terrestrial regions in East Africa, such as Msene in north-western Unyamwezi and Isanga (near present-day Iringa) in Uhehe, whose declines represented their locales' near abandonment by many long-distance traders.[19] It also contrasts with urbanising trends around Lake Victoria, which were less established except where centralising forces were strong, such as in Buganda.[20] Lake Victoria's circular shape encouraged travelling around it as much as across it, implying a lesser need for port towns. Conversely, Lake Tanganyika's thin, north–south trajectory versus most traders' east–west direction of travel encouraged traversing it. Lake Tanganyika's environment, shape, and location made its shores particularly suited to the growth of emporia during the nineteenth century.

The centrality of commerce to emporia also implies a central role for caravans in this history. Indeed, the arrival and departure of caravans to, from, and across Lake Tanganyika were crucial to the functioning of lakeshore towns. Caravans varied in size, with tens, hundreds, and – by the 1870s – thousands of porters, traders, and other workers and hangers-on populating them. The largest known pre-1890 caravan traversed the interior of East Africa in 1881 and had around 3,000 people in it.[21] This may have been superseded in size by a subsequent caravan in

[17] Burton, *Lake Regions*, 309; David Livingstone to Roderick Murchison, April–July 1870, in 'Letters of the Late Dr. Livingstone', *Proceedings of the Royal Geographical Society of London*, 18, 3 (1873–4), 274–8; Council for World Missions/London Missionary Society (hereafter: CWM/LMS) 06/02/009 Brooks to Whitehouse, 6 Aug. 1884.

[18] Verney Lovett Cameron, *Across Africa* (New York: Harper & Brothers, 1877), 206; Joseph Thomson, *To the Central African Lakes and Back: The narrative of the Royal Geographical Society's East Central African Expedition, 1878–80*, Vol. II (London: Sampson Low, Marston, Searle, & Rivington, 1881), 28.

[19] Sheriff, *Slaves, Spices and Ivory*, 176–9.

[20] Richard J. Reid and Henri Médard, 'Merchants, missions and the remaking of the urban environment in Buganda, c.1840–90', in *Africa's Urban Past*, eds. David M. Anderson and Richard Rathbone (Oxford: James Currey, 2000), 98–108.

[21] Pallaver, 'Nyamwezi participation', 522; Rockel, *Carriers of Culture*, 128.

1884, which was led by the same people, and which headed in the opposite direction, but contemporary estimates of its size are not forthcoming. More likely, the 1884 caravan was a series of interlinked caravans that passed through East Africa at staggered intervals. The significance of caravans such as these is that in the broader history of urbanisation on Lake Tanganyika shores, they were of a similar-sized population to many of the emergent towns. Thus, when the aforementioned 1881 caravan of 3,000 arrived in Uguha on the lake's western shore, it likely more than doubled the amount of people in and around Mtowa, Uguha's principal lakeshore town. The size of caravans such as these give the impression of vast 'moving cities', in a similar vein to which Richard Reid attaches the idea of 'urbanism' to the 'vast mobile military capitals' in Ethiopian history.[22] Their arrival in Lake Tanganyika's towns represented an encounter between two forms of emporia: one moving and one lacustrine.

Caravans also warrant mention because of one of their core functions: they linked the interior to the coast and the wider IOW through travel and historical themes. Stephen Rockel saw caravans as 'uniting' all East African regions and settlements that were integrated into long-distance commercial systems from a cultural perspective.[23] He identified a pervasive 'labour culture' through work 'on the road', which he conceptualised through *utani* (Swahili: joking) relationships that transcended regional and social categorisations.[24] This occurred through the interaction of various strata of society – traders, porters, other waged labourers, the enslaved; male and female – in the caravan setting, who themselves came from a variety of regions. Emporia, such as those on Lake Tanganyika's shores, were also important zones within which various regional cultures were shared and exchanged. Broadly speaking, one can discuss a 'commercial culture' that linked caravan workers and urban inhabitants.[25] Both on the road and in emporia, people culturally interacted and adapted in ways that geared themselves towards the functioning of commerce. The significance of this 'commercial culture' for this discussion is that, just as caravans did, it linked urban inhabitants between the Indian Ocean littoral and the lakeshore. Towns on East Africa's Indian Ocean littoral, as emporia with significant connections to the wider IOW, had been geared towards commerce for centuries, and in the nineteenth century interior towns, such as those that emerged on the shores of Lake Tanganyika, became likewise. The emergence of emporia and

---

[22] Reid, 'Warfare and urbanisation', 49.   [23] Rockel, 'From shore to shore', 71–3.

[24] Rockel, *Carriers of Culture*, 32.   [25] Castryck, 'Bordering the lake', 121.

caravans in East Africa's interior created the spaces for commercial and cultural interaction between Great Lakes and other IOW populations.

The following discussion is split into three sections. The first examines the influences, broadly conceived, on the structures and appearance of emergent lakeshore emporia during the nineteenth century. Much of the analysis focuses on the coastal traders' *tembes* (square-walled houses), whose design and location in lakeshore and other interior towns owed much to long- and short-term trends in the wider IOW. Additionally, on the lakeshore, their position in relation to markets and the lake reflected the lake's increasing importance in everyday and political life. This trend had parallels to patterns on East Africa's Indian Ocean littoral, where connections to the oceanic environment were a key facet of the town experience. The second and third sections examine the emergence of emporia on Lake Tanganyika's shores on a more individual basis. The second section does so with a case study on Ujiji, where influences from the wider IOW were at their most sustained and intense; the third does so through an analysis of other towns that dotted the lakeshore, and which rose and declined in importance at various points. Collectively, they show the changes over time and space that led to the emergence of emporia on the lakeshore. They also describe the settings in which the cultural exchanges described in subsequent chapters took place. Overall, they argue for the centrality of lakeshore populations and micro-environments in shaping how influences from the wider IOW contributed to the emergence of emporia on the lakeshore.

Lakeshore Emporia in IOW Context

East Africa's distinctive environments and deeper history are crucial to understanding its nineteenth-century urban emporia. Newly emergent towns were rarely built on previously unoccupied land. Like other towns in present-day Tanzania, such as Mpwapwa and Tabora, many lakeshore towns developed from clusters of previously independent villages.[26] Areas where such village clusters existed were often situated in particularly fertile or strategic tracts. Mpwapwa, for example, lay on a fertile plain, just west of a series of mountains and swamps and east of the arid region of Ugogo. It was thus one of the few parts of its locale that was adapted to both agricultural farming and cattle-keeping. Subsequently, through the demands of commerce, villages in each cluster became larger

---

[26] Rockel, *Carriers of Culture*, 137; Rockel, 'Forgotten caravan towns', 13; Karin Pallaver, 'A triangle: Spatial processes of urbanization and political power in 19th-century Tabora, Tanzania', *Afriques: Débats, méthodes et terrains d'histoire*, 11 (2020), 2.

and increasingly interlinked, to the extent that they appeared more as a conglomeration of districts or quarters within a singular emporium. In a similar vein, Karin Pallaver conceived Tabora's numerous districts as a 'triangle' of settlements that comprised a singular urban area.[27] Each district usually had specific functions, and most had their own individual marketplace – markets either being held daily or on a certain number of days per week. Limited water supplies that depended on widely dispersed wells, coupled with fire risks associated with building too many houses with straw and wooden components in close proximity, probably ensured a degree of separation between districts.[28] Nevertheless, commerce brought them increasingly together administratively, commercially, and culturally.

Influences from the wider IOW became established as conglomerations of villages increasingly took the form of distinct towns. This is firstly observable in terms of architectural influences from the East African coast. For the most part, historians and archaeologists have stressed the differences between East African coastal and interior architectural forms, with the former being characterised by stone and the latter by 'wattle and daub'.[29] However, 'wattle and daub' buildings, sometimes referred to as 'mud and thatch', 'mud and wattle', and 'earth and thatch', also had a significant role in East African coastal history.[30] In some cases, they pre-existed stone buildings, which were then built on top of them; in others, they interspersed stone buildings; and in others, they characterised the entirety of a town's urban architecture.[31] By the

---

[27] Pallaver, 'A triangle', 1–31.

[28] Pallaver, 'A triangle', 19; Catherine Coquery-Vidrovitch, *Processus d'urbanisation en Afrique*, Vol. I (Paris: L'Harmattan, 1988), 68; J. A. Moloney, *With Captain Stairs to Katanga* (London: S. Low, Marston & Co., 1893), 67.

[29] Stephanie Wynne-Jones and Jeffrey Fleisher, 'Fifty years in the archaeology of the eastern African coast: A methodological history', *Azania: Archaeological Research in Africa*, 50, 4 (2015), 520; Fleischer et al., 'When did the Swahili become maritime?', 108.

[30] See, for example: Thomas H. Wilson, 'Spatial analysis and settlement patterns on the East African coast', *Paideuma: Mitteilungen zur Kulturkunde*, 28 (1982), 201–19; James de Vere Allen, 'Swahili culture and the nature of East coast settlement', *International Journal of African Historical Studies*, 14, 2 (1981), 306–34; Burton, 'Urbanization in eastern Africa', 4, 5, 12; Jeffrey Fleisher and Adria LaViolette, 'Elusive wattle-and-daub: Finding the hidden majority in the archaeology of the Swahili', *Azania: Archaeological Research in Africa*, 34, 1 (1999), 87–108.

[31] Fleisher and LaViolette, 'Elusive wattle-and-daub', 88; Mark Horton, 'Swahili architecture, space and social structure', in *Architecture and Order: Approaches to social space*, eds. Michael Parker Pearson and Colin Richards (London: Routledge, 1997), 143–4; Stephanie Wynne-Jones, *A Material Culture: Consumption and materiality on the coast of precolonial East Africa* (Oxford: Oxford University Press, 2016), 98; Allen, 'Swahili culture', 319; Adria LaViolette and Stephanie Wynne-Jones, 'The Swahili world', in *The Swahili World*, eds. Wynne-Jones and LaViolette, 4, 9; Sinclair,

late eighteenth century, occupying a stone building on the coast was frequently synonymous with elite status.[32] However, focusing on architectural social divisions obscures wattle and daub's enduring influence among coastal elites. Many of the designs and functions of stone buildings on the coast were based on wattle and daub precedents, and where wattle and daub architecture prevailed among elites in smaller or newer towns, 'their house and town plans remain[ed] those of stone-built towns, and retain[ed] the same significance'.[33] Also, many wattle and daub buildings contained many of the same features of stone houses, such as a *baraza* (Swahili: veranda, courtyard).[34] In this context, Abdul Sheriff argued that stone and wattle and daub houses were not diametrically opposed; rather, there was a continuum between them.[35] Thus, likewise, coastal and interior architectural forms were not diametrically opposed either.[36]

Links between coastal and interior architectural styles are clearest through analysis of the coastal traders' *tembes*. The term *tembe* can be used to describe any rectangular house with a curved roof located in present-day central and west-central Tanzania. Their origins of such

'Urbanism', 186; Stephanie Wynne-Jones and Jeffrey Fleisher, 'Swahili urban spaces of the eastern African coast', in *Making Ancient Cities: Space and place in early urban societies*, eds. Andrew T. Creekmore III and Keven D. Fisher (Cambridge: Cambridge University Press, 2014), 125; Abdul Sheriff, 'The spatial dichotomy of Swahili towns: The case of Zanzibar in the nineteenth century', *Azania: Archaeological Research in Africa*, 36–7, 1 (2001), 64.

[32] Stephanie Wynne-Jones, 'The public life of the Swahili stonehouse, 14th–15th centuries AD', *Journal of Anthropological Archaeology*, 32, 4 (2013), 761; L. W. Donley-Reid, 'A structuring structure: The Swahili house', in *Domestic Architecture and the Use of Space: An interdisciplinary cross-cultural study*, ed. Susan Kent (Cambridge: Cambridge University Press, 1993), 114–26; Allen, 'Swahili culture', 319; Sarah Hillewaert, 'Identity and belonging on the contemporary Swahili coast: The case of Lamu', in *The Swahili World*, eds. Wynne-Jones and LaViolette, 607; Horton, 'Swahili architecture', 149–50.

[33] Mark Horton and John Middleton, *The Swahili: The social landscape of a mercantile society* (Oxford: Blackwell, 2000), 125; Mark Horton, *Shanga: The archaeology of a Muslim trading community on the coast of East Africa* (London: British Institute in Eastern Africa, 1996), 59.

[34] Horton, 'Swahili architecture', 143–4; Patricia Caplan, 'Life in Swahili villages', in *The Swahili World*, eds. Wynne-Jones and LaViolette, 582; Wynne-Jones and Fleisher, 'Swahili urban spaces', 114; Fleisher and LaViolette, 'Elusive wattle-and-daub', 93; Wynne-Jones, 'The public life', 759.

[35] Sheriff, 'The spatial dichotomy', 64.

[36] Steven Fabian has made a similar argument about the adoption of *barazas* by populations in the East African coastal hinterland. See: Steven Fabian, *Making Identity on the Swahili Coast: Urban identity, community, and belonging in Bagamoyo* (Cambridge: Cambridge University Press, 2019), 45.

buildings in the region may lie in Ugogo or Unyamwezi.[37] However, some nineteenth-century Europeans also used the term to distinguish between coastal traders' houses and those of various interior populations, especially on the lakeshore. The coastal traders' *tembes* had some distinguishing features. Just as in the case of many homes on the coast, most had a public-facing *baraza*, where men socialised, conducted commerce, and – in some parts of the interior – prayed.[38] Also in common with coastal precedents, they had private and store rooms at the back – the former were for women and dependents – which opened out onto an enclosed courtyard.[39] Finally, they frequently had flat roofs made from beaten clay, making them look much like the roofs of coastal buildings made from stone.[40] They used a minimum of thatch and grass, which were considered a fire risk, and were commonly used as the sole material to roof many interior populations' buildings.[41] Thus, while much coastal archaeology has focused on the importance of elite-owned stone buildings, a deeper history of wattle and daub found resonance in the interior through the construction of the coastal traders' *tembes*. The result was that the coastal traders' *tembes* were remarkably similar in layout and function to many of their stone equivalents on East Africa's Indian Ocean littoral.

For the most part, coastal traders sought central locations for their *tembes*. Doing so built on prevailing precedents from East Africa's Indian

[37] Moyd, *Violent Intermediaries*, 287; Wayne McKim, 'House types in Tanzania: A century of change', *Journal of Cultural Geography*, 6, 1 (1985), 62–6; Rockel, *Carriers of Culture*, 137; Cameron, *Across Africa*, 72; Burton, *Lake Regions*, 213, 252–3; Hore, 'Twelve tribes', 5; Edward C. Hore, *Tanganyika: Eleven years in central Africa* (London: Edward Stanford, 1892), 55; Thomson, *Central African Lakes*, I, 219.

[38] Fabian, *Making Identity*, 124–5; Roman Loimeier, 'The *baraza*: A grass root institution in East Africa', in *Lieux de sociabilité urbaine en Afrique*, eds. Laurent Fourchard, Odile Georg, and Muriel Gomez-Perez (Paris: L'Harmattan, 2009), 8. For *barazas* as sites of prayer, see Chapter 7.

[39] Wynne-Jones, 'The public life', 759–60; Wynne-Jones and Fleisher, 'Swahili urban spaces', 133; Sheriff, 'The spatial dichotomy', 65, 69–70.

[40] Burton, *Lake Regions*, 229–30; Stanley, *Dark Continent*, II, 1, 7; Cameron, *Across Africa*, 317; David Livingstone, *The Last Journals of David Livingstone in Central Africa. From eighteen hundred and sixty-five to his death. Continued by a narrative of his last moments and sufferings, obtained from his faithful servants Chuma and Susi*, ed. Horace Waller (New York: Harper & Brothers, 1875), 182; Hore, *Tanganyika*, 70; John Hanning Speke, *Journal of the Discovery of the Source of the Nile* (New York: Harper & Brothers, 1864), 69; François Coulbois, *Dix années au Tanganyika* (Limoges: Pierre Dumont, 1901), 68; Victor Jacques and Emile Storms, *Notes sur l'ethnographie de la partie orientale de l'Afrique équatoriale* (Brussels: Académie Royale de Belgique, 1886), 104; Pallaver, 'A triangle', 17; Sheriff, 'The spatial dichotomy', 68–9; Kjersti Larsen, *Where Humans and Spirits Meet: The politics of rituals and identified spirits in Zanzibar* (New York: Berghahn Books, 2008), 26; Vyncke, *Brieven van een vlaamschen*, II, 228.

[41] Pallaver, 'A triangle', 19; Brown and Brown, 'East African trade towns', 198.

Ocean littoral, where elite houses were frequently located next to large
and central mosques.[42] This, however, provided challenges in the interior context. The lack of clearly defined centres between the distinct
villages that eventually came to comprise districts in towns meant that
there was frequently no obvious centre to build around. Additionally,
unlike in Buganda and among the Yao, missionary records from
1879 and 1881 suggest that coastal traders did not build a mosque in
any lakeshore region until the colonial period.[43] Thus, where natural
centres did emerge in Lake Tanganyika's towns, they usually did so
around marketplaces, and many marketplaces increased in regional
prominence after the coastal traders settled around them. To a certain
degree, this also reflects broader trends in East Africa's Indian Ocean
littoral. Before the nineteenth century, most centres of coastal East
African stone towns did not have defined marketplaces, business being
conducted in *barazas* instead. However, increased commercialisation led
to the creation of distinct marketplaces betwixt and between houses in
central locations, as well as on some stone towns' peripheries.[44] In
Zanzibar, the most famous of these was the salt market, near to the
present-day Forodhani gardens.[45] In Bagamoyo, meanwhile, 'the caravan trade ... [created] ... a demand for increased goods and services,
which in turn resulted in the enlargement of the market, [and] a proliferation of craftsmen, shopkeepers, and labourers'.[46] Markets and marketplaces became increasingly central – figuratively and spatially – to East
African towns during the nineteenth century.

The coastal traders' *tembes* were invariably surrounded by houses of
different designs. Many of the latter on the lakeshore were of conical
shape and had steep, thatched roofs, in direct contrast to the rectangu-
larly walled and flat-roofed *tembes* of coastal trader ownership.[47] Such

---

[42] Edward John Pollard, 'The maritime landscape of Kilwa Kisiwani and its region,
Tanzania, 11th to 15th century AD', *Journal of Anthropological Archaeology*, 27, 3
(2008), 278; Mark Horton, Jeffrey Fleisher, and Stephanie Wynne-Jones, 'The
mosques of Songo Mnara in their urban landscape', *Journal of Islamic Archaeology*, 4, 2
(2017), 167.

[43] A.G.M.Afr. Augier to White Fathers, 16 Apr. 1879, *Chronique Trimestrielles*, 5
(Jan. 1880); CWM/LMS/06/02/006 Hutley, 'Mohammadanism in Central Africa: Its
professors', Aug. 1881. See also: David C. Sperling, 'The coastal hinterland and the
interior of East Africa', in *The History of Islam in Africa*, eds. Nehemia Levtzion and
Randall L. Pouwels (Athens, OH: Ohio University Press, 2000), 289.

[44] Horton and Middleton, *The Swahili*, 109, 125.

[45] For an account, see: Richard F. Burton, *Zanzibar: City, island, and coast*, Vol. I (London:
Tinsley Brothers, 1872), 104–5.

[46] Walter Brown, 'Bagamoyo: An historical introduction', *Tanzania Notes and Records*, 71
(1970), 75.

[47] Pallaver, 'A triangle', 18–19; Jacques and Storms, *Notes sur l'ethnographie*, 104.

houses were located both within and around the coastal traders' compounds. Additionally, some people from the interior adopted the practice of building *barazas* on the front of their houses.[48] This speaks to a cultural encounter between ostensible 'littoral' and 'interior' architectural forms, although the construction of flat roofs made from clay appears to have remained largely the preserve of coastal traders and their associates.[49] The result was that interior towns had a diverse and intermingled appearance, which is a reflection of the variety of regional and social influences within them. However, it is also reflective of contemporaneous trends in parts of East Africa's Indian Ocean littoral, most notably in Ng'ambo, on the east side of the creek bordering Zanzibar's Stone Town. Ng'ambo was occupied by peoples of interior, coastal, Omani, and Indian origin. It hardly had a 'centre', with distinct quarters being located around various mosques and marketplaces.[50] Moreover, the diversity of its population was reflected in its architecture, which included a variety of styles made of both stone and wattle and daub.[51] Similar patterns are observable on the fringes of, for example, Bagamoyo, Kaole, and Saadani, where a variety of architectural styles proliferated.[52] The surroundings of the coastal traders' *tembes* reflected the wide variety of actors that shaped East Africa's emporia during the nineteenth century.

On Lake Tanganyika's shores, though, the location of the coastal traders' *tembes* represents a further interaction between lakeshore and coastal settlements. Coastal traders often built their *tembes* in close

---

[48] Hore, 'Twelve tribes', 9–10; Stephanie Wynne-Jones and Sarah Croucher, 'The central caravan route of Tanzania: A preliminary archaeological reconnaissance', *Nyame Akuma*, 67 (2007), 94.

[49] This contrasts with the region around Tabora in Unyamwezi, where some Nyamwezi populations appear to have built flat-roofed houses made from mud during the nineteenth century. See: Stephen J. Rockel, 'The Tutsi and the Nyamwezi: Cattle, mobility, and the transformation of agro-pastoralisim in nineteenth-century western Tanzania', *History in Africa*, 46 (2019), 244, n. 44.

[50] Garth Andrew Myers, 'Eurocentrism and African urbanization: The case of Zanzibar's other side', *Antipode*, 26, 3 (1994), 195–215; Garth Andrew Myers, *Verandahs of Power: Colonialism and space in urban Africa* (Syracuse, NY: Syracuse University Press, 2003), 81–2.

[51] Sheriff, 'The spatial dichotomy', 78–80.

[52] Brown, 'Bagamoyo', 76; Glassman, *Feasts and Riot*, 202–9; Burton, *Lake Regions*, 28; Burton, *Zanzibar*, 269–70; Cameron, *Across Africa*, 24; Steven Fabian, 'Wabagamoyo: Redefining identity in a Swahili town, 1860s–1960s' (unpublished PhD diss., Dalhousie University, 2007), 43–4, 49; Walter Brown, 'A pre-colonial history of Bagamoyo: Aspects of the growth of an East African coastal town' (unpublished PhD diss., Boston University, 1971), 239–40; Vyncke, *Brieven van een vlaamschen*, II, 38.

proximity to the water's edge.[53] This provided significant challenges in the context of the lacustrine environment because the lake's level was subject to significant interseasonal, interannual, and interdecadal variation.[54] A *tembe* could be on the lakeshore at one point in time, hundreds of metres from it at another, and submerged at another.[55] However, the coastal traders' desire to build on the water's edge was reflective of broader patterns in oceanic histories and cultures. Proximity to the ocean in coastal towns has often been observed as being an issue of prestige, and this may have been the case for coastal traders on the lakeshore as well.[56] But it was also an issue of practicality, where in the increasingly commercialised atmosphere of the nineteenth century, access to the port and its closest market were prized. Moreover, before the nineteenth century, evidence suggests that some lakeshore populations built most of their habitations at a short distance from the lakeshore.[57] This may have been a prerogative of the need to not be boxed into the lake if they were attacked by raiders. The construction of *tembes*, other houses, and marketplaces closer to the lakeshore, therefore, represented at least a partial spatial relocation of lakeshore settlements. Towns became increasingly intertwined with the lake itself, which gave them a clearer water-facing aesthetic, making the largest among them close in appearance to some of the smaller towns of East Africa's Indian Ocean littoral. The nature of the lacustrine environment meant that emergent emporia on Lake Tanganyika's shores were especially suited to adapting aesthetic and functional influences from littoral regions of the wider IOW.

Ujiji as an IOW Emporium

Analysis of specific nineteenth-century emporia on Lake Tanganyika's shores begins with the history of Ujiji. This is for two core reasons. One relates to the nature of the source material. There are more documentary sources that refer to Ujiji than to any other lakeshore town. Most nineteenth-century Europeans who travelled to Lake Tanganyika visited

---

[53] CWM/LMS/06/02/003 Hore, 'Kigoma Bay', 9 Dec. 1878. See also: Stanley, *Dark Continent*, II, 10, 26; Livingstone, *Last Journals*, 293; CWM/LMS/06/02/004 Hutley to Whitehouse, 22 Nov. 1879, Griffith to Whitehouse, 27 Dec. 1879.

[54] Sharon E. Nicholson, 'Historical and modern fluctuations of Lakes Tanganyika and Rukwa and their relationship to rainfall variability', *Climatic Change*, 41, 1 (1999), 53–71.

[55] CWM/LMS/06/02/003 Hore, 'Kigoma Bay', 9 Dec. 1878. See also: Stanley, *Dark Continent*, II, 10, 26; Livingstone, *Last Journals*, 293.

[56] Pollard, 'The maritime landscape of Kilwa Kisiwani', 278; Pearson, *The Indian Ocean*, 31.

[57] Burton, *Lake Regions*, 314, 354; Cameron, *Across Africa*, 223.

Ujiji at some point, and two of the three European organisations to establish themselves on the lakeshore before the inception of colonial rule did so at Ujiji for at least some of the period. The other relates to Ujiji's position as Lake Tanganyika's largest and longest-standing commercial centre on the lakeshore. Its importance meant that interactions between coastal and interior populations in Ujiji occurred on a larger scale and over a longer time period than in other lakeshore towns. The strength of the encounter was such that in 1879, the 'explorer' Joseph Thomson claimed that Ujiji had 'an appearance not unlike a coast village on the Mlima [sic]' – the Mrima being the East African coastal region roughly demarcated by the area between the present-day Kenya–Tanzania border and just south of Dar es Salaam.[58] To his mind, Ujiji probably resembled some of the smaller, 'haphazard' settlements of the coast, such as Saadani and Kaole, as well as Ng'ambo.[59] Moreover, in the second half of the twentieth century, one anthropologist described Ujiji's people as 'Swahili' – an identity he argued that began to emerge during the nineteenth century.[60] Although the anthropologist was describing interior peoples who adopted coastal customs rather than immigrants from the coast, this speaks to the relevance of East Africa's littoral for understanding its history.[61]

The transition that made Ujiji appear 'coastal' to a European 'explorer' in 1879 was a dramatic one. At the beginning of the nineteenth century, what later became known as Ujiji was a series of villages, each with a composition like most other lakeshore settlements that Stanley described in 1871. To Stanley, most lakeshore settlements were 'fishing settlements under the shade of a grove of palms and plantains, banians and mimosa, with cassava gardens to the right and left of palmy forests, and patches of luxuriant grain looking down upon a quiet bay'.[62] Fishing and farming were the principal activities governing village life; trans-lake and other regional trades were only the concern of a few.[63] However, commerce became gradually more important over time, to the extent that Ujiji had developed a reputation as an important market among people living at

---

[58] Thomson, *Central African Lakes*, II, 91.
[59] Horton and Middleton, *The Swahili*, 126–7.
[60] Hino, 'Neighbourhood groups', 1–30.   [61] Castryck, 'Bordering the lake', 114.
[62] Henry Morton Stanley, *How I Found Livingstone: Travels, adventures, and discoveries in central Africa including four months' residence with Dr. Livingstone* (London: Sampson Low, Marston & Company, 1872), 381; Brown, 'Ujiji', 38.
[63] Richard Gray and David Birmingham, 'Some political and economic consequences of trade in Central Africa in the pre-colonial period', in *Pre-Colonial Trade*, eds. Gray and Birmingham (London: Oxford University Press, 1970), 3.

the coast by at least the 1840s.[64] Even so, this transition was far from linear. By the end of the 1850s, Ujiji was still no more a town than it was a concentration of broadly independent villages, and possibly in decline. In 1858, Burton described Kawele (a village that eventually became a part of the present-day district of Ujiji) as 'a relic' and as 'a few scattered hovels ... surrounded by fields of sorghum and sugar-cane, and shaded by dense groves of the dwarf, bright-green plantain, and the tall sombre elaeis, or Guinea-palm'.[65] Other nearby villages, meanwhile, had varying relations with commerce. Gungu had few traders owing to a chief's reputation for plunder, and Ugoy was much frequented by coastal traders because its chief, called Habeyya, was less extortionate.[66] Thus, up to around 1860, commercial opportunities in Ujiji were uneven, and internal structures that transcended each village had yet to emerge (see Figure 1.1).

Town life did, however, begin to develop after this point. Not coincidentally, the 1860s was the decade during which coastal traders began to settle permanently in Ujiji's lakeshore regions.[67] They settled primarily in Kawele and Ugoy, though a few occupied Kasimbo and one lived in Kigoma.[68] Stanley wrote that the coastal traders lived in Ugoy, and that natives, the enslaved, and the formerly enslaved lived in Kawele, a description that historians have generally accepted.[69] However, other descriptions and images show this to be a more ordered picture than what appeared on the ground. For example, Thomson wrote that Ujiji contained 'almost every style of African architecture', making no distinction about where different types were located; Emile Storms of the AIA wrote that various types of house were next to each other, with the Jiji largely occupying conical huts which permeated the town; and François Coulbois of the White Fathers wrote that the coastal traders and their men 'mingled' with the natives of Lake Tanganyika.[70] Some Jiji and other immigrant populations also incorporated coastal architectural

[64] James MacQueen, 'Notes on African geography', *Journal of the Royal Geographical Society of London*, 15 (1845), 371–6; V. C. Brand, W. D. Cooley, and Bernardino Freire F. A. de Castro, 'Notice of a caravan journey from the East to the West coast of Africa', *Journal of the Royal Geographical Society*, 24 (1854), 266–71.

[65] Burton, *Lake Regions*, 309.   [66] Burton, *Lake Regions*, 314.

[67] Sheriff, *Slaves, Spices and Ivory*, 186.

[68] Stanley, *Dark Continent*, II, 6; CWM/LMS/06/02/003 Hore, 'Launch of the "Calabash"', 'Kigoma Bay', 9 Dec. 1878; CWM/LMS/06/02/005 Hore to Whitehouse, 9 Feb. 1880.

[69] Stanley, *Dark Continent*, II, 1–2; Reid, *War in Pre-colonial Eastern Africa*, 116; Burton, 'Urbanisation in eastern Africa', 13; Brown, 'Ujiji', 91–2; Wynne-Jones and Croucher, 'The central caravan route', 94.

[70] Thomson, *Central African Lakes*, II, 89; RMCA ESA HA.01.017-6 Storms to AIA, 1883; Coulbois, *Dix années*, 66.

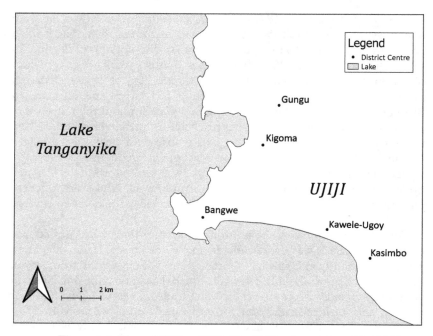

Figure 1.1 Map of Ujiji, c.1860–80. Although mentioned in LMS correspondence, the location of Cashu is unknown. Drawn by the author.

styles into their own houses, such as rectangular walls and a *baraza*, which they set up among the coastal traders.[71] Moreover, by 1878 – and probably before – Kawele and Ugoy had become one district referred to as Ujiji (for clarity's sake, it is hereafter referred to as Kawele-Ugoy).[72] Habeyya, the *teko* (Ha: district chief; sing. *umuteko*; pl. *abateko*) of Ugoy in Burton's 1858 description, had become the principal Jiji authority over both districts.[73] Also, by the late 1870s, there was only one market that

---

[71] Hore, 'Twelve tribes', 9–10; Wynne-Jones and Croucher, 'The central caravan route', 94.

[72] Hore, *Tanganyika*, 68. Environmental factors likely contributed to this transition. The lake's level rose significantly between c.1840 and 1878, and at least one missionary reported that this resulted in much of Ugoy being covered with water: CWM/LMS/06/02/003 Hore, 'Kigoma Bay', 9 Dec. 1878. See also: Chapter 2; Stanley, *Dark Continent*, II, 10, 26; Livingstone, *Last Journals*, 293; Nicholson, 'Historical and modern fluctuations', 53–71.

[73] Brown, 'Ujiji', 136; Royal Museum of Central Africa, Henry Morton Stanley Archive (hereafter: RMCA HMSA) 7. 'Journal in Lett's Diary', 17 Dec. 1871; CWM/LMS/06/02/006 Hutley to Whitehouse, 11 Feb. 1881.

served them both, which was located on the waterfront and was surrounded by the coastal traders' *tembes*.[74] The location of these *tembes* shows that the coastal traders attempted to position themselves as central to the emerging emporium (see Figure 1.2).

Similar patterns occurred in Ujiji's other villages, though with less influence from coastal traders. In 1880, Kigoma was known to have 'smaller attachments', called Cashu and Bangwe – the former being of unknown location and the latter being on the peninsula south-west of the current Kigoma centre.[75] This is notable because Bangwe was an island for much of the nineteenth century, and only a dramatic drop in the lake's level from 1878 exposed it to the possibility of 'attachment' to mainland Ujiji.[76] Bangwe did, though, have its own *teko* into at least the mid-1880s, though he may have been under the influence of Mwinyi Akida, the coastal trader living in Kigoma.[77] Edward Hore, an LMS missionary, described Mwinyi Akida as being 'more looked up to' by the Jiji than Ujiji's other coastal traders, and colonial records suggest he had a close relationship with Ujiji's central chief living in the lake's mountainous surrounds – possibly acting as his regional representative (*tware*; Ha: regional chief; sing. *umutware*; pl. *abatware*).[78] Additionally, Kigoma was governed by a locally appointed *teko*, called Bogo, who lived in Gungu on the north-eastern side of Kigoma Bay.[79] Mwinyi Akida and Bogo appear to have governed in relative harmony. Hore also wrote in 1880 that Gungu contained 'the largest houses I have yet seen built by the Wajiji [*sic*]', showing its primacy among Jiji peoples living on the lakeshore.[80] Kigoma, Gungu, and their attachments were becoming

---

[74] Stanley, *Dark Continent*, I, 399–400.

[75] CWM/LMS/06/02/005 Hore to Whitehouse, 9 Feb. 1880; ZNA AA2/29 Hore to Kirk, 9 Feb. 1880.

[76] Bangwe is reported as an island in all 'explorer' accounts of Ujiji up to 1876; from 1878 it is reported as a peninsula. For 1876 and before, see: Burton, *Lake Regions*, 313–14, 341; Stanley, *How I Found*, 393; Cameron, *Across Africa*, 178; Stanley, *Dark Continent*, II, 12. For 1878 and after, see: CWM/LMS/06/02/003 Hore 'Kigoma Bay', 9 Dec. 1878; CWM/LMS/06/02/008 Hore to Whitehouse, 18–23 June 1883. See also: Nicholson, 'Historical and modern fluctuations', 53–71; Chapter 3.

[77] CWM/LMS/06/05/5 Hore, '3 Voyages of the Calabash', 6 Aug. 1879; CWM/LMS/06/02/005 Hore to Whitehouse, 25 May 1883; Hore, *Tanganyika*, 82, 223; Geert Castryck, '"My slave sold all of Kigoma": Power relations, property rights and the historian's quest for understanding', in *Sources and Methods for African History and Culture: Essays in honour of Adam Jones*, eds. Geert Castryck, Silke Strickrodt, and Katja Werthmann (Leipzig: Leipziger Universitätsverlag, 2016), 320.

[78] CWM/LMS/06/02/005 Hore to Whitehouse, 9 Feb. 1880; ZNA AA2/29 Hore to Kirk, 25 Feb. 1880; Reid, *War in Pre-colonial Eastern Africa*, 116; Castryck, 'My slave sold all of Kigoma', 318, 320.

[79] CWM/LMS/06/02/005 Hore to Whitehouse, 9 Feb. 1880.

[80] CWM/LMS/06/02/005 Hore to Whitehouse, 26 Feb. 1880.

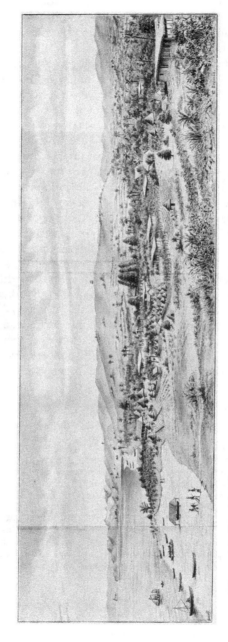

Figure 1.2 Sketch of Kawele-Ugoy, 1880s. Note the square-walled/flat-roofed *tembes* intermingled with structures of other design. In: Hore, Tanganyika, frontispiece.

increasingly integrated leading up to the 1880s. It is thus appropriate to refer to it as a distinct district called Kigoma-Gungu.

During the 1880s, Kawele-Ugoy and Kigoma-Gungu were the principal districts in the broader Ujiji emporium. Kasimbo, Cashu, and Bangwe were integrated parts of the town, though they were less significant. Coastal traders dominated Kawele-Ugoy, firstly under Mwinyi Kheri, and then, after Kheri's death in 1885, under Mohammed bin Khalfan (Rumaliza). Habeyya the Jiji *teko* of Kawele-Ugoy, being aged and inhabiting the lake's mountainous surrounds, became sidelined from town politics after an ill-fated attempt in 1880–1 to banish all but three of Ujiji's coastal traders from the town because of the perceived misdeeds of some of their bondsmen.[81] Jiji peoples remained in Kawele-Ugoy after this episode, but European visitors were frequently struck by the large immigrant populations, most notably from Manyema, the coast, and Unyamwezi.[82] Other lakeshore populations also visited Kawele-Ugoy's marketplace during the 1860s and 1870s, but they may have been more drawn to Kigoma-Gungu thereafter. This is reflected in a decline in the size of Kawele-Ugoy's marketplace from around 3,000 to 1,200 square metres between 1871 and 1876, and by it becoming more of a 'station on the road' for long-distance ivory traders than a 'position of independent importance' during the 1880s.[83] Meanwhile, both Kigoma and Cashu had 'considerable markets' from at least the late 1870s, and Gungu's market probably had regional significance.[84] It attracted traders from Urundi and Unyamwezi, and was 'the regular terminus for native [African] caravans'.[85] Regional traders may have preferred Kigoma-Gungu because it was cheaper, safer, and easier to access by boat during the post-1878 decline in the lake's level.[86] During the 1880s, Kawele-Ugoy and Kigoma-Gungu each had distinct market, human, and governance structures.

---

[81] CWM/LMS/06/02/005 Hutley to Whitehouse, 7 Nov. 1880; CWM/LMS/06/02/006 Hutley to Whitehouse, 11 Feb. 1881; Walter Hutley, *The Central African Diaries of Walter Hutley, 1877–1881*, ed. James B. Wolf (Boston: African Studies Center, 1976), 221–2; Reid, *War in Pre-colonial Eastern Africa*, 118; Bennett, *Arab versus European*, 91.

[82] RMCA ESA HA.01.017-7. 'Rapport de voyage à Oudjidji', 7 July 1883.

[83] Stanley, *Dark Continent*, II, 2; Hore, *Tanganyika*, 69; CWM/LMS/06/02/009 Brooks to Whitehouse, 6 Aug. 1884.

[84] CWM/LMS/06/02/004 Hore to Mullens, 10 Jan. 1879.

[85] CWM/LMS/06/02/005 Hore to Whitehouse, 26 Feb. 1880; CWM/LMS/06/02/004 Hore to LMS, 18 Sep. 1879; Hore, 'Twelve tribes', 9.

[86] Castryck, 'Bordering the lake', 121; Reid, *War in Pre-colonial Eastern Africa*, 116; Ruud C. M. Crul, *Limnology and Hydrology of Lakes Tanganyika and Malawi* (Paris: UNESCO Publishing, 1997), 32; CWM/LMS/06/02/004 Hutley to Whitehouse, 19 Oct. 1879; CWM/LMS/06/02/005 Hutley to Whitehouse, 7 Nov. 1880.

There were, however, links between Kawele-Ugoy and Kigoma-Gungu that governed the broader emporium. Mwinyi Akida acknowledged as much when he requested that members of the LMS ask Zanzibar's British Consul, Sir John Kirk, to petition Sultan Barghash of Zanzibar to make him *liwali* (Swahili: governor; pl. *maliwali*) of all of Ujiji town (a request that did not bear fruit).[87] Also, on occasion, Ujiji town's various power holders came together to preside over matters that concerned the broader settlement. For example, in 1880, they collectively prevented the LMS from building a permanent residence in any part of Ujiji, despite the LMS claiming to have gained permission from Bogo to build in Gungu.[88] The LMS' opposition to slave trading and to all forms of bonded labour probably persuaded Bogo to renege on this alleged promise. Additionally, again in 1880, negotiations to replace the recently deceased *ami* (Ha: central chief; sing: *umwami*; pl. *abami*) of Ujiji were held in Gungu and were overseen by Bogo, Mwinyi Akida, and Kawele-Ugoy's coastal traders.[89] The *ami* was the head of a hierarchy that nominally governed Ujiji (the province of Uha, which included the Ujiji town) from Manyovu or Nkalinzi in Lake Tanganyika's mountainous surrounds, but who only asserted his power on the lakeshore through periodic collections of tribute and appointment of his *tware*.[90] Ujiji's (the town's) various power holders conspired to elect an infant as *ami* under a regency.[91] This reduced the power of the *ami*-ship, making its principal agents dependent on Ujiji town's various representatives.[92] During the 1880s, Ujiji's urban conglomeration became a powerful political bloc.

Understanding Ujiji's history in this way has several consequences for the history of nineteenth-century East African emporia. First, it is clear that Kigoma has a significant pre-colonial history, and it is not merely the

---

[87] CWM/LMS/06/02/005 Hore to Whitehouse 26 Feb. 1880–2 Mar. 1880. Edward C. Hore of the LMS assented to this request, but the scheme does not appear to have gone further than Kirk. See: ZNA AA2/29 Hore to Kirk, 25 Feb. 1880.

[88] CWM/LMS/06/02/005 Hore to Whitehouse, 9 Feb. 1880, 26 Feb. 1880–2 Mar. 1880, 10 Mar. 1880; ZNA AA2/29 Hore to Kirk, 25 Feb. 1880, 10 Mar. 1880, 17 Mar. 1880; ZNA AC10/1 Hore to Kirk, 17 Aug. 1880; Norman R. Bennett, 'Mwinyi Kheri', in *Leadership in Eastern Africa*, ed. Norman R. Bennett (Boston: Boston University Press, 1986), 153; Reid, *War in Pre-colonial Eastern Africa*, 116–17.

[89] CWM/LMS/06/02/005 Hore to Whitehouse, 9 Feb. 1880; Bennett, 'Mwinyi Kheri', 153; Bennett, *Arab versus European*, 91.

[90] Brown, 'Ujiji', 1–37.

[91] CWM/LMS/06/02/005 Hore to Whitehouse 25 May 1880, Hore to Whitehouse, 20 July 1880.

[92] The British used the same approach in early colonial Uganda with the selection of Daudi Chwa II as *Kabaka* (king) of Buganda. This undercut central Ganda authority, leaving the British to fill the vacuum.

'colonial town' it is often made out to be.[93] Second, population estimates for late pre-colonial Ujiji are probably low. Historians have tended to accept the view that Ujiji's population was around 5,000 during the 1880s (with the caveat that the arrival and departure of caravans made this figure fluctuate dramatically), but this figure is based on missionary and 'explorer' estimates of Kawele-Ugoy only.[94] If the populations of Kigoma, Gungu, Kasimbo, Cashu, and Bangwe are added to this figure, then it is reasonable to suggest that Ujiji's population was closer to 10,000. Finally, the idea of Ujiji as an 'emporium' or an 'urban conglomeration' brings it into line with urban histories of elsewhere in East Africa.[95] Perhaps more significant, though, are the similarities between Ujiji and towns in East Africa's Indian Ocean littoral regions. Ujiji and coastal towns experienced urban growth with similar historical trajectories: architectural styles were varied and intermingled, though there was a preponderance of wattle and daub, some of which had deeper coastal precedents; marketplaces emerged in the centres of towns; and the most prominent coastal populations sought residence near to the town's centre and port. The transition was such that Ujiji's districts were increasingly oriented towards the water in a manner that has parallels with towns on East Africa's Indian Ocean littoral over the *longue durée*. In many ways, Ujiji increasingly looked like and performed the same functions as many emporia in littoral regions of the IOW.

The Fluctuating Fortunes of Other Lakeshore Emporia

Demographic growth in nineteenth-century Ujiji was to a certain degree exceptional on Lake Tanganyika's shores. No other lakeshore settlement grew to the same extent over the same time period, and none encapsulated the links between East Africa's Indian Ocean littoral and the deep interior so strongly. This can partly be attributed to that fact that coastal traders encountered and settled in Ujiji earlier, for longer, and in larger numbers than they did elsewhere on the lakeshore. However, there were longer-term issues that favoured the development of an emporium at Ujiji as well. For example, it was in a fertile valley whose soils could support a relatively high population density, and until c.1878, it had nearby islands that could act as sites of refuge in case of attack.[96] Also,

---

[93] Castryck, 'Bordering the lake', 112.
[94] Brown and Brown, 'East African trade towns', 197; David M. Anderson and Richard Rathbone, '*Urban Africa*: Histories in the making', in *Africa's Urban Past*, eds. David M. Anderson and Richard Rathbone (Oxford: James Currey, 2000), 6; Bennett, *Arab versus European*, 91.
[95] See especially: Pallaver, 'A triangle', 1–31.   [96] Brown, 'Ujiji', 1–37.

Ujiji was a natural gateway into the lake region from Uvinza, whose salt deposits had been linked to the northern half of Lake Tanganyika's commercial economy since long before the nineteenth century.[97] Ujiji thus had a familiarity with regional commerce before the expansion of the global ivory trade. Lake Tanganyika's other nineteenth-century emporia usually lacked one or more of these features. This underpinned the instability of their emergence for most of the nineteenth century. Only during the 1870s and especially the 1880s did many of them become significantly more established.

For both human and environmental reasons, large population centres did not emerge on the lakeshore until at least the 1850s, and later in most regions. On the lake's south-eastern shores, any trends towards the emergence of emporia were undermined by the arrival of Ngoni and related peoples in 1842. The new arrivals' roots lay in the *mfecane* of 1810s and 1820s southern Africa. They were highly militarised, and their arrival in regions throughout southern, central, and eastern Africa was associated with the destruction of settlements and fields, as well as the looting of cattle.[98] Lakeshore populations were particularly vulnerable, as they were on lower ground and the lake could act as a barrier to escape. Most significant centres around the south-eastern lakeshore during this time period, therefore, emerged in the lake's terrestrial hinterland.[99] Also, the resultant reforestation of lakeshore areas probably contributed to a higher prevalence of tsetse flies, which discouraged the formation of large population centres thereafter.[100] Meanwhile, when Ngoni formations attacked Ujiji in 1858, its populations were forced to temporarily flee to Bangwe Island, and the resultant destruction contributed to a change in the local chieftaincy.[101] The presence of nearby islands as potential sites of refuge in this context likely enabled it to recover in ways that other lakeshore regions did not. The steep slopes and rocky ground on most of the lake's western shores, meanwhile, discouraged the emergence of emporia for most of the nineteenth century.

Settlements were probably larger on Lake Tanganyika's north-eastern and northernmost shores up to the beginning of the 1860s. These regions

[97] Sutton and Roberts, 'Uvinza', 45–86; Chrétien, 'Le commerce du sel', 401–22.
[98] Spear, *Zwangendaba's Ngoni*, 1–43.
[99] Roy G. Willis, *A State in the Making: Myth, history, and social transformation in pre-colonial Ufipa* (Bloomington: Indiana University Press, 1981), 24 (map 4), 57 (map 5).
[100] This statement builds on work by Stephen Rockel, which noted the role of violence in the wider spread of tsetse flies in parts of west-central Tanzania later in the century. See: Rockel, 'The Tutsi and the Nyamwezi', 231–61.
[101] Burton, *Lake Regions*, 378; Stanley, *How I Found*, 393; Reid, *War in Pre-colonial Eastern Africa*, 172; Brown, 'Ujiji', 153–4.

were more fertile and protected than those on most of the south-eastern and western lakeshore. In 1871, Livingstone referred to a 'crowded population' on Urundi's shores, and Stanley referred to Bikari in Urundi (near to present-day Rumonge, which grew in significance in the 1880s) as a 'cluster of villages'.[102] These descriptions might represent early signs of villages coming together as conglomerations, but the evidence is far from conclusive. Moreover, Burton and Speke did not travel along Urundi's shoreline in 1858, choosing instead to travel westwards across the lake from near Ujiji's northern fringe because, they claimed, the Rundi had a reputation for plunder.[103] This suggests that any trends that may have existed towards the formation of larger settlements had limited connections to commercial expansion across the western IOW.[104] Uvira, meanwhile, was integrated into lacustrine commercial networks. It was a key destination for Uvinza's salt and was a producer of iron for the lakeshore market since before the arrival of coastal traders.[105] Also, by 1858, it acted as an important depot for ivory, its peoples hunting elephants beyond the lake's mountainous surrounds and supplying it to coastal traders and their associates, who then returned to Ujiji.[106] Enslaved people were also likely part of this commerce.[107] The wealth accrued by lakeshore chiefs in this context enabled them to resist demands for tribute from dynastic chiefs in the lake's hinterland at some point during the nineteenth century, although evidence for the growth of emporia at this early stage is not forthcoming.[108] The lakeshore settlement, meanwhile, did not have its own organisational structure or any form of centre.

The first certain trends towards the development of emporia to emerge outside of Ujiji likely did so around Lake Tanganyika's southern end. Liendwe was the principal settlement in this context. Referring to his visit in 1879, Joseph Thomson described it as 'the most important ... place on Lake Tanganyika [excepting Ujiji, being] formed of twenty or thirty

---

[102] Livingstone, *Last Journals*, 401; Stanley, *How I Found*, 403.
[103] Burton, *Lake Regions*, 347.
[104] This is notwithstanding the likely existence of lacustrine commercial networks involving Urundi that predated the coastal traders' arrival. See: Wagner, 'Trade and commercial attitudes', 149–66.
[105] Burton, *Lake Regions*, 354; Bolser-Brown, 'Muslim influence', 620; Jacques-Marie Francois Depelchin, 'From pre-capitalism to imperialism: A history of social and economic relations in eastern Zaire (Uvira zone, c.1800–1965)' (unpublished PhD diss., Stanford University, 1974), 155–66.
[106] Burton, *Lake Regions*, 352–5.
[107] Bishikwabo Chubaka, 'Aux origines de la ville d'Uvira selon les explorateurs et les pionniers de la colonisation Belge au Zaire (1840–1914)', *Civilisations*, 1 (1987), 105–8.
[108] Chubaka, 'Origines de la ville d'Uvira', 98–8; Burton, *Lake Regions*, 352, 354.

villages, lying along [a] rich alluvial plain'.[109] This gives the impression of a dispersed settlement or series of settlements, yet it still had characteristics that linked it to broader urbanising trends.[110] Liendwe's significance grew from the early 1870s, as it was on the landward trade route that linked East Africa's Indian Ocean littoral and Unyamwezi to Katanga and Manyema. By the end of the decade, it had a parallel hierarchy: One headed by a chief of the native Lungu populations called Kapufi, and one headed by a coastal trader known as Kabunda, who originated in Baluchistan.[111] Additionally, Victor Giraud's 1883 description of the coastal traders' 'cabins' among the Lungu's thatched 'sheds' hints at the kind of architectural intermingling that was common in East Africa's other nineteenth-century emporia (see Figure 1.3).[112] The coastal traders' influence may have contributed to initial trends that hinted at the growth of an emporium with links to the wider IOW in Liendwe from the 1860s, but they were far from enduring. Liendwe ceased having regional importance soon after the imposition of European colonial rule in the 1890s and may have been in decline as early as 1885.[113]

Other important pre-1880 settlements towards the southern end of the lake include Zombe and Pamlilo. Neither achieved much time-depth. In 1880, Zombe was described as a large, fortified town, but it was destroyed by 1883, having been attacked by Bemba raiders who came from the south.[114] Its surviving inhabitants fled inland and reformed their settlement near what is now the Kasesya border crossing between

---

[109] Thomson, *Central African Lakes*, II, 16.

[110] Karin Pallaver shows in her case study on Tabora that a dispersed settlement was not a barrier to urban forms from taking shape. See: Pallaver, 'A triangle', 1–31.

[111] Hore, *Tanganyika*, 235; Marcia Wright and Peter Lary, 'Swahili settlements in northern Zambia and Malawi', *African Historical Studies*, 4, 3 (1971), 549.

[112] Victor Giraud, *Les lacs de l'Afrique équatoriale* (Paris: Librarie Hachette, 1890), 432. These are my own translations from the French 'cases' (cabins) and 'hangars' (sheds).

[113] Mwelwa C. Musambachine, 'Nshimba (Simba) (c1820–1896) of Kilwa Island in the south-west corner of Lake Mweru, Zambia: A biography of an East African trader' (unpublished paper), 33: www.academia.edu/13153828/Nshimba_Simba_c1820_1896_of_Kilwa_Island_in_the_Southwest_Corner_of_Lake_Mweru_Zambia_A_Biography_of_an_East_African_Trader (accessed 29 Apr. 2021).

[114] CWM/LMS/06/05/21 Hore, 'Voyage to the south end of Lake Tanganyika', 12 Apr. 1880; CWM/LMS/06/02/005 Hore to Whitehouse, 2 Mar. 1880, 12 Apr. 1880, 8 May 1880; CWM/LMS/06/02/008 Hore to Whitehouse, 15 Aug. 1883; Andrew Roberts, *A History of the Bemba: Political growth and change in northeastern Zambia before 1900* (London: Longman, 1973), 149–51; Christopher St. John, 'Kazembe and the Tanganyika-Nyasa corridor, 1800–1890', in *Pre-colonial African Trade*, eds. Gray and Birmingham, 226; Willis, *A State in the Making*, 88; Wright and Lary, 'Swahili settlements', 550.

Figure 1.3 Liendwe from the lake, 1883. Original caption: 'Arrivée à la station d'Iendué'. Note the varying architectural styles in the forefront and in the distance, although the 'cabins' that Giraud describes do not appear to have been pictured. In: Giraud, Les lacs, 431.

Zambia and Tanzania, about thirty kilometres from the lakeshore. Pamlilo (sometimes referred to as Akalunga) probably grew in size and importance through Ujiji's coastal traders using it as a port town on the route to Katanga. In 1874, Cameron described meeting coastal traders and their associates in the town, but whether they settled is uncertain, and no mention is made of *tembes* being constructed. His only reference to architecture or the town's layout was to its distinctive granaries, which were cylinders built on stilts with thatched conical roofs (see Figure 1.4).[115] By the end of the 1870s, Pamlilo was in decline and coastal traders rarely visited it. This was probably the result of violence in and around the south-western lakeshore, competition from Liendwe,

[115] Cameron, *Across Africa*, 207.

Figure 1.4 A chief and a granary at Akalungu, 1874. Original caption: 'King Miriro and his Granary'. In: Cameron, Across Africa, 207. Accessed via: www.gettyimages.ca/detail/news-photo/granary-of-chief-miriro-tanzania-drawing-by-alexandre-de-news-photo/930082534? adppopup=true.

and the abandonment of the trade route between Ujiji and Katanga in favour of more northern routes towards Manyema.[116]

Some emporia became more established on Lake Tanganyika's shores during the 1880s. This transition can be attributed to traders' increased propensity for traversing the lake when travelling to and from Manyema during this decade, instead of travelling around its southern end. Travelling across the lake necessitated an increased usage of ports, around which towns emerged. In a clockwise direction from Ujiji, the most prominent towns on Lake Tanganyika's shores were Kirando, Liendwe, Katele, Mtowa, Chuinu, Uvira, and Rumonge (see Figure I.1). Some of these have been mentioned before. Their importance in the 1880s represents their ongoing participation in long-distance commerce. Those that are new to this discussion were mostly built either on the sites of pre-existing villages or next to them. In 1874, for example, Cameron described Kirando as one of many 'small villages' on Ufipa's northern lakeshore, whose endurance may be attributed to the presence of nearby islands, which served a protective role if the village was attacked. Meanwhile, he did not mention Mtowa at all. Instead, he focused on Ruanda, which was a 'considerable town' of 400–600 houses built in rows, and was about sixteen kilometres inland.[117] Rumonge, meanwhile, was a rival village to Bikari on the Urundi shoreline, and Chuinu was probably one of many settlements that Burton and Stanley described on the lake's north-western shore to the south of Uvira.[118] Despite their humble beginnings, each emerged as a significant port town during the 1880s.

There is little in the documentary record on the architecture and the layout of each of the ports and their surrounding settlements. Europeans were more likely to describe the peoples of a town and the products of its market(s) than a town itself. Limited exceptions to the archives' trajectory apply in the cases of Mtowa and Kirando. Mtowa, apart from being the location of an LMS station in 1879–85, gained its fame as a port. During the 1880s, it was a frequently used 'gate' to Manyema from Ujiji.[119] It was, for the most part, a 'camp' for people passing to and

[116] Livingstone, *Last Journals*, 189; Hamed bin Muhammed el-Murjebi, *Maisha ya Hamed bin Muhammed el Murjebi yaani Tippu Tip kwa maneno yake mwenyewe*, trans. W. H. Whitely (Dar es Salaam: East African Literature Bureau, 1974), 81; Thomson, *Central African Lakes*, II, 29.

[117] Cameron, *Across Africa*, 196, 223; Hore, 'Twelve tribes', 15–16; CWM/LMS/06/02/005 Hutley, 'Uguha and its people', 29 Sep. 1880.

[118] A.G.M.Afr. C.16-7. Journal du P. Deniaud, 15 Aug. 1879; Burton, *Lake Regions*, 351; Stanley, *How I Found*, 422–4.

[119] CWM/LMS/06/02/004 Hore to LMS, 29 Sep. 1879.

from these places.[120] In 1880, it only had about ninety habitations, and it does not appear to have grown during the subsequent decade.[121] It was, though, capable of containing 1,500 members of a passing caravan for over two months in 1881, and later it became a major site of contestation between coastal traders, their allies, and the Congo Free State.[122] The smallness of its permanent population, therefore, belied its strategic importance. Moreover, for the local Holoholo population, Mtowa became part of Ruanda, the largest individual settlement in Uguha. In the 1880s, Ruanda's chief, Kasanga, negotiated with coastal traders and missionaries over the terms of their settlement and their onward travel.[123] This marks a shift from the late 1870s when Kasanga apparently delegated matters concerning Mtowa to a chief of inferior rank.[124] In the Mtowa case, a large 'camp' of semi-permanent structures was integrated into a pre-existing settlement to make a broader conglomeration that stretched over several kilometres.

Kirando, meanwhile, had significantly more permanent residents. By the mid-1880s, it was the primary centre on a plain that stretched into the Fipa heartland and was dominated by coastal traders and their associates.[125] Kapufi, Ufipa's *eene* (Fipa: central chief; sing. *mweene*; pl. *aeene*; not to be confused with the Lungu chief at Liendwe who had the same name), also had some influence, though he was broadly aligned with the coastal traders. This is shown firstly by his appointment of Ngombe Sazi, a trader who claimed coastal origin and who had previously held positions in Kapufi's court, as Kirando's governor in 1890, and secondly, by Kapufi supporting some coastal traders' slave raids in Marungu during the late 1880s and early 1890s.[126] Additionally, Giraud's account of Kirando in 1883 contains information of an architectural encounter

[120] CWM/LMS/06/02/004 Hutley to Whitehouse, 22 Nov. 1879, Griffith to Whitehouse, 27 Dec. 1879.
[121] CWM/LMS/06/02/005 Hutley, 'Uguha and its people', 29 Sep. 1880; RMCA ESA HA.01.017–7. Storms, 'Rapport de voyage à Oudjidji', 7 July 1883; E. Trivier, *Mon voyage au continent noir: La 'Gironde' en Afrique* (Paris: Firmin-Didot & Cie, 1891), 225–6.
[122] CWM/LMS/06/02/006 Palmer to Thompson, 6 May 1881; Brown, 'Ujiji', 200; Bennett, *Arab versus European*, 251. For an earlier account in which slave traders passed what one 'explorer' counted as 800 people for enslavement through Mtowa, see: RMCA HMSA 4610. Stanley to *Daily Telegraph* and *New York Herald*, 28 Oct. 1876.
[123] CWM/LMS/06/02/004 Griffith to Whitehouse, Oct. 1879, Hutley to Whitehouse, 29 Dec. 1879; CWM/LMS/06/02/005 Griffith to Whitehouse, 28 Aug. 1880.
[124] CWM/06/05/5 Hore, '3 voyages of the Calabash', 25 Apr.–7 Sep. 1879.
[125] A.G.M.Afr. Randabel to White Fathers, 25 Oct. 1888, in *Chronique Trimestrielles*, 42 (Apr. 1889).
[126] Willis, *A State in the Making*, 156; A.G.M.Afr. Diaire de Mpala, 23 Jan. 1889; A.G.M.Afr. Diaire de Karema, 23 Oct. 1890, 7 Apr. 1891.

between coastal and interior populations. He described the compound of Makutubu, a native of Marungu who had spent time at the coast, and who had departed the condition of being enslaved by a coastal trader. Makutubu's residence was at the centre of the compound, it had a *baraza* at the front and private rooms at the back, and it was surrounded by the smaller huts of his dependents.[127] The compound's layout thus bore much similarity to coastal traders' *tembes* in, for example, Ujiji, and to many houses at the coast. However, the roof of Makutubu's residence, despite being flat like a *tembe*, was made of thatch, the customary nineteenth-century material for conical roofs in Ufipa and Marungu, not of beaten clay, like the coastal traders' *tembes* (see Figure 1.5).[128] Makutubu's residence, therefore, represents an encounter between ostensibly interior and coastal architectural designs and materials.

Finally, it is important to note that European-headed stations that emerged from 1878 onwards followed similar patterns to those already described. The members of the LMS, White Fathers, and AIA invariably negotiated with pre-existing village chiefs to establish stations in their vicinity.[129] For the missionaries, this gave them proximity to and a relationship with a group of people to whom they could proselytise, though results were invariably mixed. For the representatives of the AIA, this gave them a natural ally in their aim to assert regional military influence, which they most notably achieved around Mpala in 1884–5.[130] The most significant European stations in the 1880s were at Niamkolo (LMS), Kibanga (White Fathers), Karema, and Mpala (both AIA until 1885; White Fathers thereafter). To take one example, Kibanga was established on the edge of a village headed by a chief called Poré, which was had a population of around 600 in 1883.[131] Meanwhile, the population of the White Fathers' station, which was about a kilometre from Poré's residence, grew from 115 to 1,000 in the eighteen months between July 1886 and January 1888.[132] Although the White Fathers

---

[127] Giraud, *Les lacs*, 462–3.
[128] Giraud, *Les lacs*, 463; Roy G. Willis, *The Fipa and Related Peoples of South-West Tanzania and North-East Zambia* (London: Routledge, 2017), 25; Allen F. Roberts, 'Tabwa', in *The Encyclopedia of Vernacular Architecture*, Vol. III, ed. Paul Oliver (Cambridge: Cambridge University Press, 1997), 2012; Allen F. Roberts, 'Fipa', in *The Encyclopedia of Vernacular Architecture*, III, ed. Oliver, 1976; Livingstone, *Last Journals*, 182; Stanley, *Dark Continent*, II, 1; Coulbois, *Dix années*, 68.
[129] Peter Simchile, *A History of the White Fathers in Western Tanzania: Their work in the Vicariate of Tanganyika with special emphasis on today's dioceses of Sumbawanga and Mpanda (1870–2002)* (2002); A.G.M.Afr. Diaire de Karema, 4 Nov. 1885; A.G.M.Afr. Diaire de Mkapakwe, 10 De. 1884, 22 Jan. 1885.
[130] See: Roberts, *A Dance of Assassins*.
[131] A.G.M.Afr. Diaire de Kibanga, 17 June 1883.
[132] A.G.M.Afr. Diaire de Kibanga, 1 July 1886, 1 Jan. 1888.

Figure 1.5 Makutubu's *tembe* in Kirando, 1883. Original caption: 'Boma de Makutubu'. In: Giraud, Les lacs, 463.

governed their station for the most part independently (and Poré did likewise), they negotiated with each other on issues pertaining to the White Fathers' expansion.[133] This gives the sense of a collective structure that governed issues that affected the whole settlement, while also stressing the ongoing local influences on how emergent lakeshore towns developed. Outsiders played a critical role in the creation of emporia and other larger settlements; lakeshore populations shaped the forms that the larger settlements took.

Conclusion

There were general trends towards the growth of larger settlements on the shores of Lake Tanganyika during the nineteenth century. The centrality of commerce to this process, the water-facing environment,

[133] A.G.M.Afr. Diaire de Kibanga, 11 Feb. 1884, 3 Apr. 1886; Vyncke, *Brieven van een vlaamschen*, III, 89–93.

and the presence of traders with connections to the littoral regions of the IOW gave the emergent towns the impression of 'emporia', which have been central to IOW history over the *longue durée*. This sense of connection to the wider IOW is further visible through the architecture of the newly emergent towns. Coastal traders built their wattle and daub *tembes* based on precedents from the coast, and some lakeshore populations adapted aspects of this architectural style in the construction of their habitations. *Barazas* became frequent additions to Jiji houses, and at least one person formerly enslaved by a coastal trader made his roof flat. However, the latter did so using materials that were commonly used by other lakeshore populations rather than the methods and materials of the coastal traders. This speaks to influence of lakeshore peoples and environments over the ways in which influences from the wider IOW were incorporated into the newly emergent towns. This is further supported by the layout and location of towns, which owed a great deal to local environments, peoples, and influences, including the ongoing influence of many local authority figures. Interior East Africa's integration into the IOW's *longue durée* history of emporia occurred on distinctly local lines.

The emergence of emporia with links to the wider IOW nevertheless had significant consequences for life on the lakeshore. As examined in the rest of Part I, they contributed to the institution of two key changes in their surrounding regions. First, the emergence of larger population centres and the arrival and departure of caravans put pressure on sources of food in many locales. Thus, rural areas went through an 'agricultural revolution' that allowed farmers to supply people and locations that were directly implicated in long-distance commerce. In this sense, farmers too became embroiled in the broader emergence of a 'commercial culture' in emporia and caravans. By selling surpluses, they were increasingly geared towards the functioning of commercial systems that linked East Africa's deep interior with the wider IOW. Second, the nature of emporia on the lakeshore implied adjustments to the ways in which people living on the lakeshore engaged with the lake itself. Just as in East Africa's coastal and island regions, lakeshore populations' spiritual systems were intertwined with perceptions of their nearest body of water. As lakeshore emporia became increasingly oriented towards the lake through the construction of markets and the use of ports, and as new technologies of waterborne transport were developed to transport ever larger numbers of people and goods across the lake, such belief systems were challenged and modified, as were their associated hierarchies. These two shifts – in rural areas and in engagements with the lake – are the subjects of Chapters 2 and 3.

2   Changing Land Use in a Changing Climate

The emergence of towns and the development of long-distance trade necessitated a transformation in the agricultural economy. At the beginning of the century, farmers on the shores of Lake Tanganyika mostly tended large, scattered fields of drought-resistant crops for subsistence purposes, minimising risks of soil degradation and the effects of anomalous levels of annual or seasonal rainfall.[1] However, the growth of large population centres and the passing of caravans necessitated an increase in agricultural intensity and output around these zones. Farmers sought to achieve this through two core methods: they increased the size of their bonded labour pool by tapping into an expansion of slave raiding and slave trading networks; and they adopted crops with higher potential yields and fewer labour requirements, such as cassava, maize, and rice, to go with their indigenous staples, such as sorghum and millet. These changes were directly related to commerce. Farmers sought to maximise their yields to access markets, allowing them to participate in wider commercial structures associated with the expansion of the global ivory trade. The centrality of commercial motivations here is supported by many farmers' additional growth of tobacco, a cash crop sometimes used as currency, which had no benefits for the subsistence economy.[2] As such, during the nineteenth century, agricultural production around

---

[1] Ralph A. Austen, *African Economic History: Internal development and external dependency* (London: James Currey, 1987), 16–17.

[2] A.G.M.Afr. Diaire de Kibanga, 25 May 1886, 19 June 1887; RMCA ESA HA.01.017-7. Storms, 'Rapport sur un voyage dans la partie sud du Tanganika', 1 Apr. 1884; Depelchin, 'From pre-capitalism to imperialism', 150; Karin Pallaver, 'What East Africans got for their ivory and slaves: The nature, working and circulation of commodity currencies in nineteenth-century East Africa', in *Currencies of the Indian Ocean World*, eds. Steven Serels and Gwyn Campbell (Cham: Palgrave, 2019), 90; Karin Pallaver, 'From Venice to East Africa: History, uses, and meanings of glass beads', in *Luxury in Global Perspective: Objects and practices, 1600–2000*, eds. Bernd-Stefan Grewe and Karin Hofmeester (New York: Cambridge University Press, 2016), 207. Cash crops were grown on a much larger scale in coastal and island regions of East Africa. See: Frederick Cooper, *Plantation Slavery on the East Coast of Africa* (New Haven, CT: Yale University Press, 1977); Sheriff, *Slaves, Spices and Ivory*.

major trade routes and emergent emporia shifted from being mainly based on subsistence to becoming increasingly commercialised.[3] This represented a 'revolution' in much of the region's agricultural economy.[4]

Climate and climatic change are crucial for contextualising this agricultural revolution. Agriculture in East Africa and the wider IOW is reliant on rain brought by the Indian Ocean monsoon system. This system is underpinned by convection, caused by the temperature of land being subject to more seasonal fluctuation than the temperature of water. As land heats up in the northern hemisphere summer, hot air rises, causing wet air from the Indian Ocean to blow over southern Asia. This is the south-west monsoon. During the north-east monsoon, dry air from over the cooler Eurasian landmass blows southwards over the ocean itself. East Africa has two rainy seasons, respectively called the *mvuli* (short rains) in October–November and the *masika* (long rains) in March–May, associated with these seasonal shifts, although the short dry season (December–February) around Lake Tanganyika and other inland zones is significantly wetter than the long dry season (June–September). The *mvuli* and *masika* represent the intermediary periods between the south-west and north-east monsoons. These intermediary periods correspond to the parts of the year in which the intertropical convergence zone (ITCZ), a belt of low pressure circulating the globe near the equator in which northern and southern winds meet, passes over East Africa's latitude. The vivacity of the monsoon system at a given time is modulated by several short- and long-term global climatic teleconnections, including those associated with the El Niño Southern Oscillation (ENSO), the Indian Ocean Dipole (IOD), volcanism, sunspot activity, and long-term migrations of the ITCZ.[5]

Recent historical work has shown the importance of the Indian Ocean monsoon system for understanding Africa's relationship with the wider IOW over the *longue durée*. Gwyn Campbell has convincingly argued that long-term fluctuations in the monsoon system have underpinned several 'upturns' and 'downturns' in the IOW economy since antiquity.[6]

---

[3] Gray and Birmingham, 'Some economic and political', 1–19.
[4] The idea of an agricultural revolution here builds on other studies focusing on the introduction of New World crops to Africa. See for example: James C. McCann, *Maize and Grace: Africa's encounter with a New World crop, 1500–2000* (Cambridge, MA: Harvard University Press, 2009), 9–11; Jevan Cherniwchan and Juan Moreno-Cruz, 'Maize in precolonial Africa', *Journal of Development Economics*, 136 (2019), 137–50. In the latter article, Cherniwchan and Moreno-Cruz discuss maize's introduction to Africa in terms of an 'agricultural productivity shock' (p. 138).
[5] For a more complete description of how different factors affect rainfall in East Africa, see: Nicholson, 'Climate and climate variability', 590–635.
[6] Campbell, *Africa and the Indian Ocean World*.

The nineteenth century, however, deserves special attention, because it was a period of significant volatility in the monsoon system. The beginning of the century was marked by the final years of the Little Ice Age (LIA), a period of global cooling between c.1300 and c.1840, during which average global temperatures were sometimes up to two degrees cooler than they were in the centuries preceding it.[7] The LIA is generally associated with a weakening of the monsoon system, a more erratic climate in the IOW, and trends towards aridification in East Africa in its final decades, c.1750–1840.[8] It was succeeded by a period of generally benign environmental conditions, characterised by increased warmth and wetness in c.1840–75.[9] Following this and up to the end of the nineteenth century, frequent ENSO events and heightened levels of volcanic activity contributed to adverse climatic conditions in much of the IOW, including in East Africa, which experienced devastating droughts and floods.[10] Thus, East Africa's nineteenth-century 'agricultural revolution' occurred within a significantly shifting climatic context.

Much of the data needed to set out this climatic context have only been made available since the mid-1990s. Concern with global warming has led climatologists to seek more and better data from the past to help

[7] Sam White, 'Climate change in global environmental history', in *A Companion to Global Environmental History*, eds. J. R. McNeill and Erin Stewart Mauldin (Chichester: Wiley Blackwell, 2015), 400–2; Philipp Blom, *Nature's Mutiny: How the Little Ice Age of the long seventeenth century transformed the West and shaped the present* (New York: Liveright Publishing Corporation, 2019); H. S. Sundqvist, K. Holmgren, J. Fohlmeister, Q. Zhang, M. Bar Matthews, C. Spötl, and H. Könich, 'Evidence of a large cooling between 1690 and 1740 AD in southern Africa', *Scientific Reports*, 3, 1767 (2013), 1–6.

[8] Campbell, *Africa and the Indian Ocean World*, 134–57; Jainhui Chen, Jianbao Liu, Xiaojian Zhang, Shengqian Chen, Wei Huang, Jie Chen, Shengrui Zhang, Aifeng Zhou, and Fahu Chen, 'Unstable Little Ice Age climate revealed by high-resolution proxy records from northwestern China', *Climate Dynamics*, 53 (2019), 1517–26; Ilse Bessems, Dirk Verschuren, James M. Russell, Jozef Hus, Florias Mees, and Brian F. Cumming, 'Paleolimnological evidence for widespread late 18th century drought across equatorial East Africa', *Paleogeography, Paleoclimatology, Paleoecology*, 259 (2008), 107–20; Nicholson, 'Historical and modern fluctuations', 53–71; Andrew S. Cohen, Michael R. Talbot, Stanley M. Awramik, David L. Dettman, and Paul Abell, 'Lake level and paleoenvironmental history of Lake Tanganyika, Africa, as inferred from lake Holocene and modern stromatolites', *Geological Society of America Bulletin*, 109, 4 (1997), 444–60; Simone R. Alin and Andrew S. Cohen, 'Lake-level history of Lake Tanganyika, East Africa, for the past 2500 years based on ostracode-inferred water-depth reconstruction', *Paleogeography, Paleoclimatology, Paleoecology*, 199, 102 (2003), 31–49.

[9] Campbell, *Africa and the Indian Ocean World*, 184–5; Nicholson 'Historical and modern fluctuations', 53–71; Stefan Hastenrath, 'Variations of East African climate during the past two centuries', *Climatic Change*, 50 (2001), 209–17.

[10] Campbell, *Africa and the Indian Ocean World*, 245–54; Mike Davis, *Late Victorian Holocausts: El Niño famines and the making of the third world* (London: Verso, 2002).

model climate scenarios for the future.[11] Their analysis of climate proxies, such as ice cores, tree rings, and lake sediments, has given a clearer picture of climate in the deeper past than was available to climate historians writing in the mid-twentieth century, when climate history was last at its apex.[12] Added to more recent rain gauge data, climatologists have now reconstructed rainfall patterns in East Africa with a reasonable degree of accuracy to the beginning of the nineteenth century.[13] Limnological records from Lake Tanganyika itself add more precision here. Sharon Nicholson estimates that fluctuations in the lake's level, which are estimated for most of the late Holocene from palaeolimnological research, are broadly indicative of rainfall in its catchment, with correlation being strongest over five-year running averages.[14] Additionally, missionaries on Lake Tanganyika's shores made occasional annual measurements of rainfall during the 1870s and 1880s. Much like many other missionary sources of rainfall data in Africa, these records have yet to be incorporated into climatologists' databases.[15] They do, however, provide additional precision to the subsequent analysis in this chapter.

The crops adopted during East Africa's nineteenth-century agricultural revolution shed more light on the importance of this climatic context. Maize and rice, while having higher potential yields and (in the case of maize) requiring less labour to produce, are significantly less resistant to water stress than sorghum and millet. Thus, in adopting maize and rice, sometimes in place of sorghum and millet, East African farmers became gradually more dependent on regular rainfall. Vulnerabilities in this context became starkly apparent in the late 1870s and 1880s, when a series of global climatic anomalies disrupted the

---

[11] For a critique of their approaches, see: N. Thomas Håkansson, 'Criticizing resilience thinking: A political ecology analysis of droughts in nineteenth-century East Africa', *Economic Anthropology*, 6, 1 (2019), 7–20.

[12] The most famous mid-twentieth-century example is probably: Emmanuel Le Roy Ladurie, *Times of Feast, Times of Famine: A history of climate since the year 1000*, trans. Barbara Bray (Garden City, NY: Doubleday, 1971). More recent works include: Campbell, *Africa and the Indian Ocean World*; Sam White, *A Cold Welcome: The Little Ice Age and Europe's encounter with North America* (Cambridge, MA: Harvard University Press, 2018); Blom, *Nature's Mutiny*.

[13] Sharon E. Nicholson, Chris Funk, and Andreas H. Fink, 'Rainfall over the African continent from the 19th through the 21st century', *Global and Planetary Change*, 165 (2018), 114–27.

[14] Nicholson, 'Historical and modern fluctuations', 53–71; Alin and Cohen, 'Lake-level history of Lake Tanganyika', 31–49.

[15] Nicholson, 'Climatology: Methods', 1–38. This contrasts with the climatic histories of several other IOW regions, especially China, where archival documents have been at the forefront of reconstructing past climates.

Indian Ocean monsoon system, leading to erratic levels of seasonal and annual rainfall in East Africa, adversely affecting yields. Resultant food shortages were exacerbated in East Africa by towns' ongoing growth, by the arrival and departure of ever larger caravans, and by violence caused by increased competition for resources. Each of these factors placed higher demands on food production at a time when levels of rainfall were not conducive to meeting them. Meanwhile, the other core crop adopted for the first time by farmers in East Africa's interior during the nineteenth century, cassava, has low nutritional value and tended only to be grown as a staple in particularly infertile regions or in times of desperation. In this context, the expanded use of bonded labour had limited capacity to offset the effects of adverse climatic factors, except in specific circumstances. Although an expanded labour pool was crucial to the foundations of the 'agricultural revolution' in years of regular rainfall, the driver of its long-term success or failure was the choice of crops in a changing climate.

The importance of the climatic context to East African agriculture and thus to wider East African history cannot be understated here. The structures of the ivory trade necessitated the liberation of traders, porters, boatmen, and other specialists from agriculturally productive roles, at least for some of the year. Such people were usually densely congregated in emporia or in caravans, and they required feeding by farmers living in surrounding rural regions. If the harvests failed due to, for example, farmers growing crops that were not resistant to water stress in years of drought or overly abundant rainfall, shortages of food were likely. This had any number of consequences, many of which are elucidated in this chapter. For example, at different times, climate-related shortages of food provoked: traders to abandon their enterprises to desperately tend to their farms, undermining commerce; large numbers of hungry people with weak immune systems to travel in search of food, thus contributing to the spread of epidemics; farmers to increase their prices, contributing to inflation; heightened competition for resources, contributing to increased levels of violence; and inequalities to grow between those who were able to supplement food production through trade and labour exploitation, and those who could not. Furthermore, successive failed harvests led some traders to question the long-term viability of certain emporia, contributing to changes in different emporia's role and prominence over time. Increased reliance on high-yield crops with low resistance to water stress meant that commerce and conditions within East Africa's emergent emporia were increasingly tied to fluctuations in the Indian Ocean monsoon system.

The rest of this chapter is split into three sections, each focusing on one of the three themes addressed in this introductory section. It starts by, in turn, examining the two core features that underpinned the commercialisation of agriculture during the nineteenth century. The first of these was the expansion of slave raiding and trading in the regions around and beyond Lake Tanganyika. The centrality of enslaved labour to the agricultural revolution was such that the very act of working in the fields became associated with slave status. The second was the adoption of new crops, especially cassava, maize, and rice, in regions around towns and along commercial routes. The adoption of these crops increased potential yields while making the use of (wo)man hours in the fields more efficient. In years of reliable rainfall, both the expanded use of enslaved labour and the adoption of new crops increased yields, giving farmers increased access to markets and freeing labour to specialise in other economic pursuits for at least some of the year. However, as analysed in the third section of this chapter, periods of water stress had the capacity to undermine agricultural productivity. This section discusses the features of East Africa's agricultural revolution in the context of a changing climate, further examining how these changes affected commerce and conditions in Lake Tanganyika's emergent emporia. In so doing, it centres fluctuations of the Indian Ocean monsoon system in East African history and links trends related to food production around Lake Tanganyika's emporia to broader trends in the wider IOW.

The 'Agricultural Revolution': Acquiring Labour

The expansion of slave raiding, trading, and ownership is a well-known feature of nineteenth-century East African history. Jan Georg-Deutsch positioned the slave trade as 'important, if not crucial' to the nineteenth-century history of Unyamwezi.[16] Enslaved labour added to and replaced free Nyamwezi labour in the fields, allowing the latter to specialise in other activities for most of the year, including in long-distance trade and porterage.[17] Similarly, plantations of grains and coconuts on the coast and of spices on Zanzibar and Pemba were built on enslaved labour.[18] These were the foundations of many coastal towns' economies.[19] Many

---

[16] Jan-Georg Deutsch, 'Notes on the rise of slavery and social change in Unyamwezi', in *Slavery in the Great Lakes*, eds. Médard and Doyle, 87. See also: Reid, *War in Pre-colonial Eastern Africa*, 120.

[17] Rockel, *Carriers of Culture*, 6.

[18] Cooper, *Plantation Slavery*, 80; Sheriff, *Slaves, Spices and Ivory*, 57–9.

[19] Edward A. Alpers, 'Muqdisho in the nineteenth century: A regional perspective', *The Journal of African History*, 24, 4 (1983), 441–59; Ramachandran Menon, 'Zanzibar in the nineteenth century: Aspects of urban development an East African coast town' (unpublished MA diss., UCLA, 1978).

enslaved people were also exported through the East African coast and islands to the Arabian Peninsula, especially Oman, but also as far as Persia.[20] The sources of enslaved labour were diverse. With a couple of exceptions, rulers, plantation owners, and other free agriculturalists rarely enslaved their own kin. Nyamwezi raiders and traders imported captive people for enslavement from their region's peripheries, such as in Ufipa, Uha, and Usukuma;[21] most enslaved people taken to Zanzibar originated in the hinterland of Kilwa, as far west as the regions around the northern half of Lake Malawi;[22] and most enslaved people on the coast opposite Zanzibar were acquired in Zanzibar's slave market or in the coastal hinterland – very few were taken from the deep interior for this market, especially as far away as Lake Tanganyika.[23] These histories speak to a series of somewhat distinct slave-raiding and -trading networks in East Africa, which collectively contributed to the commercialisation of agriculture across much of the region.

Lake Tanganyika was also the site of two somewhat distinct slave-raiding and -trading networks – distinct from each other and distinct from others in East Africa. Thinking about Lake Tanganyika's history in these terms has significant consequences for understanding slave trades in the wider East African context. Popular (and some historical) accounts, including those displayed in Tanzania's museums commemorating the nineteenth century, portray Lake Tanganyika as the western limit of a long-distance slave route across present-day Tanzania.[24] The sources, though, are unequivocal – there were very few people traded as

---

[20] Cooper, *Plantation Slavery*, 115; Henri Médard, 'La traite et l'esclavage en Afrique orientale et dans l'Océan Indien: Une historiographie éclatée', in *Traites et esclavages en Afrique orientale*, eds. Médard et al., 51.

[21] Deutsch, 'Notes on the rise of slavery', 84.

[22] Edward A. Alpers, *Ivory and Slaves in East Central Africa: Changing patterns of international trade to the later nineteenth century* (Berkeley: University of California Press, 1975), 172–265; Sheriff, *Slaves, Spices and Ivory*, 158–72; John Iliffe, *A Modern History of Tanganyika* (Cambridge: Cambridge University Press, 1979), 49; Médard, 'La traite et l'esclavage', 53; Andrew Roberts, 'The Nyamwezi', in *Tanzania before 1900*, ed. Roberts, 127.

[23] Cooper, *Plantation Slavery*, 177; Fabian, *Making Identity*, 114–16; Glassman, *Feasts and Riot*, 3.

[24] These museums include the Caravan Serai and the Catholic Historic Museum in Bagamoyo, Livingstone's Tembe in Kwihara, Tabora, and the Livingstone Memorial Museum in Ujiji, Kigoma. Academic texts that have perpetuated this version of history include: Brown and Brown, 'East African trade towns', 184–8; Zöller, 'Crossing multiple borders', 306; Reid, *War in Pre-colonial Eastern Africa*, 113; Anastasia Banshchikova, 'Historical memory of the 19th century Arab slave trade in the modern day Tanzania: Between family trauma and state-planted tolerance', in *The Omnipresent Past: Historical anthropology of Africa and African diaspora*, eds. Dmitri M. Bondarenko and Marina L. Butovskaya (Moscow: LRC Publishing House, 2019), 26.

slaves along the entirety of the commercial routes between Lake Tanganyika and the Indian Ocean. Instead, almost all those brought from around Lake Tanganyika and further west were absorbed by lakeshore societies in support of their demand for agricultural labour. In an explicit example from 1879, one LMS missionary in Ujiji wrote: '[Coastal traders] going coastwise with ivory may take a few odd slaves ... along with them if profitable investments offer, but not in large numbers and I should say [they] are always parted with before reaching the coast'.[25] The enslaved taken eastwards in this context were mostly traded in Mirambo's domain and in Tabora.[26] This source is in addition to any number that comment on Ujiji as an important final destination for enslaved people and on the importance of demand in the interior of Africa, rather than on the Indian Ocean littoral, for slave-raiding and -trading activities from such towns.[27] Such sources are moreover supported by recent histories of the East African coast, which accurately point out that the commercial routes from Lake Tanganyika were predominantly ivory routes and not slave routes.[28] People living in and around Lake Tanganyika's emporia were primarily importers of enslaved people (not exporters), which served to support increases in agricultural productivity there.

The oldest slave-trading networks around Lake Tanganyika's shores focused on the lakeshore itself. One of the earliest first-hand European accounts of the lakeshore, written by Richard Burton, described Ujiji in 1858 as the major the 'slave mart' of the region.[29] At this time, Jiji traders purchased most of their people for enslavement in other northern lakeshore regions, such as in Urundi and Uvira, or enslaved people were brought to them from the Jiji hinterland of Uha.[30] There are no records

[25] CWM/LMS/06/02/004 Hore to Mullens, 16 Apr. 1879.

[26] A.G.M.Afr. C.16-7. Journal du P. Deniaud, 1 Nov. 1879.

[27] A few examples from different archives/publications include: Burton, *Lake Regions*, 318; CWM/LMS/06/02/005 Griffith to Whitehouse, 19 May 1880; A.G.M.Afr. C.16-7. Journal du P. Deniaud, 14 Jan. 1880; RMCA ESA HA.01.017-7. 'Rapport de voyage à Oudjidji', 7 July 1883. See also: Melvin E. Page, 'The Manyema hordes of Tippu Tip: A case study in social stratification and the slave trade in eastern Africa', *The International Journal of African Historical Studies*, 7, 1 (1974), 72.

[28] Steven Fabian, 'East Africa's Gorée: Slave trade and slave tourism in Bagamoyo, Tanzania', *Canadian Journal of African Studies*, 47, 1 (2013), 95–114; Sheriff, *Slaves, Spices and Ivory*, 172–90. The reasons for the discrepancy between some popular and academic accounts of the slave trade in nineteenth-century East Africa have been explored in: Philip Gooding, 'David Livingstone, UNESCO, and nation building in 19th-century Scotland and 21st-century East and Central Africa', *Journal of Indian Ocean World Studies*, 5, 2 (2021), 243–69; Jean Lindström, *Muted Memories: Heritage making, Bagamoyo, and the East African caravan trade* (Oxford: Berghahn Books, 2019).

[29] Burton, *Lake Regions*, 318.   [30] Burton, *Lake Regions*, 318.

of Jiji peoples entering into other regions and raiding for captives themselves. Rather, in the case of Urundi and Uvira, Jiji traders travelled by
canoe to other lakeshore markets, purchased people for enslavement
(and non-human goods) and brought them back to Ujiji. Violence associated with political expansion in Urundi during the early nineteenth
century may have contributed to the supply of northern lakeshore
markets in this context.[31] The arrival of coastal traders in Uvira in
c.1840 likely provided a further stimulant for raiding. The coastal traders
relied on supplies of captives brought to them by Vira traders who raided
inland.[32] Similarly, it is more probable that Ha slave traders brought
those they enslaved to the Jiji market than the other way around. All these
operations were small scale, at least initially. Burton wrote that ivory and
enslaved people were only 'occasionally ... hawked about' in Ujiji.[33]
Lacustrine transport was likely an issue here. Burton also wrote that the
Jiji's large dugout canoes, imported from Ugoma on the opposite shore,
lacked caulking, meaning that bailing water was a constant issue, possibly
limiting each canoe's potential carrying capacity.[34] This may have
limited the extent of the slave trade around Lake Tanganyika for much
of the first half of the nineteenth century.

Later in the century, slave-trading networks around Lake Tanganyika
expanded in size and scope. This was partly facilitated by advancements
in boat-building technologies. Jiji canoes were able to carry around
40–50 people by the 1870s.[35] This enabled Jiji slave traders to make
profitable journeys towards the lake's southern end.[36] Violence in and
around Ufipa, Ulungu, and Marungu in the 1870s and 1880s furthermore created a ready supply of captives, whom traders brought to the
lake to sell to passing canoes.[37] In Ufipa and surrounding regions, this

[31] Newbury, *Land beyond the Mists*, 306.
[32] Chubaka, 'Origines de la ville d'Uvira', 98–108; Depelchin, 'From pre-capitalism to imperialism', 166–75.
[33] Burton, *Lake Regions*, 310. See also: John Hanning Speke, 'Journal of a cruise on the Tanganyika Lake, Central Africa', *Blackwood's Edinburgh Magazine*, 86 (1859), 344.
[34] Burton, *Lake Regions*, 338–9.
[35] Stanley, *How I Found*, 393; RMCA HMSA 4610. Stanley to *Daily Telegraph* and *New York Herald*, 28 Oct. 1876. For more on boating technologies, see: Chapter 3.
[36] Cameron, *Across Africa*, 184; CWM/LMS/06/05/21 Hore, 'Voyage to the south end of Lake Tanganyika', 1 Apr. 1880.
[37] Cameron, *Across Africa*, 184; Stanley, *Dark Continent*, II, 34; Thomson, *Central African Lakes*, II, 34; National Archives held at the Royal Geographical Society (hereafter: NA RGS) JMS/2/144 Cameron, 'Diary of a boat journey', 18, 19, 23 Mar. 1874, 1 Apr. 1874; RMCA HMSA 17. 'Field notebook', 30 June 1876; ZNA AA2/29 Hore to Kirk, 25 Feb. 1880; CWM/LMS/06/05/21 Hore, 'Voyage to the south end of Lake Tanganyika', 1 Apr. 1880; CWM/LMS/06/02/009 Jones to Thomson, 2 Dec. 1884; Giraud, *Les lacs*, 1884; Reid, *War in Pre-colonial Eastern Africa*, 144, 171–2.

violence was generally attributed to *ruga ruga* – militarised young men, often in the service of Mirambo or Nyungu ya Mawe;[38] in Ulungu, it was associated with the attacks of Ngoni, Bemba, and coastal traders;[39] and in Marungu, coastal traders and Lusinga – a lesser-known warlord/state-builder and a contemporary of Mirambo – played a significant role.[40] Concurrently, some lakeshore populations expanded their capacity for raiding, rather than just trading for people brought to the lake by others.[41] Holoholo (Guha) populations living around the Lukuga River outlet went on joint annual raids with Rua populations from the lake's hinterland in Ugoma, to Uguha's north.[42] They kept most of those they enslaved for themselves, although they sold a minority to traders who then sold them on in Ujiji.[43] Additionally, coastal traders, their associates, and Fipa populations resident in and around Kirando in the 1880s went on occasional raids in Marungu.[44] During the 1870s and 1880s, the lakeshore was an accessible slave market for people living in its emporia, and rural areas became increasingly vulnerable to devastation at the hands of slave raiders and traders.

The permanent settlement of coastal traders in Ujiji from the 1860s precipitated an expansion of the regional scope of slave trading to the lakeshore. Coastal traders and their associates enslaved significant numbers of people from Manyema and hinterland parts of Marungu. Their actions represented the first time that people living on the lakeshore went beyond the lake's immediate hinterland to acquire people for enslavement. Their networks of credit also facilitated the payment of slave raiders in Uvira to raid in the lake's mountainous hinterland on their behalf.[45] The size of these longer-distance slave trades almost

[38] CWM/LMS/06/02/008 Hore to Whitehouse, 15 Aug. 1883; CWM/LMS/06/05/21 Hore, 'Voyage to the south end of Lake Tanganyika', 17 Mar. 1880; CWM/LMS/06/02/008 Jones to Whitehouse, 17 July 1883. For more on the *ruga ruga*, see: Moyd, *Violent Intermediaries*, 73–82.
[39] Roberts, *A History of the Bemba*, 151–60; CWM/LMS/06/05/21 Hore, 'Voyage to the south end of Lake Tanganyika', 1 Apr. 1880.
[40] Roberts, *A Dance of Assassins*, 16; Loffman, *Church, State, and Colonialism*, 88.
[41] RMCA ESA HA.01.017-7. Storms, 'L'esclavage', n.d.
[42] CWM/LMS/06/02/004 Hutley to Whitehouse, 19 Oct. 1879, 22 Nov. 1879; CWM/LMS/06/02/005 Griffith to Whitehouse, 19 May 1880, 24 Aug. 1880; CWM/LMS/06/02/005 Hutley, 'Uguha and its people', 29 Sep. 1880; A.G.M.Afr. Diaire de Kibanga, 23 Apr. 1885, 5 Jan. 1886, 27 Mar. 1886; Hutley, *Central African Diaries*, 138; Reid, *War in Pre-colonial Eastern Africa*, 90.
[43] CWM/LMS/06/02/005 Griffith to Whitehouse, 19 May 1880; CWM/LMS/06/02/005 Hutley, 'Uguha and its people', 29 Sep. 1880.
[44] RMCA ESA HA.01.017-7. Storms, 'Rapport sur un voyage dans la partie sud du Tanganika', 1 Apr. 1884.
[45] Chubaka, 'Origines de la ville d'Uvira', 98–108; Depelchin, 'From pre-capitalism to imperialism', 166–80.

certainly dwarfed those that were limited to Lake Tanganyika's shores by the late 1870s. In 1876, Henry Morton Stanley wrote of 800 captives from Manyema in Uguha waiting to be shipped to Ujiji for sale.[46] This is an improbably large number, but it still represents a significantly larger estimate than any of the numbers of people being traded to pre-existing lakeshore populations.[47] Coastal traders' construction of *dhow*-like craft – canoes with built-up sides and sails – may have made trans-lake transport of large numbers of people more feasible. Reports suggest that these craft could carry around a hundred people.[48] In 1879, one LMS missionary wrote that most coastal traders kept between twenty and a hundred people in bondage, with Mwinyi Kheri, the leader of Ujiji's coastal trader community at that time, owning closer to the higher number.[49] In 1876, Stanley estimated that Kheri kept around 120.[50] By contrast, although they were reported by an LMS missionary as 'great slave owners', individual Jiji did not enslave people in comparable numbers to the coastal traders.[51] The coastal traders' enslavement of large numbers of people on Lake Tanganyika's shores illustrates their centrality to the agricultural revolution around the lake's emporia.

Most enslaved people on the lakeshore worked either as domestics or as farmers. This is illustrated by the fact that most of the enslaved were either women or children.[52] Domestic and farm work were traditionally

---

[46] RMCA HMSA 4610 Stanley to *Daily Telegraph* and *New York Herald*, 28 Oct. 1876.

[47] Historians (see especially Reid, *War in Pre-colonial Eastern Africa*, 82) have cast doubt on the numbers quoted in Stanley's account, generally accusing him of overestimation. This applies most notably in his account of Buganda's army in 1875, which in his publication recounting his experience he claimed was 150,000-strong (Stanley, *Dark Continent*, I, 238). This figure is all the more questionable given that in his original diary, now stored in the Henry Morton Stanley Archive at the Royal Museum for Central Africa in Tervuren, Belgium, new numbers have been added to the account in a different pen to the original. Who did this to the diary and when is unknown. RMCA HMSA 15. Field Notebook (15 Aug. 1875–1 Mar. 1876), 27 Aug. 1875.

[48] NA RGS JMS/2/144 Cameron, 'Diary of a boat journey', 4, 5, 11 Mar. 1874; CWM/LMS/06/02/003 Hore, 'Launch of the "Calabash"', 9 Dec. 1878; CWM/LMS/06/02/005 Hore to Whitehouse, 20 Feb. 1880; CWM/LMS/06/02/009 Brooks to Whitehouse, 6 Aug. 1884; RMCA ESA HA.01.017-5. Storms to AIA, 16 Aug. 1884.

[49] CWM/LMS/06/02/004 Hore to Mullens, 16 Apr. 1879; ZNA AA1/23 Hore to Kirk, 14 Apr. 1879.

[50] Stanley, *Dark Continent*, II, 7. This may further illustrate Stanley's capacity for overestimation.

[51] CWM/LMS/06/02/004 Hore to Mullens, 16 Apr. 1879; ZNA AA1/23 Hore to Kirk, 14 Apr. 1879.

[52] Deutsch, *Emancipation without Abolition*, 70; Reid, *War in Pre-colonial Eastern Africa*, 120, 157; Beachey, 'The East African ivory trade', 276; Deutsch, 'Notes on the rise of slavery', 88; Marcia Wright, *Strategies of Slaves and Women: Life-stories from East/Central Africa* (New York: Lilian Barber Press, 1993), 6, 26; Page, 'Manyema hordes', 73; RMCA HMSA 4610. Stanley to *Daily Telegraph* and *New York Herald*, 28 Oct. 1876.

reserved for these demographics, and the nature of slave raiding and trading reinforced this pattern.[53] Slave raiders often killed the adult males they encountered. Slave traders and owners feared what they saw as the potentially disruptive capabilities of adult males, as well as their capacity for fleeing.[54] Meanwhile, killing them had the effect of breaking women's and children's kinship connections to their former home, decreasing the chance that they would seek to return. Furthermore, over time, both women and children had opportunities to improve the conditions of their bondage. For women, this usually occurred when they gave birth to their enslaver's kin, which could give them 'free dependent' status within their (now former) enslaver's household. From this point, their status and lives differed little from other, married, 'free' women, and their labour may have been more directed to domestic chores and childrearing than to agriculture.[55] On reaching maturity, meanwhile, boys were often employed in other domains, including as boatmen, soldiers, porters, and proxy traders. Their transition to these roles represented an improvement in their status to one that resembled more closely client than slave.[56] It may be for these reasons that some women 'welcomed' slavery and sought it out for themselves and for their children.[57] Evidence suggests that some 'free' men did likewise.[58] Slavery thus had the somewhat paradoxical potential to offer security and advancement in the long run.

One result of these dynamics was that agricultural work became intimately associated with slave status. This was especially true among men associated with one or more coastal traders. Both LMS and White Fathers' missionaries on the shores of Lake Tanganyika complained that associates of coastal traders, many of whom called themselves *ngwana* (Swahili: gentlemen, freeborn), refused agricultural work because they saw it as the work of the enslaved.[59] This was in spite of the fact that many of these people would previously have been considered slaves and

---

[53] Interview with Victoire Ndaruzinza, 4 Nov. 2013; Stephen J. Rockel, 'Enterprising partners: Caravan women in nineteenth century Tanzania', *Canadian Journal of African Historical Studies*, 34, 3 (2000), 117; Stephen J. Rockel, 'A nation of porters: The Nyamwezi and the labour market in nineteenth-century Tanzania', *The Journal of African History*, 41, 2 (2000), 174; Hore, 'Twelve tribes', 11.

[54] RMCA ESA HA.01.017-7. 'Rapport de voyage à Oudjidji', 7 July 1883; Iliffe, *A Modern History*, 50; Moyd, *Violent Intermediaries*, 81.

[55] Paul E. Lovejoy, *Transformations in Slavery: A history of slavery in Africa*, 3rd ed. (Cambridge: Cambridge University Press, 2011), 14, 34; McDow, *Buying Time*, 152; Wright, *Strategies of Slaves*, 37, 100.

[56] The transition from 'slave' to 'client' is examined more closely in Chapter 6.

[57] Wright, *Strategies of Slaves*, 26–8, 47–9.   [58] Page, 'Manyema hordes', 72.

[59] CWM/LMS/06/02/004 Hore to Mullens, 10 Jan. 1879; A.G.M.Afr. Diaire de Mkapakwe, 26 Jan. 1885.

that they were still in some form of bondage to their (former) enslaver. Other men among pre-existing lakeshore populations likely worked on farms for some of the year, such as when labour requirements were more intense during the planting and harvest seasons.[60] For the most part, though, they left the day-to-day running of the farm to women and their dependents – they themselves were predominantly fishermen and lacustrine traders.[61] Thus, the nineteenth-century 'agricultural revolution' around Lake Tanganyika's emergent emporia was built on the backs of women and an expanded supply of enslaved labour, the latter mostly being raided for around the lake and in the eastern Congo rainforests. Demand for enslaved people in this context was perpetually high from the 1860s. The growth of emporia and the arrival and departure of ever larger caravans necessitated the creation of a larger agricultural labour pool, while the structures of bondage took the enslaved out of that pool over time.

The 'Agricultural Revolution': Crops

At the beginning of the nineteenth century, East African farmers mostly grew indigenous staples – predominantly sorghum and millet. On the shores of Lake Tanganyika, the earliest first-hand reports of the region show that these were supplemented by bananas, melons, groundnuts, beans, sweet potatoes, yams, cucumbers, and more.[62] Bananas are particularly notable in this context. In the hinterland of Lake Victoria's western and northern shores, they were a staple and may have been so since around 1000 CE.[63] This is significant because bananas originated in Southeast Asia. Their presence in East Africa speaks to the Great Lakes' *longue durée* connections with the wider IOW – oft-neglected by historians.[64] However, the absence of other 'foreign' staples that were farmed in East Africa's coastal and island regions before the nineteenth century, such as cassava, maize, and rice, displays these connections' limitations. Cassava, maize, and rice only reached Lake Tanganyika and

---

[60] Rockel, 'A nation of porters', 180.

[61] Cameron, *Across Africa*, 176; Bolser-Brown, 'Muslim influence', 620.

[62] Burton, *Lake Regions*, 316.

[63] David L. Schoenbrun, 'Cattle herds and banana gardens: The historical geography of the western Great Lakes region, *ca* AD 800–1500', *The African Archaeological Review*, 11 (1993), 50–1.

[64] For archaeological and recent historical perspectives on this phenomenon, see: Chami, 'Graeco-Roman trade link', 205–15; Kusimba and Walz, 'When did the Swahili become maritime?', 429–43; Gwyn Campbell, 'Africa, the Indian Ocean World, and the "early modern": Historiographical conventions and problems', *Journal of Indian Ocean World Studies*, 1, 1 (2017), 24–37.

elsewhere on the major commercial routes to East Africa's Great Lakes region after 1800, although traditions suggest a slightly earlier arrival for maize in Buganda.[65] These crops' arrival and incorporation into the interior's agricultural regimes speak to the increased connectivity across littoral and interior regions of the western IOW during this period. How they spread was intertwined with farmers' concerns with rainfall, soil, nutritional value, seasonality, and cultural expectations. Overall, though, their adoption speaks to the increasingly commercial prerogatives motivating agricultural production.

Sorghum and millet are similar crops and are indigenous to Africa. They dominated the production of staples in the East African interior until at least the middle of the nineteenth century. Presently, numerous African countries lump the export figures for sorghum and millet together, and most nineteenth-century European 'explorers' and missionaries probably used the words 'sorghum' and 'millet' interchangeably, often using the Swahili word *mtama* to refer to both.[66] Both were (and remain) valued for their grains, which were ground and mixed with water to make a porridge or *ugali* (a stiff porridge).[67] *Ugali* is highly nutritious, being rich in carbohydrates, proteins, fats, vitamins, and minerals. In East Africa, sorghum and millet were, assuming adequate rainfall, sown during the *mvuli* in October-November, and they were harvested three to four months later. Both are resistant to drought (sorghum has the highest water-use efficiency in drought conditions of all widely grown grains in the world), and rain-fed crops thrive in regions where annual rainfall is significantly lower than around Lake Tanganyika.[68] Thus, a late onset of rains was rarely disastrous for sorghum and millet farmers, as established crops could survive in the slightly dryer months of January and February. However, both sorghum and millet require fertile soils. This may partly explain their prominence in the fertile Luiche valley around Ujiji and elsewhere on the lake's north-eastern shores, as well

---

[65] Reid, *Political Power*, 28–9.

[66] Richard F. Burton was an exception. He referred to them individually throughout *Lake Regions* and 'Lake regions of Central Equatorial Africa, with notices of the Lunar Mountains and the sources of the White Nile: Being the results of an expedition undertaken under the patronage of Her Majesty's Government and the Royal Geographical Society of London, in the years 1857–1859', *Journal of the Royal Geographical Society of London*, 29 (1859), 1–454.

[67] Burton, 'Lake regions', 398. Presently, *ugali* is usually made from maize meal.

[68] Adil Bashir Karrar, Hassan Ibrahim Mohamed, Haitham Ragab Elramlwai, and Atif Elsadig Idris, 'Rain fed sorghum (Sorghum bicolor L. Moench) crop growth yield forecasting model', *Universal Journal of Agricultural Research*, 2, 5 (2014), 154–67; N. Mbava, M. Mutema, R. Zengeni H. Shimelis, and V. Chaplot, 'Factors affecting crop water use efficiency: A worldwide meta-analysis', *Agricultural water management*, 228 (2020), 1–11.

as their absence in some other regions, such as on most of the lake's western shore, where the soils are rocky and the terrain is mountainous.[69] For most of the nineteenth century, Lake Tanganyika's largest population centres were located in regions where it was possible to grow sorghum and millet.

Cassava, also referred to as manioc, was the first nineteenth-century import to supplement sorghum and millet on Lake Tanganyika's shores. It is a New World crop and probably first arrived on the East African coast via Portuguese ships during the eighteenth century.[70] By the late 1850s, it was present on most of the well-trodden commercial routes and around emergent emporia in mainland East Africa, but it was absent, for example, in the corridor between Lakes Tanganyika and Victoria, where bananas dominated the agricultural regime.[71] These patterns suggest that cassava was a fairly recent addition to the region in the 1850s and that it was spread by traders arriving from the coast. Interior East Africans' receptivity to cassava may have been influenced by the fact that it grows quickly, with little rain, and in marginal soils. It was thus ideally suited to highly mobile populations who were vulnerable to raids from militarised rivals, such as around Lake Tanganyika's south-eastern shores when Ngoni and related peoples arrived in the region during the 1840s.[72] It was also able to grow along the lake's mountainous western shore, allowing larger population centres to emerge there for the first time. Indeed, after mid-century, cassava became a staple on parts of the south-western lakeshore and its hinterland.[73] Cassava's major drawback is its low nutritional value. Thus, cultivating cassava was less popular around Ujiji, where growing other, more nutritious crops was possible, even if it was usually available in its markets.[74] In short, the introduction of cassava to Lake Tanganyika's shores allowed larger population centres to emerge where previously there were none while sustaining people who were most vulnerable to regional violence.

Cassava was accompanied into the interior by maize. The most common type grown in nineteenth-century East Africa was flint corn, which probably first arrived on the East African coast during the late sixteenth or early seventeenth centuries.[75] Maize is similarly nutritious to

---

[69] Burton, *Lake Regions*, 309, 316; Stanley, *Dark Continent*, II, 3–4.
[70] Rory J. Hillocks, 'Cassava in Africa', in *Cassava: Biology, production and utilization*, eds. Rory J. Hillocks, J. M. Thresh, and A. Bellotti (Wallingford: CABI, 2002), 41.
[71] Hillocks, 'Cassava in Africa', 41.   [72] Spear, *Zwangendaba's Ngoni*, 1–43.
[73] A.G.M.Afr. Diaire de Mkapakwe, 5 Nov. 1884; A.G.M.Afr. Diaire de Mpala, Jan. 1890.
[74] Burton, *Lake Regions*, 316, 323; Stanley, *Dark Continent*, II, 4; Hore, 'Twelve tribes', 10.
[75] Marvin P. Miracle, 'The introduction and spread of maize in Africa', *The Journal of African History*, 6, 1 (1965), 47–8. For the effects of flint corn on north-eastern African history, see: McCann, *Maize and Grace*, 82–4.

sorghum and millet, requires similarly fertile soil, and was also planted in the nineteenth century during the *mvuli*. Additionally, like the indigenous grains mentioned, East Africans ground it down into a powder, before mixing it with water to make *ugali*.[76] Burton reported in 1858 that maize was prevalent on all major commercial routes and around emergent emporia, but Uvira was the only locale on Lake Tanganyika's shores where he mentioned its presence specifically.[77] This would also explain maize's absence from descriptions of the fields around Ujiji until the mid-1870s. By this time, maize was already being grown on Urundi's shoreline and in the fertile Lukuga River valley in Uguha.[78] Its abundance in these locations led to surpluses being sold in Ujiji's markets.[79] However, by 1878–80, the Jiji were importing sorghum from nearby terrestrial regions to supplement the maize that they grew themselves.[80] Maize's main advantage over sorghum and millet is that, under the right conditions, it requires less space and less labour to produce the same yield – or a larger yield with the same or more labour and space.[81] Indeed, it has the highest potential water-use efficiency of any cereal crop.[82] It is, however, more vulnerable to water stress, and so this efficiency decreases significantly (well below that of sorghum) under drought or flood conditions.[83] Thus, droughts and floods, especially just after it is planted during the *mvuli*, can severely affect yield, although planting again before the *masika* can offset the effects of seasonal drought on a one-annual crop regime.[84] Increased usage of maize over sorghum and millet brought more potential but also more risk to the lakeshore's agricultural output.

Rice was the final major imported crop to arrive on Lake Tanganyika's shores during the nineteenth century. The origins of rice in coastal East Africa are traditionally associated with the spread of Islam, particularly from the tenth century CE onwards, but more recent work has traced its presence in some East African islands to Austronesian migrations in the second half of the first millennium CE.[85] Rice's older association with

---

[76] Livingstone, *Last Journals*, 433.

[77] Burton, 'Lake regions', 399; Burton, *Lake Regions*, 354.

[78] Stanley, *How I Found*, 395; Stanley, *Dark Continent*, II, 4, 47; RMCA ESA HA.01.017-7. 'Rapport de voyage à Oudjidji', 7 July 1883.

[79] Stanley, *How I Found*, 436; Stanley, *Dark Continent*, II, 4.

[80] Hore, 'Twelve tribes', 9; CWM/LMS/06/02/006 Wookey to Whitehouse, 26 Jan. 1881.

[81] Cherniwchan and Moreno-Cruz, 'Maize and precolonial Africa', 138, 141–2.

[82] Mbava et al., 'Factors affecting crop water use efficiency', 1–11.

[83] McCann, *Maize and Grace*, 19.

[84] Hargurdeep S. Saini and Mark E. Westgate, 'Reproductive development in grain crops during drought', *Advances in Agronomy*, 68 (1999), 59–96.

[85] Walshaw, 'Converting to rice', 137–54; Alison Crowther, Leilani Lucas, Richard Helm, Mark Horton, Ceri Shipton, Henry T. Wright, Sarah Walshaw, Matthew Pawlowicz, Chantal Radimilahy, Katerina Douka, Llorenç Picornell-Gelabert, Dorian Q. Fuller,

Islam in historical thinking may be linked to impressions of the present and the more recent past, as rice's whiteness has been associated with purity among Muslims on East Africa's Indian Ocean littoral.[86] In the nineteenth century, coastal associations between rice and Islam were transferred into the interior. Emile Storms of the AIA reported that coastal traders and their associates refused to eat any staple other than rice, assuming it was available.[87] Also, rice was mostly only available in lakeshore towns where coastal traders or their associates were resident, and it only became available in those towns after they settled.[88] Lakeshore populations did not adopt rice cultivation independently, except around the southern extremity of the lake during in the 1880s.[89] Some Europeans also grew rice at their stations. Its vulnerability to the effects of drought compared to sorghum and millet, its higher labour requirements compared to maize, and seasonality likely played roles here. Regarding seasonality, rather than during the *mvuli*, the optimal planting time for a one-harvest crop of rice in the East African interior is before the onset of the *masika*. Its adoption by lakeshore populations would thus have necessitated a major shift in the agricultural schedule, making them reliant on abundant rainfall in one rainy season rather than spreading the risk between two. Lakeshore people's reticence to cultivate rice in the nineteenth century was likely tied to a combination of a marginal environment, additional labour requirements, and cultural expectations.

The environment's marginality is crucial for understanding the effects of maize's and rice's introduction to agricultural regimes around Lake Tanganyika's emporia. Even in the lakeshore's most fertile regions, such as in the Luiche River Valley around Ujiji, maize only produces around 40 per cent of its maximum yield under unconstrained temperature, soil, and climatic conditions.[90] Yields are significantly less than this in many other regions around the lakeshore. These kinds of adverse environmental conditions have underpinned sub-Saharan Africa's relatively low

---

and Nicole L. Boivin, 'Ancient crops provide first archaeological signature of the westward Austronesian expansion', *Proceedings of the National Academy of Sciences of the United States of America*, 113, 24 (2016), 6635–40.

[86] Walshaw, 'Converting to rice', 148.

[87] RMCA ESA HA.01.017-7. Storms, 'Les Wagoina', n.d.

[88] This is supported by oral evidence in, for example, Burundi. See: Interview with Georges Sindarubaza, 4 Nov. 2013.

[89] Burton, *Lake Regions*, 316; CWM/LMS/06/02/006 Hutley, 'Uguha and its people', 29 Sep. 1881; CWM/LMS/06/02/008 Hore to Whitehouse, 31 Aug. 1883; CWM/LMS/06/02/008 Hore to Whitehouse, 25 Sep.–11 Nov. 1883; CWM/LMS/06/02/009 Hore to Whitehouse, 2 Apr. 1884; CWM/LMS/06/02/013 Jones to Thompson, 26 Feb. 1888.

[90] Cherniwchan and Moreno-Cruz, 'Maize and precolonial Africa', 142–3.

agricultural output compared to other global regions over the *longue durée*. As the sole environmental factor with significant seasonal, annual, and decadal variation affecting crop growth in East Africa, rainfall is highly important in this context. Although there are regional and sub-regional differences, Lake Tanganyika is part of a belt that stretches across much of the interior of equatorial Africa that receives an annual average of around 1,000 millimetres of rainfall. Seasonal changes that have contributed to deviations from this mean are correlated with significantly lower maize yields in East Africa, especially under the rain-fed conditions that characterised agricultural regimes in the nineteenth century.[91] Moreover, even years of average rainfall provide adverse conditions for using rice as a staple, at least compared to regions that receive a higher annual average. In East Africa's coastal and island regions, which receive closer to 1,500 millimetres of annual rainfall, two harvests per year are possible, which are planted during the *mvuli* and the *masika*.[92] Lower average annual rainfall in the interior of Africa limited rice production to one annual harvest.

The addition of cassava, maize, and rice to Lake Tanganyika's agricultural regimes thus opened the region to a range of possibilities. Aided by high-yield crops and expanded networks of slave raiding and trading, average yields grew in most lakeshore regions for most of the nineteenth century, which facilitated the growth of emporia, including in regions where lack of soil fertility inhibited their emergence beforehand. Additionally, increased diversity of staple crops introduced the region's peoples to coastal cultural associations with certain foods, such as rice, and diversified their diets, possibly improving their resistance to disease and stimulating demographic growth for most of the period.[93] These processes had the potential to be further aided by the addition of new dynamics to the planting schedule. In theory at least, having two planting

---

[91] Bahareh Kamali, Karim C. Abbaspour, Anthony Lehmann, Bernhard Wehrli, and Hong Yang, 'Spatial assessment of maize physical drought vulnerability in sub-Saharan Africa: Linking drought exposure with crop failure', *Environmental Research Letters*, 13, 7 (2018), 1–13.

[92] Walshaw, 'Converting to rice', 147–8; Surajit K. De Datta, *Principles and Practices of Rice Cultivation* (New York: John Wiley & Sons, 1981), 11–19.

[93] The idea that the nineteenth century was a period of demographic growth in East Africa is in line with: Helge Kjekshus, *Ecology Control and Economic Development in East African History: The case of Tanganyika 1850–1950*, 2nd ed. (London: James Currey, 1996), 24–5. It is also in line with studies of West Africa, which also experienced demographic stability after the introduction of maize, despite the forced removal of millions from the region via transatlantic slave trade. See, for example: Cherniwchan and Moreno-Cruz, 'Maize and precolonial Africa', 137–50; John Thornton, 'The slave trade in eighteenth century Angola: Effects on demographic structures', *Canadian Journal of African Historical Studies*, 14, 3 (1980), 417–27.

seasons – one for maize, sorghum, and millet during the *mvuli*, and one for rice during the *masika* – could offset some of the effects of seasonal drought on annual food production. However, increased diversity of crops and seasonality did not mean more food security in the long run. The commercialisation of agriculture necessitated the prioritisation of crops with higher potential yields over crops with higher levels of resistance to water stress. This paradigm had the potential to contribute to shortages in seasons, years, and longer periods of significantly below or above average rainfall.

The Effects of a Changing Climate

Climatic and other environmental factors underpinned much about the success or otherwise of the agricultural revolution around East Africa's main commercial routes and emporia. The importance of climatic fluctuations to the broader patterns of the region's history grew during the period under review, as East African farmers transitioned away from growing crops with high water-use efficiency under drought conditions towards growing crops with high potential yields in regular rainfall years. Meanwhile, pressures on the 'revolutionised' agricultural regimes continued to mount, especially in the 1870s and 1880s. This was a period of significant urban growth, during which the numbers of people arriving and departing in caravans frequently reached into the low thousands. Thus, seasons, years, and/or long-term trends towards drought had the capacity to produce weaker harvests and food shortages at times when increasing numbers of people were demanding a supply. This could have significant consequences for people's diets and their capacities to spread and resist disease, while also affecting competition for resources, levels of violence, political stability, and structural change within emporia. Conditions in Lake Tanganyika's emergent emporia were increasingly dependent on regular rainfall from the Indian Ocean monsoon system as the century wore on.

Noting the importance of the climatic context in this history necessitates inserting global climatic teleconnections and their effects on East African rainfall into the discussion. The most important in this context are ENSO, IOD, volcanism, and sunspot activity. ENSO and IOD are anomalies of sea surface temperature (SST) and atmospheric pressure in the Pacific and Indian Oceans respectively. El Niño years, in which SSTs in the equatorial east-central Pacific Ocean are warmer than average, alongside a positive IOD, in which SSTs in the western Indian Ocean are warmer than the eastern, are associated with above average rainfall during East Africa's *mvuli* season of that year and below average rainfall in the preceding *mvuli*.[94] La Niña years, when SSTs in the east-central Pacific are below average, are associated with drought. This is the opposite of Northeast and Southeast Africa, South and most of Southeast Asia, and northern China, where El Niño is associated with below average rainfall.[95] Meanwhile, volcanic eruptions that emit large quantities of sulphur dioxide into the atmosphere and block radiation from the sun are associated with global cooling and a weakened monsoon system, thus contributing to erratic climate throughout the IOW.[96] Global temperatures are additionally affected by solar activity, with solar minimums (when there are fewer than normal sunspots) also associated with global cooling and erratic rainfall. Finally, for reasons that are not yet fully understood, drought in eastern Africa often transcends several rainy seasons. This has been especially true for the twenty-first century, though it has precedent in the late nineteenth century.[97] Such patterns necessitate looking at long-term and short-term trends in East African rainfall.

The first years of the period under review are widely associated with adverse climatic factors in the IOW. Representing the final years of the LIA, a series of extreme climatic anomalies occurred in c.1750–1840. These conditions are associated with extreme ENSO events, such as that which occurred in the 1780s and 1790s, a series of sulphur-rich volcanic eruptions, including those of Laki, Iceland in 1783 and Tambora, present-day Indonesia in 1815, and the Dalton solar minimum.[98] In the Middle East, drought in the 1780s and 1790s contributed to instability in Yemen and pushed interior populations in Oman towards littoral regions of the western IOW.[99] These trends partly underpinned Muscat's importance in oceanic trade from the late eighteenth century

---

[94] Sharon E. Nicholson and Jeeyoung Kim, 'The relationship of the El-Niño Southern Oscillation to African rainfall', *International Journal of Climatology*, 17 (1997), 117–35.

[95] Campbell, *Africa and the Indian Ocean World*, 14.

[96] Campbell, *Africa and the Indian Ocean World*, 16–17.

[97] Nicholson, 'Climate and climatic variability', 614–20.

[98] Campbell, *Africa and the Indian Ocean World*, 184; Fang XiuQi, Xiao Lingbo, and Wei ZhuDeng 'Social impacts of the climatic shift around the turn of the 19th century on the North China plain', *Science China Earth Sciences*, 56 (2013), 1044–58; Richard H. Grove, 'The great El Niño of 1789–93 and its global consequences: Reconstructing an extreme climate event in world environmental history', *The Medieval History Journal*, 10, 1–2 (2006), 75–98; Richard H. Grove and George Adamson, *El Niño in World History* (London: Palgrave Macmillan, 2018), 81–92; Vinita Damodaran, Rob Allan, Astrid E. J. Ogilvie, Gaston R. Demarée, Joëlle Gergis, Takehiko Mikami, Alan Mikhail, Sharon E. Nicholson, Stefan Norrgård, and James Hamilton, 'The 1780s: Global climate anomalies, floods, droughts, and famines', in *The Palgrave Handbook of Climate History*, eds. White, Pfister, and Mauelshagen, 517–50.

[99] McDow, *Buying Time*, 40; Steven Serels, 'Food insecurity and political instability in the southern Red Sea region during the "Little Ice Age", 1650–1840', in *Famines During the 'Little Ice Age' (1300–1800): Socionatural entanglements in premodern societies*, eds. Dominik Collet and Maximilian Schuh (Cham: Springer, 2018), 115–29.

and contributed to Omanis' increased presence in East Africa's coastal and island regions, especially in Zanzibar.[100] Omanis' and other coastal East Africans' influence on the interior of the mainland in the last years of the LIA remained limited, however. The extent to which this was tied to climatic factors is perhaps debatable. Palaeo-limnological evidence suggests that East Africa experienced a protracted dry period at this time, which may have limited expeditions inland.[101] Moreover, Nyamwezi peoples, who were the most prominent traders between the coast and the western Congo rainforests in this period, relied on indigenous drought-resistant crops, such as sorghum and millet, and they expanded institutions of enslavement to grow such crops from the early nineteenth century.[102] This suggests that Unyamwezi's agricultural economy was growing and was structured to resist the effects of protracted drought up to c.1840. Moreover, persistent drought coupled with heightened levels of instability may have contributed to increased demand for cassava. These conditions may partly explain cassava's relative abundance versus, for example, maize in the region up to the 1850s.

After c.1840, a period of warmer and wetter conditions underpinned increased agricultural productivity and commercial activity in the IOW, especially between South Asia, the Middle East, and eastern Africa.[103] In the interior of East Africa, an extended period of above average rainfall encouraged farmers to adopt higher-yield, less drought-resistant crops, such as maize. Apart from needing fertile soils, where maize was first adopted was heavily tied to each regions' annual rainfall. South-western Urundi (average annual rainfall of 1,151 millimetres), Uguha (1,068 millimetres) and Uvira (1,204 millimetres) provide adequate water for rain-fed maize in average and above average years.[104] Lesser average

[100] Bishara, *A Sea of Debt*, 1–57; McDow, *Buying Time*, 24–43.
[101] Bessems et al., 'Paleolimnological evidence for widespread late 18th century drought', 107–20; Nicholson, 'Historical and modern fluctuations', 53–71.
[102] Rockel, *Carriers of Culture*, 35–61; Rockel, 'A nation of porters', 178; Roberts, 'Nyamwezi trade', 39–74; Pallaver, 'Nyamwezi participation', 526; Deutsch, 'Notes on the rise of slavery', 83.
[103] Campbell, *Africa and the Indian Ocean World*, 176–98.
[104] All averages are taken from data provided by the Koninklijk Nederlands Meteorologisch Instituut (Royal Dutch Meteorological Institute), which has made rain gauge and temperature data from the Global Historical Climate Network (GHCN) freely available. Most of the data were collected during the twentieth century. Data for south-western Urundi are taken from the Nyanza-Lac rain gauge; Uguha's are taken from the Kalemie rain gauge. Uvira does not have its own rain gauge, the nearest one being at Fizi (about 120 km to Uvira's south-south-west and 10 km from Lake Tanganyika's nearest shore), which receives an annual average of 1,204 mm. Measurements for Uvira are complicated, as it lies on the border between the highlands and the Ruzizi River plain. Much of the former receive upwards of 1,400 mm per year; the latter receives less than 800 mm per year. See maps in: P. J. A. van

annual rainfall in and around Ujiji (952 millimetres) probably contributed to its people's reticence to adopt maize, at least initially. However, successive years and then decades of above average rainfall, which likely made early experiments with maize fruitful, coupled with increased demand for higher-yield crops in Ujiji's growing emporium, contributed to its widespread cultivation by the late 1870s. Additionally, the coastal traders' rice fields were aided in the 1860s and 1870s by frequently above average rainfall. Of greater concern to them during this period may have been that these conditions were contributing to a gradual rise in Lake Tanganyika's level, leading to some rice fields being washed away.[105] Problems in this context may have been exacerbated by the location of their fields and *tembes* next to the lakeshore.[106] Even so, the general trend between c.1840 and 1876 was for increased yields aided by a wetter than normal climate and the adoption of crops with higher productive potential. These conditions helped to feed emergent emporia and passing caravans, thus underpinning structures associated with the ivory trade.

Levels of rainfall from 1876 exposed vulnerabilities in Lake Tanganyika's agricultural revolution, contributing to instability in its emporia. A series of ENSO events and volcanic eruptions led to erratic levels of rainfall throughout the IOW up to the end of the century.[107] In this context, Mike Davis has referred to a series of 'Late Victorian Holocausts' from the mid-1870s onwards, in which ENSO-related droughts coupled with disastrous colonial grain policies contributed to widespread starvation and millions of deaths across the IOW and elsewhere.[108] A similar combination of adverse climatic factors coupled with exacerbating structures is observable in East Africa. The exacerbating structures here, though, were the transition to crops that were less resistant to water stress and increased demands placed on the food supply by the growth of emporia and the arrival and departure of ever larger caravans to facilitate the ivory trade. Added into this mix was epidemic disease. Again, this was a widespread feature of late nineteenth-century IOW history.[109] The prospect of famine provoked migration of vulnerable people, whose poorer diets decreased their resistance to disease,

Asten, A. M. Fermont, and G. Taulya, 'Drought is a major yield loss factor for rainfed East African banana', *Agricultural Water Management*, 98, 4 (2011), 542; Newbury, *Land beyond the Mists*, 288.

[105] Stanley, *Dark Continent*, II, 12; CWM/LMS/06/02/003 Hore, 'Kigoma Bay', 9 Dec. 1878.

[106] See: Chapter 1.   [107] Campbell, *Africa and the Indian Ocean World*, 245–54.

[108] Davis, *Late Victorian Holocausts*. See also: Deepti Singh, Richard Seager, Benjamin I. Cook, Mark Cane, Mingfang Ting, Edward Cook, and Mike Davis, 'Climate and the global famine of 1876–78', *Journal of Climate*, 31, 23, (2018), 9445–67.

[109] Campbell, *Africa and the Indian Ocean World*, 248–53.

thus contributing to the spread of epidemics. In Indian Ocean Africa, stretching from Egypt to southern Africa and including its islands, smallpox was the most persistent of these.[110] Around Lake Tanganyika, smallpox's spread is attributable to the movement of caravans, and it often found reservoirs in emergent emporia.[111] Ujiji and Mtowa experienced outbreaks almost annually in the 1880s, though they appear to have turned into epidemics along the entirety of caravan routes only in years of significant drought.[112] In short, environmental phenomena had a debilitating effect on lakeshore towns and commercial structures in the late 1870s and 1880s.

This period of adverse climatic factors began with one of the largest positive ENSO and IOD events in known history, which occurred in 1877–8. This ENSO-IOD event is associated with drought in South and Southeast Asia, northern China and north-eastern and south-eastern Africa, and with the deaths of around fifty million people worldwide.[113] In East Africa, and consistent with models that project the effects of ENSO and IOD events on East African climate, drought appears to have set in in 1876, before floods occurred in 1877–8.[114] Indeed, the *mvuli* of 1877 represents the second largest positive rainfall anomaly to occur in East Africa since collection of rain gauge data began in c.1874, and likely long before that as well.[115] Lack of source material from the lakeshore for late 1876 to early 1877 makes conclusions about the preceding drought

[110] Campbell, *Africa and the Indian Ocean World*, 248–53.

[111] Gerald W. Hartwig, 'Demographic considerations in East Africa during the nineteenth century', *International Journal of African Historical Studies*, 12, 4 (1979), 662–4; Kjekshus, *Ecology Control*, 132; CWM/LMS/06/02/005 Griffith to Whitehouse, 19 May 1880.

[112] Brown and Brown, 'East African trade towns', 190–3; CWM/LMS/06/02/005 Hore to Whitehouse, 20 July 1880; CWM/LMS/06/02/008 Hore to Whitehouse, 18–21 June 1883, Jones to Whitehouse, 20 Aug. 1883; RMCA ESA HA.01.017-6. Storms to AIA, 1883; CWM/LMS/06/02/009 Jones to Whitehouse 24 June 1884; CWM/LMS/06/02/012 Lea to Thompson, 2 Apr. 1887.

[113] Singh et al., 'Climate and the global famine', 9446; Davis, *Late Victorian Holocausts*, 23–116.

[114] Philip Gooding, 'ENSO, IOD, drought, and floods, in equatorial eastern Africa, 1876–8', in *Droughts, Floods, and Global Climatic Anomalies in the Indian Ocean World*, ed. Philip Gooding (Cham: Palgrave, 2022), 259–87.

[115] Nicholson, Funk, and Fink, 'Rainfall over the African continent', 114–27; Declan Conway, 'Extreme rainfall events and lake level changes in East Africa: Recent events and historical precedents', in *The East African Great Lakes: Limnology, palaeolimnology, and biodiversity*, eds. Eric O. Odada and Daniel O. Olago (Boston, MA: Kluwer Academic Publishers, 2002), 63–92. Elsewhere I have argued that it likely represented the largest positive rainfall anomaly since at least c.1800. See: Gooding, 'Tsetse flies, ENSO, and murder', 31–2. This summation is supported by limnological sources. See, for example: Nicholson, 'Historical and modern fluctuations', 53–71; Sharon E. Nicholson, 'Historical fluctuations of Lake Victoria and other lakes in the northern Rift Valley of East Africa', in *Environmental Change and Response in East African Lakes*, ed. J. T. Lehman (Dordrecht: Kluwer Academic Publishers, 1998), 7–35.

uncertain, but evidence from further east suggests drought forced maize farmers to delay planting until December, which would have been catastrophic for yields owing to the dryness of January and February in that year.[116] Additionally, this same evidence, coupled with that of Henry Morton Stanley's August 1876 reports from Ujiji, suggests that the effects of drought and consequential hunger and migration contributed to an epidemic of smallpox along caravan roots and in emporia.[117] The floods of 1877–8, meanwhile, were likely disastrous for maize farmers, whose crops, having been planted as the *mvuli* began, would have been vulnerable to being submerged and thus also to suffocation, disease, stunted growth, and the production of smaller yields.[118] Some farmers may have offset these effects by replanting after the floods had passed. Evidence from Unyamwezi suggests that maize was still growing in July 1878, long after the normal harvest but aided by the June of that year being abnormally wet.[119] Additionally, smallpox does not appear to have been so rife in 1877–8. References to outbreaks decrease in number significantly after early 1877. It is likely that replanting occupied labour that would otherwise have travelled, while flooding made travel more difficult, decreasing the appeal of migration if food was scarce. Assuming their fields were not washed away before the planting season, flooding likely affected the coastal traders' rice farms less, as it would have been planted during the *masika*, after most of the excessive rains had passed.[120]

After the 1877–8 ENSO-IOD event, agricultural regimes in East Africa were put under further pressure by a sustained period of below average rainfall. That the regions in Lake Tanganyika's catchment experienced this trend is supported by the decline of the lake's level in this period and by the drying up of freshwater wells in Ujiji.[121] Additionally, this trend is in line with much of the IOW, in which adverse

---

[116] Church Missionary Society Archive (hereafter: CMS) C/A6/O/18 O'Neill to Wright, 29 Dec. 1876; CMS C/A6/O/21 Smith to Wright, 9 Feb. 1877; CMS C/A6/O/22 Shergold Smith to Wright, 1 Jan. 1877.

[117] CMS C/A6/M/M1 Holmwood to Hutchinson, 19 Aug. 1876; CMS C/A6/O/16 Mackay to Wright, 18 Sep. 1876; CMS C/A6/O/16 Mackay to Wright, 14 Oct. 1876; CMS C/A6/O/13 Kirk to Wright, 22 Nov. 1876; Stanley, *Dark Continent*, II, 62; RMCA HMSA 33. Stanley to *Daily Telegraph* and *New York Herald*, 13 Aug. 1876.

[118] R. L. Nielsen, 'Effects of flooding or ponding on corn prior to tasseling' (May 2019): www.kingcorn.org/news/timeless/PondingYoungCorn.html (accessed 10 July 2020); Pasquale Steduto, Theodore C. Hsiao, Elias Fereres, and Dirk Raes, *Crop Yield Response to Water: FAO irrigation and drainage paper 66* (Rome: Food and Agriculture Organization of the United Nations, 2012), 118–19; McCann, *Maize and Grace*, 19.

[119] CMS C/A6/O/16 Mackay to Wright, 20 July 1878; Edward C. Hore, *Missionary to Tanganyika 1877–1888*, ed. James B. Wolf (London: F. Cass, 1971), 49.

[120] See also: Gooding, 'ENSO, IOD, drought, and floods', 258–97.

[121] Nicholson, 'Historical and modern fluctuations', 53–71.

climatic conditions contributed to a series of famines, most notably in India, and contributed to crises in, for example, Madagascar, Egypt, Ethiopia, Ottoman Kurdistan, and China.[122] In East Africa, the *mvuli* rains failed the most frequently, with deficits occurring in 1878, 1879, 1881, 1883, 1885, 1887, 1890, and 1892. The *masika* rains were generally more reliable, though 1880 and 1888 were seasons of below average rainfall, and significant droughts occurred in 1883 and 1884. As with the aftermath of the 1877–8 ENSO-IOD event, the seasonality of the droughts put more pressure on maize farmers than on rice farmers. The repeated failure of the *mvuli* rains delayed when maize farmers planted, hindering their crop's early growth, which is crucial for an abundant harvest.[123] The more reliable *masika* rains, meanwhile, aided rice farmers. Therefore, generally speaking, coastal traders probably did not experience climatic pressure on their farms to the same degree as pre-existing lakeshore populations. Moreover, their commercial networks and the larger number of people some of them enslaved may have alleviated some climatically driven pressures when the *masika* did fail. Even so, consecutive seasons of drought in East Africa, such as with the failed *mvuli-masika* in 1879–80 and the *masika-mvuli-masika* in 1883–4, had the capacity to affect agricultural production for nearly everyone around Lake Tanganyika's emporia.

Below average rainfall in East Africa in late 1879 was related to an 'extreme' La Niña event in that year.[124] This La Niña event is associated with drought and instability in Egypt, Java, and Ottoman Kurdistan.[125] In East Africa, the drought during the *mvuli* lasted into the following *masika*. The regional data established from rain gauges in Zanzibar, Mombasa, and Buganda suggest that rainfall was only slightly below average in both seasons.[126] However, missionary rain gauge data suggest that the drought around Lake Tanganyika was much deeper there than elsewhere – as it also appears to have been in Ugogo.[127] In 1879, Edward Hore of the LMS measured 756 millimetres of annual rainfall in Ujiji; and in 1880, he calculated a probability of 694 millimetres based on his

---

[122] Davis, *Late Victorian Holocausts*; Campbell, *Africa and the Indian Ocean World*, 245–54; Zozan Pehlivan, 'El Ninõ and the nomads: Global climate, local environment, and the crisis of pastoralism in late-Ottoman Kurdistan', *Journal of the Economic and Social History of the Orient*, 63, 3 (2020), 316–56.

[123] Steduto et al., *Crop Yield Response to Water*, 118–19.

[124] Joëlle L. Gergis and Anthony M. Fowler, 'A history of ENSO events since A.D. 1525: Implications for future climate change', *Climatic Change*, 92 (2009), 368.

[125] Pehlivan, 'El Ninõ and the nomads', 337 (table 1.1).

[126] Nicholson, Funk, and Fink, 'Rainfall over the African continent', 120.

[127] Clive A. Spinage, *African Ecology: Benchmarks and historical perspectives* (New York: Springer, 2012), 139; Gooding, 'Tsetse flies, ENSO, and murder', 32.

measurements up to and including October and adding the average rainfall for November and December based on his measurements from 1878 and 1879.[128] All these figures are significantly lower than Ujiji's average annual rainfall of 952 millimetres, based on twentieth-century measurements. Moreover, accounting for the broader regional trends and for the fact that the *mvuli* of 1880 was a season of above average rainfall, they suggest that the below average rainfall for both years can be attributable to drought in the 1879–80 *mvuli-masika* seasons around Lake Tanganyika. Drought conditions prevailed for the entire maize and rice growing seasons in October–May 1879–80.

Evidence that drought conditions in 1879–80 contributed to an under-supply of food in late 1880 to early 1881 comes from reports written in Ujiji. In October 1880, Jiji traders closed the market in Kawele-Ugoy. According to Walter Hutley of the LMS, their actions were a response to ill-treatment by the coastal traders' bonded labourers in the market. Subsequently, coastal traders based in Kawele-Ugoy took up the issue with Bogo, the *teko* (district chief) of Kigoma-Gungu, who was at that time receiving a visit from representatives of the *ami* (central chief) of the Ujiji kingdom. The Jiji chiefs supported the Jiji traders and sought to banish all but three coastal traders and their associates from Ujiji – a decree that they later retracted.[129] It is significant, though, that the tension started in the market, where farmers sold their surpluses. Inflation had been an issue for buyers in previous years, and a weak harvest likely exacerbated these trends.[130] These conditions contributed to thievery and violent conflict in the market leading up to October 1880. Subsequently, these violent tendencies were exacerbated around the emporium in early 1881, as members of a 3,000-strong caravan travelling from Manyema to Zanzibar raided lakeshore farms owing to their inability to afford the prices set for food.[131] The poverty and well-armed nature of many caravan workers further contributed to the violence. Their movements also facilitated an epidemic of smallpox, with the death count being so great in Ujiji that corpses were left to rot on the edge of town.[132] Many Jiji fled to the surrounding mountains and to other lakeshore

---

[128] Hore, *Tanganyika*, 145.

[129] Hutley, *Central African Diaries*, 221–2; CWM/LMS/06/005 Hutley to Whitehouse, 7 Nov. 1880.

[130] Stanley, *Dark Continent*, II, 2.

[131] CWM/LMS/06/02/006 Griffith to Whitehouse, 24 Jan. 1881; CWM/LMS/06/02/006 Hutley to Thompson, 28 Feb. 1881; CWM/LMS/06/02/006 Griffith to Whitehouse, 6 May 1881.

[132] CWM/LMS/06/02/005 Hore to Whitehouse, 20 July 1880.

regions as a result.[133] Nevertheless, it is significant that the fighting in Ujiji's surrounding fields continued even after the departure of most of the caravan, and it only stopped after the harvest at the end of the 1881 *masika*.[134] This was the first harvest since that of April–May 1879 that was not hindered by below average rainfall or by the violence of a large passing caravan, and, as such, it relieved pressure on scarce resources. A more abundant maize and rice harvest, aided by regular levels of rainfall during the 1881 *masika*, likely helped to defuse the tension.

In the aftermath of the 1880–1 violence, the head of Ujiji's coastal trader community, Mwinyi Kheri, attempted to set a regular tariff for food in Ujiji's markets.[135] This was probably intended as a measure to limit inflationary trends and competition for resources in times of shortage, such as that which Ujiji had just experienced. That he failed to do so is evident from developments that occurred during the failed *masika-mvuli-masika* of 1883–4.[136] The drought began in the year before an El Niño event, which is broadly in line with models for the effects of El Niño in East Africa during the *mvuli* season.[137] This El Niño event is also associated with drought in India, Australia, Mauritius, the Philippines, and Japan.[138] Additionally, although its effects are not fully understood, the eruption of the Krakatau volcano in the Sunda Strait in 1883 almost certainly contributed to weakened rainfall in East Africa during these years. The sulphur-rich dust cloud emitted into the atmosphere cooled global temperatures, disrupted atmospheric circulation and contributed to erratic rainfall in much of the IOW.[139] In any case, the drought of 1883–4 in East Africa was part of a broader trend towards lower levels of rainfall in much of the IOW in these and subsequent years.

---

[133] A.G.M.Afr. C.16-7. Journal du P. Deniaud, 9 Mar. 1881.

[134] CWM/LMS/06/02/006 Griffith to Whitehouse, 6 May 1881.

[135] CWM/LMS/06/02/006 Hutley to Thompson, 21 June 1881.

[136] Evidence for the ongoing fluctuation of prices in Ujiji also comes from: A.G.M.Afr. C.16-38. Guillet to White Fathers, 2 Jan. 1884; A.G.M.Afr. C.16-39. Guillet to White Fathers, 24 Jan. 1884.

[137] Nicholson and Kim, 'The relationship of the El-Niño Southern Oscillation', 117–35.

[138] Matthew S. Hopper, 'Cyclones, drought, and slavery: Environment and enslavement in the western Indian Ocean, 1870s to 1920s', in *Natural Hazards and Peoples in the Indian Ocean World: Bordering on danger*, eds. Greg Bankoff and Joseph Christensen (New York: Palgrave, 2016), 268.

[139] Natalie Schaller, Thomas Griesser, Andreas Marc Fischer, Alexander Stickler, and Stefan Brönnimann, 'Climate effects of the 1883 Krakatoa eruption: Historical and present perspectives', *Vierteljahrsschrift der Naturforschenden Gesellschaft in Zürich*, 154, 1–2 (2009), 31–40; Campbell, *Africa and the Indian Ocean World*, 179, 182–3; Stephen J. Rockel, 'A forgotten drought and famine in East Africa, 1883–85', in *Droughts, Floods, and Global Climatic Anomalies*, ed. Gooding, 289–343.

There are no rain gauge data from Lake Tanganyika for the 1883–4 drought, but regional and circumstantial evidence from the lakeshore attests to its severity. It is associated with another smallpox epidemic: as in 1879–80, corpses were left to rot on Ujiji's periphery.[140] Famine also prevailed in some of East Africa's more arid regions, especially in Ugogo and in the coastal hinterland of present-day south-eastern Kenya and north-eastern Tanzania.[141] In Ujiji and Mtowa, shortages of food were likely exacerbated by the arrival of a large caravan, or series of caravans, travelling from the coast to Manyema.[142] Just as in 1880–1, the result was spiralling prices for food in the towns' markets.[143] Deaths by starvation of caravan workers were also common.[144] Consequently, in August 1884, Ujiji was described as 'deserted and decayed', with most of its principal traders having departed for Manyema.[145] The market at Kawele-Ugoy never regained its regional prominence as an ivory depot, becoming instead a 'station on the road' to Nyangwe and Kasongo.[146] Mwinyi Kheri appears to have been the only inhabitant of Ujiji immune to these effects. In August 1884, one visiting missionary recorded him as supplying 'great quantities of food'.[147] The fact that Mwinyi Kheri owned rice fields, lived next to the lake, and enslaved large numbes of people, may have helped him to offset the effects of climatic pressures on his farms. It is possible (although it is not recorded) that he demanded that those he enslaved use lake water to drench his rice paddies. Alternatively, his wealth garnered from the ivory trade may have enabled him to purchase food, despite higher prices.

Towards the southern end of the lake, the deleterious effects of the regional drought only appear to have prevailed in the following year, 1885–6. Reasons for this are unclear, though they may be associated with the after-effects of the Krakatau volcanic eruption and an ENSO-related drought in parts of South-Central Africa at this time.[148]

---

[140] A.G.M.Afr. C.16–84. Guillet to White Fathers, 17 Apr. 1884.
[141] Gregory H. Maddox and Ernest M. Kongola, *Practicing History in Central Tanzania: Writing, memory, and performance* (Portsmouth, NH: Heinemann, 2006), 96; Hopper, 'Cyclones, drought, and slavery', 268–9; Spinage, *African Ecology*, 139.
[142] CWM/LMS/06/02/009 Hore to Whitehouse, 23 Apr. 1884; RMCA ESA HA.01.017-11. Cambier to Storms, 10 Sep. 1884; RMCA ESA HA.01.017-27. Journal du Lieut. Storms, 29 May 1885.
[143] CWM/LMS/06/02/010 Jones to Thompson, 10 Feb. 1885.
[144] A.G.M.Afr. C.16-84. Guillet to White Fathers, 17 Apr. 1884.
[145] CWM/LMS/06/02/009 Brooks to Whitehouse, 6 Aug. 1884.
[146] Hore, *Tanganyika*, 69; Annie B. Hore, *To Lake Tanganyika in a Bath Chair* (London: Sampson Low, Marston, Searle & Rivington, 1886), 159.
[147] CWM/LMS/06/02/009 Brooks to Whitehouse, 6 Aug. 1884.
[148] David J. Nash, Kathleen Pribyl, Georgina H. Endfield, Jørgen Klein, and George C. D. Adamson, 'Rainfall variability over Malawi during the late 19th century', *International Journal of Climatology*, 38, S1 (2018), 629–42.

In Kirando, for example, the emergent emporium was built on rice cultivation, which coastal traders and their associates developed sometime during the first half of the 1880s.[149] In late 1885, White Fathers missionaries reported that the people living in Kirando were experiencing a famine and that traders based there had abandoned their commercial enterprises to tend to their rice farms.[150] They also wrote that maize, grown alongside indigenous crops and cassava in surrounding fields, had been taken out of circulation in the market and replaced with sorghum, at least until the expected harvest in January.[151] The ongoing use of an indigenous, hardier crop to supplement the crops of higher yield likely lessened the drought's most deleterious effects. Similarly, in the White Fathers' nearby station of Karema, shortages resulted in the missionaries being obliged to purchase food from surrounding regions. Just as in Kirando, rice was crucial to Karema's growth, and it is likely that the rice harvest of that year was inadequate.[152] Their reliance on crops grown by local populations in the surrounding regions occurred despite 'the country [having] very little' and the prices being 'exorbitant'[153] Drought in 1883–4 and 1884–5 affected the entirety of the lakeshore, albeit at different times, but it was felt especially deleteriously in towns that had adopted rice and maize in previous years. High prices prevailed and some towns became reliant on supplies of indigenous crops grown in the lake's hinterland.

It is also worth mentioning the consecutive seasons of below average rainfall in East Africa across the 1887–8 *mvuli-masika* seasons. This anomaly is associated with a 'very strong' La Niña episode, which also contributed to drought conditions in China, Ottoman Kurdistan, Northeast Africa, Unyamwezi, and Buganda.[154] However, for most of

---

[149] CWM/LMS/06/05/21 Hore, 'Voyage to the south end of Lake Tanganyika', 1 Apr. 1879; RMCA ESA HA.01.017-7. Storms, 'Rapport sur un voyage dans la partie sud du Tanganika', 1 Apr. 1884.

[150] A.G.M.Afr. Diaire de Karema, 3 Oct. 1885; A.G.M.Afr. Diaire de Karema, 11 Dec. 1885.

[151] A.G.M.Afr. Diaire de Karema, 11 Dec. 1885.

[152] RMCA ESA HA.01.017-9. Beine to Storms, 19 May 1884; RMCA ESA HA.01.017-5. Ramaekers to AIA, 18 Jan. 1882.

[153] A.G.M.Afr. Randebel to White Fathers, 23 Sep. 1885, *Chronique Trimestrielles*, 29 (Jan. 1886); A.G.M.Afr. Randebel to White Fathers, 28 Dec. 1885, *Chronique Trimestrielles*, 31 (July 1886); RMCA ESA HA.01.017-21. Randebel to Storms, 4 Jan. 1886.

[154] Gergis and Fowler, 'A history of ENSO events since A.D. 1525', 368; Pehlivan, 'El Niño and the nomads', 337 (table 1.1); A.G.M.Afr. Diaire de Kipalapala, 21 Feb. 1888, *Chronique Trimestrielles*, 40 (Oct. 1888); A.G.M.Afr. Diaire de Kamoga au Bukumbi, 5 Feb. 1888, *Chronique Trimestrielles*, 39 (July 1888); Henri Médard, 'La peste et les missionnaires: Santé et syncrétisme medical au royaume du Buganda à la fin du XIXe siècle', *Outre-mers*, 92, 346–7 (2005), 91.

equatorial East Africa, the scale of the anomaly pales versus that of 1883–4 (or 1884–5 in the Lake Tanganyika's southern half), and missionary rain gauge data suggest its effects were uneven or possibly nonexistent around Lake Tanganyika. Measurements taken on Kavala Island, an island near to Uguha's shoreline, state that the island received 1,323 millimetres of rainfall in 1886, 1,327 millimetres in 1887, and 1,473 millimetres in 1888.[155] The steady increase in rainfall in these years is inconsistent with the idea that 1887–8 was a period of anomalously low rainfall. Additionally, all these figures are significantly higher than the annual average of the island's nearest twentieth-century rain gauge at Kalemie, where average annual rainfall is 1,067 millimetres. The measurements can, however, be accepted on the basis that shortages of food were not recorded around the southern half of the lake in 1887–8 – in fact one missionary source suggests that food was abundant at the lake's southern end around this time.[156]

The evidence from Lake Tanganyika's northern half is somewhat murkier. There appears to have been shortages of food in some locales, and smallpox appears to have been especially prevalent between Mtowa and Ujiji in these years, but the causes are not particularly clear.[157] White Fathers missionaries stationed in Kibanga noted famine in the regions around their station, especially on the Ubwari peninsula, but attributed this to raids by Guha and Rua populations coming from the south and by the associates of coastal traders who had recently settled in the region.[158] In the case of the latter, they claimed that the coastal traders' associates' decision to raid was based on the fact they had not cultivated at all, not because their crops had failed.[159] Given that they were usually better armed than those they encountered, and given farming's association with slave status, they may have considered raiding to be a more optimal strategy for acquiring food in the early years of their settlement. However, as the White Fathers never actually visited the coastal traders' associates' station in these years, it is also possible that adverse climatic factors undermined their first attempts at establishing an efficient agricultural regime. Meanwhile, in March 1889, one LMS missionary reported that there was an abundance of rice at Ujiji, with Rumaliza being the primary supplier.[160] Again, this could indicate that climatic conditions were not as adverse as elsewhere in East Africa and in some

---

[155] Hore, *Tanganyika*, 145.
[156] CWM/LMS/06/02/014 Jones to Thompson, 14 Nov. 1887.
[157] CWM/LMS/06/02/012 Lea to Thompson, 2 Apr. 1887.
[158] A.G.M.Afr. Diaire de Kibanga, 11 June 1883, 13 Aug. 1886.
[159] A.G.M.Afr. Diaire de Kibanga, 13 Nov. 1888, 15 Nov. 1888, 19 Nov. 1888.
[160] CWM/LMS/06/02/014 Carson to Thompson, 9 Mar. 1889.

other IOW regions, but it could also be attributed to the possible use of lake water to drench rice fields next to the lakeshore. In any case, if trends towards drought existed at all in 1887–8, they were probably uneven across the lakeshore and not as strong as in 1879–80 and 1883–5.

Conclusion

In sum, both the expansion of slave trading and the adoption of high-potential yield crops in c.1840–76 facilitated an agricultural revolution around East African trade routes and emergent emporia. Farmers located in these regions used these developments to produce agricultural surpluses, which they sold into markets in emporia and to caravans, giving them access to the goods of the world economy. This represented a commercialisation of their agricultural regimes. However, the way commercialisation took place also had the double effect of increasing farmers' agricultural regimes' vulnerability to the effects of water stress. These vulnerabilities were exposed in the late 1870s and 1880s as global climatic anomalies increased the frequency of droughts and floods, and as demands for marketed food grew, which owed itself to the growth of emporia and the creation of ever larger caravans. Even so, the effects of these changes around Lake Tanganyika were uneven. The seasonality of the droughts meant that maize farmers (predominantly pre-existing lake-shore populations) were affected by adverse climatic conditions more than rice farmers (predominantly coastal traders and their associates). Moreover, some of the latter may have been able to use the larger supplies of enslaved labour to use lake water to drench their rice fields, which were located closer to the lake.

There are two further conclusions to draw from this. First, these patterns of human–environment interaction shed light on the power dynamics within emergent emporia. Although, as discussed in Chapter 1, lakeshore elites and wider populations remained prominent in their emporia's affairs, the 1880s were a period in which coastal traders became increasingly assertive and influential. This is usually attributed to their credit, debt, and exchange networks that extended into the wider IOW. The analysis here suggests that there were additional, more funda-mental layers to their influence; namely, their growing of rice and use of enslaved labour working on farms within the context of an erratic cli-mate. These factors helped to create for them higher levels of food security, making their residence on the lakeshore more sustainable at a time when other lakeshore populations were struggling. Second, the introduction of crops from the New World and the wider IOW made the history of East Africa move more closely with fluctuations in the

Indian Ocean monsoon system over time. Increasing reliance on regular rainfall to support 'revolutionised' agricultural regimes meant that food production around Lake Tanganyika's emergent emporia were increasingly linked to broader historical patterns occurring in the wider IOW. The late nineteenth century is widely known as a period of climatic, social, and political turbulence in the IOW. This chapter shows inland East Africa to have been a part of these broader patterns, albeit one associated more with the spread of capitalism via the global ivory trade than with formal colonialism, which only became established in the region from the 1890s.

3   Traversing the Lake

Phenomena associated with the expansion of the global ivory trade reshaped how people encountered and perceived Lake Tanganyika. Throughout the nineteenth century, the lake was a source of food, a distinct commercial zone, and a site of religious and political innovation, but the prerogatives that affected these aspects of lakeshore people's lives shifted over time. At the beginning of the century, fishing in small, locally made canoes dominated economic activities on the lake; by the century's end, fishermen were accompanied by traders in larger craft, which were built with materials and technologies from different parts of the lakeshore and the wider IOW. As an illustration of these diverse influences, sails put on Lake Tanganyika's boats in the latter part of the nineteenth century were often made from cloth made in New England cotton mills, having been traded through the hands of Indian financiers and Omani and East African traders, and then taken to the lakeshore.[1] Additionally, while beliefs in the existence of spirits in the lake were ubiquitous among lakeshore populations before the period under review, the arrival of coastal traders, with their beliefs in Islam and associated *zimu* (Swahili [Bantu root]: spirits; sing. *mzimu*; pl. *mizimu*) and *jini* (Swahili [Arabic root]: spirits; sing: *jini*; pl. *majini*) reshaped how these spirits were perceived, as well as who was believed to have power over them.[2] Encounters with the lake went beyond the practical and economic, entering also the spiritual and political.

Much about this history can be examined in terms of boats and changes to boating technologies. Boats on Lake Tanganyika took numerous forms. Jiji fishermen, for example, made 3–5 metre-long dugout canoes from the trunks of trees growing near Ukawende to fish for *dagaa*

---

[1] CWM/LMS/06/02/003 Hore, 'Launch of the "Calabash"', 9 Dec. 1878. Coastal traders also sometimes used cloth made in England or India, see: NA RGS JMS/2/144 Cameron, 'Diary of a boat journey', 4–5 Mar. 1874.

[2] For a summary of *zimu* and *jini* in coastal, Swahili culture, see: John Middleton, *African Merchants of the Indian Ocean: Swahili of the East African coast* (Long Grove: Waveland Press, 2004), 122–4.

Figure 3.1 A dugout fishing canoe. Original caption: 'A dug-out canoe. This is used for fishing. The land on the opposite side of the lake is not visible. The men have scientifically distributed their weight to preserve proper balance.' In: Swann, *Fighting the Slave-Hunters*, 51.

in nearby waters (see Figure 3.1).[3] Rundi fishermen constructed catamarans by lashing several dugout canoes together for similar purposes.[4] The most famous boats on Lake Tanganyika, though, were those made from *mvule* trees (*milicia excelsa*), which grew in Ugoma and elsewhere on the lake's western shore. Their thick trunks were ideal for the construction of large dugout canoes of up to twelve metres in length, to which planks, masts, sails, and other modifications could be added.[5] There was a ready market for Goma dugouts around much of Lake Tanganyika, but they were especially demanded in Ujiji, where they were crucial to the community's sense of identity. Traditions told in Ujiji trace the founding of the town to the voyage of an intrepid traveller, Mshelwampamba, who, on seeing smoke rising on the western shore, traversed the lake on a

---

[3] Brown, 'Ujiji', 42. An LMS missionary noted a lack of wood around the Ujiji centre: CWM/LMS/06/02/003 Hore to Mullens, 17 Sep. 1878. When in need, members of the LMS instead acquired it further south: CWM/LMS/06/02/005 Hore to Whitehouse, 20 July 1880.

[4] Hore, 'Twelve tribes', 12.

[5] Burton, *Lake Regions*, 338–9; Stanley, *How I Found*, 393; RMCA HMSA 4610. Stanley to *Daily Telegraph* and *New York Herald*, 28 Oct. 1876; Jacques and Storms, *Notes sur l'ethnographie*, 99; Alfred J. Swann, *Fighting the Slave-Hunters in Central Africa: A record of twenty-six years of travel and adventure round the Great Lakes and of the overthrow of Tip-tu-tib, Rumaliza, and other great slave-traders* (Philadelphia: J.B. Lippincott Company, 1910), 77.

locally made fishing canoe. When he returned, he did so with people from the western shore (who were invited to stay and live in Ujiji) on larger craft that were ideal for traversing the lake.[6] These larger craft were Goma canoes. This tradition speaks both to the importance of connections across the lake in the conceptual foundations of some lakeshore communities and to the centrality of boats and technological innovations to making these connections.[7]

Goma canoes were subsequently a core vector through which many people living on the lakeshore encountered and perceived the lake. Jiji fishermen used them for ambitious expeditions to seasonal fishing locations towards the lake's southern end.[8] They were also important trading vessels to Jiji and coastal traders alike. Even though later in the nineteenth century, coastal traders introduced sailing technologies, inspired by the ubiquitous *dhows* of the western Indian Ocean, they implanted most of these innovations on Goma canoes.[9] Moreover, the launching of Goma canoes was a religious event, presided over by *ganga* (Swahili: religious specialists [Muslim or non-Muslim]; sing. *mganga*; pl. *waganga*) in Ugoma and by *teko* (district chiefs) in Ujiji. In Ujiji, the Jiji *teko*'s power rested on being the sole authorities who were believed to be able to appease the lake's spirits for successful fishing and commercial expeditions.[10] The arrival of coastal traders, Islam, and boating technologies challenged perceptions of their authority vis-à-vis the lake's spirits. The power of some almost certainly withered as a result – the declining influence of Habeyya in Kawele-Ugoy during the 1880s, discussed in Chapter 2, is evidence for this. Yet, others, such as Bogo in Kigoma-Gungu, likely wielded the new influences to their advantage, converting to Islam and promoting trans-lake commerce in Goma canoes.[11] Coastal technological and religious influences were new

---

[6] Brown, 'Ujiji', 36–7; Wagner, 'Trade and commercial attitudes', 155; Hino, 'Neighbourhood groups', 2; Interview with Rashidi Hamisi bin Kasa, 12 Nov. 2013; Interview with Hamisi Feuse Kabwe Katanga, 14 Nov. 2013; Interview with Zuberi Shabani Aburula, 12 Nov. 2013; Interview with Branbati Ali Kiola and Isa Pama Kiola, 12 Nov. 2013; Interview with Selimani Kadudu Musa, 13 Nov. 2013; Interview with Musa Isa Rubinga, 14 Nov. 2013.

[7] For a more general overview of the multifaceted importance of boats in oceanic histories, see: Sivasundaram, Bashford, and Armitage, 'Introduction', 8–13.

[8] Brown, 'Ujiji', 44; Hore, 'Twelve tribes', 42.

[9] Sheriff, *Dhow Cultures*; CWM/LMS/06/02/003 Hore, 'Launch of the "Calabash"', 9 Dec. 1878; Swann, *Fighting the Slave-Hunters*, 83.

[10] Michele Wagner, 'Environment, community and history: "Nature in mind", in nineteenth- and early twentieth-century Buha, western Tanzania', in *Custodians of the Land: Ecology and culture in the history of Tanzania*, eds. Gregory H. Maddox, James L. Giblin and Isaria N. Kimambo (London: James Currey, 1996), 191.

[11] Wagner, 'Environment, community and history', 191. See also: Chapter 1.

additions to a pre-existing religious framework focused on beliefs in spirits in the lake.

These patterns suggest a high degree of compatibility between coastal and lakeshore belief systems.[12] This argument contests some of the older East Africanist historiography, which often dichotomised the 'Islamic coast' with the 'non-Islamic interior'.[13] However, it is supported by the presence in coastal belief systems of *zimu* and *jini*. These were (and in some cases remain) nature spirits that occupied distinctive geographical features near to the coast.[14] Many, including the most powerful, were believed to live in the Indian Ocean.[15] Such *jini* were said to guide oceanic commercial voyages, if appeased correctly.[16] Muslims and non-Muslims alike, including Africans and Omanis, flocked to consult famous *ganga* who communicated with *jini* along the East African coast and islands during the nineteenth century.[17] Some *ganga* and *jini* remain prominent in coastal Muslim lives today.[18] Coastal traders entering the interior of East Africa for the first time during the nineteenth century brought these beliefs with them. As they arrived at Lake Tanganyika, they encountered a familiar water-facing environment occupied by peoples who similarly believed in waterborne nature spirits. This is not to argue that coastal and lakeshore belief systems were the same. Indeed, there were significant differences – but they were not, in general, irreconcilable. Coastal traders and their associates (including their bondsmen), though, played a prominent role in making these reconciliations. As they did so, they became ever more prominent actors in shaping lakeshore people's relationships with Lake Tanganyika's spirits. The results of this transition were twofold. First, it contributed to the coastal traders' increased influence over lakeshore affairs, especially in the 1870s and 1880s; and, second, it contributed to the ironing out of regional differences in the ways that lakeshore peoples sought to appease the lake's spirits. During the nineteenth century, lakeshore people's practices as they pertained to their collective beliefs in spirits in Lake Tanganyika

---

[12] Wagner, 'Environment, community and history', 190–1.

[13] For a summary critique of this approach, see: Rockel, 'From shore to shore', 73–7.

[14] See, for example: Middleton, *African Merchants*, 121–8; Patricia Caplan, *African Voices, African Lives: Personal narratives from a Swahili village* (London: Routledge, 1997), 109; Edward A. Alpers, '"Ordinary household chores": Ritual and power in a 19th-century Swahili possession cult', *The International Journal of African Historical Studies*, 17, 4 (1984), 690; Brown, 'Bagamoyo', 79–80; Glassman, *Feasts and Riot*, 71, 77.

[15] Linda Giles, 'Spirit possession on the Swahili coast: Peripheral cults or primary texts?' (unpublished PhD diss., University of Texas at Austin, 1989), 64–5.

[16] Meier, *Swahili Port Cities*, 33.   [17] Meier, *Swahili Port Cities*, 32–3, 90–1.

[18] Meier, *Swahili Port Cities*, 32.

became more integrated as they took on influences from East Africa's Indian Ocean littoral.

Into this mix, one also has to add the effects of a changing environment. Human encounters with the lake were seasonal. Although Jiji fishermen fished locally throughout the year, they and other boatmen generally only travelled between lakeshore regions during the long dry season from the end of May to the beginning of October, when the southwesterly winds were more reliable and the requirements on their labour in the fields were fewer. During the rainy season, sudden changes of wind direction and storms were common and endangered lacustrine journeys.[19] This seasonal pattern was well adapted to trade, as the caravan season, too, occurred during the dry season.[20] In terms of more longterm environmental changes, the water level of Lake Tanganyika is subject to significant interannual and interdecadal variation. After being generally low in the last years of the LIA, c.1780–1840, the annual average of the lake level rose for most of mid-century.[21] This process was facilitated by the wetter conditions of the period and by the natural development of a reed and mud dam at the entrance to the Lukuga River, the lake's only outlet. The excessive nature of the rains during the extreme ENSO-IOD anomaly of 1877–8, however, contributed to the collapse of this reed and mud dam, leaving a rocky sill 13.9 metres below where the level of the lake previously stood.[22] Consequently, rapids and eddies formed where before the current was barely perceptible.[23] Coupled with below average rainfall in subsequent years, this caused the level of the lake to decrease by 8.6 metres over the next six years, or 10.9 metres over the next sixteen – a significantly greater decline than in East Africa's other Great Lakes during this period.[24] This change exposed beaches where before there were ports, and connected islands opposite Ujiji and Mtowa to the mainland.[25] As will be seen, this had

---

[19] CWM/LMS/06/02/008 Hore to Whitehouse, 30 Dec. 1883; CWM/LMS/06/02/009 Hore to Whitehouse, 23 Apr. 1884; A.G.M.Afr. Diaire de Mpala, 23 Jan. 1889.

[20] Rockel, 'A nation of porters', 177.

[21] Nicholson, 'Historical and modern fluctuations', 57.

[22] Nicholson, 'Historical and modern fluctuations', 62; Crul, *Limnology and Hydrology*, 34.

[23] Stanley, *Dark Continent*, II, 45; Edward C. Hore, 'Lake Tanganyika', *Proceedings of the Royal Geographical Society and Monthly Record of Geography*, 4, 1 (1882), 11–12; NA RGS CB6/1167 Hore to RGS, 27 May 1879; ZNA AA1/23 Hore to Kirk, 27 May 1879; ZNA BK1/12 Thomson to Kirk, 27 Mar. 1880.

[24] C. Gillman, 'The hydrology of Lake Tanganyika', in *Tanganyika Territory Geological Survey Department*, 5 (1933), 6; Sharon E. Nicholson and Xungang Yin, 'Rainfall conditions in equatorial East Africa during the nineteenth century as inferred from the record of Lake Victoria', *Climatic Change*, 48 (2001), 388.

[25] CWM/LMS/06/02/005 Griffith to Whitehouse, 28 Aug. 1880; CWM/LMS/06/02/008 Hore to Whitehouse, 18–21 June 1883.

consequences for trade and for perceptions of different leaders' ability to appease the lake's spirits.

The following discussion is split into two sections. The first section examines the origins and nature of beliefs in Lake Tanganyika's spirits; the second examines how these phenomena evolved in response to the arrival of coastal traders and the expansion of the global ivory trade. With the additional use of anthropological sources, they both examine a history of changing belief systems in the context of evolving commercial, technological, and environmental circumstances. Boats, as the key media through which people living on the lakeshore encountered the lake throughout the period, are a core vector of analysis. As their designs became increasingly shaped by the needs of commercial expeditions, so too Lake Tanganyika's religious framework became increasingly linked to the vagaries of commerce. This process can be described as the 'commercialisation' of spiritual belief, a phenomenon more commonly associated with colonial and post-colonial Africa, but which nevertheless represents the ways in which religious power became increasingly intertwined with success in commerce.[26] Moreover, in stressing the importance of spirits in the lake to political life on the lakeshore, this chapter builds on a historiography that stresses high levels of 'structural continuity' in East African institutions during the nineteenth century.[27] Belief systems arriving from littoral regions of the IOW did not replace indigenous ones; they were integrated into them. On Lake Tanganyika's shores, this speaks to the cosmological compatibilities between Indian Ocean–facing and lacustrine-facing cultures.

Spirits in the Lake

In myths of origin, the founding of societies near to oceans is often associated with supernatural activity in and around the sea. Ancient Mesopotamians believed the ancient world to have been covered with water until an ocean goddess was torn in half, creating land; the chief god among ancient Hindus was Veruna, the God of water and the ocean, among other things; and Comorian folklore traces the origins of the archipelago's largest island to a *jini* dropping a jewel in the ocean.[28]

---

[26] Jean Allman and John Parker, *Tongnaab: The History of a West African God* (Bloomington: Indiana University Press, 2005), 236.

[27] Juhani Koponen, *People and Production in Late Precolonial Tanzania: History and structures* (Helsinki: Finnish Society of Development Studies, 1988), 361.

[28] For a recent and useful resource on these myths of origin and others like them, see: Eric Roorda (ed.), *The Ocean Reader: History, culture, politics* (Durham, NC: Duke University Press, 2020), 5–40. For more details on the Comoros myth, see: Gillian Marie

According to recorded traditions, many people living on the shores of Lake Tanganyika believed the lake and its societies to have been formed through similar, 'oceanic' themes. Henry Morton Stanley, for example, recorded a belief among Jiji canoemen that Lake Tanganyika emerged through the wrath of a spirit who flooded a rich and fertile plain because its secrecy had been betrayed by an infidel woman.[29] More recently, an anthropologist identified beliefs at the lake's southern end that traced the founding of Lungu society to the meeting between a migrant queen and the god of the lake.[30] Among Tabwa and Fipa peoples, meanwhile, supreme beings associated with creation, the sun, and the sky are said to have created the spirits that inhabit the lake and its shores.[31] Lake Tanganyika and its spirits were key to understandings of the origins of lakeshore peoples and their cosmologies.

Spirits in Lake Tanganyika were believed to inhabit the liminal space between land and lake at capes, peninsulas, and small islands. They were regarded as 'nature spirits' (as opposed to other kinds of spirits, such as ancestor spirits) in all of the lakeshore's distinct languages. To the Jiji, they were *sigo* (sing. *ikisigo*; pl. *ibisigo*) or *shinga* (sing. *ishinga*; pl. *amashinga*); to the Fipa and Lungu, they were *leza* (pl. *amaleza*); and to the Tabwa and Holoholo, they were *ngulu*.[32] The most prominent nature spirits in Lake Tanganyika were Sewakaao and Wampembe in Ufipa, Kapembwa in Ulungu, Tembwe in Marungu, Mzimu at the northern tip of Ubwari, and Kabogo, which was believed to inhabit a cape and an island at two locations on the lake's eastern shore (hereafter referred to as, respectively, Kabogo (N) and Kabogo (S)).[33] These capes,

---

Shepherd, 'The Comorians in Kenya: The establishment and loss of an economic niche' (unpublished PhD diss., London School of Economics, 1982), 46.

[29] Stanley, *Dark Continent*, II, 12–15. The centrality of canoe men and other 'water-borne workers' to oceanic cosmologies in East Africa's Great Lakes region is supported by evidence from Lake Victoria. See: Michael G. Kenny, 'The powers of Lake Victoria', *Anthropos*, 72, 5–6 (1977), 717–33.

[30] Roy G. Willis, 'The great mother and the god of the lake: Royal and priestly power in Ulungu', *Zambia Journal of History*, 4 (1991), 21–2; Roy G. Willis, *Some Spirits Heal, Others Only Dance: A journey into human selfhood in an African village* (Oxford: Berg, 1999), 57–71.

[31] Roberts, 'Heroic beasts', 129–42, 150–2; Lechaptois, *Aux rives du Tanganika*, 165–75.

[32] G. C. K. Gwassa and J. F. Mbwiliza, 'Social production, symbolism and ritual in Buha: 1750–1900', *Tanzania Notes and Records*, 79–80 (1976), 18; Lechaptois, *Aux rives du Tanganika*, 169; Allen F. Roberts, '"Fishers of men": Religion and political economy among colonized Tabwa', *Africa*, 54, 2 (1984), 49–70; Schmitz and Overbergh, *Les Baholoholo*, 231–3; Wagner, 'Environment, community and history', 178–81, 191.

[33] Speke, 'Journal of a cruise', 349; Stanley, *Dark Continent*, II, 67; RMCA HMSA 33. Stanley to *Daily Telegraph* and *New York Herald*, 7 Aug. 1876; A.G.M.Afr. C.16-7. Journal du P. Deniaud, 9 Oct. 1879, 21 Oct. 1879; Roberts, 'Heroic beasts', 134–42; Lechaptois, *Aux rives du Tanganika*, 170–2; Vyncke, *Brieven van een vlaamschen*, II, 240–1; Willis, 'The great mother', 21–30; Willis, *The Fipa and Related Peoples*, 31.

peninsulas, and islands were also departure points for turning into open sea. Travellers thus saw appeasement of spirits at these locations as essential for their safety on the most dangerous part of their journey.[34] Around Lake Tanganyika, this contributed to the creation of spatial divisions. Travellers' journeys across the lake between capes made imaginary lines between different lakeshore peoples and regions. This was reinforced by the shapes of capes and peninsulas as physical features. They were often the furthest north or south that lakeshore peoples could definitively identify from their settlements, meaning that they were a natural limit to their everyday conceptions of space.[35] The result was the creation of two 'oceanic' regions, split by the imaginary line between Kabogo (S) and Tembwe. Up to the mid-nineteenth century, those to the north of this line referred to the lake as Tanganyika; those to the south referred to it as Liemba.[36] Peoples on either side of the imaginary line viewed the lake beyond it as 'endless', much like an ocean.[37]

Lakeshore peoples saw the appeasement of the lake's spirits as essential for their respective societies' well-being. Thus, ceremonies and rituals were common at particularly important times of the year, such as before fishing and rainy seasons, at the time of annual pilgrimage, and at times of war, or to mark important economic and cultural activities, such as fishing or the launch of a new canoe.[38] Deaths were often attributed to displeased or malignant spirits. Many lakeshore peoples believed that such malignant spirits manifested in the form of crocodiles or snakes, or occasionally hippos, which came on land and 'devoured' those that caused their wrath. They similarly believed that the animals they embodied would only return to the lake once the spirit was aptly compensated.[39] Storms that endangered lacustrine journeys and destroyed boats were also frequently associated with the activities of displeased spirits.[40] The power of lacustrine spirits in this context is further

---

[34] Meier, *Swahili Port Cities*, 32.   [35] Roberts, 'Heroic beasts', 129–31.

[36] Roberts, 'Heroic beasts', 132–5. These differing conceptions confused European 'explorers', especially David Livingstone, who believed for most of his time in eastern Africa that Tanganyika and Liemba were two different lakes.

[37] Roberts, 'Heroic beasts', 89.

[38] A.G.M.Afr. Diaire de Mpala, 23 Nov. 1885, 19 Oct. 1888, Oct. 1890; A.G.M.Afr. Diaire de Kibanga, 22 Aug. 1886; Hore, *Tanganyika*, 106; Swann, *Fighting the Slave-Hunters*, 77–8; Roberts, 'Fishers of men', 53–4; Willis, *Some Spirits Heal*, 67; Interview with Georges Ntigarika, 7 Nov. 2013; Interview with Daniel Rucintingo, 7 Nov. 2013.

[39] Lechaptois, *Aux rives du Tanganika*, 168; A.G.M.Afr. Diaire de Massanze, 11 Feb. 1881; A.G.M.Afr. Diaire de Kibanga, 11 Feb. 1884, 7 Feb. 1887; Interview with Simeon Sindimwo and Venant Baragasirika, 5 Nov. 2013; Interview with Raphael Ntangibingura, 5 Nov. 2013; Roberts, 'Heroic beasts', 136 (esp. n. 2), 139; Willis, *The Fipa and Related Peoples*, 31.

[40] Swann, *Fighting the Slave-Hunters*, 77–8; Jacques and Storms, *Notes sur l'ethnographie*, 84.

established by the attitudes of some inland populations. The central chiefs of both Ujiji and Urundi (*ami*), who both lived in the lake's mountainous surrounds, forbade themselves from viewing the lake at all because they believed that the lake's spirits would kill them if they did.[41] According to one missionary source, similar beliefs may have existed in Uguha's hinterland regions.[42] In a cruel twist, Mwezi Gisabo did die in 1908 soon after being the first Rundi *ami* to view the lake, having contracted malaria when he visited what later became known as Bujumbura.[43] In any case, in the nineteenth century, this ambivalence from inland populations served to distinguish lakeshore inhabitants' engagements with the lake further. People living on the lakeshore were alone in seeking to appease the lake's spirits by interacting with them.

Canoes and lacustrine travel were crucial to lakeshore people's interactions with the lake's spirits. The construction and use of a Goma canoe began with cutting down an *mvule* tree in the lake's mountainous surrounds. The trunk was then dragged down to the lakeshore, where carpenters, using a combination of axes, adzes, and fire, transformed it into a dugout canoe.[44] The canoes were then painted white, decorated with numerous insignia, and blessed by a *ganga*.[45] Once constructed, they were characterised as 'infants', meaning that only youths were allowed to carry them onto the lake.[46] Thereafter, one missionary account suggests that youths on their first journeys were obliged to drink the water of the lake at the location of each spirit they encountered.[47] Subsequently, and according to several accounts, boatmen made offerings of valuable goods by dropping them into the lake.[48] This latter practice built on regional patterns, in which local *ganga* made offerings of often specific goods and materials to the spirit they were most familiar

[41] Hutley, *Central African Diaries*, 65; Nigel Watt, *Burundi: The biography of a small African country*, 2nd ed. (London: Hurst & Company, 2016), 6.

[42] CWM/LMS/06/02/008 Griffith to Whitehouse, 7 Feb. 1883.   [43] Watt, *Burundi*, 6.

[44] Hore, *Tanganyika*, 106–7; Swann, *Fighting the Slave-Hunters*, 77; A.G.M.Afr. Diaire de Mpala, 1 Oct. 1889; CWM/LMS/06/02/003 Hore, 'Launch of the "Calabash"', 9 Dec. 1878; Burton, *Lake Regions*, 338–9; Speke, 'Journal of a cruise', 344.

[45] Hore, *Tanganyika*, 107; Swann, *Fighting the Slave-Hunters*, 77–8; Wagner, 'Environment, community and history', 191–2.

[46] Swann, *Fighting the Slave-Hunters*, 77.

[47] A.G.M.Afr. Diaire de Massanze, 17 Oct. 1881.

[48] See, for example: NA RGS JMS/2/144 Cameron, 'Diary of a boat journey', 19 Mar. 1874, 1, 3, 4 Apr. 1874; A.G.M.Afr. C.16-7. Journal du P. Deniaud, 9 Oct. 1879, 21 Oct. 1879; A.G.M.Afr. Diaire de Massanze, 17 Oct. 1881; Hermann Von Wissmann, *My Second Journey through Equatorial Africa from the Congo to the Zambesi in the Years 1886 and 1887*, trans. Minna J. A. Bergmann (London: Chatton & Windus, 1891), 258; RMCA ESA HA.01.017-7. Storms, 'Rapport de voyage à Oudjidji', 7 July 1883; Jacques and Storms, *Notes sur l'ethnographie*, 84.

with.[49] Offerings to Kapembwa among the Lungu, for example, included seeds and a perfumed oil made by an old woman, while offerings to Wampembe among the Fipa included goats and cows.[50] In short, people living on the lakeshore sought to appease the lake's spirits through a combination of ceremonies, canoe design, and offerings.

Some political leaders on the lakeshore rested their power on appeasement of the lake's nature spirits. According to anthropologist Allen F. Roberts, Tabwa informants told him that 'the meaning ... of chiefship [is] his prerogative to contact *ngulu*'.[51] In Ulungu, meanwhile, royalty and priesthood were (and remain in 'traditional Lungu culture') two distinct parts that comprised social authority and power.[52] Similarly, in Ujiji, the word *teko* (district chief) literally translates as 'earth-priest (s)'.[53] The *teko*'s spiritual role gave them authority over all matters pertaining to the environment in their district. In terrestrial spaces, this meant they had power over harvests and grazing rights; near to Lake Tanganyika, it meant they also had power over matters pertaining to the lake itself.[54] The *ami*'s power, centred in the lake's mountainous surrounds, counted for little in everyday matters on the lakeshore and was acknowledged largely only through the periodic payment of tribute, which was paid through his *tware* (regional chiefs).[55] Similar structures pervaded Urundi, where locally appointed chiefs living near to the lakeshore (also called *teko*) used their base to frequently usurp the king's authority during the nineteenth century.[56] In terms of the Jiji *teko*'s connection to the lake, though, those living near to the lakeshore led rituals in the manner of *ganga* before the disembarkation of a canoe, and may have occasionally led ceremonies at peninsulas in which goods were offered to spirits.[57] These practices were meant to appease the lake's spirits, enabling safe and profitable passage for expeditions from Ujiji around and across the lake.

---

[49] See, for example: Willis, *Some Spirits Heal*, 64–5; Roberts, 'Heroic beasts', 138–9.

[50] Willis, *Some Spirits Heal*, 64–5; Lechaptois, *Aux rives du Tanganika*, 173. Oral sources in Burundi also suggested the importance of sacrificing livestock to spirits in the lake. Interview with Georges Ntigarika, 7 Nov. 2013.

[51] Roberts, 'Fishers of men', 51.   [52] Willis, *Some Spirits Heal*, 68.

[53] Wagner, 'Environment, community and history', 182; Gwassa and Mbwiliza, 'Social production', 16, 18.

[54] Wagner, 'Environment, community and history', 182; W. B. Tripe, 'The death and replacement of a divine king in Uha', *Man*, 39, 2 (1939), 22; J. H. Scherer, 'The Ha of Tanganyika', *Anthropos*, 54, 5–6 (1959), 856–7; RMCA HMSA 4718. Stanley, 'The dark continent and its people, or, Africa and the Africans', 19.

[55] Burton, *Lake Regions*, 323–4; CWM/LMS/06/02/006 Hutley to Whitehouse, 11 Feb. 1881; Bolser-Brown, 'Muslim influence', 627.

[56] Newbury, *Land beyond the Mists*, 287–8.

[57] Wagner, 'Environment, community and history', 191.

Commerce was an integral feature of these lacustrine engagements. Jiji traders had been traversing the northern regions of the lake since long before the arrival of the first coastal traders in c.1830. The Jiji *teko*'s role in this context was to appease the lake's spirits to facilitate trans-lake transactions. They received payment for conducting pre-launch ceremonies, and evidence suggests that on at least some occasions they travelled on the lake to offer goods to the spirits directly. On their journey from Ujiji to Uvira in 1858, Burton and Speke were accompanied by Kannena, a Jiji chief living on the lakeshore.[58] Burton wrote that at Mzimu (the northern tip of the Ubwari peninsula), Kannena demanded additional goods as payment for safely traversing the lake.[59] However, Kannena was 'heavily in debt' by the time they reached Uvira.[60] It is likely that, unbeknownst to Burton, Kannena dropped the goods he gave him in sacrifice to Mzimu's spirit. This was his thanks for safe passage and his request for further good fortune on their journey.

The arrival of coastal traders from c.1830 strengthened some Jiji *teko*'s position, at least initially. The consequential increase in the volume of trade and in the frequency of lacustrine voyages called for ever more canoes and ever more ceremonies to protect them. As commerce expanded, perceptions in Ujiji of the *teko*'s power over the lake's spirits grew.[61] Moreover, the Jiji *teko* demanded payment for conducting these ceremonies, including (and increasingly) in expensive products brought from the wider, globalising world, such as glass beads from Venice and Hamburg and cotton cloths from Gujarat and Oman.[62] Ownership of these kinds of goods became associated with prestige and chiefly status.[63] Jiji chiefs sought further access to them through various forms of taxation, such as for the rights to trade in the market, to use the harbour, and to employ Jiji boatmen, and by reinvesting that which they acquired by

---

[58] Burton almost certainly erroneously referred to Kannena as a *tware* rather than a *teko*. *Tware* were regional chiefs acting on behalf of the central chief living in the lake's mountainous surrounds. Travel on the lake was not prescribed for in their role. Burton's conclusion may have been driven by his (and other Europeans') fascination with kingship in Africa. He referred to the central chief of Ujiji as 'The Great Mwami or Sultan of Ujiji'. Subsequent evidence analysed in this book shows that these central chiefs hardly had 'great' power in lakeshore regions. See: Burton, *Lake Regions*, 323.

[59] Burton, *Lake Regions*, 350.   [60] Burton, *Lake Regions*, 354.

[61] Wagner, 'Environment, community and history', 191–2.

[62] Speke, 'Journal of a cruise', 343–5; Burton, *Lake Regions*, 338, 350; RMCA HMSA 73. Field Notebook, 17 Dec. 1871; Gwassa and Mbwiliza, 'Social production', 17; Wagner, 'Environment, community and history', 191. See also: Chapter 5.

[63] David M. Gordon, 'Wearing cloth, wielding guns: Consumption, trade, and politics in the south central African interior during the nineteenth century', in *The Objects of Life in Central Africa: The history of consumption and social change, 1840–1890*, eds. Robert Ross, Marja Hinfelaar, and Iva Peša (Leiden: Brill, 2013), 29–30. See also: Chapter 5.

these means in trans-lake commercial expeditions.[64] Thus, their conditions for presiding over matters pertaining to the lake's spirits were increasingly tied to the exchange of expensive, imported commodities. This is further reflected in the goods offered to the spirits. It is notable that Kannena demanded and then likely sacrificed glass beads from Burton at Mzimu.[65] Other, later accounts show that Jiji and other lakeshore populations also sacrificed agricultural produce and livestock as well as such imported goods, but this example is the first among many that show the importance of valuable imports for directly appeasing the lake's spirits. As will be seen, this was a pattern that continued to strengthen later in the nineteenth century. Appeasing the lake's spirits became increasingly intertwined with commerce and the imported goods that facilitated it.

The Influence of Coastal Traders and Their Associates

During the second half of the nineteenth century, the 'commercialisation' of interactions with Lake Tanganyika's spirits contributed to a shift in spiritual authority and practice among people living on the lakeshore. In the 1870s and 1880s, indigenous lakeshore peoples ceased being the most prominent 'appeasers' of the lake's spirits. This distinction fell instead to coastal traders and their associates, many of whom referred to themselves as *ngwana* (freeborn Muslims) despite being in forms of bondage.[66] In 1882, for example, one member of the White Fathers wrote, '[i]t is not the [locals] who have the greatest fear of the spirits, it is mainly Wangouana [*sic*]'.[67] Similarly, Adolphe Léchaptois, also of the White Fathers, wrote in the early twentieth century: 'The [coastal] traders of Ujiji ... offer up to ten *dotis* of cloth ... for the happy success of their expeditions to the south of the lake; and, on their return, add in acts of grace [to the spirit], powder, ivory, and one or two slaves.'[68] These kinds of offerings somewhat reflect patterns in parts of the western Indian Ocean, where East African Muslims sent out small boats with

---

[64] Burton, *Lake Regions*, 313–14, 338, 342; NA RGS JMS/2/114 Cameron, 'Diary of a boat journey', 10 Mar. 1874; Cameron, *Across Africa*, 179; CWM/LMS/06/02/004 Hore to Mullens, 16 Apr. 1879; CWM/LMS/06/02/005 Hore to Whitehouse, 9 Feb. 1880; Hutley, *Central African Diaries*, 80; CWM/LMS/06/02/010 Jones to Thompson, 10 Feb. 1885; Bolser-Brown, 'Muslim influence', 626; Wagner, 'Environment, community and history', 190–2.

[65] Burton, *Lake Regions*, 350.   [66] See: Chapter 6.

[67] A.G.M.Afr. Diaire de Massanze, 17 Oct. 1882.

[68] Léchaptois, *Aux rives du Tanganika*, 172. See also: RMCA ESA HA.01.017-7. Storms, 'Resistance des marcheurs en caravan', n.d.; Stanley, *Dark Continent*, II, 67. A *doti* is a length-measurement of cloth equivalent to around 3.7 metres.

offerings to *jini* living in the sea.[69] However, they also reflect patterns of offering to spirits that people originating on Lake Tanganyika's shores had already identified. There was clearly a high degree of compatibility between 'oceanic' belief systems in this context. Coupled with commercial, technological, and environmental change, this compatibility allowed coastal traders and their associates to take prominent roles in the appeasement of Lake Tanganyika's spirits, which enhanced perceptions of their spiritual power and political authority. The effect was an increasingly commercialised spiritual framework that took on influences from the wider IOW, which also integrated varying practices from different parts of the lakeshore.

The process of commercialisation helped to facilitate the coastal traders' increased prominence in the appeasement of the lake's spirits. They were the principal importers of expensive goods from the wider IOW, including beads, cotton cloth, guns, and gunpowder. As such goods became more commonplace in the offerings made to spirits during trans-lake journeys, they were in the most ideal position to make them. Their ownership of such goods may also have been associated with religious power, given their importance to perceptions of the Jiji *teko*'s authority. It is perhaps additionally notable that the action of dropping goods to the lake's spirits is the most commented-on aspect of Lake Tanganyika's spiritual framework in 'explorer' and missionary sources written in the 1870s and 1880s.[70] This may partly reflect the visibility of such practices to Europeans on lacustrine journeys. *Ganga* practices on the lakeshore may have been more secretive – certainly the experiences of some twentieth-century anthropologists suggest that the secrecy of some rituals may have shaped the archive.[71] However, it may also represent an increased emphasis on offerings as crucial aspects of spirit appeasement. This could have been caused by an increase in the frequency in lacustrine expeditions, the gradual commercialisation of interactions with the lake's spirits, and this practice's compatibility with similar practices in the western Indian Ocean. In any case, as the traders with the largest

[69] Patricia Caplan, *Choice and Constraint in a Swahili Community: Property, hierarchy and cognatic descent on the East African coast* (Abingdon: Routledge, 2018), 100; Alpers, 'Ordinary household chores', 683.

[70] NA RGS JMS/2/144 Cameron, 'Diary of a boat journey', 19 Mar. 1874, 1, 3, 4 Apr. 1874; A.G.M.Afr. C.16-7. Journal du P. Deniaud, 9 Oct. 1879, 21 Oct. 1879; A.G.M.Afr. Diaire de Massanze, 17 Oct. 1881; Wissmann, *My Second Journey*, 258; RMCA ESA HA.01.017-7. Storms, 'Rapport de voyage à Oudjidji', 7 July 1883; Jacques and Storms, *Notes sur l'ethnographie*, 84; Lechaptois, *Aux rives du Tanganika*, 172.

[71] See, especially: Willis, *Some Spirits Heal*, 157–71.

commercial networks on the lakeshore, coastal traders and their associates were ideally placed to appease the lake's spirits through making offerings.

The prerogatives of commerce also led coastal traders to undermine some aspects of the Jiji *teko*'s spiritual role. Until the 1860s, coastal traders purchased their Goma canoes in Ujiji, paying taxes to Jiji *teko* for the right to do so, and for the right to employ Jiji boatmen. In subsequent decades, they sought to cut the Jiji *teko* out of these transactions. One way they did this was through purchasing Goma canoes directly in Ugoma and elsewhere on the lake's western shore. They then launched them on the lake without a Jiji *teko*'s rituals and without paying for them to be conducted. This does not mean that they did away with all indigenous customs, however, including in regard to decorating canoes for spiritual purposes. Alfred Swann of the LMS reported *ganga* painting 'two immense eyes on the bow' of Goma canoes.[72] These were *oculi*, which were ubiquitous on Indian Ocean *dhows*. They were meant to 'guard the soul of the boat and to drive off any malignant spirits which endanger[ed] the vessel'.[73] It is unknown whether the *ganga* who painted these eyes considered themselves Muslim, like the coastal traders, or not. However, it is likely that the practice of painting *oculi* on Lake Tanganyika's boats arrived with the coastal traders' influence. *Ganga*, whether indigenous to the lakeshore or originating in littoral regions of the IOW, adapted Lake Tanganyika's pre-existing spiritual practices vis-à-vis the decoration of canoes for ritual purposes to take on influences from the wider IOW. Taking place on the lake's western shore, these adaptations took some Jiji *teko* out of some of the core practices meant to appease the lake's spirits.

Influences from the wider IOW also affected the designs of craft traversing Lake Tanganyika. The coastal traders' demand for canoes opened new canoe construction centres and markets. According to reports, they frequently bought dugouts from regions further north (towards the Massanze region) and south (as far as northern Marungu) than Ugoma's main export centre, which supplied Ujiji's market.[74] The dugouts made in these alternative regions were smaller than those exported from Ugoma's core, but they were apparently more structurally

---

[72] Swann, *Fighting the Slave-Hunters*, 77.

[73] Dionisius A. Agius, 'Decorative motifs on Arabian boats: Meaning and identity', in *Natural Resources and Cultural Connections of the Red Sea*, eds. Janet Starkey, Paul Starkey, and Tony Wilkinson (Oxford: Archaeopress, 2007), 105.

[74] Stanley, *Dark Continent*, II, 2; CWM/LMS/06/02/005 Griffith to Whitehouse, 28 Aug. 1880; Giraud, *Les lacs*, 519–20.

Figure 3.2 A coastal trader's sailing craft. Original caption: 'A slave
dhow. A slave dhow dug out of a large tree in the Goma mountains
opposite Ujiji, and built up at the sides. Sails are made of American
calico. Two Arabs are on the quarter-deck, and a sailor is bringing on
shore a tusk of ivory. These vessels sail swiftly before the wind, often
escaping from the pinnaces of our men-of-war.' In: Swann, *Fighting the
Slave-Hunters*, 83.

capable of taking on significant modifications, such as the additions of
keels, rudders, masts, sails, and planks to the sides (see Figure 3.2).[75]
These modifications made canoes more manoeuvrable, increased their
carrying capacity to around 100–120 people, and – in the case of those
with masts and sails – made them significantly faster. It took around
twenty-four hours to traverse the lake between Kabogo (N) and Uguha in
a canoe powered by paddles; whereas, depending on wind, it took
between five and ten hours to do so in a canoe powered by sail, supplemented by oars.[76] In 1858, there was only one sailing craft on Lake

[75] NA RGS JMS/2/144 Cameron, 'Diary of a boat journey', 4, 5, 11 Mar. 1874. CWM/
LMS/06/02/003, Hore, 'Launch of the "Calabash"', 9 Dec. 1878; CWM/LMS/06/02/
005 Hore to Whitehouse, 20 Feb. 1880.
[76] CWM/LMS/06/02/004 Griffith to Whitehouse, 1 Nov. 1879; A.G.M.Afr. Diaire de
Kibanga, 17 Mar. 1885; Giraud, *Les lacs*, 496–7. The White Fathers wrote that it took
around eight hours to travel in a vessel of this kind between their station in Massanze and

Tanganyika; by December 1878 there were fifteen in Ujiji's harbour, not counting others in other lakeshore regions.[77] Additionally, soon after this latter time, Rumaliza had constructed a *dhow* closer in style to those found in the Indian Ocean. Its base was made from tied or nailed planks, and, as such, was the first craft on Lake Tanganyika designed explicitly for trans-lake travel that was not made from the base of a Goma canoe. Missionaries reported it as the 'superior' and 'most beautiful' boat on the lake.[78] They were clearly impressed by the adaptation of technologies from the wider IOW to the lacustrine environment.[79]

Again, these adaptations undermined aspects of the Jiji *teko*'s role, while possibly enhancing perceptions of the coastal traders' and their associates' spiritual power. Sailing craft were exclusively owned by coastal traders, and they were manned by their bondsmen (this is excepting the few owned by European missionaries, discussed later in this section). Initially, coastal traders favoured labour brought from littoral regions of the IOW for manning sailing craft because of their experience on *dhows* in the ocean.[80] This experience had trained them to man sails and use oars while sitting backwards. It contrasted with the methods of Jiji boatmen, who used paddles while facing forwards.[81] Later

Rumonge in Urundi, which is of a slightly lesser distance: A.G.M.Afr. C.16-7. Journal du P. Deniaud, 19 Feb. 1880.

[77] Speke, 'Journal of a cruise', 351–2; Richard F. Burton and John Hanning Speke, 'Extracts from reports by Captains Burton and Speke, of the East Africa expedition, on their discovery of Lake Ujiji, &c, in Central Africa', *Proceedings of the Royal Geographical Society*, 3, 3 (1858–9), 112–13; CWM/LMS/06/02/003, Hore, 'Launch of the "Calabash"', 9 Dec. 1878. See also: Vyncke, *Brieven van een vlaamschen*, II, 231.

[78] NA RGS CB6/1167 Hore to RGS, 10 Dec. 1879; CWM/LMS/06/02/004 Hore to Whitehouse, 11 Dec. 1879; Hutley, *The Central African Diaries*, 158; A.G.M.Afr. C.16-7. Journal du P. Deniaud, 21 Feb. 1880, 10 Apr. 1881; CWM/LMS/06/02/005 Palmer to Whitehouse, 4 Nov. 1880.

[79] It is notable that the extent and influence of these innovations on Lake Tanganyika is exceptional for the East African Great Lakes. Studies into new forms of lacustrine transport have been much more numerous for Lake Victoria, but sails do not appear to have been added to any craft there until the late 1870s – and then it was only to one craft. There, lacustrine transport continued to be dominated by (non-sailing) Ganda canoes, which went through their own modifications during the nineteenth century, making them more adapted to long-distance trade across the entirety of Lake Victoria. See, for example: Gerald W. Hartwig, 'The Victoria Nyanza as a trade route in the nineteenth century', *The Journal of African History*, 11, 4 (1970), 535–52; C. F. Holmes, 'Zanzibari influence at the southern end of Lake Victoria: The lake route', *African Historical Studies*, 4, 3 (1971), 477–503; Reid, 'The Ganda on Lake Victoria', 349–63; McDow, *Buying Time*, 190–214.

[80] Speke, 'Journal of a cruise', 352; CWM/LMS/06/02/004 Hore to Mullens, 16 Apr. 1879; Swann, *Fighting the Slave-Hunters*, 53; Erik Gilbert, *Dhows and the Colonial Economy in Zanzibar, 1860–1970* (Athens, OH: Ohio University Press, 2004), 36–51.

[81] CWM/LMS/06/02/005 Hutley, 'Uguha and its people', 29 Sep. 1880.

on, labourers with experience in the Indian Ocean trained some of the coastal traders' bondsmen, most of whom originated in Manyema.[82] These patterns of labour recruitment reduced coastal traders' reliance on the labour of Jiji boatmen and on the Jiji *teko* as a supplier of labour. Moreover, they associated the coastal traders and their associates with the largest and fastest of all craft on Lake Tanganyika. Missionary sources suggest that this may have had spiritual implications. When members of the LMS constructed an iron steamer in Ulungu during the 1880s, Swann reported that the locals did not believe it would float because of the material it was made from. When one observer was proved wrong, he apparently said: 'You put medicine in it.'[83] Such 'medicine', or *dawa* (Swahili), often created by the practices described earlier, was believed capable of appeasing the lake's spirits.[84] Thus, innovations to boats, including those made by coastal traders and their associates, may have been associated with spiritual power.

One effect of faster transport and increased frequency of commercial journeys was the flattening of regional differences in interactions with the lake and its spirits. Traditions among Tabwa populations associate the nineteenth century with the obliteration of the imaginary line between Tembwe and Kabogo (S), which, up to that point, had divided the lake's northern (Tanganyika) and southern (Liemba) halves. Subsequently, the entirety of the lake was referred to as Tanganyika.[85] The use of the northern term suggests the centrality of phenomena from the north, especially from Ujiji, in making sustained connections between these zones. This pattern is further reflected in the language used to refer to the lake's spirits. Increasingly, people living on the lakeshore referred to Lake Tanganyika's spirits as *zimu*. This word, of Bantu root, was known to both Great Lakes and coastal populations before the nineteenth century. In the Great Lakes region, it referred to ancestral spirits located in natural features, including lakes; on the coast, it usually referred to nature spirits on land – those in the sea were referred to as *jini*.[86] During the nineteenth century, *zimu*'s usage became more widespread

---

[82] CWM/LMS/06/02/004 Hore to Mullens, 16 Apr. 1879; ZNA AA1-23 Kirk to Marquis of Salisbury, 7 Nov. 1879; A.G.M.Afr. C.16-7. Journal du P. Deniaud, 12 Apr. 1881; A.G.M.Afr. Diaire de Massanze, 27 July 1882.

[83] Swann, *Fighting the Slave-Hunters*, 99–100.

[84] A.G.M.Afr. Diaire de Kibanga, 7 Feb. 1887; Swann, *Fighting the Slave-Hunters*, 91–2.

[85] Roberts, 'Heroic beasts', 132–5.

[86] David L. Schoenbrun, 'Conjuring the modern in Africa: Durability and rupture in histories of public healing between the Great Lakes of East Africa', *The American Historical Review*, 111, 5 (2006), 1424; Willis, *Some Spirits Heal*, 72, n. 7; Willis, *The Fipa and Related Peoples*, 31; Caplan, *African Voices*, 171; Alpers, 'Ordinary household chores', 684–6.

around Lake Tanganyika. It was used alongside indigenous terms for spirits, such as *ngulu* and *leza*, in the lake's southern half.[87] In Ujiji, it replaced *sigo* and *shinga* to refer to lacustrine spirits, even if such terms continued to be used to refer to nature spirits inland.[88] This reflects the coastal traders' longer-term and more sustained influence in Ujiji versus other lakeshore and inland regions. *Zimu*'s familiarity to both lakeshore and coastal peoples made it the ideal term to collectively refer to Lake Tanganyika's various spirits as the coastal traders' influence became more entrenched.

Coastal influences in Ujiji may also have been strengthened by the post-1878 decline in the lake's level. Environmental change in this context was disastrous for the port opposite Kawele-Ugoy, the site of the coastal traders' largest lakeshore settlement and Ujiji's most prominent market. This port was notable for its shallowness, meaning that small fluctuations in the lake's level had the capacity to create a large beach between the water and solid ground. By the mid-1880s, this beach was about 100 metres deep, leaving the approach exposed to strong south-westerly winds during the trading and long-distance fishing season.[89] It became decreasingly practical to dock sailing craft there, to the extent that European missionaries ceased using it from around 1883, instead docking their craft in Kigoma's deeper and more sheltered port.[90] Subsequent colonial governors preferred Kigoma to Ujiji for similar reasons, hence the construction of the harbour in the former place.[91] First-hand descriptions of how this environmental change affected perceptions of spiritual power in Kawele-Ugoy are not forthcoming. Yet, shifts, if they occurred, may have been disastrous for Habeyya, Kawele-Ugoy's *teko*. The accounts of Père Deniaud and Ameet Vyncke of the White Fathers suggest that Jiji boatmen attributed the decline of the lake to spiritual forces.[92] Additionally, referring to parts of Lake Tanganyika's south-western shore, Roberts wrote that 'changes in man's relationship to the earth spirits are synonymous with changes in Tabwa chiefship'.[93]

---

[87] Roberts, 'Fishers of men', 49, Lechaptois, *Aux rives du Tanganika*, 169; Schmitz and Overbergh, *Les Baholoholo*, 231–3.

[88] Gwassa and Mbwiliza, 'Social production', 79–80; Scherer, 'The Ha of Tanganyika', 892–3.

[89] Brown, 'Ujiji', 2; CWM/LMS/06/02/006 Griffith to Thompson, 12 Aug. 1881.

[90] CWM/LMS/06/02/008 Hore to Whitehouse, 18–23 June 1883, 5 Dec. 1883; CWM/LMS/06/02/011 Hore to Thompson, 23 Oct. 1886; CWM/LMS/06/02/012 Carson to Thompson, 11 Sep. 1887.

[91] Gooding, 'History, politics, and culture', 11.

[92] A.G.M.Afr. C.16-7. Journal du P. Deniaud, 20 Feb. 1880; Vyncke, *Brieven van een vlaamschen*, II, 231.

[93] Roberts, 'Fishers of men', 51.

If this can be used as precedent for other lakeshore regions where the role of the chief was similar, the retreat of the lake and its consequences for the travel of the lake's largest and fastest craft could have been interpreted as representative of the lake's spirits' wrath. It is perhaps notable that from around this time, Habeyya mostly withdrew from everyday affairs in Kawele-Ugoy, leaving matters in the hands of the coastal traders. Bogo, the *teko* of Kigoma-Gungu, whose port remained deep and sheltered, did not experience the same fate.[94] There is thus significant circumstantial evidence to suggest that changes in the lake level weakened perceptions of some Jiji *teko*'s spiritual authority, contributing to the coastal traders' rise in this context.

It is finally worth noting the role of Europeans in the development of boating technologies. Like the coastal traders, they brought significant innovations. Edward Hore of the LMS, for example, claimed that he was the first to add a second sail to a Goma canoe; the coastal traders apparently only used one at the time of his arrival.[95] Similarly, Emile Storms of the AIA added four sails to a canoe they called the *Strauch*. His ability to do so was rooted in the use of ambatch trees as caulking, which reduced leakages, allowing the base of the canoe to sit deeper in the water. The *Strauch* could carry 150 men and so was probably about 25 per cent larger than the coastal traders' largest craft made from the base of a Goma canoe (the carrying capacity of Rumaliza's *dhow* is unknown).[96] The AIA were also the first to make a boat on Lake Tanganyika out of iron. They made the *Cambier*, a steamer of around 6.5 metres in length, in 1881, although breakages and inefficiencies soon made it obsolete. The LMS persevered with this technology, however. In 1883, they launched *The Morning Star*, an iron sailing boat; and in 1887 they launched the SS *Good News*, a steamer (from 1885, they had used the shell of the SS *Good News* as a sailing boat) (see Figure 3.3). All these craft were part of larger fleets. The representatives of European organisations present on the lakeshore in the 1870s and 1880s also rented, purchased, and modified Goma canoes. Just as with Lake Tanganyika's most prominent traders, travelling around the lake with speed, efficiency, and safety was of utmost importance to the first Europeans who settled on the lakeshore.

European innovations to boating technologies inadvertently brought them into contact with Lake Tanganyika's spiritual framework. Unlike

---

[94] See: Chapter 1.
[95] CWM/LMS/06/02/003 Hore, 'Launch of the "Calabash"', 9 Dec. 1878; CWM/LMS/06/02/010 Hore to Thompson, 10 Feb. 1885; Hore, *Tanganyika*, 251.
[96] RMCA ESA HA.01.017-6. Storms to AIA, 15 Nov. 1883; RMCA ESA HA.01.017-6. Storms to AIA, Jan. 1885.

Figure 3.3 The London Missionary Society's iron boats. Original caption: 'The "Morning Star" at anchor. The "Morning Star" was dragged overland from Zanzibar to Ujiji, 823 miles. The S.S. "Good News" is in dry dock, quarried out of rock, floated by pith-wood after being wrecked. Salvage operations took four months, as natives had to work under water. The Author is in white, and near him is Alexander Carson, B.Sc, who died near this spot. From the opposite hills, Livingstone first saw the Lake.' In: Swann, *Fighting the Slave-Hunters*, 83.

coastal traders and their associates, they did not see or understand their belief systems as compatible with beliefs in nature spirits. Yet, as the earlier quotation about beliefs in the 'medicine' in the LMS's iron boat indicates, this did not stop people living on the lakeshore from integrating European phenomena into their existing spiritual framework.[97] Additionally, many African converts to Christianity on Lake Tanganyika's shores continued to practise rituals associated with beliefs in lacustrine spirits.[98] In Gregory Maddox's terms, they 'domesticated'

[97] Swann, *Fighting the Slave-Hunters*, 99–100.
[98] A.G.M.Afr. Diaire de Mpala, 23 Nov. 1885, 23 Aug. 1888; CWM/LMS/06/02/014 Jones to Thompson, 23 Jan. 1889; Iliffe, *A Modern History*, 86–7; McCaskie, 'Cultural encounters', 679.

Christianity into an existing belief system.[99] This process frustrated missionaries. Perhaps notably, they principally blamed the *ngwana* for it occurring.[100] Their doing so was partly a symptom of racialised preconceptions. They saw the 'blending' of belief systems, including between Islam and nature spirits (which they mistakenly saw as distinct), as unnatural, and they believed that the *ngwana's* presence encouraged new Christian converts to follow their precedent. Yet, it also shows the *ngwana*'s influence on the nature of Lake Tanganyika's spiritual framework in the 1870s and 1880s. By this time, they were the principal propagators of beliefs in lacustrine spirits and of the offerings meant to appease them. These practices had been strengthened in previous years through heightened levels of commercial activity and through the introduction of technological and spiritual influences from the wider IOW. Their influence shows the compatibility of East African coastal and lacustrine belief systems and the integration of somewhat distinct regional beliefs in lacustrine spirits into a broader spiritual framework covering the entirety of Lake Tanganyika.

Conclusion

The people of Lake Tanganyika's shores understood the lake as 'endless', as an ocean, looking north or south from their lakeshore vantage points. In conceptualising the lake as such, this chapter shows the compatibility between lakeshore people's perceptions of the lake and Indian Ocean littoral populations' perceptions of the ocean. Like in the wider IOW, Lake Tanganyika's somewhat distinct subregions became increasingly connected during the nineteenth century by physical lines of trade across it. This process sparked a process of spiritual innovation, adapting pre-existing beliefs in spirits in the lake to influences from the wider IOW. These adaptations were expressed in changes to canoe design and decoration, the language used to refer to the spirits, the prominence of offering commodities to the spirits, and the types of labour used on boats. Apart from indicating influences from the wider IOW, these changes contributed to the coastal traders' increased influence in many

---

[99] Gregory H. Maddox, 'The church and Cigogo: Fr. Stephen Mlundi and Christianity in Central Tanzania', in *East African Expressions of Christianity*, eds. Thomas Spear and Isaria N. Kimambo (Oxford: James Currey, 1999), 150, 162–3. See also: Thomas Spear, 'Toward the history of African Christianity', in *East African Expressions*, eds. Spear and Kimambo, 3–24; Chapter 5 for more discussion of patterns of 'domestication'.

[100] CWM/LMS/06/02/005 Hutley to Whitehouse, 12 Aug. 1880; CWM/LMS/06/02/009 Jones to Whitehouse, 24 June 1884; CWM/LMS/06/02/012 Jones to Thompson, 14 Nov. 1887; CWM/LMS/06/02/014 Jones to Thompson, 23 Jan. 1889.

lakeshore regions' affairs – although, as will be seen in the next chapter, this was not always a peaceful process. Nevertheless, in an interlinked development, appeasement of the lake's spirits became increasingly commercialised, and coastal traders and their followers became the principal commercial agents and spiritual authorities on the lake. The changing environment may also have been key to this process, especially in the late 1870s and 1880s. Declining lake levels may have contributed to a power vacuum in some lakeshore regions, into which coastal traders inserted themselves.

This chapter concludes Part I, 'Demarcations of Space'. As in Chapters 1 and 2, there has been an emphasis on the changing environment. In Chapter 1, this was expressed primarily through human actions – the development of 'emporia', the introduction of new architectural influences, and the movement of the centres of settlements towards the lakeshore. In Chapter 2, it was expressed through human–environment interaction – an 'agricultural revolution' in the context of a volatile climate. Both environmental and human factors have also been central to this chapter, with the focus on changing perceptions of the lake while the lake itself was changing. 'Perceptions' in this chapter are especially important. These perceptions were dependent on a changing cultural context associated with the influence of commerce and belief systems from the wider IOW on pre-existing spiritual beliefs and practices from the lakeshore. This, then, sets the thematic scene for Part II, which focuses on encounters and exchanges, many of them cultural, in the changing spaces described here.

Part II

Interactions

4   Competition and Conflict on the
       Western Frontier

The coastal traders were a heterogeneous body of people. In the early nineteenth century, most among them originated on the East African coast and islands.[1] In most historical discourse, such traders have been referred to as 'Swahili'.[2] Later in the century, Swahili traders were overshadowed by traders who traced their kinship links to other regions in the IOW littoral, including Hadramis, Balucchis, and especially Omanis.[3] Omanis had been visiting the East African coast for centuries, and there was an Omani governor in Zanzibar from the end of the seventeenth century.[4] Their influence in the region grew in significance after c.1830, moreover, when Said bin Sultan, the sultan of Oman, moved his capital to Zanzibar, enabling Omanis to gradually usurp the role of the pre-existing Swahili rulers there. Thence, four of Said's sons, Said Majid (r.1856–70), Said Barghash (r.1870–88), Said Khalifa (r.1888–90), and Said Ali (r.1890–3) were the first sultans of Zanzibar, independent of Oman. Barghash was especially important for establishing *liwalis* (governors) in mainland coastal emporia, whose power undermined the influence of some pre-existing Swahili elites. Moreover, during Barghash's reign, Omani traders became some of the most

---

[1] Sheriff, *Slaves, Spices and Ivory*, 173.

[2] See, for example: McDow, *Buying Time*, 99. In a previous publication, I referred to those labelled as Swahili here as 'Rima'. I chose the latter to reflect geographical origins on the Mrima coast – roughly demarcated as the East African coastal region between the present-day Kenya/Tanzania border and just south of Dar es Salaam. In some ways, this is more appropriate than using 'Swahili' to distinguish coastal East Africans from Omanis, as 'Swahili culture' underwent several changes during the nineteenth century that were influenced by Omanis. However, 'Rima' is also a somewhat invented word – one that is not in common use, at least not since the nineteenth century. It is thus thought more prudent here to use a term that is more well known and whose complex histories are more widely appreciated. See: Philip Gooding, 'The ivory trade and political power in nineteenth-century East Africa', in *Animal Trade Histories in the Indian Ocean World*, eds. Martha Chaiklin, Philip Gooding, and Gwyn Campbell (Cham: Palgrave, 2020), 260–9.

[3] Sheriff, *Slaves, Spices and Ivory*, 190.

[4] See: Abdul Sheriff, 'History of Zanzibar to 1890', *Oxford Research Encyclopedia of African History* (2020), 1–42.

prominent coastal traders in the East African interior. As at the coast, their rise came partly at the expense of Swahili populations. Analysis of these shifts speaks to interlinked patterns of competition and conflict between Omani and Swahili populations in East Africa across Indian Ocean littoral and interior regions during the nineteenth century.

Scholars writing in the last twenty years have increasingly come to grips with the idea of disunity within coastal trader communities in the interior. Their doing so has contested older histories, which tended to treat the coastal traders as a homogenous group of 'Arabs'.[5] Richard Reid, for example, wrote that the coastal trader communities of Tabora and Ujiji were 'riddled with intrigue, ... internal tensions and rivalries'.[6] Thomas McDow has more recently shed some light on what underpinned these divisions, by examining an 'undercurrent ... of contest over the status and authority of [Swahilis] in comparison to [Omanis]'.[7] In so doing, he traced competitions and conflicts between coastal traders in the East African interior to broader patterns occurring on East Africa's Indian Ocean littoral. His work, though, is based on limited source material, as it focuses largely on one mid-century caravan and two coastal trader settlements in present-day west-central Tanzania, using, for the most part, Richard Burton's *Lake Regions* as a reference.[8] Consequently, he defers to some of the older historiography for a later period and for other regions, which emphasises cooperation and congeniality between coastal traders as a collective body of 'Arabs'.[9] This chapter contests this aspect of McDow's work, extending instead the 'undercurrent' of 'contest' that he identified up to the early 1890s to Lake Tanganyika and further west.

The complex relationship between Omanis and Swahilis in East Africa's Indian Ocean littoral during the nineteenth century is a relatively

---

[5] See, for example: Brown, 'Ujiji', 164–208; Sutton and Roberts, 'Uvinza', 75; Beachey, 'The East African ivory trade', 272–3; Karin Pallaver, 'Muslim communities, long-distance trade and wage labour along the central caravan road: Tanzania, 19th century', *Storicamente*, 8 (2012), 2. A limited exception here is: Bennett, *Mirambo of Tanzania*, 53. Here, Bennett rightly argues that the coastal traders in Tabora were disorganized and disunited in the face of Mirambo's threat, and that there was much infighting between them. However, it took a generation until historians started building on this aspect of his research.

[6] Reid, *War in Pre-colonial Eastern Africa*, 115–17.

[7] McDow, *Buying Time*, 99. This is cogent with my oral sources collected in Ujiji and its surrounds, where informants tended only to use the moniker 'Arab' when describing someone of Omani descent, at the exclusion of other coastal traders. See: Interviews with Saidi Hamisi Kunga, 11 Nov. 2013; Rashidi Juma Hei al-Reith, 12 Nov. 2013; Hamisi Ali Juma al-Hey, 14 Nov. 2013.

[8] McDow, *Buying Time*, 97–107.

[9] McDow, *Buying Time*, 99. Specifically, he cites: Brown, 'Ujiji', 110.

well-known history. 'Interaction' – cultural, religious, familial – is a pervasive theme of the encounter. Intermarriages between Omani and Swahili populations were common, as were conversions of Omanis from Ibadhism to the Shafi'i branch of Sunni Islam, which predominated in East Africa. Additionally, coastal Swahili culture took on significant 'Omani' elements with the rise of *ustaraabu* (Swahili: 'to assimilate oneself to the Arabs, to become an Arab, to adopt the customs of the Arabs') as a cultural signifier of prestige.[10] 'Undercurrents' of conflict, however, were always present, especially among social and political elites. The male heads of Swahili households, for example, often refused to allow their daughters to marry Omani rulers and officials, knowing that to do so would lead to them losing control of their property; and Sultan Barghash imprisoned or deported some prominent Omani Ibadhi scholars who associated with Shafi'is.[11] Trade was also a significant arena of conflict. Swahili traders were generally determined to keep it in their hands as middlemen between the East African interior and the wider IOW.[12] However, the establishment of customs houses and (during the reign of Sultan Barghash) *liwalis* in coastal East African towns had the long-term effect of limiting Swahili traders' revenues and undermining their networks of credit and patronage heading into the East African interior.[13] By the 1880s, many Swahili social elites had become 'hopelessly in debt' and impoverished.[14]

That most historians have yet to trace shifting Omani–Swahili power dynamics on East Africa's Indian Ocean littoral to interior regions may be attributable to several factors. For instance, the European-authored sources about interior regions frequently use 'Arab' and 'Swahili' interchangeably, sometimes using them to refer to the coastal traders as a whole and sometimes to specific factions within them. Only with analysis of kinship connections, a core organising principle of the coastal traders' commercial networks, can divisions between Omani and Swahili traders in the interior be understood.[15] Thus, efforts have been made in the following discussion to, where possible, include traders' clan and family names. McDow's pioneering research and François Bontinck's French

---

[10] Randall L. Pouwels, *Horn and Crescent: Cultural change and traditional Islam on the East African coast, 800–1900* (Cambridge: Cambridge University Press, 1987), 129; Randall L. Pouwels, 'The East African coast, c.750–1900', in *The History of Islam in Africa*, eds. Nehemia Levtzion and Randall L. Pouwels (Athens, OH: Ohio University Press, 2000), 251.

[11] Horton and Middleton, *The Swahili*, 86; Anne K. Bang, *Sufis and Scholars of the Sea: Family networks in East Africa, 1860–1925* (London: Routledge, 2003), 94–6.

[12] Horton and Middleton, *The Swahili*, 86.   [13] Fabian, *Making Identity*, 78–9.

[14] Horton and Middleton, *The Swahili*, 87; Glassman, *Feasts and Riot*, 24, 153.

[15] McDow, *Buying Time*, 118–20.

translation of Hamed bin Muhammad el-Murjebi's (Tippu Tip's) autobiography are key here.[16] Nevertheless, some historians also probably
assumed that there was more to bind coastal traders than divide them,
given their origins in littoral regions of the IOW and their distinct urban,
maritime, and Islamic culture(s). Further, there is significant evidence of
cooperation between different coastal trader groups in the interior, especially in the earlier part of the nineteenth century and in distant regions
from the Indian Ocean. Omanis and Swahilis travelled in the same
caravans, they sometimes advanced each other credit, and they fought
together in wars versus hostile interior populations.[17] In many ways,
these acts of cooperation represented a 'pioneer ethic' that underpinned
Omani–Swahili relations as they entered unknown (to them) regions.[18]
This 'pioneer ethic', however, had its limits. It was less pervasive later in
the nineteenth century, when most coastal traders were hardly 'pioneering' into new regions but instead were settling into established towns and
travelling on well-known paths.[19] By this time, factions of coastal traders
were more likely to compete with each other for control of known ivory
supplies and trade routes, contributing to a hardening of conflicts
between Omani and Swahili factions.

Conflicts between Omani and Swahili traders took distinctly violent
forms in the interior. As will be seen in the following discussion, the acts
of bondsmen had the capacity to provoke death sentences and sentences
of bodily mutilation; disputes arose over the right to administer violence
among interior populations; and at least one war, lasting three years,
broke out between Omani and Swahili traders' respective followings.
These patterns contrast with the nature of the Omani–Swahili relationship in East Africa's IOW littoral, where conflicts tended to be negotiated
through formal institutions (the coastal riots and subsequent Abushiri
Rebellion in 1888–90, discussed in the Epilogue of this book, being an
exception). This divergence partly speaks to broader themes in
nineteenth-century East African Great Lakes history. In Richard Reid's
terms, the regions around the central commercial route comprised a
'corridor of [violent] conflict'. Although Reid relies largely on analysis
of militarised East African states, such as Buganda and those of Mirambo
and Nyungu ya Mawe, to make this point, conflicts between coastal

---

[16] McDow, *Buying Time*, 117–44; Hamed bin Muhammed el-Murjebi, *L'autobiographie de
Hamed ben Mohammed el-Murjebi Tippo Tip (ca. 1840–1905)*, trans. François Bontinck
(Brussels: Académie Royale des Sciences d'Outre Mer, 1974).
[17] Brown, 'Ujiji', 164–5; Murjebi, *L'autobiographie*, 42.
[18] A. G. Hopkins, *An Economic History of West Africa*, 2nd ed. (Abingdon: Routledge,
2020), 111.
[19] Decker, 'The "autobiography"', 746–7.

traders can also be considered a part of this history.[20] But it also speaks to the position of the East African Great Lakes in relation to the wider IOW. Forming a frontier region on the IOW's western edge, the Great Lakes were where competition between Omanis and Swahilis played out in particularly robust ways. The recency of their arrival in the region, the lack of formal institutions from the IOW's littoral core to follow them, and the highly competitive nature of ivory trading lent itself to the proliferation of violence. Citing another of Reid's works, one can argue that violence between coastal traders and their followings in IOW frontier regions, such as around Lake Tanganyika, was the 'surface manifestation of deeper ... tectonics' whose roots lay in the IOW's littoral core.[21]

An appreciation of these broader IOW dynamics around the East African Great Lakes adds significantly to understandings of Lake Tanganyika's history and of networks of kinship, credit, and debt in the western IOW. Specifically, it sheds light on the nature and direction of trade routes and on the shifting relationships between coastal traders and the peoples among whom they lived. With this in mind, the following discussion is split into three sections, ordered chronologically. The first section refers to the period c.1830–60, during which time Lake Tanganyika was the western limit of most coastal traders' commercial networks. Most only visited the lake's eastern shore, returning to more established centres further east once they had traded there. Only a few pioneers crossed the lake, with Omanis largely heading south-west and Swahilis heading west. To most, though, Lake Tanganyika was a natural barrier to the further expansion of IOW commercial networks in these decades. The second section refers to the period c.1860–80, during which time a faction of Swahili traders dominated most coastal trader settlements and trade routes around and across Lake Tanganyika. This was for ecological reasons on the lakeshore, for political reasons in lake's surrounding regions, and for economic reasons that developed from the previous period. These factors make the Lake Tanganyika case study stand out somewhat, in that prevailing Swahili influence endured here longer than it did elsewhere in East Africa's interior. The period represents some lakeshore regions' direct and sustained integration with commercial networks emanating from the wider IOW for the first time. Finally, the third section analyses the period c.1880–90, in which an Omani faction of traders, with credit ties to Kutchchh and political ties

[20] Reid, *War in Pre-colonial Eastern Africa*, 112–13.
[21] Reid, *Frontiers of Violence*, 23. For a summary of similar themes in India's past, see: Joseph McQuade, *A Genealogy of Terrorism: Colonial law and the origins of an idea* (Cambridge: Cambridge University Press, 2020), 6.

to the Zanzibar sultan, gradually took over from their Swahili counter-parts. Lake Tanganyika in this context became a crucial intermediary zone connecting littoral regions of the IOW to East Africa's most abundant supply of ivory. Nevertheless, this aspect of Lake Tanganyika's history was complicated by the actions of Europeans with increasingly imperial ambitions. As the analysis of the 'frontier' suggests, these transitions in the 1880s were violent and highly contested processes.

'Flying Caravans' and Early Pioneers, c.1830–1860

Lake Tanganyika was largely peripheral to coastal trader influence until c.1860. Although by this time coastal traders had been visiting the lakeshore for around thirty years, very few – if any – settled there permanently up to that point. Most instead only visited the eastern lakeshore in 'flying caravans' from Tabora or Msene in Unyamwezi.[22] This meant they arrived at the lakeshore, usually in Ujiji, traded their wares, and returned to their original settlement in Unyamwezi. Only a very few crossed the lake. Those who did so headed either in a south-western or western direction, respectively towards Katanga or Manyema. Burton recorded in 1858 that coastal traders on Lake Tanganyika's eastern shore and further east regarded such traders as 'debtors and desperate men'.[23] The lake's peripheral nature to coastal traders in this context stands in contrast to some surrounding regions, including Unyamwezi and Katanga, which had permanent coastal trader settlers from as early as the 1840s. Reasons of economics, practicality, environment, and feasibility played a role in Lake Tanganyika's comparatively minimal importance to coastal traders at this time. Only the most ambitious traders took these factors on, and some met early deaths as a result.[24] However, as will be seen in subsequent sections, some of those who survived became among Lake Tanganyika's most influential coastal traders in later decades.

Until just after mid-century, the coastal traders' position in most of the East African interior was highly vulnerable. They were few in number – Tabora, their most notable settlement up to this point, only had around two-dozen permanent coastal trader residents in 1858.[25] Also, their

---

[22] Burton, *Lake Regions*, 315–16. See also: Alison Smith, 'The southern section of the interior, 1840–84', in *History of East Africa*, Vol. I, eds. Roland Oliver and Gervase Mathew (Oxford: Clarendon Press, 1963), 272.

[23] Burton, *Lake Regions*, 374. See also: Sheriff, *Slaves, Spices and Ivory*, 175.

[24] Livingstone, *Last Journals*, 265, 291; Sheriff, *Slaves, Spices and Ivory*, 186; Reefe, *Rainbow and the Kings*, 163.

[25] Burton, *Lake Regions*, 229.

caravans tended to contain only around a hundred people, including porters. Travel to Lake Tanganyika in this context was considered dangerous. Tabora's coastal traders discouraged Burton and John Hanning Speke from travelling to Ujiji in 1858 due to 'dangers on the road'.[26] At this time, these dangers were mostly attributable to Ngoni formations, who, since the 1840s, had been travelling in the corridor between Lake Tanganyika and Unyamwezi and, in late 1858, attacked Ujiji itself.[27] Caravans had to be heavily armed for their protection, which was an expensive undertaking, undermining profitability.[28] Moreover, the return journey had the potential to be more dangerous than the outward. European 'explorers' noted that Nyamwezi *pagazi* (porters) were liable to desert if they spent too long in Ujiji.[29] This was because, apart from earning wages from porterage, they also brought their own goods to trade for ivory and captives.[30] Those who purchased captives were obliged to return to Unyamwezi quickly to reduce the costs of feeding them on the road and to limit the time during which they might escape. Jiji and other lakeshore populations, meanwhile, refused to work as porters.[31] Acquisition of goods from the lakeshore for transport eastwards was thus a dangerous and uncertain undertaking.

Those who sought to cross Lake Tanganyika and enter regions further west encountered further difficulties. Travel across the lake was expensive – traders had to pay Jiji boatmen wages and Jiji chiefs tribute for the right to do so.[32] Also, Nyamwezi *pagazi* often refused to travel on the lake.[33] The dangers of capsizing in dugout canoes and of 'the unknown' on the other side of the lake likely played a role here, as did their

[26] Burton, *Lake Regions*, 222. See also: Burton and Speke, 'Extracts from reports', 111–12; Reid, *War in Pre-colonial Eastern Africa*, 111.

[27] Burton, *Lake Regions*, 378; Stanley, *How I Found*, 393; Spear, *Zwangendaba's Ngoni*, 1–43; Roland Oliver, 'Discernible developments in the interior, c.1500–1840', in *History of East Africa*, I, eds. Oliver and Mathew, 208–11; Brown, 'Ujiji', 153–4; Reid, *War in Pre-colonial Eastern Africa*, 172.

[28] Verney Lovett Cameron, 'Livingstone east coast aid expedition', *Proceedings of the Royal Geographical Society of London*, 18, 3 (1873–4), 281; Stephen J. Rockel, 'Caravan porters of the *Nyika*: Labour, culture and society in nineteenth century Tanzania' (unpublished PhD diss., University of Toronto, 1997), 24, 74, 77; Sheriff, *Slaves, Spices and Ivory*, 163; Pallaver, 'Nyamwezi participation', 522.

[29] Burton, *Lake Regions*, 326; RMCA HMSA 18. Field notebook, 'Notes summary', n.d.

[30] Burton, *Lake Regions*, 326; Rockel, *Carriers of Culture*, 52–5.

[31] Burton, *Lake Regions*, 326; RMCA HMSA 4611. Stanley to *Daily Telegraph* and *New York Herald*, 30 Oct. 1876.

[32] Burton, *Lake Regions*, 323–4, 338; Cameron, *Across Africa*, 179; Bolser-Brown, 'Muslim influence', 623, 626.

[33] Burton, *Lake Regions*, 374; RMCA HMSA 4719. Stanley, 'Incidents of the journey through the dark continent', 17; Stanley, *Dark Continent*, II, 67.

commitments to return to their farms for the planting season.[34] Distance and uncertainty in this latter context discouraged travel across Lake Tanganyika, which could potentially put a significant obstacle in the way of their return journey. If coastal traders hoped to travel west of Lake Tanganyika, therefore, they had to form caravans composed entirely of their bondsmen, which was often more expensive in the long run than it would otherwise have been to employ free-waged Nyamwezi *pagazi*.[35] The one obvious way for coastal traders to account for these issues was to own or construct their own vehicles for traversing the lake. Up to c.1860, only one, Hamed bin Sulayyam (clan name unknown), an Omani, had achieved this through the construction of a sailing craft.[36] He based himself on Kasenge Island, just off the Uguha mainland, and traded in Urua, a region beyond the western lakeshore on the way to Manyema and Katanga. However, he, along with some other famous coastal traders of this era, including one by the name of Salim bin Habib el-Afifi, was killed by those with whom he traded.[37] Even the most ostensibly established traders around Lake Tanganyika were highly vulnerable in these distant and (to them) relatively unknown lands.

These obstacles and dangers did not prevent a small few coastal traders establishing commercial links with regions beyond Lake Tanganyika's western shore. Those that did so can be split into two groups – those that went in a south-western direction towards Katanga and those that went in a western direction towards what later became known as Manyema. Those that went south-westwards were predominantly Omani. Katanga at this point was already a famous exporter of ivory, people for enslavement, and copper. Copper from Katanga was traded in Ujiji and Unyamwezi in as early as 1800.[38] Portuguese traders had also visited Katanga by arriving from its south-east in 1806.[39] The Omani traders coming from the north-east in the 1840s likely travelled by canoe from Ujiji down to Kabogo (N) or Kabogo (S), before turning westwards

[34] Burton, *Lake Regions*, 35–6, 240, 251, 260, 372; Stanley, *Dark Continent*, II, 67; Rockel, *Carriers of Culture*, 55, 59.

[35] Stephen J. Rockel, 'Slavery and freedom in nineteenth century East Africa: The case of the Waungwana caravan porters', *African Studies*, 68, 1 (2009), 100. See also: Chapter 6.

[36] Speke, 'Journal of a cruise', 351–2.

[37] Livingstone, *Last Journals*, 265; Sheriff, *Slaves, Spices and Ivory*, 172; Reefe, *Rainbow and the Kings*, 163.

[38] Rockel, *Carriers of Culture*, 44–5; Roberts, 'Nyamwezi trade', 56; Alpers, *Ivory and Slaves*, 180; Smith, 'The southern section', 265–6.

[39] Rockel, *Carriers of Culture*, 44–5; Roberts, 'Nyamwezi trade', 56; Alpers, *Ivory and Slaves*, 180; Smith, 'The southern section', 265–6; Ian Cunnison, 'Kazembe and the Portuguese 1898–1832', *The Journal of African History*, 2, 1 (1961), 61–76.

towards Uguha or Marungu.[40] The most famous among them were Mohammed bin Saleh el-Nebhani and Said bin Habib el-Afifi (Salim bin Habib's brother). After encountering hostility from a chief called Nsama in Itawa in around 1845–6, they fled to Kazembe's kingdom in Katanga.[41] For the next twenty-or-so years, they used Kazembe's as a commercial base, amassing a fortune that attracted other Omani traders to the region via Lake Tanganyika's southern extremity.[42] However, Nsama's hostility prevented them from making sustained links with the lake, and in the 1860s, a change in the chiefship in Kazembe resulted in the seizure of much of their wealth and with restrictions being put on their movements.[43] It was not until a larger group of Omani traders arrived from the east and south-east in 1867 that they were able to return to Lake Tanganyika.

Less is known about the coastal traders that made westward links in the direction of Manyema during this period. The evidence, such as it is, suggests that they were more successful than the Omanis heading south-westwards. The key traders here were Mwinyi Kheri bin Mwinyi Mkuu el-Ghaskani, his brother Mwinyi Mokaia, and Mwinyi Akida bin Tayari (clan name unknown). All three were Swahili traders, likely originating in Pangani.[44] None were mentioned in either Burton or Speke's accounts of Ujiji in 1858. They were also apparently unknown to these Europeans' 'Arab' informants. However, several later accounts state they were in the region from the 1840s.[45] They were mostly occupied with trade in Uvira at the north end of the lake, from which point they ventured westward towards Manyema. This aligns with several studies of Uvira's history, which state that coastal traders probably arrived in the region in the early 1840s.[46] Burton also reported the presence of two young coastal traders in Uvira during his 1858 visit, who were sent there to acquire ivory.[47] This suggests the existence of a functioning ivory trade route between the elephant-rich regions to Uvira's west and the northern lakeshore, the kind of which did not exist between Katanga and Lake Tanganyika's south-western shore. No doubt this was aided by Vira populations

[40] Livingstone, *Last Journals*, 50.   [41] Murjebi, *L'autobiographie*, 202.

[42] Sheriff, *Slaves, Spices and Ivory*, 187.

[43] Livingstone, *Last Journals*, 237; Cameron, *Across Africa*, 174; Sheriff, *Slaves, Spices and Ivory*, 186; St. John, 'Kazembe and the Tanganyika-Nyasa corridor', 218.

[44] Brown, 'Ujiji', 127–8, esp. n. 2; Castryck, 'My slave sold all of Kigoma', 319.

[45] Livingstone, *Last Journals*, 327; CWM/LMS/06/02/005 Hore to Whitehouse, 9 Feb. 1880; Bennett, 'Mwinyi Kheri', 147; Bolser-Brown, 'Muslim influence', 628.

[46] Chubaka, 'Origines de la ville d'Uvira', 98–108; Depelchin, 'From pre-capitalism to imperialism', 166–75.

[47] Burton, *Lake Regions*, 352–4.

themselves, who were known elephant hunters in the lake's mountainous surrounds.[48] In any case, among the coastal traders, Swahili traders appear to have been the principal agents who tapped into and expanded these networks.

Diversion and Reconnection, c.1860–1880

During the mid-1860s, the existence of abundant, high-quality, and cheap ivory in Manyema became common knowledge in regions beyond Lake Tanganyika's eastern shore.[49] From this point on, it became increasingly important for coastal traders to travel to the other side of the lake, rather than to visit it in 'flying caravans' and leaving crossing it only to the most pioneering or reckless (depending on your point of view) among them. Several factors affected how different coastal traders encountered Lake Tanganyika in this context. Some were in common with the years discussed in the previous section. The logistical and economic difficulties of crossing the lake remained, and they were exacerbated by the fact that coastal traders travelled in ever larger caravans. Some had upwards of 1,000 people in them by the late 1870s, making traversing the lake on existing craft decreasingly practicable.[50] Further complicating encounters with Lake Tanganyika was the rise of Mirambo in western Unyamwezi, which brought violent instability to the route between Tabora and Ujiji.[51] There were also changes in East Africa's Indian Ocean littoral, which had consequences for Omani traders in the interior. Said bin Sultan died in 1856, and in 1859, Said Barghash attempted a coup versus his brother and Said's successor, Said Majid. When it failed, Barghash was exiled to Bombay for two years and many of his supporters fled to the East African interior, especially to Tabora.[52] Collectively, these factors contributed to Omanis dominating much of the coastal traders' activities in the East African interior, although most of Lake Tanganyika remained peripheral to their influence. Instead, Swahili traders were the most prominent coastal traders on the lakeshore, especially in the lake's northern regions.

[48] Livingstone, *Last Journals*, 327.
[49] Stanley, *How I Found*, 380; Bennett, *Arab versus European*, 113–14; Iliffe, *A Modern History*, 49.
[50] Pallaver, 'Nyamwezi participation', 522.
[51] Bennett, *Mirambo*; Reid, *War in Pre-colonial Eastern Africa*, 108–41.
[52] Speke, *Journal of the Discovery*, 107; Murjebi, *L'autobiographie*, 43; McDow, *Buying Time*, 104; Sheriff, *Slaves, Spices and Ivory*, 212; B. G. Martin, *Muslim Brotherhoods in Nineteenth-Century Africa* (Cambridge: Cambridge University Press, 1976), 166–8.

Even before Barghash's failed coup, Omanis dominated Tabora's coastal trader community. Msene's community, by contrast, located in western Unyamwezi, was dominated by Swahilis. According to Burton, the Swahili of Msene had a 'natural antipathy' to the Omanis of Tabora, hence their abandonment of the latter settlement.[53] Mirambo's rise in the late 1860s, however, spelled this latter community's end. Mirambo's capital, Urambo, was in its vicinity, and it soon dominated regional affairs, taking away Msene's viability as a place of commercial importance.[54] Mirambo then fought several wars with the Nyamwezi kingdom of Unyanyembe, in which Tabora was situated, especially in 1871–5.[55] Apart from engaging in the war, Tabora's Omani traders' response to this situation was to more or less abandon the route to Ujiji and elsewhere on Lake Tanganyika's north-eastern shores. They instead pioneered overland routes around the lake's south end, where they may also have encountered the occasional caravan coming from Lake Malawi and from Kilwa.[56] The most prominent trader in this context was Hamed bin Muhammad el-Murjebi, more commonly known as Tippu Tip (see Figure 4.1). Hamed was a relatively unknown veteran of earlier pioneer journeys beyond Lake Tanganyika's western shore, but he soon grew in prominence.[57] From 1867, he marched a 700-strong caravan from Tabora around Lake Tanganyika's southern end, finally establishing a post in Kasongo on the Lualaba River in Manyema. On their way, his followers established a post at Liendwe and successfully fought wars in Ugalla in southern Unyamwezi and versus Nsama in Itawa.[58] They also negotiated the freedom of older Omani pioneers in Katanga, including Mohammed bin Saleh.[59] These developments allowed the latter and his contemporaries to rebuild their connections with Lake Tanganyika, and they soon returned to Ujiji.[60]

Once they settled in Ujiji, the old Omani traders were generally overshadowed by Swahili traders who had already established their presence

---

[53] Burton, *Lake Regions*, 229, 269; Livingstone, *Last Journals*, 420; Alfred Chukwudi Unomah, 'Economic expansion and political change in Unyanyembe: (Ca.1840–1890)' (unpublished PhD diss., University of Ibadan, 1972), 221; McDow, *Buying Time*, 104–7.

[54] Sheriff, *Slaves, Spices and Ivory*, 179.

[55] Bennett, *Mirambo*, 53; Unomah, 'Economic expansion', 217–19, 235, ch. 5; Sutton and Roberts, 'Uvinza', 72–3; Reid, *War in Pre-colonial Eastern Africa*, 115–16.

[56] Wright and Lary, 'Swahili settlements', 549; Sheriff, *Slaves, Spices and Ivory*, 186, 191.

[57] Sheriff, *Slaves, Spices and Ivory*, 186.

[58] Murjebi, *Maisha*, 17–21; Livingstone, *Last Journals*, 171–82; Iliffe, *A Modern History*, 47; Sheriff, *Slaves, Spices and Ivory*, 188.

[59] McDow, *Buying Time*, 122–3; Murjebi, *Maisha*, 28–9.

[60] Murjebi, *L'autobiographie*, 193.

Figure 4.1 Hamed bin Muhammad el-Murjebi, also known as
Tippu Tip. www.gettyimages.ca/detail/news-photo/swahili-zanzibari-
trader-tippu-tip-circa-1890-after-a-news-photo/126318656?
adppopup=true.

in Uvira and towards Manyema.[61] The reasons for this power dynamic
were both regional and local. The success of the Swahili pioneers in
Uvira and further west in previous years led to the establishment of
Nyangwe in c.1866.[62] This town was (and remains) about sixty-five
kilometres from Kasongo, and, like the latter, it was on the banks of
the Lualaba River in Manyema.[63] Its most prominent coastal trader was a
Swahili trader called Mwinyi Dugumbi (clan name unknown), who may

---

[61] See, for example: CWM/LMS/06/02/004 Hore to Mullens, 16 Apr. 1879.
[62] Murjebi, *L'autobiographie*, 240. Several sources note Nyangwe as dominated by Swahili
    traders, including: Murjebi, *Maisha*, 79; Stanley, *Dark Continent*, II, 117; Cameron,
    Across Africa, 263–4.
[63] Cameron, *Across Africa*, 271–5; RMCA HMSA 18. Field Notebook, 18 Oct. 1876;
    Murjebi, *L'autobiographie*, 240–1.

have originated in Windi, near Saadani on the Swahili coast.[64] Links between Ujiji, Uvira, and Nyangwe made Ujiji's Swahili traders the richest coastal traders on the lakeshore, allowing them more prominence in the town's affairs. They built on this by establishing close relations among the Jiji. Mwinyi Kheri married a daughter of a Jiji chief during Verney Lovett Cameron's visit in 1874, and Mwinyi Akida apparently at some point dispatched troops, guns, and ammunition to protect Ujiji's central chief (*ami*) from an attack of Rundi populations from the north.[65] This latter act of leadership may have led to him being appointed as the Jiji *ami*'s regional representative (*tware*) in Kigoma.[66] Strong relationships with Jiji populations and commercial prowess underpinned Swahili traders' prominence around Lake Tanganyika's northern shores in the 1860s and 1870s.

The relationship between Omani and Swahili traders in Ujiji was frequently hostile. This is partly evident from the parts of town that they inhabited. Most of the Swahili traders lived in Kawele-Ugoy, while the Omanis lived in Kasimbo. Mwinyi Akida lived somewhat separately in Kigoma. In any case, the coastal trader districts of Kawele-Ugoy and Kasimbo might be described as 'bifurcated settlements', a term that McDow used to describe the relationship between the Omani settlement of Tabora and the Swahili settlement of Msene.[67] But, where distance (around 110 kilometres) kept open hostilities to a minimum between these two coastal trader communities in the 1850s an 1860s, such possibilities did not apply to Ujiji in the 1860s and 1870s. By the end of this period, many of the original pioneers who had returned from Katanga and Manyema in the 1860s had died. Mwinyi Mokaia died in Tabora in 1873 and Mohammed bin Saleh died sometime between 1874 and 1876. From this latter point on, the Swahili faction in Kawele-Ugoy was led by Mwinyi Kheri. The Omani faction, meanwhile, was led by Abdullah bin Suleiman el-Khangeri, a possibly younger trader whose time of arrival on the lakeshore is unknown.[68] In 1878, Edward Hore of the LMS wrote that Kheri and Abdullah were 'the leaders of two opposing factions' among the coastal traders.[69] This opposition occasionally broke out into bloodshed, most notably in 1876, when Mwinyi Kheri mustered a force of Jiji soldiers versus the Omani faction in Kasimbo owing to accusations of thievery on the part of one of Abdullah's bondsmen. The first verdict

[64] Murjebi, *L'autobiographie*, 98, 199, 240; Stanley, *Dark Continent*, II, 118.
[65] Cameron, *Across Africa*, 174; Castryck, 'My slave sold all of Kigoma', 321–2.
[66] Castryck, 'My slave sold all of Kigoma', 321–2.
[67] McDow, *Buying Time*, 104–7. See also, Pallaver, 'A triangle', 10.
[68] Murjebi, *L'autobiographie*, 259.
[69] CWM/LMS/06/02/003 Hore to LMS, 9 Dec. 1878.

was to cut off Abdullah's right hand, though the end result was a death sentence for the offending bondsman.[70] As Abdullah stated to one LMS missionary later on, the power of the Swahili faction in these contexts contributed to Omanis largely withdrawing from the town's affairs.[71]

Acknowledgement of Swahili prominence in Ujiji in the 1860s and 1870s sheds further light on the direction of trade routes to, from, across, and around Lake Tanganyika during this period. First, towards the east – Ujiji's Swahili traders appear to have been indifferent to travel to Tabora and the coast. This was probably informed by the 'dangers on the road' around Mirambo's domain, but it was also informed by indifference to the Omani-dominated coastal trader community in Tabora and their ongoing conflicts with Mirambo. According to Verney Lovett Cameron, writing of his experiences in 1874:

The prevailing feeling among [Ujiji's coastal traders regarding eastward travel] did not seem to be one of fear that they that they might be robbed by [Mirambo] on the road to Unyanyembe, but rather that they should be compelled by Said ibn Salim [Tabora's Omani governor] to remain there instead of going to Zanzibar, so as to increase the numerical strength at his disposal.[72]

Ujiji's coastal traders had no interest in Mirambo's war with Unyanyembe, including the latter's coastal trader community in Tabora, except for the ways it impinged on their commercial aims. They also likely feared reprisal attacks if it became known to Mirambo that they were partaking in the war. Evidence for this comes from missionary reports in 1880–1, during which time rumours abounded that Sultan Barghash was sending Zanzibari troops to confront Mirambo about the deaths of two AIA representatives in his domain.[73] Rumours of Mirambo's proximity and the possibility of reprisals on Ujiji owing to such actions sparked terror among Ujiji's inhabitants – coastal traders and locals alike. As the rumours swirled, many sold off their goods and prepared to evacuate to one of Ujiji's nearby islands.[74] Indifference to Omanis based further east contributed to Ujiji becoming

---

[70] Stanley, *Dark Continent*, II, 8–9; Bennett, 'Mwinyi Kheri', 153.
[71] CWM/LMS/06/02/004 Hore to Mullens, 16 Apr. 1879.
[72] Cameron, *Across Africa*, 171.
[73] CWM/LMS/06/02/005 Hutley to Whitehouse 11 Dec. 1880, Wookey to Whitehouse, 27 Dec. 1880; CWM/LMS/06/02/006 Southon to Whitehouse, 1 Jan. 1881; Bennett, *Mirambo*, 113–19; Reid, *War in Pre-colonial Eastern Africa*, 70, 117.
[74] ZNA AA1/23 Hore to Kirk, 14 Apr. 1879; CWM/LMS/06/02/004 Hore to Mullens, 16 Apr. 1879; CWM/LMS/06/02/005 Griffith to Whitehouse, 19 May 1880, Hutley to Whitehouse, 7 Nov. 1880, Hutley to Whitehouse, 11 Dec. 1880; ZNA AA1/28 Southon to Kirk, 29 Nov. 1880, Hore to Kirk, 20 Nov. 1880; RMCA ESA HA.01.017-7. Storms, 'Rapport de voyage à Oudjidji', 7 July 1883; Reid, *War in Precolonial Eastern Africa*, 172.

somewhat of an eastern 'terminus' for trade from Nyangwe and its vicinity through Uvira during the 1860s and 1870s.

Across Lake Tanganyika from Ujiji, the Omani–Swahili rivalry coupled with new commercial dynamics contributed to the abandonment of south-western routes towards Katanga. Livingstone's account suggests that Ujiji's Swahili traders attempted to open this route in the late 1860s, following in the direction of Mohammed bin Saleh and his contemporaries around twenty years before. However, they were forced to return empty-handed as Omani traders in Itawa, having arrived in the region overland around Lake Tanganyika's southern end, had purchased all the ivory and refused to sell it except at the prices they hoped to charge at the coast.[75] Subsequently, and until the 1880s, most traders travelling towards Katanga travelled overland. Ujiji's Omani traders, meanwhile, sought access to Kasongo (and Manyema more broadly) primarily through Uguha and the Lukuga River valley. This contributed to the opening of a new arena of competition. The region between Nyangwe and Kasongo represented the meeting point of Omani and Swahili routes into Manyema. Tippu Tip's autobiography suggests that there was a high degree of enmity between the two factions.[76] He claimed that he rejected the Swahili traders' overtures to join them (presumably under their influence) in Nyangwe, and instead he chose to set himself up in a nearby region.[77] He then sought strategic marriages to embed himself in local political structures at the expense of his competitors.[78] The success with which he did so is not only shown by his commercial prowess but also by the fact he was able in 1874 to use his jurisdiction to force some Swahili traders based in Nyangwe to compensate Manyema populations for attacking them.[79] These accounts suggest that Omani traders gained an early upper hand over their Swahili counterparts in Manyema.[80] This was a pattern that continued in the 1880s, during which time it also spread to Lake Tanganyika shores.

Violence on the Lakeshore, c.1880–1890

Factors both within and outside the lacustrine environment reshaped Lake Tanganyika's position in relation to trade routes used by coastal

---

[75] Livingstone, *Last Journals*, 189. See also: Murjebi, *L'autobiographie*, 56, 202–3. For an example of some Swahili traders trying (and failing) to get around the Omani influence in Itawa in later years, see: Andrew Roberts, 'The history of Abdullah ibn Suliman', *African Social Research*, 4 (1967), 245.

[76] See, for example: Murjebi, *Maisha*, 135.   [77] Murjebi, *L'autobiographie*, 98–9.

[78] McDow, *Buying Time*, 136–43.   [79] Cameron, *Across Africa*, 270–3.

[80] For a more detailed summary of Tippu Tip's experiences in Manyema and surrounding regions, see: Loffman, *Church, State, and Colonialism*, 44–6.

traders during the 1880s. To the east of the lakeshore, wars between Mirambo and Unyanyembe decreased in intensity from c.1875, and they ceased entirely on Mirambo's death in December 1884.[81] This reopened the route between Tabora and Ujiji, allowing Tabora's Omani traders greater access to northern lakeshore regions than in previous years. Once there, they contributed to an ongoing pattern of technological development, in which boats on Lake Tanganyika, including with the addition of sails and other modifications, became increasingly adapted to the trans-lake transport of large numbers of people and goods.[82] Omani traders and political leaders, meanwhile, became increasingly concerned with occurrences on the lakeshore. Said Barghash, the sultan of Zanzibar (see Figure 4.2), in line with patterns elsewhere on the East African mainland and provoked by letters from European missionaries sent in 1880, sought increased influence over the lakeshore's coastal trader communities. Tippu Tip also became concerned with conditions around the northern end of Lake Tanganyika after traversing it in 1881 on his route to Zanzibar. While at his destination, he worked with the Zanzibar sultan and Indian financiers in the latter's court to facilitate the long-distance ivory trade from Manyema to Zanzibar via the northern end of Lake Tanganyika. As their capacities grew in this context, the previously dominant Swahili faction of traders based in Ujiji became sidelined in the region's commercial and political affairs.

The role of Europeans complicates this history somewhat. Official European interference in the mainland's affairs opposite Zanzibar began with Sultan Barghash using British help to impose *liwalis* in coastal towns.[83] For the British, this ensured a regional ally and represented a claim of Zanzibari sovereignty on the mainland to counteract other potential claims made by their European competitors. These claims, however, amounted to little in the mid-1880s, when it became apparent that Zanzibari political influence hardly extended beyond each coastal towns' limits and as the European 'Scramble for Africa' developed.[84] Coastal traders on the shores of Lake Tanganyika were cognisant of these developments, and their commercial networks and the relationships within their communities were affected accordingly. The 1888–90 Abushiri Rebellion in coastal regions (which was ostensibly against the imposition of German colonial rule but was also rooted in long-term

---

[81] ZNA AA1/42 Kirk to Foreign Office, 30 June 1885; Bennett, *Mirambo*, 53; Unomah, 'Economic expansion', 224.

[82] See: Chapter 3.

[83] Horton and Middleton, *The Swahili*, 86; Glassman, *Feasts and Riot*, 150.

[84] Fabian, *Making Identity*, 78–9.

Figure 4.2 Said Barghash, sultan of Zanzibar (r. 1870–88). https://upload.wikimedia.org/wikipedia/commons/6/6a/Barghash_bin_Said_of_Zanzibar.jpg.

developments dating from Said bin Sultan's reign; see Epilogue), for example, resulted in a German blockade, limiting coastal traders' access to their sources of credit in Zanzibar.[85] At the same time, the British African Lakes Company fought wars with coastal traders around Lake Malawi, and in the early 1890s, Belgian forces fought with coastal traders in Manyema to establish the Congo Free State. How to engage with these influences was a matter of significant debate and resulted in new fissures emerging within Lake Tanganyika's coastal trader communities, especially, as will be seen, among Omani traders.

---

[85] Glassman, *Feasts and Riot*; Fabian, *Making Identity*, 175–210.

Sultan Barghash influenced the initial rise in Omani engagements with Lake Tanganyika in the 1880s. The sultan's interest in this context developed through complaints directed to him from LMS missionaries stationed in Ujiji and because of his allegiance with Britain dating from the early 1870s. After the imposition of *liwalis* in coastal towns in the 1870s, the British considered all the people living and/or born in these towns to be the sultan's subjects. With this in mind, Barghash also appointed a *liwali* to Tabora in 1872 to govern the people there who came under these jurisdictional terms.[86] Letters sent by members of the LMS based in Ujiji to Sir John Kirk, the British consul in Zanzibar, in 1880, however, threatened to undermine this façade of influence over coastal peoples in the interior. The letters stated that Mwinyi Kheri and his associates were preventing the LMS from building a mission station in Gungu, against the local chief's wishes.[87] As discussed in Chapter 1, such claims were almost certainly off-base. Nevertheless, they were an embarrassment to Barghash. They suggested that some coastal peoples could work actively against British interests. If the matter was not resolved, Kirk wrote, he would cease to recognise the sultan's authority in Ujiji.[88] Such would have been a dangerous precedent in the context of the developing European imperial discourse of the period. Barghash's response was to appoint Mwinyi Kheri as *liwali* of Ujiji, Uvira, and Uguha.[89] This changed little about the internal structure of Ujiji's coastal trader community, reflecting the limited ability of both Barghash and the British to enact change there at this point. It did, however, mark the point of the sultan's first official engagement with the lakeshore and of its potential importance to him and wider imperial structures in later years.

Omani influence around the northern lakeshore grew subsequently with the passing of a 3,000-strong caravan led by Tippu Tip between Uguha and Ujiji on its way to Zanzibar in 1881. By this time, Tippu Tip had established a commercial domain in Manyema, in which he took on an increasingly political role. He imposed, for example, a monopoly on ivory and ivory trading.[90] In so doing, he claimed the same rights as some of the most prominent East African political leaders of the period, such as

---

[86] Gooding, 'History, politics, and culture', 9.

[87] ZNA AA1/28 Hore to Kirk, 7 Dec. 1880; CWM/LMS/06/02/005 Hore to Whitehouse, 10 Mar. 1880.

[88] ZNA Kirk to Hore, 21 June 1880, Barghash to Kheri, Akida, the natives of Ujiji, and the Arabs, 17 June 1880, Barghash to Abdullah bin Nassib, June 1880.

[89] CWM/LMS/06/02/006 Griffith to Thompson, 29 May 1881; Reid, *War in Pre-colonial Eastern Africa*, 117; Bolser-Brown, 'Muslim influence', 628.

[90] Wissmann, *My Second Journey*, 210, 218; Murjebi, *L'autobiographie*, 96.

Mirambo and the *kabakas* (kings) of Buganda.[91] Additionally, just like these other leaders, he established his rights significantly through violence.[92] His arrival in Ujiji in 1881 sparked similar patterns in Lake Tanganyika's northern regions. The main actors in this context were Abdullah bin Suleiman, the leader of the Omani faction in Ujiji based in Kasimbo since the mid-1870s, and two brothers of the el-Barwani clan, Nassur and Mohammed bin Khalfan (the latter later being known as Rumaliza, see Figure 4.3), who had only recently settled on the lakeshore. Tippu Tip did not know Rumaliza and his brother personally before he met them in Ujiji, though he knew their kin through family connections, shared lines of credit, and the recommendations of his peers.[93] Abdullah, Nassur, and Rumaliza then set about establishing Omani influence on the western lakeshore. Abdullah led a party to Mtowa in Uguha through to Manyema, along the route that Tippu Tip had just passed.[94] The Khalfans, meanwhile, established Omani influence in Chuinu in Massanze, and from there carved out a more direct route to Manyema.[95] Rumaliza then travelled to Zanzibar with Tippu Tip; Abdullah and Nassur returned to the lakeshore after accompanying them as far as Tabora.[96] The routes from Mtowa and Chuinu then competed with the route from Uvira as the most prominent route to Manyema from Lake Tanganyika's western shore.

Ujiji's Swahili faction of traders did not watch these developments idly. Indeed, Tippu Tip's autobiography suggests a degree of personal enmity along Omani–Swahili lines between Rumaliza and Mwinyi Kheri, with the former claiming that the latter was not 'well-disposed' to him.[97] Nevertheless, Ujiji's Swahili traders, too, sought to expand their influence around the northern lakeshore through violence during this period. In 1881–2, they fought wars in the lakeshore regions of Uvira and Urundi, the latter being en route to the former over the lake.[98] They were well acquainted with these regions, owing to the existence of their

---

[91] Bennett, *Mirambo*, 73; Apolo Kagwa, *The Customs of the Baganda*, trans. Ernest B. Kalibala, ed. May Mandelbaum (New York: AMS Press, 1969), 31–2.

[92] Reid, *War in Pre-colonial Eastern Africa*, 113.

[93] Murjebi, *L'autobiographie*, 113; Martin, *Muslim Brotherhoods*, 166; McDow, *Buying Time*, 139–42.

[94] CWM/LMS/06/02/006 Griffith to Thompson, 1 Aug. 1881; Marcia Wright, 'East Africa 1870–1905', in *The Cambridge History of Africa*, Vol. VI, *From 1870–1905*, eds. Roland Oliver and Neville Sanderson (Cambridge: Cambridge University Press, 1985), 563.

[95] A.G.M.Afr. C.16-7. Journal du P. Deniaud, 12 Apr. 1881; A.G.M.Afr. Diaire de Massanze, 26 June 1881, 26 Mar. 1882, 6 Apr. 1882; Brown, 'Ujiji', 167–9, 176.

[96] Murjebi, *L'autobiographie*, 123.   [97] Murjebi, *L'autobiographie*, 113.

[98] A.G.M.Afr. Diaire de Massanze, 29 May 1881, 20–3 July 1881, 21–9 Aug. 1881, 18 Sep. 1881, 10 Oct. 1881, 24 Apr. 1882, 29 Apr. 1882.

Figure 4.3 Mohammed bin Khalfan el-Barwani, also known
as Rumaliza. www.gettyimages.ca/detail/news-photo/portrait-of-
mohammed-bin-hassan-rumaliza-an-important-news-photo/
526582340?adppopup=true. Also in: ZNA AV3/4 Rumaliza.

long-established trade route via Uvira to Nyangwe. They then imposed
chiefs who were favourable to their commercial aims, and they settled
among them. From around this point, Mwinyi Kheri spent more of his
time in Uvira than anywhere else, including Ujiji.[99] He largely left
governance of Ujiji's coastal trader community to Mwinyi Hassani,
who came from Mbweni (near Pangani) and who Stanley referred to as

---

[99] Mwinyi Kheri's absence from Ujiji compelled the White Fathers visit him in Uvira in
early 1880. See: A.G.M.Afr. C.16-7. Journal du P. Deniaud, 2 Feb. 1880. For a later
example, see: A.G.M.Afr. Guillet to White Fathers, 10 Apr. 1884, *Chronique
Trimestrielles*, 23–4 (Oct. 1884).

one of Mwinyi Kheri's 'young ... relations'.[100] The LMS's record occasionally refers to Mwinyi Hassani as a 'secretary', who acted as Mwinyi Kheri's representative.[101] Mwinyi Kheri's other major ally in this context was his nephew, Bwana Mkombe, who since 1880 had been attempting to establish a permanent presence in Rumonge.[102] Bwana Mkombe subsequently saw himself as Rumonge's governor, acting under Mwinyi Kheri's authority.[103] In short, where in the early 1880s the Omani faction broadly focused their attention on western regions of the northern lakeshore, the Swahili faction occupied themselves with the lake's northern extremity and its north-eastern regions.

There were some areas of ambiguity between these broad regional divisions, however. Mwinyi Kheri remained, at least according to the Zanzibar sultan's directives, the *liwali* of Uguha. He apparently attempted to assert this authority in late 1881 by directing Mwinyi Hassani to discourage the local chief from allowing the LMS a plot of land on which to build. The LMS account of this episode suggests the Omani faction did not support Mwinyi Kheri's efforts, further stating that 'there [were] endless feuds between the Arabs [Omanis] and the Wamrima [Swahili]'.[104] The LMS settled soon after, and the Swahili faction's influence in Uguha subsequently appears to have been minimal. Further north, in 1880, Bwana Mkombe had a direct role in selecting a favourable chief in Massanze after the death of a previous incumbent.[105] Subsequent to the Khalfans' wars, however, neither Bwana Mkombe nor Mwinyi Kheri's other associates appear to have had much influence in the region. The White Fathers stationed nearby were more concerned with the actions of Rumaliza's followers based in Chuinu.[106] Bwana Mkombe's exit from this region, however, may have been negotiated, at least initially. After carving out a domain around and beyond Chuinu, Rumaliza headed northwards to help with the Swahili faction's war in

---

[100] Stanley, *Dark Continent*, II, 8; Brown, 'Ujiji' 128, n. 2.
[101] CWM/LMS/06/02/004 Hore to Mullens, 16 Apr. 1879; CWM/LMS/06/02/006 Griffith to Thompson, 13 Nov. 1881.
[102] A.G.M.Afr. C.16-7. Journal du P. Deniaud, 20 Feb. 1880; Vyncke, *Brieven van een vlaamschen*, II, 15.
[103] A.G.M.Afr. C.16-7. Journal du P. Deniaud, 31 July 1880; CWM/LMS/06/02/006 Griffith to Thompson, 12 Aug. 1881; A.G.M.Afr. Guillet to White Fathers, 10 Apr. 1884, *Chronique Trimestrielles*, 23–4 (Oct. 1884); A.G.M.Afr. Coulbois to White Fathers, 18 May 1884, *Chronique Trimestrielles*, 26 (Apr. 1885).
[104] CWM/LMS/06/02/006 Griffith to Thompson, 13 Nov. 1881.
[105] A.G.M.Afr. C.16-7. Journal du P. Deniaud, 10 July 1880, 21 Oct. 1880; 11–13 Nov. 1880.
[106] A.G.M.Afr. Diaire de Massanze, 27 July 1882, 28 Nov. 1882, 7 Jan. 1883.

Uvira.[107] Tippu Tip also claimed to have left 140 followers in Ujiji to help with the Swahili traders' offensive.[108] It is possible that Ujiji's Swahili traders lessened their claims to parts of the western lakeshore in exchange for assistance in strengthening their existing and long-term influence in Urundi and Uvira.

Subsequent changes in Omani–Swahili politics on the lakeshore were heavily tied to developments in East Africa's Indian Ocean littoral. Tippu Tip and Rumaliza arrived in Zanzibar in early 1882. The former was there to settle his debts with Tharia Topan, a Kachcchi financier who was also one of Sultan Barghash's closest advisors.[109] The subsequent allegiance between these three individuals represented a fateful conjunction of Indian financial and Omani political and commercial interests. Barghash sought greater influence in the interior partly as a buffer against European imperialism, and the success of Tippu Tip's expeditions to date encouraged Tharia Topan to fund more of the former's ivory trading activities.[110] The latter's firm's funds contributed to the creation of several of the largest known caravans in the nineteenth-century East African context to traverse the region in 1884.[111] Moreover, Sultan Barghash's and Tharia Topan's collective interests gave Tippu Tip the resources and mandate to expand his influence in the interior in the name of the Zanzibar sultan, which he did most notably by extending Omani commercial interests as far as present-day Kisangani.[112] In this context, some historians have regarded Tippu Tip as Sultan Barghash's 'satrap' (provincial governor) in the eastern Congo rainforests.[113] Lake Tanganyika was a crucial intermediary zone to this region, providing, with its lacustrine environment, distinct challenges for the development of long-distance commercial networks. Thus, Tippu Tip appointed his accomplice, Rumaliza, to ensure the efficient travel of traders, credit, and ivory across the lake. On his arrival at the lakeshore in late 1884, Rumaliza used this position to claim he had a mandate from Sultan

---

[107] CWM/LMS/06/02/006 Griffith to Thompson, 29 May 1881; A.G.M.Afr. Diaire de Massanze, 26 June 1881, 27 June 1881.

[108] Murjebi, *Maisha*, 99.

[109] Murjebi, *L'autobiographie*, 170; Wright, 'East Africa', 562; Sheriff, *Slaves, Spices and Ivory*, 107–9; Iliffe, *A Modern History*, 46; Brown, 'Ujiji', 113–14; Deutsch, *Emancipation without Abolition*, 33.

[110] Sheriff, *Slaves, Spices and Ivory*, 107–9.

[111] CWM/LMS/06/02/009 Jones to Whitehouse 12 Apr. 1884, Hore to Whitehouse, 23 Apr. 1884; A.G.M.Afr. Guillet to White Fathers, 10 Apr. 1884, *Chronique Trimestrielles*, 23–4 (Oct. 1884).

[112] ZNA AA1/36 Kirk to Earl Granville, 23 Oct. 1884, Tipo Tipo to Barghash, undated; Heinrich Brode, *Tippoo Tib: The story of his career in Central Africa, narrated from his own accounts*, trans. H. Havelock (London: Edward Arnold, 1907), 160.

[113] Horton and Middleton, *The Swahili*, 87; Wright, 'East Africa', 562–3.

Barghash to govern Lake Tanganyika's shores.[114] His claims and his relationship to Tippu Tip, the Zanzibar sultan, and Tharia Topan represented a significant expansion of Omani influence around Lake Tanganyika.

The resources made available to Rumaliza enabled him to challenge the settlements made between Ujiji's Omani and Swahili factions during and after the 1881–2 wars. Soon after arriving in the Congo rainforests in 1884, Tippu Tip apparently sought to send around 900 *frasilahs* of ivory to Zanzibar via Lake Tanganyika. At the same time, Rumaliza claimed to him that Ujiji's Swahili faction were trying to strip him of the right to do so across Massanze, Urundi, and Uvinza. Consequently, Tippu Tip sent around 500 armed men to his aid.[115] The bulk of the fighting thereafter occurred in Urundi, which, since 1880, had been within Bwana Mkombe's zone of influence. However, even though it was on the Swahili faction's long-known route from Ujiji to Uvira, by the mid-1880s, it was also on the route to Chuinu, from where Rumaliza and his brother had carved a new route to Manyema. Competition for control of this crucial zone precipitated three years of violent conflict between the Omani and Swahili traders' respective followings.[116] During these years, both Mwinyi Kheri and Bwana Mkombe died – Mwinyi Kheri in Uvira in September 1885 and Bwana Mkombe in Ujiji in January 1886.[117] Both deaths were unrelated to the fighting, but they nevertheless undercut the Swahili leadership during this crucial period of violence. In April 1886, Rumaliza declared himself to be the governor of Massanze and the Urundi lakeshore, claiming tribute from local populations as a sign of his power.[118] Soon after, Ujiji's Swahili faction revoked their claims in Urundi in exchange for the right to trade there in Rumaliza's name.[119] A combination of enlarged Omani resources and untimely deaths in the Swahili faction ensured Omani dominance of northern Lake Tanganyika's coastal trader communities from the mid-1880s.[120]

---

[114] A.G.M.Afr. Coulbois to White Fathers, 2 Sep. 1884, *Chronique Trimestrielles*, 26 (Apr. 1885); CWM/LMS/06/02/009 Jones to Thompson, 2 Dec. 1884; RMCA ESA HA.01.017-5. Storms, 'Construit des bateaux pour revitailler l'Itawa en bateaux', 1884.

[115] Murjebi, *L'autobiographie*, 137–8.

[116] A.G.M.Afr. Coulbois to White Fathers, 2 Sep. 1884, *Chronique Trimestrielles*, 26 (Apr. 1886); RMCA ESA HA.01.017-17. Swann to Storms, 28 June 1885; A.G.M.Afr. Diaire de Kibanga, 29 Apr. 1886, 4 Feb. 1887, 1 Apr. 1887.

[117] RMCA ESA HA.01.017-20. Moinet to Storms, 15 Sep. 1885; A.G.M.Afr. Diaire de Kibanga, 26 Jan. 1886.

[118] A.G.M.Afr. C.16-133. Charbonnier to White Fathers, 30 Apr. 1886; A.G.M.Afr. Diaire de Kibanga, 13 Aug. 1886.

[119] A.G.M.Afr. C.19-439. 'Voyage à Oujiji', 1888; Brown, 'Ujiji', 178.

[120] See also: CWM/LMS/06/02/014 Swann to Thompson, 30 Jan. 1889.

In subsequent years, Rumaliza sought to consolidate his power at the north end of the lake and to extend it to its southern half. Following the collapse of the Swahili leadership in Uvira, he quickly stepped into the power vacuum there.[121] He attempted to impose favourable chiefs and to charge them annual tribute.[122] Around Lake Tanganyika's southern half, his power was much more diffuse. For example, he negotiated a favourable settlement for Kirando's coastal traders and their associates versus the White Fathers when the former wanted to settle in Katele, near to the White Fathers' station at Mpala, in 1890.[123] He was also known to visit Lake Tanganyika's southern extremity.[124] From there, he made connections with Omani traders based in Liendwe and elsewhere on the overland route to Manyema around Lake Tanganyika's southern end.[125] He was apparently trusted enough that Tippu Tip's representatives there occasionally forwarded ivory from their domains for dispatch coastwards.[126] Advancements in boating technologies and the opening of the route between Ujiji and Tabora may have made the transport of ivory from beyond Lake Tanganyika's southern and south-western shores in this direction more efficient than via the overland route. Of course, this represented the reopening of the south-western trans-lake route from Ujiji towards Katanga, followed by Mohammed bin Saleh and his contemporaries in the 1840s. During the late 1880s to early 1890s, Omani interests connected to the wider IOW were a pervasive feature of political life on the lakeshore. Their influence at this time probably represents the closest that one sole power has ever come to governing all of Lake Tanganyika's shoreline at one time.

Rumaliza, though, was far from a popular influence on the lakeshore. This is partly evident from a series of wars and disputes with lakeshore populations that arose over the collection of tribute, particularly around the northern end of the lake.[127] However, his unpopularity is further apparent from his relations with Ujiji's coastal trader community. The policy of transferring ivory through Ujiji to Zanzibar grated with traders who had no intention of returning to littoral regions of the IOW and who

[121] A.G.M.Afr. Diaire de Kibanga, 13 Aug. 1886, 7 Sep. 1886, 24 Sep. 1886.
[122] A.G.M.Afr. Diaire de Kibanga, 23 Nov. 1888; CWM/LMS/06/02/015 Swann to Thompson, 1 Aug. 1890, Swann to Thompson, 2 Aug. 1890.
[123] A.G.M.Afr. Diaire de Mpala, Jan. 1890. This conflict went back several years. See: A.G.M.Afr. Diaire de Mpala, 11 Aug. 1887; RMCA ESA HA.01.017-20. Moinet to Storms, Sep. 1888.
[124] CWM/LMS/06/02/016 Swann to Thomson, 31 Aug. 1891, Jones to Thompson, 5 Oct. 1891; A.G.M.Afr. Diaire de Karema, 2 Nov. 1893.
[125] Trivier, *Mon voyage*, 268–72.   [126] Roberts, 'The history of Abdullah', 245.
[127] A.G.M.Afr. Diaire de Kibanga, 23 Nov. 1888; CWM/LMS/06/02/015 Swann to Thompson, 1 Aug. 1890, Swann to Thompson, 2 Aug. 1890; Brown, 'Ujiji', 169–70.

did not rely on the supply of additional credit to trade. This applied especially to many Swahili traders, who had, since the 1860s, used Ujiji as an eastern terminus for trade. Commenting on this situation in 1889, LMS missionary Alfred Swann claimed that Ujiji's Swahili traders '[did]-n't care a jot for Zanzibar', and thus also its sultan and the structures underpinning Rumaliza's influence.[128] But it also increasingly applied to many Omanis in the context of encroaching European influence. German actions versus the Abushiri Rebellion at the coast and the African Lakes Company's war versus coastal traders around Lake Malawi shed doubt on the future viability of all coastal traders' commercial networks and fostered resentment towards Europeans. As a result, rumours that Ujiji's coastal traders intended to kill European missionaries on the lakeshore abounded, especially in 1889, at the height of the Abushiri Rebellion. Instead of responding to these concerns, however, Rumaliza initially sought to ride the wave of change. He courted the representatives of the LMS to recommend him to the British consul in Zanzibar, so that Zanzibar's new sultan, Said Khalifa, would declare him governor of the northern half of Lake Tanganyika.[129] In the late 1880s, Rumaliza sought a prominent place in the newly emergent world order, with limited concern for his compatriots.

Once Europeans' imperial ambitions were fully apparent, however, Rumaliza changed course towards a more confrontational approach. He and his followers fought battles with members of the Congo Free State and the Belgian Antislavery Society in the Lukuga River Valley in 1892, and he joined some of his kin to fight battles against Belgian forces at present-day Kisangani, Nyangwe, and Kasongo in 1893–4.[130] Again, however, Rumaliza's approach went increasingly against the wishes of Lake Tanganyika's coastal trader communities. By the 1890s, and after the crushing of Abushiri Rebellion and the removal of Omani *liwalis* from coastal towns, European imperialism appeared more of an inevitability than it had in the late 1880s. In this context, many coastal traders sought to accommodate the new influences as best as possible rather than risking their lives against them. At Lake Tanganyika's southern end, for

---

[128] CWM/LMS/06/02/014 Swann to Thompson, 14 Aug. 1889.
[129] CWM/LMS/06/02/014 Swann to Thompson, 30 Jan. 1889, Jones to Thompson, 7 Feb. 1889, Carson to Thompson, 9 Mar. 1889, Swann to Thompson, 14 Aug. 1889, Mather to Thompson, 14 Aug. 1889.
[130] ZNA AC1/7 Kirk to Foreign Office, 3 July 1892; Brown, 'Ujiji', 188–91, 204; Leda Farrant, *Tippu Tip and the East African Slave Trade* (London: Hamish Hamilton, 1975), 121; C. T. Brady, *Commerce and Conquest in East Africa: With particular reference to the Salem trade with Zanzibar* (Salem: Essex Institute, 1950), 206–7; Loffman, *Church, State, and Colonialism*, 68, 87–8.

example, traders based around Liendwe used European transport to further the ivory trade.[131] The leader of a similar drive in Ujiji was Msabah bin Njem el-Sheheni, an old Omani inhabitant of Kasimbo, who may have been at the lakeshore since the 1840s. In previous years, he was known as an ally of Abdullah bin Suleiman (and therefore also, in the early 1880s, of Tippu Tip and Rumaliza). Indeed, following Abdullah's military venture into Uguha in 1881, he set up a station there, just beyond the lakeshore, on the route to Manyema.[132] When Rumaliza fled to Ujiji from what had by then become the Congo Free State in 1894, the new German colonial government had already installed Msabah as the town's governor. Rumaliza was disgraced, forced to return to Zanzibar in hiding, and disowned by some of his closest associates, including Tippu Tip, who later accused him of embezzlement and of being a 'warmonger'.[133] Nevertheless, despite Rumaliza's unceremonious decline, Msabah's rise in Ujiji was still reflective of one broader trend to have developed over the previous decade: Omanis had usurped their Swahili counterparts as the most influential among Ujiji's coastal traders. By the early 1890s, though, they had become subjects of European colonial rule.

Conclusion

The Lake Tanganyika case study adds further dynamics to historical understandings of the relationship between Omanis and Swahilis in the wider IOW during the nineteenth century. Scholars of littoral regions of the IOW have done much to unpick the nuanced blend of cultural, religious, and familial interaction in this history, as well as the inherent tensions in their relationships. Many of these latter tensions related to the actions and perceptions of the Omani/Zanzibari sultan, and, as McDow argues, they contributed to an 'undercurrent' of competition and conflict. Focusing on the frontiers on the IOW adds a dynamic of violence to this discussion. The further from the littoral core of the IOW the coastal traders travelled and the later in the nineteenth century they did so, the more these 'undercurrents' took on more robust forms. The lack of formal institutions from the littoral following them into the interior, the

---

[131] Roberts, 'The history of Abdullah ibn Suliman', 245.
[132] Murjebi, L'autobiographie, 259; ZNA AC10/1 Hore to Kirk, 17 Aug. 1880; CWM/ LMS/06/02/006 Griffith to Thomson, 12 Aug. 1881; Brown, 'Ujiji', 176; Thomas F. McDow, 'Arabs and Africans: Commerce and kinship from Oman to the East African interior, c.1820–1900' (unpublished PhD diss., Yale University, 2008), 164–5.
[133] Murjebi, Maisha, 93; Roberts, 'The history of Abdullah ibn Suliman', 245.

violence of some contemporary African states, the increased stakes associated with the ivory trade over time, and the emerging question about what to do about encroaching European imperialists all played a role in this context. Nevertheless, as these tensions and this violence manifested, broader patterns were visible across the littoral–frontier divide. In both regions, Omanis became increasingly influential over their Swahili counterparts, which owed a great deal to their long-distance connections across the wider IOW to Zanzibar, Oman, and north-western India. This theme of violence will be picked up most notably in the Epilogue to this book. In turning to the coastal riots that marked the outbreak of the Abushiri Rebellion of 1888–90, it shows how violence, having developed gradually among coastal traders on the shores of Lake Tanganyika and elsewhere in the interior, exploded dramatically onto a core littoral region of the IOW.

Lake Tanganyika as a distinct environmental subregion had a significant role in shaping the direction of commercial networks spanning the western IOW. In the early 'pioneer' years of the East African ivory trade, it represented a barrier to most traders emanating from the IOW's littoral core; from c.1860 to c.1880, Ujiji represented an eastern terminus of trade from Manyema, while many traders sought to avoid the lake entirely by travelling the landward route around its southern extremity; and in the 1880s, it was a crucial intermediary zone between East Africa's Indian Ocean littoral and Manyema, the East African region with the most abundant supply of high-quality ivory. Several factors contributed to these transitions: the growth of emporia, agricultural change and, technological developments to lacustrine craft (each respectively addressed in Chapters 1, 2 and 3); in addition to political conditions in hinterland regions and coastal traders' increased capacity to influence the regions in which they resided. But an appreciation of wider Swahili–Omani encounters across the western IOW adds further, previously unexplored dynamics. They shed light on, for example, why the trans-lake route between Ujiji and Marungu towards Katanga fell into disuse in the 1860s; the diverging historical experiences of coastal trader communities in Ujiji and Tabora; and the direction of and reasons underpinning violence between coastal traders and northern lakeshore populations in the 1880s. Competition and conflict between and among coastal trader communities in the interior of East Africa shaped the direction and influence of commercial networks whose roots lay in IOW's littoral core.

5   Global Commodities in East African Societies

Of all the facets of East Africa's relationship with the wider IOW during the nineteenth century, most is probably known about the ways in which Africans' patterns of consumption shaped production in far-off places. Historians writing in the last fifteen years have done much to show how changing consumer demand in Africa for global commodities, such as glass beads, cotton cloths, and firearms, influenced the development of the global economy.[1] In so doing, they have challenged older, developmentalist narratives that only saw Africans as the 'victims' of asymmetrical global exchanges.[2] In Jeremy Prestholdt's terms:

> Though we tend to think of cloth, beads, and brass wire as finished manufactured goods distinct from the 'raw' materials Africans exported, it is more appropriate to think of them as only partially manufactured, since they often had to be radically redesigned in India, East African centers of trade, or on caravan trails before they could be sold in local markets.[3]

This statement stresses Africans' agency in globalising processes, shaping where and how global commodities destined for East African markets were manufactured. It also implicates structures whose bases were in the IOW – for example in Bombay and Zanzibar, and on East African caravan routes – as mediators in the distribution of global commodities to East African consumers. Moreover, how Africans demanded these products was shaped by their own changing fashions, economies, and socio-political structures, which, in turn, shaped and reshaped the production of different goods in different locales.[4] East African consumers

---

[1] See, for example: Prestholdt, *Domesticating the World*; Machado, *Ocean of Trade*; Pallaver, 'From Venice to East Africa', 192–217.

[2] For a critique, see: Prestholdt, *Domesticating the World*, 60–87. Also cited in: Walz, 'Route to a regional past', 54–5.

[3] Prestholdt, *Domesticating the World*, 68.

[4] See also: Machado, *Ocean of Trade*, 121; Maria Suriano, 'Local ideas of fashion and translocal connections: A view from upcountry Tanganyika', in *Translocal Connections across the Indian Ocean: Swahili speaking networks on the move*, ed. Francesca Declich (Leiden: Brill, 2018), 163–5.

were active participants in the globalising nineteenth century, even if the long-term effect of globalisation fostered (and continues to foster) inequalities between Africa and much of the rest of the world.

The key global commodities under discussion in this chapter are glass beads, cotton cloths, and guns. Beads made from glass were principally manufactured in Europe, especially Venice, which had been a global leader in glass bead manufacturing since the Middle Ages. Having faced decline in the eighteenth century, industrialisation breathed new life into Venice's glass bead industry in the nineteenth century, and facilitated the growth of competitors, for example in Hamburg.[5] According to Nadia Maria Filippini, in 1874, East Africa received just under 10 per cent of Venice's glass bead exports.[6] However, significantly more than that would have arrived there having been transhipped through India, England, and elsewhere in Europe, which received in that same year respectively around 23 per cent, 18 per cent, and 14 per cent of Venice's glass bead exports.[7] Writing of his experience in the late 1850s, Richard Burton claimed that there were around 400 varieties of beads in circulation in East Africa.[8] Some were significantly more valuable than others, though prices were not universal. Some beads, highly valued in Zanzibar, for example, were sometimes untradable in the interior owing to local (dis)tastes.[9] In any case, East Africans used beads as currency, in jewellery, and as decorative materials on everyday objects, such as on belts and musical instruments. Some of the most valuable, moreover, were demanded specifically by chiefs for display and distribution as symbols of their status.[10]

Imported cotton cloths, meanwhile, were principally manufactured in the north-eastern USA, north-western India, and England. Up to the American Civil War (1861–5), unbleached cotton cloth made around Salem, Massachusetts dominated the East African market, although it invariably passed through the hands of Indian and/or Omani financiers, firms, and institutions in Zanzibar before reaching East African consumers. Following the Civil War's disruption to the USA's cotton economy, Bombay upped its exports, building on centuries of Indian

---

[5] Pallaver, 'From Venice to East Africa', 197–8; Karin Pallaver, '"A recognised currency in beads" – Glass beads as money in nineteenth-century East Africa: The central caravan road', in *Money in Africa*, eds. Catherine Eagleton, Harcourt Fuller, and John Perkins (London: The British Museum, 2009), 26.

[6] Nadia Maria Filippini, 'Un filo di perle da Venezia al mondo', *La Ricerca Folklorica*, 34 (1996), 6.

[7] Pallaver, 'From Venice to East Africa', 200–1.   [8] Burton, 'Lake regions', 424.

[9] Pallaver, 'From Venice to East Africa', 212–13.

[10] Pallaver, 'From Venice to East Africa', 210.

connections with East Africa through India's supplies of cotton.[11] England, too, sought greater access to the East African market at this point, though largely through cotton that they first exported to India, where it was dyed for the East African market. English attempts at dying the cloth themselves apparently did not please East African consumers.[12] Following the recovery of the American cotton economy in the 1870s through the larger ports of New York and Providence, American, Indian, and Indian-dyed English cotton pervaded East African markets.[13] East African consumers used imported cotton cloth in clothing and as a larger denomination of currency than beads.[14] East African chiefs, moreover, demanded more elaborate cloths with distinctive patterns and styles.[15] Many of these were made in Oman, as well as in India.[16] Such cloths were often blended cotton and silk, and were used in chiefly attire and as gifts to secure commercial allegiances across the region.

Finally, the first guns to arrive in East Africa were flintlock muskets, which had been used by European militaries during the Napoleonic Wars. They presumably started entering the East African interior with the first trader coastal caravans, but they were not numerous in the Great Lakes region until at least the 1860s.[17] Breach-loaders and the occasional repeating rifle also circulated from the mid-1880s.[18] East African consumers used such guns in war and in hunts. The most famous wielders of guns near to Lake Tanganyika in these contexts were the *ruga ruga* – young armed men in the employ of statesmen such as Mirambo and Nyungu ya Mawe.[19] The *ruga ruga* were both soldiers and elephant

---

[11] Sarah Fee, 'Filling hearts with joy: Handcrafted "Indian textiles" exports to central eastern Africa in the nineteenth century', in *Transregional Trade and Traders: Situating Gujarat in the Indian Ocean from Early Times to 1900*, eds. Edward A. Alpers and Chhaya Goswami (New Delhi: Oxford University Press, 2019), 185; Prestholdt, *Domesticating the World*, 78–87; Katharine Frederick, *Twilight of an Industry in East Africa: Textile manufacturing, 1830–1940* (Cham: Palgrave Macmillan, 2020), 124–5; Clarence-Smith, 'The textile industry of eastern Africa', 264–5.

[12] Prestholdt, *Domesticating the World*, 66; Fee, 'Filling hearts with joy', 165.

[13] For the rise of New York and Providence, see: Prestholdt, *Domesticating the World*, 77.

[14] For cloth as a currency, see: Pallaver, 'What East Africans got', 76–7; Frederick, *Twilight of an Industry*, 126–36.

[15] Sarah Fee, '"Cloths with names": Luxury textile imports in eastern Africa, 1800–1885', *Textile History*, 48, 1 (2017), 49–84.

[16] Fee, 'Cloths with names', 75–6.

[17] Giacomo Macola, *The Gun in Central Africa: A history of technology and politics* (Athens, OH: Ohio University Press, 2016), Kindle edition, loc. 872; Reid, *War in Pre-colonial Eastern Africa*, 50; R. W. Beachey, 'The arms trade in East Africa in the late nineteenth century', *The Journal of African History*, 3, 3 (1962), 451–2.

[18] Beachey, 'The arms trade', 452; Reid, *Political Power*, 221; Moyd, *Violent Intermediaries*, 132.

[19] Reid, *War in Pre-colonial Eastern Africa*, 51; Michael Pesek, 'Ruga-ruga: The history of an African profession, 1820–1918', in *German Colonialism Revisited: Africa, Asian, and*

hunters.[20] However, the efficacy of guns in these contexts was often limited. Imported firearms were notoriously unreliable and susceptible to catastrophic malfunctions.[21] Also, powder was frequently in short supply, meaning that those armed with firearms often resorted to using alternative ammunition, such as stones and pieces of copper, iron, and brass.[22] Thus, many soldiers were still using swords, spears, shields, and bows and arrows, and hunters were using pits, spears, and poisoned arrows to kill elephants as European colonial armies arrived in the 1890s.[23] Instead of these practical uses, guns' greater significance was often more symbolic. Gun ownership frequently became associated with status, prestige, and power.

The extent to which the importation and usage of glass beads, cotton cloth, and firearms was transformative for East African societies is debatable. It should not be surprising that jewellery, clothes, arms, forms of currency, and items of decoration and prestige existed in the interior of East Africa before the expansion of the global ivory trade. Iron and copper goods, salt, *mbugu* (barkcloth), and *seketa* cloth (made from indigenously grown cotton in Ufipa) were all important in these contexts. The vitality of the industries that produced these products was such that many of them endured throughout the nineteenth century and well into the European colonial period, and in some cases beyond. Ufipa produced *seketa* cloth and upland Urundi produced *mbugu* into the 1930s, for example, while Katanga and Uvinza still produce copper and salt respectively.[24] The archaeological record additionally suggests that such goods of local make were in wider circulation around Lake Tanganyika than those brought from the coast during the nineteenth century. Stephanie Wynne-Jones and Sarah Croucher, digging near in Ujiji and its surrounds in the 2000s, found 'a cross-section of ceramics' from the nineteenth century that were 'mostly locally-produced, although a few imports were found'.[25] Thus, beads, cloth, and guns hardly replaced or

---

oceanic experiences, eds. Nina Berman, Klaus Mühlhahn, and Patrice Nganang (Ann Arbor: University of Michigan Press, 2014), 85–100; Moyd, *Violent Intermediaries*, 67, 75–84.

[20] Gooding, 'The ivory trade', 255–7.   [21] Reid, *Political Power*, 221–2.

[22] Reid, *War in Pre-colonial Eastern Africa*, 50; CWM/LMS/06/02/005 Southon, 'History, country, and people of Unyamwezi', 28 Mar. 1880.

[23] Gooding, 'The ivory trade', 256; Gissibl, *The Nature of German Imperialism*, 52–3; Reid, *Political Power*, 61.

[24] For *seketa*, see: Frederick, *Twilight of an Industry*, 167–203. For *mbugu*, see: Wagner, 'Trade and commercial attitudes', 158–9.

[25] Wynne-Jones and Croucher, 'The central caravan route', 94. See also: Sarah Croucher, 'Ujiji 2008': https://scroucher.faculty.wesleyan.edu/research/ujiji-2008/ (accessed 14 Oct. 2020).

invented new forms of consumption in East Africa. Instead, they supplemented what existed before, often adding new layers to existing patterns. As scholars such as Prestholdt for cloth and Giacomo Macola for guns have shown, East Africans 'domesticated' global commodities: they integrated them into existing cultural frameworks rather than using them to replace them.[26] African cultural expectations shaped significantly how and why global commodities circulated in their regions.

A further influence in this context was that of the coastal traders and their associates. Imported beads and cloths had been circulating in the East Africa's Indian Ocean littoral centuries before coastal traders started entering the East African interior. In this time, littoral populations had attributed cultural meanings to many global commodities. For example, by the nineteenth century, unbleached cotton cloth from the USA tied under the armpits (women) or around the waist (men) had become synonymous with slave status in nineteenth-century Zanzibar.[27] As coastal traders took imported beads, cloths, and guns into the interior, they brought such cultural associations with them. This influenced the ways in which some interior East Africans integrated global commodities into their societies. The coastal traders' influence in this context was especially strong in regions where they were the dominant importers of global commodities, such as around Lake Tanganyika from the 1860s. At the same time, however, coastal traders adapted their cultural practices in the interior. The same USA-made cloth that was associated with servitude on East Africa's IOW littoral, for example, was highly valued by all sectors of society on the lakeshore. Thus, coastal traders attributed new meanings and uses to beads, cloth, and guns as they encountered people on the lakeshore, who themselves sought to incorporate them into their cultures for their first time. How global commodities were perceived on the lakeshore was shaped by a cultural hybrid borne out of lakeshore populations' 'domestication' and coastal traders' cultural adaptation to interior contexts.

This chapter is organised into three sections, each focusing on a different category of global commodity. The first discusses the influence of glass beads. Beads were the least expensive and most widely available of imported global commodities in East Africa. Some arrived in interior regions via interconnections between regional trades in previous

---

[26] Prestholdt, *Domesticating the World*, 8; Macola, *The Gun in Central Africa*, loc. 261–75.
[27] Laura Fair, 'Remaking fashion in the Paris of the Indian Ocean: Dress, performance and the cultural construction of a cosmopolitan Zanzibari identity', in *Fashioning Africa: Power and the politics of dress*, ed. Jean Allman (Bloomington: Indian University Press, 2014), 14–15; Laura Fair, 'Dressing up: Clothing and gender in post-abolition Zanzibar', *The Journal of African History*, 39, 1 (1998), 68, 76.

centuries, but their circulation grew significantly during the nineteenth century. People living around Lake Tanganyika primarily used beads as currency. In so doing, northern lakeshore populations added an additional layer to the existing practice of using salt for the same purpose. Beads were less influential in lakeshore people's jewellery and decorations over the long term, although some were present in certain contexts. The second section discusses imported cotton cloths, which were sometimes used as a higher denomination of currency to beads. In contrast to beads, though, they had a significant influence on lakeshore people's fashions, at least during and after the 1860s, and especially in lakeshore emporia. Up to that point, cloths of local make, such as *mbugu* and *seketa*, were more prominent. How lakeshore peoples adopted different imported cloths was linked to previous styles of wearing clothes of indigenous make, to changes in global supply, and to fashions promoted by coastal traders and their associates. The final section discusses guns, the most valuable and least circulated of the three main imported global commodities on the lakeshore. Apart from those that were distributed to chiefs to secure allegiances, guns were almost monopolised by coastal traders and their followers, including by their bondsmen. This created an association between gun ownership and being a member of a coastal trader's following. As lakeshore populations demanded the most symbolic and valuable of imported global commodities, they increasingly turned to the coastal traders and their associates for cultural reference.

Glass Bead Currencies, Jewellery and Decorations

Interior East Africans had several currencies before the arrival of imported glass beads. The most important were salt and iron. Both products were highly valued and located only in specific locations. Their absence in Unyamwezi, for example, has elsewhere been interpreted as a stimulant to Nyamwezi participation in early long-distance trade. Seeking salt and iron, they were obliged to travel to other regions to acquire them.[28] Later in the century, iron products, specifically *jembe* (iron hoes), became a standard currency on many trade routes spanning present-day mainland Tanzania.[29] Around the northern end of Lake Tanganyika, salt was more important. Vinza collectors and traders

---

[28] Roberts, 'Nyamwezi trade', 45–8.

[29] Koponen, *People and Production*, 123; Wagner, 'Trade and commercial attitudes', 158; Rockel, 'Caravan porters', 30–1; Pallaver, 'What East Africans got', 85, 87; R. M. A. van Zwanenberg with Anne King, *An Economic History of Kenya and Uganda, 1800–1970* (London: Macmillan, 1975), 151.

brought it to Ujiji primarily in exchange for palm oil.[30] Jiji populations then packaged the salt in leaves, making the finished object resemble a loaf of bread. Jiji boatmen and, later, coastal traders used the packaged salt to purchase all manner of commodities from other lakeshore regions, including agricultural produce, livestock, iron, *mbugu*, ivory, and people for enslavement.[31] The importance of salt in these contexts endured at least into the 1880s – the White Fathers' archive shows that salt was a regular currency across the northern lakeshore during this decade.[32] Beads supplemented and added to these processes. Vinza salt was less important around Lake Tanganyika's southern regions. The main sources of salt for these regions were Ivuna on the western shores of Lake Rukwa in Ufipa and around Lake Mweru towards Katanga.[33] There is no known evidence that lakeshore populations used these sources of salt for currency. Around Lake Tanganyika's southern end, beads likely had a more transformative effect on systems of exchange.

The most prominent bead currency on the lakeshore was in beads known locally as *sofi*. These beads were made from glass in Venice, where they were referred to as *cannettone*. They resembled broken pipe stems and came in a variety of colours and sizes. They could be white, red, blue, or dark blue, and they were between eight and thirteen millimetres in length.[34] In Zanzibar, during the late 1850s, they were sold in white packets at 2–3 Maria Theresa dollars (MTDs) per *frasilah* (roughly sixteen kilograms).[35] They acquired more value in the interior, however. In Ujiji, individual *sofi* beads were referred to as *masaro*, but they were usually sold on strings (*khete*) or in bunches of ten strings (*fundo*). In 1858, a *khete* was the length of a string equivalent to the distance between the thumb and the elbow, or two times around the neck.[36] This was equivalent to 55–60 beads.[37] By the 1870s, these measurements and associated processes became more standardised. From this time, a *khete*

[30] Burton, *Lake Regions*, 45, 47–9; Roberts, 'Nyamwezi trade', 54.
[31] A.G.M.Afr. C16-7. Journal du P. Deniaud, 7 Oct. 1880; Interview with Raphael Ntangibingura, 5 Nov. 2013.
[32] A.G.M.Afr. C16-7. Journal du P. Deniaud, 14 Sep. 1879, 18 Sep. 1879, 7 Oct. 1880, 27 Dec. 1880, 19 Jan. 1881, 27 Jan. 1881, 27 Mar. 1881; A.G.M.Afr. Diaire de Massanze, 25 Jan. 1881, 11 June 1881, 12 June 1881, 15 July 1881, 25 Sep. 1881; A.G.M.Afr. Diaire de Kibanga, 2 Nov. 1885, 1 Jan. 1886, 24 May 1886, 25 May 1886. See also: Vyncke, *Brieven van een vlaamschen*, III, 2–3.
[33] Sutton and Roberts, 'Uvinza', 67–8.
[34] J. R. Harding, 'Nineteenth-century trade beads in Tanganyika', *Man*, 62 (1962), 104; Karlis Karklins, 'Identifying beads used in the 19th-century central East Africa trade', *Beads*, 4, 49–50 (1992), 53–4; Pallaver, 'From Venice to East Africa', 207.
[35] Burton, *Lake Regions*, 530.   [36] Burton, *Lake Regions*, 113–14.
[37] Burton, *Lake Regions*, 530.

was made of exactly twenty *sofi* beads.[38] *Masaros*, *khetes*, and *fundo*s of *sofi* beads subsequently became the standard currency for transactions in Ujiji's market. Money changers on the markets' edge further facilitated this process. They set the daily rate of *sofi* beads versus other commodities, including salt, iron, copper, and cotton cloth. Traders were obliged to exchange with money changers their goods for *sofi* beads to trade in the market. Money changers made profits from this process.[39] Larger-denomination currencies were used for transactions of more expensive items outside of Ujiji's markets. Such transactions included imported cotton cloths for ivory and people for enslavement, which often took place in coastal traders' *barazas*.[40] But for everyday exchanges of agricultural produce and other small items, *sofi* beads became Ujiji's standard currency.

Elsewhere around Lake Tanganyika's northern shores, *sofi* and other beads acted as a supplement to salt. The White Fathers frequently returned to Ujiji from their stations in Rumonge, Massanze, and Kibanga during the late 1870s and 1880s to acquire 'salt and *masaros*', which facilitated commercial transactions in their locales.[41] Northern lakeshore populations likely demanded *sofi* beads partly to gain access to Ujiji's markets without going through the emporium's money changers. Some lakeshore Rundi populations also wore *sofi* as jewellery.[42] Earlier in the period, though, beads known as *samisami* were more important for linking Ujiji to other northern lakeshore regions. According to Burton and Stanley, these were the most expensive beads by weight available in Zanzibar for mainland East African markets.[43] They were red with a white centre, and they came in various sizes. Writing in 1962, J. R. Harding traced their origins to Venice, writing that they were made from glass, although Burton described them being made from coral.[44] If the latter, then their origins are less clear. Despite *samisami* beads' value in East Africa's Indian Ocean littoral, they were little desired in Ujiji. Both Burton and Stanley reported that lakeshore Jiji valued a *khete* of *samisami* less than a *khete* of *sofi*.[45] The only northern

---

[38] Stanley, *Dark Continent*, II, 4; Hore, 'Twelve tribes', 9.
[39] Cameron, *Across Africa*, 176; Hore, 'Twelve tribes', 9; A.G.M.Afr. C.16–7. Journal du P. Deniaud, 7 Feb. 1879; Roberts, 'Nyamwezi trade', 64; Bolser-Brown, 'Muslim influence', 622; Koponen, *People and Production*, 122; Pallaver, 'What East Africans got', 83–4.
[40] Cameron, *Across Africa*, 176; Gordon, 'Wearing cloth, wielding guns', 24–5.
[41] See note 32.
[42] A.G.M.Afr. Journal du P. Deniaud, 7 Oct. 1880; Hore, 'Twelve tribes', 12.
[43] Burton, *Lake Regions*, 113, 529–30; Stanley, *Dark Continent*, II, 509.
[44] Harding, 'Nineteenth-century trade beads', 104; Burton, *Lake Regions*, 113.
[45] Burton, *Lake Regions*, 326, 530; Stanley, *Dark Continent*, II, 4.

lakeshore populations to have valued *samisami* highly appear to have been Jiji boatmen and Rundi and Vira chiefs in the 1850s and 1860s, the latter of whom wore them as symbols of their status.[46] In this context, Jiji boatmen acquired *samisami* beads at a discounted rate in Ujiji's markets and traded them to northern lakeshore chiefs in exchange for goods of higher value in Ujiji, especially ivory. Imported cotton cloths were put to similar usage at this time.[47] Differing fashions and uses for imported commodities among different lakeshore populations enabled some traders to make significant profits while also incentivising trans-lake trade.

The only other bead with significant importance to lakeshore markets during the nineteenth century were known as *matunda* or *mzizima*. *Matunda* were ring-shaped, either dark blue or near white, and were made in Hamburg.[48] In 1858, they were valued in Zanzibar at 7–9 MTDs per *frasilah* – cheaper by weight than *samisami* but more expensive by individual bead.[49] Their elaborate nature brought significant luxury demand among lakeshore populations. Burton reported Jiji populations using *matunda* in their jewellery.[50] By the 1880s, moreover, Holoholo (Guha) and Tabwa populations demanded *matunda* for use in necklaces, belts, and musical instruments.[51] In the latter context, *matunda* beads became useful tradable commodities for traders based in Ujiji seeking goods from the western and south-western lakeshore – principally maize and people for enslavement.[52] As a result, Emile Storms of the AIA reported in 1883 that most items in Ujiji were purchasable with *sofi*, but that the most expensive goods, such as enslaved people, guns, and ivory, were 'procured with mitounda [*sic*] and cloths'.[53] This report suggests that demand for *matunda* beads in Ujiji grew as opportunities to use it as currency in Uguha and Marungu developed. This increased *matunda* beads' worth to the extent that they became valued in

---

[46] Burton, *Lake Regions*, 320, 326, 331, 340, 346, 354.

[47] Burton, *Lake Regions*, 338; Speke, 'Journal of a cruise', 343; Bolser-Brown, 'Muslim influence', 623, 626.

[48] Karklins, 'Identifying beads', 52.

[49] Burton, *Lake Regions*, 530. Henry Morton Stanley claimed the beads he referred to as *matunda* did not have much value in Ujiji. This statement was almost certainly made in error. He described *matunda* as small, blue, brown, and white, which does not align with other descriptions (Stanley, *Dark Continent*, II, 4). He thus appears to have been confused between beads. See also: Karklins, 'Identifying beads', 52.

[50] Burton, *Lake Regions*, 320, 347, 372.

[51] CWM/LMS/06/02/005 Hutley, 'Uguha and its people', 29 Sep. 1880; Hore, 'Twelve tribes', 15; Jacques and Storms, *Notes sur l'ethnographie*, 26; Brown, 'Ujiji', xvii.

[52] CWM/LMS/06/02/005 Hutley, 'Uguha and its people', 29 Sep. 1880.

[53] RMCA ESA HA.01.017-7. Storms, 'Rapport de voyage à Oudjidji', 7 July 1883. See also: Vyncke, *Brieven van een vlaamschen*, II, 228, and III, 34–5.

comparative terms to cotton cloth. Traders in Ujiji thus took advantage of demand for *matunda* beads in other lakeshore regions to facilitate trans-lake trade, much as they had before with *samisami*, and much like they continued to do with salt. In short, lakeshore populations incorporated glass beads into their everyday lives in ways that contributed to the standardisation of currency in Ujiji and facilitated trade between different lakeshore regions.

Apart from using them as currency, lakeshore and other East African populations also used glass beads in jewellery and in decorations to everyday objects. This is partly evident from the earlier discussion of necklaces in Ujiji, Urundi, and Uvira, and of *matunda*-adorned objects in Uguha and Marungu. Yet, imported glass beads only had limited roles in these contexts. When they were used, they were generally only additions to existing fashions rather than replacements. Iron products from Uvira and copper products from Katanga remained some of the principal human-decorative objects among lakeshore populations throughout the nineteenth century. Holoholo men, for example, were famous for their headdresses, which were put together with iron, copper, and wooden pins.[54] By the early 1880s, such headdresses were apparently often further decorated with 'bands of cowries and beads'.[55] Additionally, iron and copper bracelets and anklets, known as *sambo*, were frequently noted as popular among most lakeshore populations.[56] Beads appear to have been little desired as replacements or accompaniments to these items. Some lakeshore populations additionally desired animal products on necklaces. Jiji and Rundi populations apparently often wore crescent-shaped hippopotamus teeth in the 1870s and 1880s.[57] Ivory jewellery appears to have declined in popularity over time, however, as ivory itself became valued more as an export good. Beads may have replaced some ivory fashions in this context, as they appear to have done in Unyamwezi, though the evidence from the lakeshore is unclear.[58] Regardless, the significance of these patterns should not be overstated. Appreciably more beads were traded as currency than were worn.[59] Additionally, by the 1890s, most lakeshore Jiji had ceased wearing glass beads in any form.[60]

[54] Cameron, *Across Africa*, 213–14; Stanley, *Dark Continent*, II, 52–3; Hore, 'Twelve tribes', 10, 14–15.

[55] Hore, 'Twelve tribes', 15.

[56] Burton, *Lake Regions*, 354; RGS NA JMS/2/144 Cameron, 'Diary of a boat journey', 22 Apr. 1874; Hore, 'Twelve tribes', 10.

[57] Cameron, *Across Africa*, 208; Hore, 'Twelve tribes', 10–12.

[58] Gooding, 'The ivory trade', 253–4; Pallaver, 'From Venice to East Africa', 202–3.

[59] Pallaver, 'From Venice to East Africa', 204; Burton, 'Lake regions', 424.

[60] Roberts, 'Nyamwezi trade', 64.

They and other lakeshore populations saw beads' value principally in terms of currency, a trend which lasted well into the colonial period.[61]

Cotton Clothing

Like glass beads from Venice and Hamburg, cotton cloths from western India, the USA, and England had a dual purpose in lakeshore societies. Lakeshore populations used both as currency and in fashions. In terms of currency, cotton cloths were frequently used as larger denominations than beads. Traders used them to purchase expensive commodities, such as people for enslavement and ivory, and to pay tribute to chiefs or for labour.[62] Traders also used money changers to convert cotton cloths into beads so that they could buy everyday objects of lesser value in Ujiji's markets. Several scholars have argued as a result that Ujiji's bead currency was based on a cloth standard.[63] The degree of the linkage here, though, has probably been overstated. As some contemporary accounts show, other commodities, including many whose origins lay in the interior of East Africa, such as iron and copper goods, were equally convertible into beads at the edge of Ujiji's markets.[64] The prominence of cloth in historical discussions of Ujiji's market currency may be attributable to the fact that the European authors of the archive primarily used cloth to acquire beads, and thus they commented on exchange values between beads and cloth more frequently than between beads and other goods. Additionally, as will be seen in the following discussion, the values of different imported cotton cloths varied significantly over time. The key driver of value in this context was fashion, not exchange values in relation to beads. Changing fashions in cloths were linked to changes in global supply, the cultural influence coastal traders and their associates, and the ongoing vitality of other clothing industries around Lake Tanganyika's shores.

The peoples living near the shores of Lake Tanganyika had three core, indigenous clothing industries during the nineteenth century. These

---

[61] Pallaver, 'From Venice to East Africa', 208.

[62] See previous section for currency. For payment of tribute, see, for example: Burton, *Lake Regions*, 313–14; Cameron, *Across Africa*, 179; Bolser-Brown, 'Muslim influence', 623, 626; Michael Pesek, 'Cued speeches: The emergence of *shauri* as colonial praxis in German East Africa, 1850–1903', *History in Africa*, 33 (2006), 399–400. For payment for labour, see for example: CWM/LMS/06/02/006 Southon to Thomson, 17 May 1881; CWM/LMS/06/02/008 Griffith to Whitehouse, 18 July 1883; A.G.M.Afr. C.16–7. Diaire de P. Deniaud, 27 May 1879.

[63] Koponen, *People and Production*, 122; Bolser-Brown, 'Muslim influence', 622; Roberts, 'Nyamwezi trade', 64; Pallaver, 'What East Africans got', 83.

[64] Cameron, *Across Africa*, 177; A.G.M.Afr. C.16–7. Journal du P. Deniaud, 31 Jan. 1879.

were respectively for the manufacture of *mbugu* (barkcloth) in Urundi, *seketa* (cotton cloth) in Ufipa, and softened animal skins throughout the lakeshore region. In Urundi, *mbugu* was principally worn by the wealthy and chiefly classes. Up to at least mid-century, most people wore animal skins.[65] Similar patterns may have pervaded Ujiji, whose traders acquired *mbugu* on Urundi's lakeshore and from Rundi traders in their markets.[66] Referring to his visit in 1858, Burton wrote that Jiji populations wore 'softened skins and tree-bark', the order perhaps suggesting that skins were more common, as in Urundi.[67] However, by the 1880s, sheets of *mbugu* tucked under one arm and tied over the opposite shoulder were ubiquitous among Ujiji's rural populations.[68] The latter's production of surplus crops for sale to townspeople and passing caravans likely gave them access to more valuable cloths.[69] *Mbugu* was also known in Holoholo and other north-western lakeshore fashions at a contemporaneous time, some of which may have been manufactured among inland Tabwa populations.[70] Regarding *seketa*, growing and weaving cotton appears to have been ubiquitous in much of Ufipa during the second half of the nineteenth century, including its lakeshore regions.[71] In the 1870s and 1880s, *seketa* was the primary dress of most of Ufipa's lakeshore inhabitants.[72] Lack of evidence inhibits making claims about earlier periods, although it is likely that similar conclusions would apply. *Mbugu* and *seketa* industries thrived during the second half of the nineteenth century and likely before.[73]

The vivacity of these cloth-making industries initially limited demand for imported cotton. In 1858, Burton wrote that traders in Ujiji '[lose] by cloth' in commercial transactions, as the imports he brought with him had little value. He claimed that this was because the lakeshore Jiji were 'contented' to wear softened animal skins and *mbugu*.[74] The only cloths to have significant usage to traders at this time were elaborately patterned cloths, or 'cloths with names'.[75] Their somewhat singular nature appealed to chiefs, who demanded them as tribute and wore them as

---

[65] Wagner, 'Trade and commercial attitudes', 158–9.
[66] Burton, *Lake Regions*, 320; Hore, 'Twelve tribes', 8–11.
[67] Burton, *Lake Regions*, 325.   [68] Hore, 'Twelve tribes', 9.   [69] See: Chapter 2.
[70] CWM/LMS/06/02/006 Griffith to Thompson, 12 Aug. 1881; Vyncke, *Brieven van een vlaamschen*, III, 36–7; Allen F. Roberts, 'Precolonial Tabwa textiles', *Museum Anthropology*, 20, 1 (1996), 47–59.
[71] Willis, *A State in the Making*, 151–5; Livingstone, *Last Journals*, 463; Cameron, *Across Africa*, 196.
[72] Frederick, *Twilight of an Industry*, 167–70.
[73] Katherine Frederick has recently made this argument explicitly in reference to Ufipa's *seketa* cloth. See: Frederick, *Twilight of an Industry*, 169.
[74] Burton, *Lake Regions*, 325.   [75] Fee, 'Cloths with names', 49–84; Burton, 114–15.

symbols of their status. Such cloths were often blended silk and cotton. They were made in a variety of locations, including in north-western India, Oman, and England.[76] Burton reported that the most common 'named cloth' was called *barsati*, which was blue with a broad red stripe, and was made in India (later versions may have been made in England and dyed in India).[77] A more valuable 'named cloth' in Burton's time was known as *debwani*, a cloth with a small blue and white check made in Oman.[78] According to Burton, Jiji *teko* (district chiefs) were already wearing such cloths when he and John Hanning Speke visited the lake-shore.[79] It is possible that the Jiji chiefs' preference for imported 'cloths with names' represented a departure from a previous chiefly fashion for clothing made from *mbugu*. If true, then this may have further contrib-uted to Jiji farmers gaining greater access to *mbugu* in subsequent years. *Mbugu* may have become more ubiquitous in Ujiji as it became less associated with chiefly status and more subject to general demand.

The first imported cotton cloth to receive popular appeal on the lakeshore was known in East Africa as *kaniki*. This was an indigo-dyed cotton cloth made in north-western India, where it was known as *canne-quim*. Its origins lie in the fifteenth and sixteenth centuries, from which time north-western Indian cloths were crucial to commercial relation-ships across littoral regions of the western IOW.[80] During the second half of the nineteenth century, the major processing centres were in Bombay and Kutchchh. Some additional *kaniki* was made in England before being dyed in these centres.[81] This Indian-dyed English cloth is often referred to in the sources as *satini*. *Kaniki* and *satini* were valued similarly around Lake Tanganyika.[82] By the 1870s, most Jiji living in its lakeshore emporium wore *kaniki* in the style that they had previously worn *mbugu*,

---

[76] Fee, 'Cloths with names', 50.

[77] Burton, *Lake Regions*, 114; Fee, 'Cloths with names', 53, 65.

[78] Burton, *Lake Regions*, 115; Fee, 'Cloths with names', 53, 75–6.

[79] Burton, *Lake Regions*, 320. For Urundi at a later point, see: A.G.M.Afr. C.16-7. Journal du. P. Deniaud, 26 May 1879.

[80] Subrahmanyam, 'Between eastern Africa and western India', 804–15; William G. Clarence-Smith, 'The expansion of cotton textile production in the western Indian Ocean, c.1500–c.1850', in *Reinterpreting Indian Ocean Worlds: Essays in honour of Kirti N. Chaudhuri*, eds. Stefan Halikowski Smith and K. N. Chaudhuri (Newcastle Upon Tyne: Cambridge Scholars Pub., 2011), 84–106; Michael N. Pearson, *Port Cities and Intruders: The Swahili Coast, India, and Portugal in the early modern era* (Baltimore, MD: Johns Hopkins University Press, 1998), 48.

[81] Fee, 'Filling hearts with joy', 192–5.

[82] CWM/LMS/06/02/005 Griffith to Whitehouse, 20 Nov. 1880; CWM/LMS/06/02/008 Griffith to Whitehouse, 18 July 1883; RMCA ESA HA.01.017-6. Storms to AIA, 15 Nov. 1883.

that is, under one arm and over the other shoulder.[83] They thus incorporated *kaniki* into an existing dress-style. By contrast, most Jiji people living just five or six kilometres from the lakeshore continued wearing *mbugu* throughout the period, perhaps because of preference, or because they lacked the means to purchase *kaniki*.[84] Wearing *kaniki* in this context became a symbol of the urban Jiji's participation in the commercial culture that pervaded East African emporia and caravans.[85] There may also have been global dynamics to this process. The lakeshore Jiji's incorporation of imported cotton cloth into their dress occurred during and immediately after the American Civil War, during which time there was a shortage of American-manufactured cloth and an increase in the supply of Indian- and British-manufactured cloth in East Africa. By 'domesticating' *kaniki*, lakeshore Jiji partly responded to the vagaries of international supply, at least initially.

American-manufactured cloth was more popular in other lakeshore regions in the late 1860s and 1870s, as well as in Ujiji during the 1880s. East Africans referred to American cloth as *merikani*. In the USA, it was known as *calico*, or white, unbleached sheeting. From the beginning of the nineteenth century until the American Civil War, *merikani* dominated East Africa's imported cotton cloth markets, at least where imported cotton cloth was in demand at all (thus not in Ujiji).[86] It was valued in East Africa partly for its durability. It is perhaps for this reason that coastal traders favoured it in the interior, and that they and their counterparts resident in East Africa's Indian Ocean littoral dressed their bonds(wo)men in it.[87] But where in littoral regions *merikani* consequently became associated with servility and thus also low social status, similar patterns did not pervade the shores of Lake Tanganyika or elsewhere in the interior. In East Africa's Great Lakes region, it was highly valued by people of wealthier and more prestigious status. Coastal traders and their followers, for example, often cut it into the shape of a dress shirt, known as a *kanzu*, in line with styles at the coast. Some of their bonds(wo)men did similarly.[88] For example, Sheryl

---

[83] Stanley, *Dark Continent*, II, 3, 7; Hore, 'Twelve tribes', 10; RMCA ESA HA.01.017-7. Storms, 'Rapport de voyage à Oudjidji', 7 July 1883; Jacques and Storms, *Notes sur L'ethnographie*, 32.

[84] Hore, 'Twelve tribes', 9.   [85] Frederick, *Twilight of an Industry*, 124.

[86] Prestholdt, *Domesticating the World*, 72–8.

[87] Fair, 'Remaking fashion', 14–15; Fair, 'Dressing up', 68, 76; Jonathon Glassman, 'The bondsman's new clothes: The contradictory consciousness of slave resistance on the Swahili coast', *The Journal of African History*, 32, 2 (1991), 310–12; McCurdy, 'Transforming associations', 98.

[88] A.G.M.Afr. C.16-7. Diaire de P. Deniaud, 27 May 1879; NA RGS CB6/2173 Thomson to Kirk, 27 Mar. 1880, 26 May 1880; CWM/LMS/06/02/006 Hutley,

Figure 5.1 Women wearing imported cotton cloth in Rumaliza's court. In: Edward Hore, 'An Arab friend in Central Africa', Chronicle of the London Missionary Society (August 1891), 236. With thanks to University Library Frankfurt for providing a copy of the image.

McCurdy has shown that Manyema women in Ujiji during the 1880s and 1890s, many of whom were in some form of bondage, were at the forefront of incorporating *merikani* cloth into elaborate fashions, which enhanced their status (see Figure 5.1).[89] Indeed, access to cloth, especially *merikani*, was likely a core motivation for joining and staying in a coastal trader's following. Among other peoples, wealthy Fipa populations wore *merikani* tied around their necks over loin cloths made of *seketa*, and north-western lakeshore populations added cotton garments

'Mahommadanism in Central Africa: Its influence', Aug. 1881; RMCA ESA HA.01.017-7. Storms, 'Rapport de voyage à Oudjidji', 7 July 1883; CWM/LMS/06/02/009 Jones to Thompson, 2 Dec. 1884; A.G.M.Afr. Diaire de Mkapakwe, 26 Jan. 1885; CWM/LMS/06/02/013 Wright to Thompson, 4 Nov. 1888; Jacques and Storms, *Notes sur l'ethnographie*, 32.

[89] McCurdy, 'Transforming associations', 98; Sheryl McCurdy, 'Fashioning sexuality: Desire, Manyema ethnicity, and the creation of the "kanga," "ca." 1880–1900', *International Journal of African Historical Studies*, 39, 3 (2006), 441–69. The idea of using dress to enhance social status is cogent with patterns in East Africa's Indian Ocean littoral during the colonial period. See: Laura Fair, *Pastimes and Politics: Culture, community, and identity in post-abolition urban Zanzibar* (Athens, OH: Ohio University Press, 2001), 64–109.

to dress styles dominated by skins and barkcloth.[90] They thus added an additional layer to their existing fashions. Reporting more broadly on the Lake Tanganyika region, Victor Jacques and Emile Storms of the AIA wrote that *merikani* cloth was a 'luxury clothing that not everyone could afford'.[91] In short, by the late 1870s, wearing *merikani* cloth, often in the style proffered by coastal traders and their followers, became a symbol of prosperity.

The increasing association between *merikani* and wealthy status partly explains changing values of imported cotton cloths in Ujiji's market in the late 1870s to early 1880s. In 1878–80, a *doti* (approx. 3.5 metres) of *kaniki* was equivalent to 9–11 *fundo* of *sofi*, while *merikani* was equivalent to 12–15 *fundo*.[92] However, by 1883, the value of *kaniki* had declined to around four *fundo*, while *merikani* maintained its value.[93] According to one source, by this later time, *merikani* had become the most fashionable cloth in Ujiji.[94] This is probably an overstatement – there are no other sources that support it, and in a subsequent publication, the author of this source noted the prominence of *kaniki* among lakeshore Jiji.[95] However, it may somewhat reflect patterns occurring in Kawele-Ugoy, the district of Ujiji in which the coastal traders and their followers were most influential. At the same time, *kaniki*'s declining value may also be attributable to a possible glut in the market. The reopening of the trade route between Tabora and Ujiji in the late 1870s (discussed in Chapter 4) gave increased access to traders and their commodities coming from the east to the northern lakeshore region. If this caused an oversupply of imported cotton cloth in Ujiji, the value of *kaniki* would have been most affected, as there were fewer willing buyers of *kaniki* in other lakeshore markets. High demand for *merikani* among other lakeshore populations may have enabled traders to sell their excess in other lakeshore regions.[96] Lake-wide demand for *merikani* may have helped maintain its value in the face of increasing supply in the 1880s.

The importance of *merikani* in Lake Tanganyika's fashions provides an interesting counterpoint to trends on East Africa's Indian Ocean littoral. *Merikani* was the material and dress of the enslaved and of other bonds (wo)men in Zanzibar and on the coast. Elite littoral populations

[90] Thomson, *Central African Lakes*, II, 285; Willis, *A State in the Making*, 152; Vyncke, *Brieven van een vlaamschen*, III, 36–7.
[91] Jacques and Storms, *Notes sur l'ethnographie*, 32.   [92] Hore, 'Twelve tribes', 9.
[93] Hore, *Tanganyika*, 71–2; RMCA ESA HA.01.017-6. Storms to AIA, 1883; RMCA ESA HA.01.017-7. Storms, 'Rapport de voyage à Oudjidji', 7 July 1883.
[94] RMCA ESA HA.01.017-7. Storms, 'Rapport de voyage à Oudjidji', 7 July 1883.
[95] Jacques and Storms, *Notes sur l'ethnographie*, 32.
[96] CWM/LMS/06/02/012 Carson to Thompson, 5 Jan. 1887.

demanded instead more elaborate 'cloths with names'.[97] By contrast, coastal traders in the interior only wore 'cloths with names' on special occasions – they deemed *merikani*, being more durable, as suitable for daily life.[98] For context, and as Sarah Fee recently wrote, Nyamwezi porters famously 'wore rags' on the march, only to change into higher-quality cloths when they reached home.[99] The coastal traders likely did likewise. Nevertheless, like with the people put into servility on East Africa's Indian Ocean littoral, many among the coastal traders' bonds(wo)men also wore *merikani*. Here, though, this cannot be attributed to an association between lower status and *merikani*-made clothing. *Merikani* was the most valued of all widely available imported cloths in the East African interior. Thus, wearing clothes made from *merikani* was associated with wealthy status. In this way, coastal traders and those they encountered around Lake Tanganyika and elsewhere in the interior reimagined and redefined cultural meanings associated with *merikani* that originated on East Africa's Indian Ocean littoral. This had the effect of making the coastal traders' bonds(wo)men appear wealthy and prestigious. The apparent contradiction between bonded status and prestige is a theme that is explored in more depth in Chapter 6. As will be seen in the remainder of this chapter, though, associations between the coastal traders' bondsmen and prestige on Lake Tanganyika's were also reinforced by patterns of gun ownership.

Guns as Weapons and Symbols

Like imported cotton cloth, guns had a delayed impact on the lakeshore. Among some lakeshore populations, this may be attributed to taste. Guns in nineteenth-century East Africa were notoriously unreliable, and powder was often in short supply. Thus, some preferred swords, shields, spears, and other weapons of local make in times of war. Additionally, among others, including the Ngoni near to Lake Tanganyika's southern end, using guns except in court ceremonies may have contravened established notions of masculinity and honour, thus limiting demand.[100] Elsewhere, however, demand for guns appears to have been high, even if supply did not match it. At least one missionary believed that the principal reason underpinning Manyema migrants' movements in traversing Lake Tanganyika was their desire to acquire a

---

[97] Fee, 'Cloths with names', 59, 60, 63, 64, 78–9.
[98] See, for example: Swann, *Fighting the Slave-Hunters*, 85.
[99] Fee, 'Cloths with names', 79.   [100] Macola, *The Gun in Central Africa*, ch. 5.

gun.[101] Earlier on, Burton wrote that although Jiji people living on the lakeshore desired guns, the coastal traders 'avoid[ed] granting their demands'.[102] That this policy endured and was successful is attested to by a missionary account published in 1883, which stated that the missionary had 'never seen an Mjiji [*sic*] in possession of a gun' and that the coastal traders had 'been able to prevent the introduction of firearms where it suited their purpose'.[103] This pattern stands in contrast to other inland East African regions, especially Buganda, Unyamwezi, and parts of the Tabora–Ujiji corridor, where guns were much more widespread.[104] On the lakeshore, coastal traders likely sought to limit guns' circulation for their security and to maintain guns' high value as items of prestige.

Given their value and their association with prestige, it may be unsurprising that chiefs were the first among lakeshore populations to regularly acquire guns. In the 1850s and 1860s, Jiji chiefs around what became the Ujiji emporium, Lungu chiefs around Liendwe, and Tabwa chiefs around Pamlilo demanded guns as tribute from coastal traders in exchange for favourable commercial relations, as they did with certain beads and 'cloths with names'.[105] Outside of these demographics, only coastal traders and their followers were prominent gun-owners. In 1879, an LMS missionary wrote in Ujiji that 'to the people of the coast, carrying a gun is the normal practice and is no more threatening than carrying an umbrella in England'.[106] Carrying a gun was part of the coastal traders' everyday garb – an addition to coastal fashions borne out of an adaptation to living in the interior. Additionally, coastal traders frequently armed their bondsmen to protect their caravans, which were made up primarily of free-waged porters from the interior.[107] Many of the latter were armed, but many also were not, and it certainly was not a condition of their labour.[108] Guns, in this context, were symbols of the coastal traders' bondsmen's status in the caravan and of their affiliation to one or more

---

[101] CWM/LMS/06/02/005 Hutley to Whitehouse, 20 Feb. 1880; Hutley, *Central African Diaries*, 105, 145, 158.

[102] Burton, *Lake Regions*, 321.

[103] Hore, 'Twelve tribes', 10. See also: Reid, *War in Pre-colonial Eastern Africa*, 51.

[104] See, for example: Reid, *War in Pre-colonial Eastern Africa*, 50; Gordon, 'Wearing cloth, wielding guns', 25–38.

[105] Burton, *Lake Regions*, 321; Reid, *War in Pre-colonial Eastern Africa*, 52; Gordon, 'Wearing cloth, wielding guns', 29–30; Macola, *The Gun in Central Africa*, loc. 1162–70; Roberts, *A History of the Bemba*, 203, 206, 306.

[106] CWM/LMS/06/02/004 Hore to Whitehouse, 10 Jan. 1879.

[107] Murjebi, *L'autobiographie*, 47–9. Some European missionaries reinforced this pattern. See, for example: CMS C/A6/O/16 Mackay to Wright, 18 Aug. 1876; CMS C/A6/O/22 Shergold Smith to Wright, 22 Aug. 1876.

[108] See, for example: CWM/LMS/06/02/004 Southon to Whitehouse, 1 Nov. 1879.

coastal traders. The coastal traders' control over the supply of guns in this context led many Manyema migrants to seek positions of labour or bondage under them, in the hope of acquiring a gun for themselves.[109] Gun ownership among non-chiefs on the lakeshore became synonymous with being a coastal trader or affiliated with a coastal trader – bonded or otherwise. Guns were a core element of lakeshore people's encounters and impressions with cultural phenomena arriving from littoral regions of the IOW.

Given coastal traders' influence over the supply of guns around Lake Tanganyika, their movements shaped significantly their incorporation into lakeshore societies and cultures. The first lakeshore regions to significantly feel guns' presence were around the lake's southern end, as Tippu Tip and his associates developed the landward route to Manyema during the second half of the 1860s. Tippu Tip recorded his violent encounter with Chief Nsama in Itawa, who had in previous years prevented some of Tippu Tip's Omani compatriots from trading between Katanga and south-western Lake Tanganyika.[110] Nsama's soldiers were largely armed with bows and arrows, while those of Tippu Tip were armed with guns. Tippu Tip claimed that the guns killed around 200 and that at least 800 more were killed by being trampled by those fleeing. This contrasted with apparently only two dead and two wounded (including Tippu Tip himself) from among Tippu Tip's following.[111] Notwithstanding the exaggerations here (other accounts suggest a rather closer battle), the sound and shocking initial effect of a volley guns likely covered up for some of their mechanical failings, at least when the coastal traders were at war with people who were unfamiliar with them.[112] Later on, coastal traders secured favourable commercial relations through distributing guns to regional chiefs around the southern half of Lake Tanganyika.[113] When disputes with other regional powers arose, they relied on such chiefs providing men with a range of arms, including swords, shields, and spears, to help them, although they themselves were largely armed with guns.[114] Guns were no more than a supplement to existing arms in the context of wider battles and patterns of warfare.

---

[109] CWM/LMS/06/02/005 Hutley to Whitehouse, 20 Feb. 1880; Hutley, *Central African Diaries*, 105, 145, 158.

[110] See: Chapter 4.   [111] Murjebi, *L'autobiographie*, 51.

[112] Roberts, 'The history of Abdullah', 243, 251; Livingstone, *Last Journals*, 182; Gordon, 'Wearing cloth, wielding guns', 31–2. Richard Reid has noted similar patterns of guns causing more shock than death in conflicts between Buganda and Bunyoro at a roughly contemporaneous time. See: Reid, *Political Power*, 196.

[113] CWM/LMS/06/02/005 Hore to Whitehouse, 8 May 1880.

[114] See, for example: Roberts, 'The history of Abdullah', 244–5; A.G.M.Afr. Diaire de Mpala, 11 Aug. 1887; A.G.M.Afr. Diaire de Mpala, Jan. 1890.

Towards the northern end of Lake Tanganyika, guns only became widespread from the beginning of the 1880s. This is the point from which coastal traders sought to violently impose commercial hegemony across the lakeshore regions of Ujiji, Urundi, Uvira, Massanze, and Uguha.[115] In the lead-up to this process, missionaries reported ominously of coastal traders in Ujiji 'arming' their bondsmen.[116] Daily life in Ujiji consequently became increasingly militarised. Missionaries reported on frequent fights in and around the market, with the coastal traders' bondsmen and other associates using their guns to settle personal disputes.[117] Outside Ujiji, the coastal traders and their followers used guns in their wars with lakeshore populations. One missionary wrote in 1886 that some populations in Ubwari charged the coastal traders' followers with spears and arrows, having blocked their ears with cotton so that they could not hear their adversaries' gunshots. Perhaps inevitably, the result was a massacre.[118] However, when coastal traders attacked larger and more organised populations in, for example, the interior of Urundi and towards Ruanda (present-day Rwanda) in the mid-1880s, they were rebuffed after a series of humiliating defeats.[119] These patterns suggest that many of the guns that circulated Lake Tanganyika at this time were more noisy and confusing for adversaries than they were effective killing machines, at least when the opposition to gun-wielders was effectively organised.[120] Even so, the gun itself clearly had a striking psychological effect on lakeshore populations. The fact that their distribution was limited largely to coastal traders and their followers served to enhance these people's status. Guns gave their owners prestige, whether chief, coastal trader, or one of the latter's followers or bondsmen.

These patterns of guns' distribution on the lakeshore stand out from several other East African interior regions. Although they rarely replaced existing arms made from wood and iron, guns reached wider demographics elsewhere. In Mirambo's and Nyungu ya Mawe's respective polities, for example, guns were a common feature of *ruga ruga*'s

---

[115] See: Chapter 4.

[116] CWM/LMS/06/02/004 Hutley to Whitehouse, 19 Oct. 1879; A.G.M.Afr. Journal du P. Deniaud, 31 July 1880, 5 Dec. 1880, 25 Jan. 1881.

[117] CWM/LMS/06/02/004 Hutley to Whitehouse, 19 Oct. 1879; CWM/LMS/06/02/005 Hore to Whitehouse, 26 May 1880; CWM/LMS/06/02/007 Griffith to Thomson, 16 Oct. 1882.

[118] A.G.M.Afr. Diaire de Kibanga, 1 Oct. 1888.

[119] A.G.M.Afr. Diaire de Massanze, 30 May 1881; A.G.M.Afr. Diaire de Kibanga, 18 Dec. 1886, 18 Jan. 1887, 10 July 1887.

[120] Reid, *War in Pre-colonial Eastern Africa*, 51; Reid, *Political Power*, 219–20.

weapons.[121] Similarly, Buganda's and Bunyoro's armies, both centred in present-day Uganda, had significant numbers of gun carriers.[122] The fact that these gun carriers were core elements of centralised polities may partly explain the divergent patterns between these regions and those around Lake Tanganyika. Mirambo, the Ganda kings, and likely Nyungu sought to arm their soldiers with guns. They saw doing so as crucial to the maintenance of their respective states.[123] By contrast, chiefs around Lake Tanganyika sought guns primarily as objects of prestige to demarcate their status. They did not create standing armies to which guns could be distributed. Thus, the coastal traders were the first on the lakeshore to explore the value of distributing guns to a wider demographic, but they did so in a limited way, supplying guns only to men in their followings. This probably gave them some military advantages, especially when they introduced guns into a region for the first time and when they came up against smaller populations in many lakeshore regions. But the deeper influence of their distribution of guns was probably symbolic. Ownership of guns was synonymous with prestige among most lakeshore societies from soon after they were introduced. The coastal traders' distribution and usage of guns from c.1860 onwards served to enhance their and their followers' prestige in the eyes of other lakeshore populations.

Conclusion

Broader regional and temporal contexts are crucial to understanding how the arrival of global commodities influenced Lake Tanganyika's societies during the nineteenth century. Lakeshore people's pre-existing and ongoing structures, fashions, and industries shaped the ways in which they demanded and used imported glass beads and cotton cloths as currencies and in fashions. Additionally, the ways in which coastal traders introduced and distributed cotton cloths were tied to patterns that first developed on East Africa's Indian Ocean littoral. However, both coastal traders and those they encountered on the lakeshore adapted these littoral patterns to the interior. *Merikani* worn in particular ways demarcated servile, inferior status on East Africa's Indian Ocean coast and islands. By contrast, around Lake Tanganyika and other interior regions, *merikani* was the most valuable of all the widely available cloths

---

[121] Reid, *War in Pre-colonial Eastern Africa*, 51–2; Pesek, 'Ruga-ruga', 85–100.
[122] Reid, *War in Pre-colonial Eastern Africa*, 52.
[123] Reid, *Political Power*, 12, 224; Richard J. Reid, 'Mutesa and Mirambo: Thoughts on East African warfare and diplomacy in the nineteenth century', *The International Journal of African Historical Studies*, 31, 1 (1998), 74.

and was associated with prestige. Thus, although many of the coastal traders' bonds(wo)men were dressed in *merikani* around Lake Tanganyika, this did not mean that servility was intrinsically associated with social inferiority. Indeed, as evidence from the distribution of guns among people living on the lakeshore further indicates, the coastal traders' bondsmen were able through ownership of certain imported goods to enhance their social status. Additionally, by the 1880s, demand for imported glass beads, cotton cloth, and guns was almost ubiquitous around the lakeshore, even if different lakeshore populations demanded different varieties or styles. These differences helped to facilitate trans-lake trade and prices in different lakeshore regions. That chiefly fashions for *samisami* beads in Uvira and Urundi during the 1850s and 1860s and fashions for *matunda* beads in Uguha during the 1870s and 1880s affected price and demand for these beads in Ujiji is testament to this. The domestication of global commodities helped to facilitate increased economic connectivity around and across Lake Tanganyika's shores during the nineteenth century.

Putting these patterns into a wider IOW perspective, what is analysed here is illustrative of trends described by scholars such as Jeremy Prestholdt and Pedro Machado in the last fifteen years. Clearly, East Africans, in 'domesticating' global commodities, shaped how and where such commodities were produced and circulated in a rapidly globalising world. Whether patterns of consumption on Lake Tanganyika's shores on their own shaped global production is less clear. The author is not aware of any document that would indicate that cotton dyers in Kutchchh or glass bead makers in Venice geared their productive capacities for lakeshore consumers specifically. The likelihood is that such a document does not exist and that in fact, these centres of production manufactured their products for East Africa more generally, rather than for specific regions within it. There are further dynamics to consider here, however. Key to this are the agents through which global commodities arrived in the interior of East Africa. On the shores of Lake Tanganyika, coastal traders, as the primary importers of glass beads, cotton cloth (especially *merikani*), and (again, especially) guns, had a significant role in shaping how and why lakeshore populations demanded them. Lakeshore populations did not just 'domesticate' the global commodity; they also 'domesticated' patterns of consumption related to such commodities as they were introduced to them by coastal traders and their followers. This was part of a broader pattern of cultural exchange and interaction between traders who originated in littoral regions of the IOW and those they encountered on the lakeshore.

6   Structures of Bondage

Nineteenth-century societies on the shores of Lake Tanganyika were built on the work of bondsmen and bondswomen (bonds(wo)men).[1] This statement aligns with themes addressed in Chapter 2, in which it was argued that the status of being a slave became intertwined with agricultural labour. This chapter, though, examines other forms of bondage in the context of different types of labour, such as porterage, boating, proxy trading, and soldiery. Previous historical studies focusing on East Africa have referred to many of the labourers working in these roles as 'slaves'.[2] This is also the terminology that European 'explorers' and missionaries used in their publications and unpublished journals and letters, which form the bulk of the source material for this book. But studies on slavery and other forms of 'unfree' labour in IOW history published in the last two decades have contested the trajectory of such regional historiographies. They have argued that they impose a terminology developed to describe slavery in the ancient Mediterranean and the Americas during the era of the transatlantic slave trade on IOW societies.[3] They further contend that, in the IOW, there were numerous gradations of servitude or forms of bondage that existed between 'slave' and 'free', and, as such, these latter two terms have 'limited analytical utility'.[4] To distance themselves from western Atlantic models, IOW scholars have examined different conditions of bondage between slavery and freedom, including serfdom, clientage, debt bondage, and

---

[1] An earlier version of this chapter was published as: Philip Gooding, 'Slavery, "respectability", and being "freeborn" on the shores of nineteenth-century Lake Tanganyika', *Slavery and Abolition*, 40, 1 (2019), 147–67. Reprinted with permission. www.tandfonline.com.

[2] See, for example: Médard and Doyle (eds.), *Slavery in the Great Lakes*; Rockel, 'Slavery and freedom', 87–109.

[3] For a summary and a critique, see: Sivasundaram, 'The Indian Ocean', 42–6.

[4] Campbell, 'Introduction: Slavery and other forms', xxv. See also: Clarence-Smith, *Islam and the Abolition*, 2, 72; Suzanne Miers, 'Slavery: A question of definition', *Slavery and Abolition*, 24, 2 (2003), 4–5; Gwyn Campbell, 'Introduction: Bondage and the environment', in *Bondage and the Environment*, ed. Campbell, 1–4.

concubinage.[5] This chapter does likewise. Most labourers living on the shores of nineteenth-century Lake Tanganyika were not concerned with the distinction of either being 'slave' or 'free'. Rather, they were concerned with who they were bonded to, the conditions of their bondage, and what this meant for their social status.

The debate over the utility of the terms, bondage and slavery, to describe the variety of servile forms on Lake Tanganyika's shores comes down to a question of definition. East Africanist historians have, up to now, used a broad definition of slavery. Those regarded as enslaved include all those who experienced what Orlando Patterson described as 'social death': Through the act of being enslaved, their links to their homelands and their kin were broken, and they endured 'outsider' status in their new societies.[6] This includes, for example, 'agricultural slaves', 'armed slaves' (bondsmen with guns), and the occasional 'slave caravan leader' (viongozi).[7] By contrast, most IOW historians have used a much narrower definition of slavery and refer to it as only one form of bondage. They equate 'slavery' with 'chattels', meaning that slaves by their definition had no rights and could be bought and resold at their enslaver's will.[8] This is also the popular definition of slavery, and it characterised plantation slavery in the Americas during the era of the transatlantic slave trade.[9] IOW scholars have frequently used it to describe bondage in the agricultural sector, such as on the Mascarene Islands during the nineteenth century and those described in Chapter 2 of this book.[10] They additionally acknowledge that many other bonds(wo)men may have experienced 'social death' and have been enslaved at some point, but that some such people also experienced a kind of 'social resurrection' over time.[11] This meant that they gradually acquired kinship, status, and

---

[5] Miers, 'Slavery: A question', 1–16.

[6] Orlando Patterson, *Slavery and Social Death: A comparative study* (London: Harvard University Press, 1982), xvii–xix. See also: Lovejoy, *Transformations*, 1; Miers, 'Slavery: A question', 1.

[7] For agricultural slaves, see: Chapter 2. For armed slaves, see: Reid, *War in Pre-colonial Eastern Africa*, 143, 157; Iliffe, *A Modern History*, 48; Page, 'Manyema hordes', 79. For slave caravan leaders, see: Rockel, 'Slavery and freedom', 100; Médard, 'Introduction', in *Slavery in the Great Lakes*, eds. Médard and Doyle, 11.

[8] Campbell, 'Introduction: Bondage and the environment', 2–3.

[9] Frederick Cooper, 'The problem of slavery in African studies', *The Journal of African Studies*, 20, 1 (1979), 106; Igor Kopytoff and Suzanne Miers, 'African "slavery" as an institution of marginality', in *Slavery in Africa: Historical and anthropological perspectives*, eds. Suzanne Miers and Igor Kopytoff (Madison: University of Wisconsin Press, 1977), 3–77.

[10] Campbell, 'Introduction: Slavery and other forms', xii, xv.

[11] Lovejoy, *Transformations*, 13–15; Campbell, 'Introduction: Slavery and other forms', xxii.

personhood, which allowed them to leave the condition of slavery and to enter a different form of bondage.

The decision here to follow recent IOW trends rather than longer-standing East Africanist ones is supported by analysis of the oral record. In Ujiji, my informants sought to minimise the role of slavery in their town's history.[12] They claimed as evidence that many people regarded in the East Africanist historiography as 'slaves' inherited the coastal traders' property, which, according to Islamic law, disqualified them from being considered as enslaved.[13] This process of inheritance is verifiable from early colonial archival sources.[14] Even so, informants still characterised the nineteenth century as the period of the slave trade. They did so because of a belief that people were enslaved in present-day eastern DRC and then sold overland into littoral regions of the IOW.[15] This is the 'official' record contained in Tanzania's museums and in some historical research. As noted in Chapter 2, however, this long-distance slave trade from Lake Tanganyika to East Africa's Indian Ocean littoral was minimal, at least compared to the trade around Lake Tanganyika itself and compared to southern long-distance routes to Kilwa. Furthermore, some informants in both Burundi and Ujiji claimed that the long-distance slave trade through their towns (which historical research shows was minimal) was driven by demand in the USA.[16] Collectively, these misconceptions are representative of a feedback loop. Some of Ujiji's current inhabitants have equated slavery with popular images from the Americas. Their minimisation of slavery's importance in their town's history is borne out of a well-founded belief that conditions that correspond to these images were not prevalent there. Meanwhile, their belief that a long-distance slave trade existed is associable with a need to reconcile their claims about their own region's history with the

---

[12] Interview with Rashidi Hamisi bin Kasa, 12 Nov. 2013; Interview with Branbati Ali Kiola and Isa Pama Kiola, 12 Nov. 2013; Interview with Rashidi Juma Hei Al-Reith, 12 Nov. 2013; Interview with Hamisi Ali Juma al-Hey, 14 Nov. 2013.

[13] Interview with Rashidi Hamisi bin Kasa, 12 Nov. 2013; Interview with Hamisi Ali Juma al-Hey, 14 Nov. 2013. Rules regarding the inheritance of property in other Islamic contexts in Africa contradict the idea that the people referred to in this chapter can be regarded as slaves. See: Bruce S. Hall, *A History of Race in Muslim West Africa, 1600–1960* (Cambridge: Cambridge University Press, 2011), 238.

[14] Castryck, 'My slave sold all of Kigoma', 318–23; McCurdy, 'Transforming associations', 18.

[15] Interview with Branbati Ali Kiola and Isa Pama Kiola, 12 Nov. 2013; Interview with Musa Isa Rubinga, 4 Nov. 2013.

[16] Interview with Remy Ngirye, 4 Nov. 2013; Interview with Simeon Sindimwo and Venant Baragasirika, 5 Nov. 2013; Interview with Silas Bujana, 5 Nov. 2013; Interview with Saidi Hamisi Kunga, 11 Nov. 2013. See also: Banshchikova, 'Historical memory', 39–41.

'official' record. The use of 'slavery' as a catch-all term to describe diverse forms of bondage in the nineteenth century has contributed to conflicts over the term's usage and meaning in the East African present.[17]

The roots of current discourses regarding slavery in nineteenth-century East Africa can be traced to the European-authored sources and how historians have interpreted them. From an East Africanist perspective, Stephen Rockel has been at the forefront of deconstructing these discourses. In his seminal monograph, *Carriers of Culture*, he contested what he described as an 'obsession with slavery' in East Africanist historical writing.[18] He argued that 'along the grain' readings of missionary and colonial archives had led to an overemphasis on slavery in East African history. Victorian-era Europeans arrived in East Africa with preconceptions about the nature of slavery in the region. For Protestant missionaries especially, anti-slavery was part of a broader ideology bound up with the 'Livingstonian' tenets of Christianity, civilisation, and commerce.[19] They thus had an interest in emphasising the prevalence of slavery in their communications with Europe to justify their raison d'être as Christian anti-slavery crusaders.[20] Within this context, they often conflated different forms of bondage with slavery, particularly if they did not immediately recognise them as a form of free-waged labour.[21] Subsequently, European colonial powers used the term 'slavery' to describe diverse social and labour forms in Africa, which helped them to justify colonial rule to their publics on the basis of abolitionist sentiment.[22] As such, the use of 'slavery' as a broad term to describe a variety of servile forms can partly be regarded as a legacy of colonialism. Rockel's contribution in this context was to analyse the position of Nyamwezi *pagazi* (porters). Up to the publication of *Carriers of Culture*, Nyamwezi *pagazi* had been regarded in much of the East Africanist historiography as slaves.[23] Rockel instead showed them to

---

[17] See also: Benedetta Rossi, 'Introduction: Rethinking slavery in West Africa', in *Reconfiguring Slavery: West African trajectories*, ed. Benedetta Rossi (Liverpool: Liverpool University Press, 2009), 3; Henri Médard, 'Introduction', in *Traites et Esclavages*, eds. Médard et al., 25; Kopytoff and Miers, 'African "slavery"', 3–77.

[18] Rockel, *Carriers of Culture*, 20. Similar arguments have been made in the trans-Saharan context. See: Ghislaine Lydon, *On Trans-Saharan Trails: Islamic law, trade networks, and cross-cultural exchange in nineteenth-century western Africa* (Cambridge: Cambridge University Press, 2009), 122–3.

[19] Gooding, 'David Livingstone, UNESCO, and nation-building', 250–1.

[20] Rockel, *Carriers of Culture*, 13–14, 20, 22; McCaskie, 'Cultural encounters', 686; Wright, *Strategies of Slaves*, 4; Chrétien, *L'Invention de l'Afrique*, 33.

[21] Rockel, *Carriers of Culture*, 9–10; Wright, *Strategies of Slaves*, 8; Médard, 'Introduction', in *Traites*, 12–16.

[22] Rockel, *Carriers of Culture*, 8–23.   [23] See, for example: Glassman, *Feasts and Riot*, 62.

be free-waged labourers who used their status to leverage better wages and conditions as caravan workers.

While pioneering, Rockel's work represents only one methodology of deconstructing the prevalent role given to slavery in East Africanist historical writing. In a subsequent article, he addressed the issue of *ngwana* (gentlemen) porters, whom he described as 'slaves or freed slaves'.[24] The idea of being *ngwana* on East Africa's IOW littoral implied 'respect' and 'freeborn' status. To Rockel, the *ngwana* caravan workers were 'islamicised' people of various origin who had 'acculturated into coastal society'.[25] He did not, however, examine the ways in which some of these 'slaves' came to be free or the processes that contributed to their eventual 'freedom'. Subsequent research has thus gone in a different conceptual direction when exploring such dynamics. Fahad Ahmad Bishara and Thomas McDow, for example, in examining patterns on East Africa's Indian Ocean littoral, argued that many people claiming to be *ngwana* sought to maintain conditions of bondage to their (former) enslaver. Doing so had the potential to acquire them access to credit, and thus, given the centrality of commerce to cultural life, also to respect and personhood.[26] Such people rarely sought 'freedom' by European missionaries' or colonial rulers' definitions of the term, even though it could have been available to them. For them, 'liberty' was to be found within the confines of their bondage. To modify Rockel's model, then, the *ngwana* were not 'slaves,' in that they had access to degrees of respect and personhood, but nor were they 'freed slaves'. Rather, they were more often 'former slaves' who had, over time, negotiated more favourable conditions of bondage.

Situating these patterns on the shores of Lake Tanganyika adds further dynamics. On the lakeshore, personhood was more accessible to people whom coastal traders had enslaved or formerly enslaved than it was on East Africa's Indian Ocean littoral. This is because, in littoral regions, several institutions served to distinguish 'free' persons from bonds(wo)men. Attendance of certain mosques, cultural events, and festivals, for example, was reserved only for 'free' residents of the coast.[27] People who had been enslaved at some point in their life were denied access to them. Only the children of a bondswoman, if fathered by a free man, could gain access to 'freeborn' status – and this transition was far from certain.[28]

---

[24] Rockel, 'Slavery and freedom', 87.   [25] Rockel, *Carriers of Culture*, 17.

[26] Bishara, *A Sea of Debt*, 76; McDow, *Buying Time*, 152–3.

[27] Glassman, *Feasts and Riot*, 4, 134.

[28] Glassman, *Feasts and Riot*, 85–6, 128; Deutsch, *Emancipation without Abolition*, 65, 69, 73; Elisabeth McMahon, *Slavery and Emancipation in Islamic East Africa: From honor to respectability* (Cambridge: Cambridge University Press, 2013), 15; Lovejoy,

Dynamics around Lake Tanganyika and in other interior regions, by contrast, enabled bonds(wo)men to acquire full personhood for themselves and not just their children. The coastal institutions that marked the free from the bonded did not follow the coastal traders inland. Missionary sources suggest that no mosque was constructed in the lakeshore region until the colonial period, for example.[29] Additionally, coastal traders and other enslavers were motivated to fast track those they enslaved into positions of respect. They needed to prevent their bonds(wo)men from running away, an especially difficult task given the brutality of the slave trade that brought many people to the lakeshore and the opportunities that such people had for free-waged labour in caravans. Material and social inducements were key to this process. Moreover, coastal traders required specialised boatmen, soldiers, and proxy traders – occupations that implied social status above that of enslaved people working in the fields. A lack of institutions that marked certain bonded from 'free' populations and the nature of labour required on the lakeshore facilitated many bonds(wo)men's access to markers of respect and personhood over relatively short periods of time.

Returning to my oral sources, informants in Ujiji were most vociferous in contesting the 'official' history regarding the relationships between coastal traders and Manyema populations. As noted in Chapter 2, coastal traders mostly enslaved people from Manyema. Rather than in terms of slavery, however, informants discussed the coastal trader–Manyema relationship in terms of marriage, family, and closeness.[30] Their doing so has links to the demographics of my informants – most were of either Omani, Manyema, or of mixed Omani-Manyema descent. In the present, they collectively form a distinctive, town-based Muslim community.[31] Thus, their discourse has important present-day implications. Minimising slavery's importance serves to limit disrepute across Omani-Manyema lines and to emphasise the town's Muslim character. Nevertheless, my informants' claims also speak to the brevity of the 'slave experience' for many bonds(wo)men in the nineteenth century. They suggest that, even if slavery was a feature of their lives, as indicated in the archive and by

Transformations, 4; Patrick Manning, *Slavery and African Life: Occidental, oriental and African slave trades* (Melksham: Cambridge University Press, 1990), 117.

[29] A.G.M.Afr. Augier to White Fathers, 16 Apr. 1879, *Chronique Trimestrielles*, 5 (Jan. 1880); CWM/LMS/06/02/006 Hutley, 'Mohammadanism in Central Africa: Its professors', Aug. 1881; Sperling, 'The coastal hinterland', 289. See also: Chapter 7.

[30] Interview with Rashidi Hamisi bin Kasa, 12 Nov. 2013; Interview with Branbati Ali Kiola and Isa Pama Kiola, 12 Nov. 2013; Interview with Hamisi Ali Juma al-Hey, 14 Nov. 2013.

[31] Hino, 'Neighbourhood groups', 1–30.

analysis of the conditions of agricultural labour, it was neither the defining nor the most enduring one. In the words of a male formerly enslaved informant cited by Norman Bennett, '[becoming enslaved] happened once, and all was soon over. Then you were given a home, food, cloths, etc., and above all a *gun*; you were a man.'[32] The transition to personhood defined this informant's life, not the experience of slavery. How the trauma of being enslaved in the first place affected formerly enslaved people psychologically thereafter remains an open question – and one which the sources do not allow a sure answer to.[33] Even so, my informants' rejection of 'slavery' as an analytical term to describe the prevailing conditions of labour in their region's past necessitates looking beyond the 'slave–free' binary to analyse labour and social relations in nineteenth-century East Africa.

The following discussion is split into two sections. The first analyses some of the social and labour relations that coastal traders encountered on the lakeshore when they arrived there. The focus is on Jiji boatmen, who until at least the 1860s and 1870s were the key source of labour for conveying traders across the lake. At the beginning of the period, Jiji boatmen's labour was governed by Jiji *teko* (district chiefs), who acted as 'landlords' over land and water, and presided over labour in their domains accordingly. Over time, however, with the influence of coastal traders and the commercial world that made more connections across Lake Tanganyika and between the lake and the wider IOW, such bonds waned. Many boatmen sought alternative conditions of labour over time, some of which amounted to a different form of bondage. One such form is the subject of the second section – bondage to the coastal traders or to one of their associates, who themselves were often in some form of bondage. Again, much of the focus is on the labour required for making connections around and across the lake – boatmen, proxy traders, and (especially in the 1880s) soldiers. While the structures that underpinned

---

[32] Bennett, *Arab versus European*, 10 (emphasis in the original). See also: Lovejoy, *Transformations*, 13–15; John Iliffe, *Honour in African History* (Cambridge: Cambridge University Press, 2005), 133–9; Deutsch, *Emancipation without Abolition*, 66–74; David L. Schoenbrun, 'Violence, marginality, scorn and honour: Language evidence of slavery to the eighteenth century', in *Slavery in the Great Lakes*, eds. Médard and Doyle, 46.

[33] Katherine Jean Allen rightly criticised the article on which much of this chapter is based for not engaging with the long-term psychological effects of enslavement amongst people who were formerly enslaved. See: Katherine Jean Allen, 'Routes to deliverance: The development of social mobility among East African slave porters by way of missionary caravans, 1877–1906' (unpublished MA diss., Clemson University, 2020), 42. Richard Reid has elucidated limits of the source material for analysing trauma among young men and women who experienced violence in the nineteenth century. See: Reid, *War in Precolonial Eastern Africa*, 99.

the conditions that such labourers experienced had their roots in East Africa's Indian Ocean littoral, they developed in distinct ways around Lake Tanganyika. Making such statements builds on several other studies of slavery and bondage 'on the frontiers' of the Islamic world, in which local customs and conditions contributed to divergences from the *sharia* or from prevailing customs in regions where Muslims were a majority, such as East Africa's Indian Ocean littoral.[34] On the lakeshore, many bonded labourers claimed, and were encouraged to claim by their (former) enslavers, 'freeborn' social status. Here then, a distinction is made between conditions of labour and the social status that is usually seen to be inherent with such conditions. Being able to claim 'freeborn' social status within the confines of bondage was more favourable to many bonds(wo)men than any notion of 'legal' freedom.

Bondage in Jiji Society

Structures of bondage in East Africa pre-date the expansion of the global ivory trade and the arrival of coastal traders in the Great Lakes region.[35] These later phenomena did, however, contribute to transitions within those long-standing structures. Historians have, in general, noted the increasing levels of brutality inherent in servile forms during the nineteenth century. The expansion of slave raiding and trading as well as increased demand for agricultural labour provoked an increase in the levels of coercion and violence in labour and social relations.[36] The case of Jiji boatmen offers a counterpoint to such histories. Nineteenth-century European commentators were enamoured with the skilled nature of Jiji boatmen's labour and their geographical knowledge of Lake Tanganyika.[37] Divorced as they were from discussions of slavery, twentieth-century historians consequently characterised them as free-waged labourers or as 'independent carriers and traders'.[38] This

---

[34] Phrase taken from: Paul E. Lovejoy, ed. *Slavery on the Frontiers of Islam* (Princeton: Markus Wiener Publishers, 2004).

[35] See, for example: Schoenbrun, 'Violence, marginality, scorn and honour', 38–75.

[36] See, for example: Medard, 'Introduction', in *Slavery in the Great Lakes*, eds. Medard and Doyle, 15–16. Edward A. Alpers, 'Debt, pawnship and slavery in nineteenth-century East Africa', in *Bonded Labour and Debt in the Indian Ocean World*, eds. Gwyn Campbell and Alessandro Stanziani (London: Pickering and Chatto, 2013), 31–44.

[37] Burton, *Lake Regions*, 321; Stanley, *Dark Continent*, II, 6; Hore, 'Twelve tribes', 11.

[38] Brown, 'Ujiji', 52–3; Bolser-Brown, 'Muslim influence', 623–6; Brown and Brown, 'East African trade towns', 185. This pattern is in line with other studies of boatmen in African history. See: Patrick Manning, 'Merchants, porters, and canoemen in the Bight of Benin: Links in the West African trade network', in *The Workers of African Trade*, eds. Catherine Coquery-Vidrovitch and Paul E. Lovejoy (Beverly Hills: Sage Publications, 1985), 51.

characterisation, though, fails to acknowledge Jiji boatmen's obligations to their *teko* (district chief) and the latter's role vis-à-vis the environment. Lakeshore *teko*'s role as 'earth-priests' gave them rights over the products of Jiji boatmen's labour, principally fish and traded goods, in the form tribute. Additionally, the *teko* exerted rights over the distribution of Jiji boatmen's labour, negotiating their wages and their rights to search elsewhere for waged employment. It was only with the expansion of the global ivory trade that Jiji boatmen were able to challenge these conditions of bondage, using their specialised skills as leverage to reshape the conditions of their labour for their benefit.

From sometime around the mid-seventeenth century, the *teko*'s role over the environment in Ujiji and the other kingdoms of Uha gave them command over the labour resident in their domain.[39] Similar patterns existed in Uguha.[40] Unlike in Unyamwezi, where land was owned privately by individuals, *teko* had a determining role over all land and labour.[41] This was especially true on the lakeshore, distant as it was from the *ami* (central chief), whose presence and source of authority in highland regions may have inspired rebellions versus overbearing *teko*.[42] The pervasiveness of the *teko*'s influence over labour in lakeshore regions, however, is attested by the position of Jiji boatmen. The lakeshore Jiji *teko* charged traders and European missionaries for the right to employ Jiji boatmen, which added to the cost of paying the boatmen individually – a rate which was also negotiated by the *teko*.[43] If the *teko*'s demands were not met, they had the power to withdraw their boatmen's labour.[44] In the lakeshore Jiji system, this followed a clear logic. Up to just after mid-century, the Jiji *teko* were regarded as the sole powers who could appease the lake's spirits, much as they appeased the spirits in their terrestrial domains.[45] This gave them the same rights over labour on water as on land. Additionally, boatmen up to this point also worked the land when supplementary labour was required, such as during the planting and harvesting seasons. The Jiji *teko*'s power over boatmen's labour was thus contingent on the organisation labour to account for seasonal cycles of labour on land and water.

---

[39] Gwassa and Mbwiliza, 'Social production', 14–16, 18.
[40] CWM/LMS/06/02/010 Jones to Thompson, 10 Feb. 1885.
[41] Pallaver, 'A triangle', 31, n. 146; Paul Reichard, *Deutsch-Ostafrika: Das land und seine bewohner* (Leipzig: O. Spammer, 1892), 358.
[42] CWM/LMS/06/02/004 Hore to Whitehouse, 18 Nov. 1879; Gwassa and Mbwiliza, 'Social production', 14.
[43] Burton, *Lake Regions*, 338, 354, 357.
[44] Hutley, *Central African Diaries*, 78–80; CWM/LMS/06/02/004 Hore to Mullens, 10 Jan. 1879, Hore to Mullens, 25 Feb. 1879, Hore to Mullens, 16 Apr. 1879.
[45] Wagner, 'Environment, community and history', 191.

Several factors in the second half of the nineteenth century destabilised these patterns. The expansion of slave raiding and trading meant that agriculture on Ujiji's lakeshore became less dependent on the seasonal labour of boatmen. This labour, instead, fell to those the Jiji enslaved. As a result, Jiji boatmen became increasingly employed on the lake across seasons and for longer periods of time. The Jiji *teko* sought to tap into these opportunities, acting as a patron who provided credit and by employing boatmen as clients and proxy traders to trade in other lakeshore regions on their behalf.[46] They may also have attempted to negotiate more favourable rates for Jiji boatmen employed by others in an attempt to ensure their loyalty despite their long absences. In negotiations with the LMS in February 1879, for example, Habeyya, the *teko* of Kawele-Ugoy, demanded that boatmen under his jurisdiction be paid with the same type of cloths with which the LMS paid him and in the same quantity.[47] Such parity may have been designed to enhance the status of the boatmen in his district who were bonded to him. Yet, in general, Jiji boatmen's obligations to their *teko* declined over time. As discussed in Chapter 3, perceptions of some Jiji *teko*'s power over the lake's spirits declined in this period, owing to the emergence of coastal traders and their associates as new spiritual powers, and in the context of declining lake levels after 1878. As some *teko*'s power waned over the affairs of their districts, so did their powers over the Jiji boatmen.

There are several pieces of evidence from the late 1870s and 1880s that attest to this transition. In the February 1879 example cited earlier, Habeyya was not the only alternative party seeking compensation for the employment of Jiji boatmen. Mwinyi Hassani, acting as Mwinyi Kheri's surrogate as the leader of Ujiji's coastal trader community, also demanded an equal number of cloths to the *teko* and each individual boatman.[48] Ujiji's coastal trader leadership thus became involved in shaping the conditions of the Jiji boatmen's bondage. Additionally, some Jiji boatmen sought to challenge how Jiji *teko* negotiated their labour. Some did so by demanding more wages once they had left Ujiji. For example, in May 1879, the White Fathers were dumbfounded when the Jiji boatmen who conveyed them to southern Urundi refused the cloth that they had agreed to pay them in Ujiji. Instead, the boatmen demanded an increase in the quantity and quality of cloth, refusing *satini* and demanding the 'cloths with names' that they paid to chiefs.[49] Elsewhere, LMS missionary accounts in Uguha state that some Jiji

[46] CWM/LMS/06/05/21 Hore, 'Voyage to the south end of Lake Tanganyika', 1 Apr. 1879.
[47] Hutley, *Central African Diaries*, 79–80.   [48] Hutley, *Central African Diaries*, 79–80.
[49] A.G.M.Afr. C.16-7. Journal du P. Deniaud, 27 May 1879.

boatmen travelled across the lake to seek and negotiate waged labour at their (short-lived) missionary station at Mtowa.[50] Many others, meanwhile, sought a different form of bondage under a coastal trader, which, as will be seen the following section, may have given them increased access to cloth, guns, and other valuable imported commodities.[51] Consequently, many Jiji boatmen's connection to their land and to their *teko* declined as they sought alternative opportunities for personal enrichment around the lake.

The Coastal Traders' Bondsmen: Becoming *Ngwana*

Most of the coastal traders' associates, followers, and labourers came from Manyema. They arrived on Lake Tanganyika's shores having been brutalised by the conditions of the ivory trade in their own region.[52] They usually came as part of a caravan led by a coastal trader or one of his associates. Many – mostly women and children – came as captives. Adult men tended to join caravans for their security when their houses, villages, and/or farms had been destroyed, though some also came voluntarily as traders.[53] Many died on the route, and European 'explorers' wrote that many more of those who made it to the lakeshore were malnourished and afflicted by disease, to the extent that they resembled 'bony skeletons'.[54] In addition to these physical depredations, such people experienced 'social death' as they departed Manyema and arrived at the lakeshore, where they were considered 'outsiders'. Rumours swirled of such people's 'savagery' and their 'cannibalism'.[55] They were referred to as *shenzi* (barbarians; savages), a term that East African coastal and island populations also used to describe non-Muslims from the interior.[56] Additionally, when they entered bondage, they were usually regarded as *tumwa* (Swahili; sing. *mtumwa*; pl. *watumwa*; lit: 'one who is used or is sent'), which is usually translated as slave, and which represented the

---

[50] CWM/LMS/06/02/006 Hutley to Thompson, 21 June 1881; CWM/LMS/06/02/006 Griffith to Thompson, 12 Aug. 1881.

[51] CWM/LMS/06/02/006 Hutley, 'Mahommadanism in Central Africa: Its influence', Aug. 1881.

[52] Rockel, *Carriers of Culture*, 132; Brown, 'Ujiji', 120.

[53] Page, 'Manyema hordes', 73; Reid, *War in Pre-colonial Eastern Africa*, 157; McCurdy, 'Transforming associations', 71; Wright, *Strategies of Slaves*, 6, 26.

[54] RMCA HMSA 4610. Stanley to *Daily Telegraph* and *New York Herald*, 28 Oct. 1876; Cameron, *Across Africa*, 280–1; Hutley, *Central African Diaries*, 90, 105; Livingstone, *Last Journals*, 319–20, 352–3; Wissmann, *My Second Journey*, 246.

[55] Stanley, *Through the Dark Continent*, II, 67; A.G.M.Afr. C.16-7. Journal du P. Deniaud, 22 Dec. 1880; McCurdy, 'Transforming associations', 74–8.

[56] McCurdy, 'Transforming associations', 68–74.

lowest social rung on East Africa's Indian Ocean littoral.[57] Yet, many *tumwa* acquired 'respectability', personhood, and kinship in lakeshore societies remarkably quickly. They did so by claiming to be *ngwana* (gentlemen), a term denoting respectability and freeborn status among coastal populations and traders. In East Africa's Indian Ocean littoral regions, embodying *ngwana* necessitated being born free. By contrast, the coastal traders' labourers on the lakeshore claimed *ngwana* status as bonds(wo)men. They refashioned what it meant to be *ngwana*, respected, and 'freeborn' within the confines of their bondage.

The refashioning of routes to respectability was partly rooted in precedents in East Africa's coastal and island regions. Coastal populations referred to the people from the interior, or *shenzi*, who they enslaved as *tumwa*. They put such people to work in the agricultural sector. *Tumwa* and *tumwa*-dom became an increasingly important aspect of society on East Africa's Indian Ocean littoral during the nineteenth century, as plantations became central to the region's commercial economy.[58] Over time, though, some *tumwa* were able to acquire titles that gave them enhanced status and alternative conditions of bondage. Boys who learnt the skills of artisans were often referred to as *fundi* (artisan), and young, enslaved women often acquired the status of *jakazi* (female domestic slave; maidservant) if they trained in domestic labour. Men employed as watchmen, messengers, servants, or cooks acquired the status of *twana* (male domestic slave; vassal). Many of these bondsmen were regarded as clients rather than as slaves. *Suria* (concubines) also had a relatively privileged status versus *tumwa* and other bonded labourers. In all these instances, the modification of labour roles away from agricultural occupations allowed bonded people to differentiate themselves from the lowlier *tumwa*. These processes were also accompanied with assimilation to coastal cultural forms, such as through conversion to Islam. Such bonds(wo)men, though, were rarely allowed to become *ngwana*. On this continuum between slavery and freedom, only the children born of free men (*ngwana*) and female *tumwa*, *jakazi*, or *suria* could acquire freeborn status and thus full personhood. These children's access to 'freeborn' status was born out of their integration into coastal and wider IOW kinship networks at the exclusion of their interior, '*shenzi*' heritage.[59]

Coastal traders entering the East African interior in the nineteenth century adapted this social continuum to the contexts they encountered.

[57] Deutsch, *Emancipation without Abolition*, 65–74.   [58] Cooper, *Plantation Slavery*, 264.
[59] Deutsch, *Emancipation without Abolition*, 67–74; Glassman, *Feasts and Riot*, 85–96; McMahon, *Slavery and Emancipation*, 11–14.

Around Lake Tanganyika, people who had been enslaved by coastal traders were able to acquire *ngwana* status for themselves over time. Evidence from the lakeshore and the wider Islamic world suggests that this process took around five to seven years, and likely varied according to the attitudes and specific labour needs of individual coastal traders, as well as the bonds(wo)men's degree of assimilation to the coastal traders' expectations. For example, White Fathers missionaries stationed in Kibanga reported in 1888 that some *ngwana* traders came to their station and demanded that their labourers be given the opportunity to leave if they had spent five years in the missionaries' company.[60] Such claims may have been based on what these *ngwana* had experienced with their coastal trader patrons, or on the conditions they imposed on their own bonds(wo)men. Elsewhere, Captain Jules Ramaeckers of the AIA designed a system by which the Association's labourers were to acquire freedom after six years at its stations. During the intervening period, labourers were to be given gradually more rights, such as the right to own land on the AIA's plot after three years, more responsibilities, and fewer obligations to perform agricultural work.[61] Ramaeckers' reasons for designing this system were based on the need to limit runaways and to gain loyalty from their labourers. These were also concerns that coastal traders held with their bonded labourers. It is thus logical that Ramaeckers' system was based on one that was already employed by the coastal traders, even if he may have tried to tailor or improve it based on the AIA's specific needs.[62]

Speaking more broadly, the possibility of personhood, which in most contexts meant freedom, after around seven years is widely established in certain past Islamic societies. This possibility mostly applies to regions in which Muslims were only just entering, where they were a minority of the population, or where their institutional support was weak. All these conditions applied to the coastal traders on the shores of Lake Tanganyika. In such contexts, pre-existing customs, precedent, and practicalities as they pertained to slavery and other forms of bondage have often prevailed over the *sharia* as a necessity for Muslims' ongoing survival. These processes have occasionally resulted in the granting of rights and freedoms to enslaved people after relatively short periods of

[60] A.G.M.Afr. Diaire de Kibanga, 30 Oct. 1888.
[61] RMCA ESA HA.01.017.5. Ramaeckers to AIA, 18 Jan. 1882. See also: Bennett, *Arab versus European*, 106; Edvard Gleerup, 'A journey across Tanganyika in 1886', trans. Per Hassing, ed. Norman R. Bennett, *Tanzania Notes and Records*, 56 (1962), 130–1.
[62] See also: Livingstone, *Last Journals*, 223–4; CWM/LMS/06/02/006 Griffith to Thompson, 13 Mar. 1882; RMCA ESA HA.01.017-7. Storms, 'Les Wagoina', n.d.; Rockel, 'Slavery and freedom', 97–8.

time, often under a decade.[63] Case studies from the Ottoman world, especially from the empire's frontiers and during its later years, are prominent in this context.[64] Patterns of enslavement in Algeria, Egypt, parts of Anatolia, and elsewhere incorporated mechanisms towards manumission during the nineteenth century.[65] Additionally, processes towards the emancipation of enslaved people were additionally often faster when the slave(s) in question converted to Islam or when they displayed heroism in battle.[66] Again, as discussed in more depth in Chapter 7, many enslaved people and other bonds(wo)men converted to Islam while bonded to coastal traders. At the same time, the coastal traders' need for armed followings, especially during their 1880s commercial and military expansion around the northern lakeshore, gave bondsmen opportunities to demonstrate their commitment to their patron's cause. The conditions of enslavement 'on the frontiers of Islam' often necessitated the development of direct routes to personhood.[67]

On the lakeshore, the coastal traders' need to fast track the people they enslaved to positions of higher status was complicated by several factors. Primary among these was the brutality of the slave trade that brought many Manyema people to the lakeshore. This brutal process was a problem for Lake Tanganyika's coastal traders because it encouraged many of the people they enslaved to run away. Indeed, runaways were a constant issue for enslavers. Enslaved men and women could relatively easily run away in a caravan, in which they could take advantage of opportunities for free-waged labour. Men primarily did so as traders and porters; women did so as traders, porters, cooks, and domestic workers.[68] The draws for Manyema men were particularly strong here. As discussed in Chapter 5, many Manyema men sought ownership of a gun. If they did not feel as though this was possible through bondage to a coastal trader, the clearest passage to gun ownership was through using earned wages to buy one in one of Unyamwezi's arms markets, such as at Urambo and in Unyanyembe.[69] Market towns, meanwhile, were known

[63] Clarence-Smith, *Islam and the Abolition*, 66.

[64] See, for example: Clarence-Smith, *Islam and the Abolition*, 67; Richard Hellie, *Slavery in Russia 1450–1725* (Chicago: University of Chicago Press, 1982), 517–18; Y. Hakan Erdem, *Slavery in the Ottoman Empire and Its Demise 1800–1909* (London: Palgrave MacMillan, 1996), 154–7; Alan W. Fisher, 'Muscovy and the Black Sea slave trade', *Canadian-American Slavic Studies*, 6, 4 (1972), 576, 585.

[65] Clarence-Smith, *Islam and the Abolition*, 66–70.

[66] Clarence-Smith, *Islam and the Abolition*, 69.   [67] Lovejoy, *Slavery on the Frontiers*.

[68] Rockel, *Carriers of Culture*, 117–30.

[69] CWM/LMS/06/02/005 Hutley to Whitehouse, 20 Feb. 1880; Reid, *War in Pre-colonial Eastern Africa*, 45–6.

for their high levels of sexual activity and prostitution.[70] Some women may have sought an exit from enslavement by these means, thereby developing their own routes to 'respectability'.[71] Given the brutality of the slave trade, it would have been hard for coastal traders to persuade those they had recently enslaved to not take up one of these options. According to Marcia Wright, guarantees of security for women and their children may have helped induce women to stay under conditions of bondage.[72] Such women may also have been more amenable to work in the fields, where they would work alongside and under similar conditions to 'free' women, even if they did not have the same status as them. Additionally, they may have acquired respect over time, especially if they gave birth to a 'free' child of their enslaver's kin.[73] By doing so, such women may have been regarded as *jakazi* or *suria* instead of *tumwa*, and some may have acquired 'free dependent' status.

By contrast, coastal traders' inducements to enslaved men occurred outside the fields and household. Work in these domains was regarded as the work of women, the enslaved, or both. Forcing enslaved men to work in them, especially after the brutality of their journey to the lakeshore, would likely have been difficult, hence the need for alternative material and social inducements. Provision of clothing, especially that which was made from *merikani* cloth (the most expensive widely available cloth on the lakeshore), was an immediate strategy to ameliorate relations between coastal traders and their bondsmen.[74] In the longer term, coastal traders taught many of their bondsmen about Islam.[75] Assuming it was received enthusiastically, this had the double effect of assimilating their bondsmen to their culture, thus building trust between them. This enabled them to employ their bondsmen in more 'high-risk' occupations, such as in porterage, boating, soldiery, or proxy trading.[76] Coastal traders supplied their soldiers with firearms and their proxy traders with credit to be traded on their behalf. The men in these

---

[70] Stanley, *How I Found*, 388; Hutley, *Central African Diaries*, 106; Brown and Brown, 'East African trade towns', 196; Glassman, *Feasts and Riot*, 4.

[71] This idea builds on themes in studies of female prostitutes in East African colonial urban centres, in which '[prostitutes], far from being degraded by the transformation of sexual relations into a sale of services, ... held their own in "respectable society" with men' (Janet M. Bujra, 'Women "entrepreneurs" of early Nairobi', *Canadian Journal of African Studies*, 9, 2 (1975), 215). See also: Luise White, *The Comforts of Home: Prostitution in colonial Nairobi* (Chicago: University of Chicago Press, 1990).

[72] Wright, *Strategies of Slaves*, 26–8, 47–9. See also: Miers, 'Slavery: A question', 7.

[73] Deutsch, *Emancipation without Abolition*, 60; Lovejoy, *Transformations*, 14–15.

[74] Glassman, 'Bondsman's new clothes', 310–12.   [75] See: Chapter 7.

[76] ZNA AA1/23 Hore to Kirk, 14 Apr. 1879; Jacques and Storms, *Notes sur l'ethnographie*, 66–7.

professions had the capacity, therefore, to kill or economically damage their coastal trader patron with the tools of their labour. Trust was thus a necessity before coastal traders could contemplate allowing bondsmen to embark on these activities. They were, though, further aided by the fact that these were desirable occupations for many bondsmen. Porters, boatmen, soldiers, and proxy traders could socially differentiate themselves from the lowly *tumwa* working in the fields, thus allowing them to claim that they had left slave status. It was a practical necessity of coastal traders' capacities and their commercial aims to advance their bondsmen's status quickly.

The coastal traders' labour needs also encouraged their labourers to develop independent agency over time. This applied particularly from the beginning of the 1880s, when coastal traders armed their bondsmen to entrench their position and develop commercial routes and emporia across the northern half Lake Tanganyika. Many of these bondsmen were armed with guns, a key symbol of respect on the lakeshore.[77] The coastal traders then left these soldiers to govern trading stations, most notably Rumonge and Chuinu.[78] In the archive, these 'governor bondsmen' are frequently referred to as *ngwana*, a sign of the term they used refer to themselves.[79] This is despite the fact that many of the commentators who made these references wrote that such people remained bonded to coastal traders, a phenomenon they struggled to reconcile with the idea of *ngwana* being 'freeborn', as was the case on East Africa's Indian Ocean littoral.[80] From this point on, the coastal traders' *ngwana* bondsmen frequently raided for captives, ivory, and food. Their successes meant that they soon came to dominate their respective regions militarily.[81]

---

[77] CWM/LMS/06/02/004 Hutley to Whitehouse, 19 Oct. 1879; CWM/LMS/06/02/005 Hore to Whitehouse, 26 May 1880; CWM/LMS/06/02/007 Griffith to Thomson, 16 Oct. 1882; A.G.M.Afr. C.16-7. Journal du P. Deniaud, 2 June 1879, 31 July 1880, 5 Dec. 1880, 25 Jan. 1880, 1 Aug. 1881; RMCA ESA HA.01.017-7. Storms, 'Rapport sur un voyage dans la partie sud du Tanganika', 1 Apr. 1884; A.G.M.Afr. Diaire de Kibanga, 1 Oct. 1888; A.G.M.Afr. Diaire de Mpala, Jan. 1890.

[78] A.G.M.Afr. C.16-7. Journal du P. Deniaud, 12 Apr. 1881; CWM/LMS/06/02/006 Griffith to Thompson, 12 Aug. 1881; A.G.M.Afr. Guillet to White Fathers, 10 Apr. 1884, *Chronique Trimestrielles*, 23–4 (Oct. 1884); A.G.M.Afr. Coulbois to White Fathers, 18 May 1884, *Chronique Trimestrielles*, 26 (Apr. 1885); Interview with Daniel Rucintingo, Rumonge, 7 Nov. 2013.

[79] A.G.M.Afr. Diaire de Massanze, 26 June 1882, 27 June 1882, A.G.M.Afr. Diaire de Kibanga, 3 Dec. 1887, 10 Nov. 1888, 23 Nov. 1888.

[80] CWM/LMS/06/02/006 Hutley, 'Mahommadanism in Central Africa: Its influence', Aug. 1881; A.G.M.Afr. Diaire de Mkapakwe, 26 Jan. 1885; RMCA ESA HA.01.017-7. Storms, 'Les Wagoina', n.d.

[81] A.G.M.Afr. C.16-7. Journal du P. Deniaud, 12 Apr. 1881; A.G.M.Afr. Diaire de Massanze, 26 June 1881, 27 June 1882; A.G.M.Afr. Diaire de Kibanga, 3 Dec. 1887, 10 Nov. 1888, 23 Nov. 1888.

Such patterns came with dangers for coastal traders. In December 1887, for example, Rumaliza lamented his inability to control his bondsmen in and around the Ubwari peninsula, which brought him into disrepute with the White Fathers stationed in Kibanga.[82] Nevertheless, in general, the coastal traders probably encouraged their *ngwana* bondsmen to act violently and somewhat independently in these contexts. Doing so decreased their bondsmen's reliance on their credit lines, and it generally helped to safeguard and expand their long-distance commercial networks.

Thinking beyond the confines of their relationship to coastal traders, *ngwana* bondsmen also developed respect and personhood among other lakeshore populations. By the mid-1880s, some of the most successful *ngwana* bondsmen had attracted their own followings. They, too, acquired bonds(wo)men, who, like their patrons, often saw themselves as *ngwana*.[83] The respect to which the bonded *ngwana* were held is further shown through many lakeshore people's assimilation to the *ngwana*'s cultural forms, such as their customs, ideas, dress, songs, and language.[84] One Protestant missionary referred to this phenomena in terms of a spread of '*ngwana*-ism', which to him and his colleagues was a heretical version of Islam contrary to that which was practised on East Africa's Indian Ocean littoral (this perspective is challenged in Chapter 7).[85] Missionaries lamented the prevalence of these kinds of cultural and spiritual exchanges between bonded *ngwana* and lakeshore populations, as such exchanges limited their capacity to gain Christian converts.[86] They thus tried to establish stations far from the *ngwana*'s influence, which caused them to abandon Ujiji as a potential missionary station during the mid-1880s. Even so, their ability to escape the

---

[82] A.G.M.Afr. Diaire de Kibanga, 3–8 Dec. 1887, 23 Dec. 1887; Vyncke, *Brieven van een vlaamschen*, III, 93–5.

[83] A.G.M.Afr. Diaire de Karema, 8 Dec. 1888; Stephanie Wynne-Jones, 'Lines of desire: Power and materiality along the Tanzania caravan route', *Journal of World Prehistory*, 23, 4 (2010), 223; Page, 'Manyema hordes', 72, 80.

[84] CWM/LMS/06/02/009 Jones to Thompson, 2 Dec. 1884. See also: CWM/LMS/06/02/006 Hutley, 'Mahommadanism in Central Africa: Its influence', Aug. 1881; CWM/LMS/06/02/006 Hutley, 'Mahommadanism in Central Africa: Its professors', Aug. 1881; A.G.M.Afr. Diaire de Mkpakwe, 26 Jan. 1885; RMCA ESA HA.01.017-7. Storms, 'Les Wagoina', n.d; Vyncke, *Brieven van een vlaamschen*, III, 9–10.

[85] CWM/LMS/06/02/014 Jones to Thompson, 23 Jan. 1889.

[86] RMCA ESA HA.01.017-7. Storms, 'Rapport de voyage à Oudjidji, 7 July 1883; CWM/LMS/06/02/009 Jones to Whitehouse, 24 June 1884; CWM/LMS/06/02/009 Jones to Thompson, 2 Dec. 1884; A.G.M.Afr. Randabel to White Fathers, 28 Dec. 1885, *Chronique Trimestrielles*, 31 (July 1886); A.G.M. Afr. Diaire de Kibanga, 9 July 1886; CWM/LMS/06/02/013 Carson to Thomson, 20 Aug. 1888; A.G.M.Afr. Diaire de Karema 8 Dec. 1888; CWM/LMS/06/02/01 Jones to Thompson 23 Jan. 1889.

ngwana's cultural influence elsewhere on the lakeshore decreased over the course of the decade. The missionaries were reliant on *ngwana* labour to sustain their stations (for which they paid wages and a fee to their patron), and the geographical scope of the towns with large *ngwana* populations by c.1890 – all of the lakeshore's principal emporia – meant that no lakeshore region was far from their influence.[87] The perception of the *ngwana* as 'respected' and of representing personhood came to permeate the whole lakeshore, even though many were bonded.[88]

The core factors underpinning the bonded *ngwana*'s respectability among lakeshore populations during the 1880s were twofold. The first pertains to material culture. Through their bondage, *ngwana* acquired access to expensive cloths, especially *merikani*, and guns. As discussed in Chapter 5, both these items were symbolic of wealth and prestige. Moreover, the limited circulation of guns around the lakeshore in markets meant that many lakeshore populations believed that the easiest way to acquire one was to enter a social contract with a coastal trader or one of their bondsmen. In this way, guns also became symbolic of having *ngwana* or freeborn status, even if the gun owner was under some form of bondage.[89] No doubt such patterns contributed to the desirability of becoming *ngwana* and the weakening of the bonds between Jiji boatmen and their *teko*, described earlier. The second reason underpinning bonded *ngwana*'s respectability pertains to patterns of religious and spiritual interaction. As discussed in Chapter 3, the coastal traders and their bondsmen became the principal actors in the appeasement of spirits who were believed to inhabit Lake Tanganyika. They did so by adopting and adapting a pre-existing religious framework centred on the lake to fit their cultural expectations and to account for influences from the wider IOW. They demonstrated their power over the lake's spirits through offerings, rituals, and canoe construction – much like lakeshore populations had done previously but on a larger and more universal scale. Perceptions of their spiritual power and authority inevitably brought admiration, thus also attributions of respect and personhood.

Finally, it is worth stressing that the *ngwana*'s aquiring of respect and 'freeborn' status should not be conflated with them becoming 'free' – at least not in the commonly used sense of the word. Despite gaining opportunities for legal freedom after five to seven years, most *ngwana* on Lake Tanganyika's shores chose to remain in some form of bondage

---

[87] CWM/LMS/06/02/009 Jones to Whitehouse, 24 June 1884; A.G.M.Afr. Diaire de Karema, 8 Dec. 1888.

[88] See also: Jan Vansina, *Paths in the Rainforests: Towards a history of political tradition in equatorial Africa* (London: James Currey, 1990), 228.

[89] See also: Murjebi, *L'autobiographie*, 85, 97.

with a coastal trader.[90] They stayed bonded because of the opportunities inherent in doing so. For example, remaining tied to a coastal trader could give them access to privately owned land (which was not available among the Jiji, for example) and to the coastal traders' lines of credit.[91] In the commercialised world of nineteenth-century East Africa, access to such credit was, in and of itself, a symbol of personhood. Additionally, remaining in bondage probably provided greater opportunities for enrichment. The voluntary and opportunity-providing nature of this form of bondage necessitates not referring to it within a 'slave-free' paradigm. 'Clientage' would be a more accurate term, although only with the caveat that its usage should not imply a fixed form of bondage.[92] The fact that some bonded *ngwana* inherited coastal trader property means that the form of clientage described here does not fully correspond to clientage in Islamic west and north-west Africa (referred to as '*wala*'), nor does it correspond to the rights available to *twana* clients in East African coastal and island regions.[93] Additionally, coastal traders treated some clients with more respect than others by granting them access to differing amounts of credit.[94] Even so, the nature of the coastal trader–*ngwana* bonds(wo)men relationship meant that, despite claiming to be 'freeborn', few bond(wo)smen actually sought freedom. Instead, they sought 'respect' and the implied social status of being 'freeborn'. Acquiring this status was more important to their claims of being freeborn than actually being 'free' from bondage.

Conclusion

The key argument of this chapter is that analysing labour and social relations in nineteenth-century East Africa in terms of a binary between

---

[90] Jacques and Storms, *Notes sur l'ethnographie*, 66–7; Jérôme Becker, *La vie en Afrique ou trois ans dans l'Afrique Centrale*, II (Paris: J. Lebègue & Co., 1887), 45–6; Coulbois, *Dix années*, 64; Gleerup, 'A journey across Tanganyika', 131; Iliffe, *A Modern History*, 47; Page, 'The Manyema hordes', 80–1; Rockel, 'Slavery and freedom', 95. This pattern has wider applicability on the African Continent. See: Rossi, 'Introduction', 2.

[91] Norman R. Bennett, 'Captain Storms in Tanganyika', *Tanzania Notes and Records*, 54 (1960), 51; RMCA ESA HA.01.017-5. Ramaeckers to AIA, 18 Jan. 1882; Gleerup, 'A journey across Tanganyika', 130–1; McCurdy, 'Transforming associations', 60, 68–74; Bennett, *Arab versus European*, 106; Lovejoy, *Transformations*, 233; Vansina, *Paths in the Rainforests*, 228.

[92] Lovejoy, *Transformations*, 4–5.

[93] Hall, *A History of Race*, 237–9; Chouki El Hamel, *Black Morocco: A history of slavery, race, and Islam* (Cambridge: Cambridge University Press, 2013), 49.

[94] For more on the social importance of credit among coastal traders and their kin living on East Africa's IOW littoral, see: Glassman, *Feasts and Riot*, 24, 57–8, 71–4, 173; Bishara, *A Sea of Debt*, 76; McDow, *Buying Time*, 152–3.

'slave' and 'free' does not account for the complexity of bonded forms that existed in this region and time period. The 'feedback loop' referred to in the oral record, which has been caused by using 'slavery' as the key analytical term to describe different forms of bondage since the nineteenth century, shows the potentially dangerous consequences of continuing a discourse focused on slavery. In the long run, this chapter's core proposal of 'clientage' as an alternative analytical focus for understanding some forms of bondage may be shown to be as unsatisfactory and cumbersome as 'slavery'. Yet there are at least three interrelated arguments for thinking of social and labour relations in terms of 'clientage' and other forms of bondage more than has been the case in the past. First, it may allow for a correction in the oral record. East Africans, such as my informants in Ujiji, would no longer have to reconcile an 'official' record that focuses on slavery with popular images of slavery from the Americas during the era of the transatlantic slave trade. Second, it would respond to many nineteenth-century bondsmen's rejection of slave status, which they partly expressed through their refusal of agricultural work – an occupation that became synonymous with slavery, especially among men. It is arguable that imposing the term 'slave' on such bonds(wo)men is another example in histories of slavery of 'archival violence', in which paradigms whose roots are in the archive obscure the true character of certain bonds(wo)men's histories.[95] Rejecting the 'violence' of the archive would allow historians to challenge the paradigms of 'slave versus free' and to incorporate more complex accounts that elucidate a range of experiences, social statuses, and labour conditions.[96] Finally, 'clientage' and other types of bondage are hardly less reductive than 'slavery' as analytical tools, and yet histories about slavery dominate the discourse. If used alongside existing studies of slavery, emphasising clientage more in the future would promote a greater appreciation of the diversity of labour and social forms in the interior.[97] This would also allow historians to cease having to qualify their statements about how social and labour forms in East Africa were inherently different from those in the Americas, even though they use the same terminologies.

---

[95] Marisa J. Fuentes, *Dispossessed Lives: Enslaved women, violence, and the archive* (Philadelphia: University of Pennsylvania Press, 2016).

[96] This is a direct adaptation of Fuentes' claims vis-à-vis 'archival violence' enacted upon enslaved women in the Americas. She wrote: 'Incorporating concerns of power and the reproduction of quotidian and archival violence, moves us outside the paradigms of resistance into more complex accounts that offer a range of experiences, responses to domination, and articulations of humanity' (Fuentes, *Dispossessed Lives*, 142).

[97] For a similar call for more investigation into the histories of clientage and patronage, see: Medard, 'Introduction', in *Slavery in the Great Lakes*, eds. Médard and Doyle, 16–17.

There are dangers with simply emphasising the complexity of bonded forms in nineteenth-century East Africa and the wider IOW, however. Key among them is that doing so does the opposite of focusing on either 'slavery' or 'clientage'. While these terms may be too reductive in that they reduce a wide range of labour and social forms into one (or two) term(s), emphasising complexity on its own lacks precision. It is for this reason that case studies are required to unpick complexities in different circumstances. It is hoped that the case study provided in this chapter is regarded as one that does this. Making connections across the lake – whether commercial, administrative, or military – necessitated the adaptation of existing social and labour forms. This applied to forms that were indigenous to the lake, in the case of Jiji boatmen, and those that had their origins on the East Africa's Indian Ocean littoral, in the case of the coastal traders' bonds(wo)men. The latter forms came to dominate much of the lakeshore, though with significant differences with how they were originally conceived on East Africa's coast and islands. The coastal traders' labourers', associates', and followers' claims of being *ngwana*, and thus of being 'freeborn', on the shores of Lake Tanganyika did not mean that they were necessarily 'free'. Indeed, many remained in bondage, and voluntarily so. In this instance, their claims of being freeborn were not about technical accuracy but about a demand that they were to be respected. They expressed this respectability through their dress, their ownership of guns, their interactions with spirits in the lake, and (as analysed more closely in Chapter 7) their conversion to Islam. Their success in doing so is shown by the high levels of wealth, prestige, and power some among them acquired. On the shores of Lake Tanganyika, the transition to 'respectability' was more important in the lives of the coastal traders' bonds(wo)men from Manyema than the experience of slavery when they first arrived at the lakeshore. Slavery was brief, while 'respectability' and the transition to it were enduring.

Thinking about these patterns in the wider IOW context necessarily invokes certain contradictions. It is important to note that these patterns did not occur on East Africa's Indian Ocean littoral. To East African coastal and island populations, the fact that these people on the lakeshore claiming to be *ngwana* were from the interior and were clearly in some form of bondage meant that they could not regard them as 'freeborn'. Even if some might not have regarded them as *shenzi* or *tumwa*, they were clearly not, in their eyes, *ngwana*. At best, they were *twana* – vassals or clients, a status which denied them access to important markers of personhood on East Africa's coastal and island regions, such as to certain mosques and festivals, and denied them the right to inherit their former enslaver/patron's property. Indeed, as Geert Castryck shows, the children of coastal traders living in coastal regions sometimes challenged *ngwana* bondsmen's right to inherit their father's property on the lakeshore in the early colonial period, although they generally failed to win their cases.[98] Additionally, key markers of respect that distinguished *ngwana* in some parts of the interior, such as gun ownership (which applied especially around Lake Tanganyika), did not apply on East Africa's Indian Ocean littoral. As Jonathon Glassman argues, and as explored in greater depth in the Epilogue, the social contradiction of interior people's claims of *ngwana* identity versus having their claims rejected in coastal regions was a crucial factor that provoked riots in coastal towns in 1888.[99] During the nineteenth century, people claiming to be *ngwana* used guns as a tool to assert their respectability and personhood in the confines of their bondage on the shores of Lake Tanganyika. In 1888, they did likewise in parts of the littoral core of the IOW.

A focus here on bondage, then, complicates somewhat current East Africanist understandings of slavery during the nineteenth century. It challenges universalist definitions of slavery, arguing that a 'slave' by one person's definition often does not equate to a 'slave' by another's. Even though nineteenth-century Europeans, Indian Ocean littoral populations, and most East Africanist historians have labelled many of the people described in this chapter as 'slave' or 'free', these terms were not used in the same way on the shores of Lake Tanganyika – whether in the nineteenth century or by my informants in 2013. Although this is a somewhat revolutionary way of thinking about labour and social status in East Africanist circles, precedents can be found elsewhere in the IOW, especially 'on the frontiers' of Islam. Building on this latter historiography, this chapter shows how coastal traders were forced to adapt their paradigms of bondage established on East Africa's Indian Ocean littoral through their encounters with Great Lakes peoples and environments. Coastal traders' weak institutional backing on the lakeshore and their need for specialised labour necessitated granting people considered bonded, and therefore unfree on the East African coast and islands, 'freeborn' social status. Of course, bonds(wo)men's agency cannot be understated here. Much like in Rockel's analysis of Nyamwezi *pagazi*, in which he argues porters used their leverage to acquire better wages and conditions, the coastal traders' bonds(wo)men manoeuvred enslaved people's propensities for running away and the coastal traders' need for

---

[98] Castryck, 'My slave sold all of Kigoma', 317–36.
[99] Glassman, *Feasts and Riot*; Fabian, *Making Identity*, 175–210.

specialised labour to acquire material and social advantages.[100] They were conscious of coastal traders' reliance upon them, and they acted accordingly. In maintaining their position as bonds(wo)men in coastal traders' followings, they challenged routes to respectability and personhood whose origins lay on East Africa's Indian Ocean littoral.

[100] Rockel, *Carriers of Culture*.

7   An Islamic Sea

The emergence and spread of Islam are central to the history of the IOW.[1] Edward Alpers, building on the work of K. N. Chaudhuri and others, recently referred to the Indian Ocean as an 'Islamic Sea' over the *longue durée*. This 'Islamic Sea' was characterised by Muslims making commercial and religious connections across oceanic space from soon after Islam's founding in the Arabian Peninsula in the seventh century until deep into the 'early modern' period. Arab Muslims formed diasporic trading communities in as far east as present-day Indonesia and Guangzhou, China from the seventh–eighth centuries.[2] The earliest evidence for mosques on the coast and islands of East Africa is contemporaneous with this development.[3] In subsequent years, though, it was not Arabs who were the main drivers in making the sea 'Islamic'. Rather, it was local converts to Islam. New converts 'integrated' and 'domesticated' Islam into their existing belief systems. In the past, historians discussed such patterns in terms of syncretism – the idea that Islam existed side by side with indigenous beliefs.[4] More recently, scholars have analysed the ways in which beliefs in Islam modified pre-existing belief systems and vice versa, thus stressing the diversity of Islamic beliefs and practices across different global regions and the importance of local contexts for Islam's spread. These patterns of acculturation, they have argued, were crucial for the dissemination of Islam and for local populations being able to spread it among themselves.[5] This chapter seeks to

---

[1] Parts of this chapter were published as: Philip Gooding, 'Islam in the interior of precolonial East Africa: Evidence from Lake Tanganyika', *The Journal of African History*, 60, 2 (2019), 191–208. Reprinted with permission.

[2] Alpers, *The Indian Ocean*, 41–5; Chaudhuri, *Trade and Civilisation*.

[3] Horton, *Shanga*, 420.

[4] See, for example: Clifford Geertz, *Islam Observed: Religious development in Morocco and Indonesia* (Chicago: University of Chicago Press, 1971), 13.

[5] See, for example: Felicitas Becker, 'Commoners in the process of Islamization: Reassessing their role in light of evidence from southeastern Tanzania', *Journal of Global History*, 3 (2008), 227–45; Rudolph T. Ware III, *The Walking Qur'an: Islamic education, embodied knowledge, and history in West Africa* (Chapel Hill: University of North

situate this history of Islam within this recent trend. It emphasises the agency of new converts in shaping Islamic beliefs and practices, and it stresses the importance of local environments and belief systems for understanding the different ways it has been interpreted over time and space. How Islam spread around Lake Tanganyika was indelibly shaped by new converts' encounters with the lake and its peoples.

Examining a history of Islam around Lake Tanganyika adds significant layers to regional and macro-regional historiographies. This is because few historians – of East Africa and of the wider IOW – have included the interior of 'pre-colonial' East Africa within a broader history of Islam. In an extract that is characteristic of the general attitude towards Islam's history in the region before c.1890, David Sperling wrote in 2000: 'Because of the limitation of our sources and the consequent lack of knowledge, the history of Islam necessarily lies hidden behind the secular and commercial activities whose details are so much better known.'[6] The apparent impossibility of reconstructing a history of Islam for the interior of nineteenth-century East Africa has led some historians to conclude that Islam had little impact in this context.[7] When Islam is acknowledged to have left an imprint, it has only made a qualified entry into the historiography. Melvin Page and David Northrup respectively referred to 'semi-Islamized' and 'partly-Islamicized' populations in Manyema, and Stephen Rockel wrote of 'familiarity with Islam' rather than Islamic conversion among certain populations in present-day west-central Tanzania.[8] There is a sense in the historiography of Islam only making a limited entry into the lives of interior East Africans during the nineteenth century.[9] 'Semi' or 'partly' Islamised interior populations have been viewed as 'nominal' rather than 'fully fledged' Muslims.

These patterns in the East Africanist historiography sit uneasily with recent histories of Islam in other regions and time-periods, many of which are in the IOW. Scholars writing about such contexts have critiqued the idea of 'semi-Islamisation' among new converts. In her seminal case study on south-eastern German East Africa, Felicitas Becker

---

Carolina Press, 2014); M. C. Ricklefs, 'Rediscovering Islam in Javanese history', *Studia Islamika*, 21, 3 (2014), 397–418; Prange, *Monsoon Islam*.

[6] Sperling, 'The coastal hinterland', 297.

[7] Pallaver, 'Muslim communities', 2, 7; Pallaver, 'New modes of production', 31, 45; Sperling, 'The coastal hinterland', 290; J. Spencer Trimingham, *Islam in East Africa* (Oxford: Clarendon Press, 1964), 56. For a critique of this perspective with a focus on colonial Burundi, see: Castryck, 'Living Islam', 263–98.

[8] Page, 'Manyema hordes', 74; Northrup, *Beyond the Bend*, 24; Rockel, 'Slavery and freedom', 88.

[9] Sperling, 'The coastal hinterland', 288; Trimingham, *Islam in East Africa*, 26–7.

argued that 'the notion of a nominal conversion is dubious'.[10] In so doing, she pointed out that 'becoming Muslim' questioned new converts' ways of living, social relationships, and ritual practices, even if they did not become 'model Muslims' by academic Islamicists' standards.[11] In this context, even if pre-existing rituals or practices were not abolished by conversion to Islam, they were often modified to fit how new converts interpreted their new religion. Using similar perspectives, Rudolph Ware noted how spirit possession among Muslim converts in West Africa evolved in ways that were influenced by Islam; M. C. Ricklefs explored how received Islamic practice was adapted by Javanese populations to fit their pre-conceived knowledge of the spiritual world; and Sebastian Prange argued that in monsoon Asia, 'local receptions, understandings, and practices were crucial to [Islam's] historical development'.[12] In the final example, Prange developed the idea of 'monsoon Islam' as a way of conceptualising the ways in which trade, travel, and cultural encounters influenced the spread of Islam in the IOW. These themes, of course, are highly cogent with factors underpinning encounters between Muslim coastal traders and Great Lakes populations in the interior of nineteenth-century East Africa. Taken collectively, these recent studies show that the ongoing evolution of ostensibly local practices has been seen as vital to each region's Islamic history rather than as representative of only nominal conversions or of syncretic belief systems.[13]

Understanding the interaction between Islam and local belief systems as crucial to the history of Islam is at the core of this chapter. Coastal traders were the first Muslims to arrive on the lakeshore. They were a mixture of Ibadhis and Shafi'i Sunnis. Omanis comprised most of the former and Swahilis comprised most of the latter, though these distinctions were far from absolute.[14] Many from among both denominations were also influenced by the arrival of Sufi scholars to Zanzibar during the second half of the nineteenth century.[15] Africanist historians such as J. Spencer Trimingham have seen the lack of a proselytising ethic among

---

[10] Becker, 'Commoners', 229.   [11] Becker, 'Commoners', 229.

[12] Ware III, *The Walking Qur'an*, 5; Ricklefs, 'Rediscovering Islam', 397–418; Prange, *Monsoon Islam*, 3.

[13] See also: Lovejoy, *Transformations*, 30; Mark R. Woodward, *Java, Indonesia and Islam* (Dordrecht: Springer, 2011), 40–4.

[14] Horton and Middleton, *The Swahili*, 49; Pouwels, 'The East African coast', 262–3; Trimingham, *Islam in East Africa*, 1–2.

[15] Bang, *Islamic Sufi Networks*, 32–5; Glassman, *Feasts and Riot*, 138–9; Roman Loimeier, 'Africa south of the Sahara to the First World War', in *The New Cambridge History of Islam*, Vol. V, *The Islamic World in the Age of Western Dominance*, ed. Francis Robinson (Cambridge: Cambridge University Press, 2011), 286–8; Pouwels, 'The East African coast', 263.

Ibadhis and Shafi'is as a barrier to conversion in East Africa's nineteenth-century interior, including around Lake Tanganyika.[16] However, focusing on the attitudes of coastal traders denies interior populations agency, underestimating their capacity to convert themselves through their encounters with newly arrived Muslims. The key actors in this context are the coastal traders' bonds(wo)men and other followers, most of whom came from Manyema. As discussed in Chapter 6, such people often referred to themselves as *ngwana*, denoting 'freeborn' status, even though most among them remained in some form of bondage. Additionally, the paradigms of the older historiography fail to acknowledge the ways in which coastal traders adapted their religious practices to the lakeshore and other interior contexts. The absence of mosques and other institutions on the lakeshore necessitated that they readjust their everyday religious practices. Coastal traders and their bonds(wo)men adapted Islamic belief and practice to their position within the lakeshore environment.

Exploring these adaptive dynamics leads to the conclusion that Islam is much more important to understandings of the history of East Africa's Great Lakes during the nineteenth century than has previously been acknowledged. Even so, Lake Tanganyika likely has a privileged position within this broader regional history. The growth of emporia within the water-facing, lacustrine environment meant that the urban, 'oceanic' way of life that characterised Islamic society on East Africa's Indian Ocean littoral was more adaptable to the lakeshore region than it was to nearby terrestrial zones. Islam's importance on the lakeshore was such that Lake Tanganyika had the appearance, by the 1880s, of an 'Islamic Sea' in the heart of Africa, similar in conception to the wider IOW over the *longue durée*. This is not to imply homogeneity of religious belief on the lakeshore. As argued in Chapter 1, Lake Tanganyika's emporia were cosmopolitan places (as were emporia in the wider IOW) in which people with different origins and belief systems intermingled. Rather, it is to acknowledge that people professing faith in Islam were integral to the composition of Lake Tanganyika's principal population centres – its emporia – and to the creation of physical lines of connection between different lakeshore regions through commerce. *Ngwana* bonds(wo)men were crucial in the making of this 'Islamic Sea'. Apart from being the

---

[16] Trimingham, *Islam in East Africa*, 55. See also: Bimangu and Tshibangu, 'Contribution à l'histoire', 228; August H. Nimtz, *Islam and Politics in East Africa: The Sufi order in Tanzania* (Minneapolis: University of Minnesota Press, 1980), 8–9; Ayre Oded, *Islam in Uganda: Islamization through a centralized state in pre-colonial Africa* (New York: J. Wiley & Sons, 1974), 64–5; Pallaver, 'Nyamwezi participation', 517.

principal actors who developed the coastal traders' commercial networks around and across Lake Tanganyika as boatmen, proxy traders, and soldiers, they were also crucial to associating some of these processes with their understandings of their Islamic faith. The ways they encountered the lake and viewed the terms of their bondage were increasingly seen through the lens of Islam.

The remainder of this chapter is split into two sections. The first analyses the methodological approaches used for ascertaining the lives of new converts to Islam on the lakeshore. It starts with a critique of the ways in which perspectives dating from the nineteenth century have influenced the dearth of scholarship on Islam in the 'pre-colonial' East African interior. Labelling people under various forms of bondage as 'slaves' has led to assumptions that such people were not Muslim, given the illegality of Muslim enslavement according to Islamic law. By contrast, closer analysis of bonds(wo)men's claims of *ngwana* status, discussed in Chapter 6, allows for a reappraisal and a recognition that some people ostensibly confined by conditions of bondage could claim to be 'freeborn' Muslims. The argument here is supported by Ujiji's oral record, which stresses the importance of Islamic learning in encounters between coastal traders and Manyema populations. The second section analyses the nature of Islamic belief and practice on the lakeshore. It shows that, even though adherence to many of the key tenets of orthodox Islam, including Islam's five pillars, may have been uneven, new converts additionally demonstrated their faith through other means. Their housing, their dress, their diet, their claims of being *ngwana*, and their interactions with spirits that they and other lakeshore populations believed inhabited the lake were crucial in this context. In short, conversion to Islam was part of a broader process of material, cultural, and religious exchange between people arriving from littoral regions of the IOW and those they encountered on the lakeshore.

Locating Muslim Converts on the Lakeshore

The absence of *ngwana* bondsmen in previous discussions of Islam in the interior of East Africa owes itself significantly to the legacies of nineteenth-century perspectives and sources. People living in East Africa's Indian Ocean littoral regions rejected bonded *ngwana*'s conversions. They labelled them as heterodox or even blasphemous.[17] This was part of a broader discourse that claimed that such people could not be

---

[17] Glassman, *Feasts and Riot*, 134.

ngwana owing to their interior, *shenzi* origins and their experience of being enslaved and/or in bondage. In littoral populations' eyes, only free populations of the coast and islands could be regarded as freeborn Muslims in East Africa. European 'explorers' and missionaries, in documenting these attitudes, generally bought into the rhetoric that underpinned them. They generally regarded the *ngwana* bonds(wo)men of coastal traders as 'slaves', neglecting to understand the complexity of their bondage as discussed in Chapter 6.[18] If the nineteenth-century Europeans' perspective is accepted (which it should not), then it barred the coastal traders' bonds(wo)men from being considered Muslim according to Islamic law – it being illegal in Islamic law for Muslims to be enslaved.[19] Stressing the importance of the *ngwana* bonds(wo)men's agency over their labour and social status around Lake Tanganyika, however, modifies the potential avenues for their conversion to Islam. If they claimed *ngwana* and therefore 'freeborn' status, they also claimed the right to convert to Islam according to Islamic law, even though many among them remained in some form of bondage to a coastal trader.

Placing emphasis on the capacity of bonds(wo)men to convert to Islam perhaps unsurprisingly differs methodologically from the few previous attempts to examine Islamic histories in East Africa before the colonial period. Much of the older historiography focuses on the conversions of political elites where the forces of centralisation were strong. Edward Alpers, for example, argued that the intersection of pre-existing chiefly and religious values among the Yao around the northern end of Lake Malawi 'favourably predisposed [them] for the spread of Islam among them'.[20] Similarly, Ayre Oded claimed that widespread conversion to Islam in Buganda in the 1860s and 1870s was tied to the *kabaka*'s (king's) own adoption and promotion of Islamic beliefs and practices.[21] In this sense, conversion was seen as tied to prevailing norms, which were to a large degree centralised, even if subaltern individuals had their own

---

[18] See, for example: CWM/LMS/06/02/006 Hutley, 'Mohammadanism in Central Africa: Its influence', Aug. 1881.

[19] This is notwithstanding the fact that some Muslims sometimes broke the law and enslaved other Muslims or forced new converts within their followings to remain in bondage. See, for example: Paul E. Lovejoy, 'Slavery, the Bilād al-Sūdān and the frontiers of the African diaspora', in *Slavery on the Frontiers*, ed. Lovejoy, 17–18.

[20] Edward A. Alpers, 'Towards a history of the expansion of Islam in East Africa', in *The Historical Study of African Religion*, eds. T. R. Ranger and Isaria N. Kimambo (Berkeley: University of California Press, 1972), 176.

[21] Oded, *Islam in Uganda*, 127.

motivations for conversion.[22] Lake Tanganyika's polities lacked the degree of centralisation that Buganda and the Yao had. Even though Michele Wagner notes that some lakeshore Jiji *teko* acculturated some aspects of Islam, they did not have the required level of authority to enact mass conversion.[23] As neither the Ibadhi nor Shafi'i coastal traders were particularly motivated to convert populations from a spiritual standpoint either, the agency of the bonded *ngwana* in desiring conversion is implied. The bonded followers of coastal traders were at the forefront of Islamic conversion on the lakeshore.

Locating new converts to Islam in the archive is a process that is filled with ambiguity. The reasons for this are related to the ways in which European 'explorers' and missionaries used the term *ngwana* (or its Swahili or Anglicised derivatives, including, *mgwana*, *waungwana* and *wangwana*) as a label for some of the people they encountered. They often restrained themselves from referring to the coastal traders' bondsmen as *ngwana*, even if some acknowledged that they were Muslim or accepted 'some Islamic doctrine' and, on other occasions, that this was the term that they used to describe themselves.[24] For example, in 1880, William Griffith, an LMS missionary based at the time at Mtowa, wrote: 'Besides the coast people, there are vast numbers of Arabs' slaves, dependents, and followers, improperly called by the natives "*Wangwana*" [*sic*].'[25] Europeans were often loath to attribute *ngwana* status to people from the interior who they saw as slaves, despite local populations using this terminology and regarding them as having 'free-born' social status. Moreover, Europeans frequently referred to Swahili traders as *ngwana*, a term that, in their eyes, distinguished them from Omani 'Arabs'.[26] Thus, when news of a caravan of *ngwana* traders was rumoured to be in a particular locality, it is unknown whether the author of the source was trying to refer to a caravan of coastal people or of individuals referred to here as *ngwana* or bonded *ngwana*. On other

---

[22] Jonathon L. Earle, *Colonial Buganda and the End of Empire: Political thought and historical imagination in Africa* (New York: Cambridge University Press, 2017), 147.

[23] Wagner, 'Environment, community and history', 191.

[24] CWM/LMS/06/02/006 Hutley, 'Mahommadanism in Central Africa: Its influence', Aug. 1881; A.G.M.Afr. C.16-73. Guillet to White Fathers, 20 Aug. 1881; CWM/LMS/06/02/014 Jones to Thompson, 23 Jan. 1889.

[25] CWM/LMS/06/02/005 Griffith to Whitehouse, 5 Nov. 1880. See also: RMCA ESA HA.01.017-7. Storms, 'Les wagoina', n.d.

[26] A.G.M.Afr. Journal du R. P. Coulbois, 3 June 1884, *Chronique Trimestrielles*, 26 (Apr. 1885). For the inherent problems of such categorisations, see: James de Vere Allen 'Town and country in Swahili culture', in *Symposium Leo Frobenius: Perspectives of contemporary African studies* (Cologne: Pullach, 1974), 298–301; Bennett, 'Mwinyi Kheri', 148.

occasions, Europeans used the term *ngwana* to refer to the coastal traders' 'emancipated' bondsmen, who also originated on East Africa's Indian Ocean littoral.[27] In such instances, they tapped into coastal paradigms that associated the idea of being *ngwana* with coastal origins and being legally free. Looking for new converts in the archive does not, therefore, necessarily align with a search with references to *ngwana*.[28]

There are, however, two core features of the archive that make new converts visible to historians, apart from the occasional reference that refers to *ngwana* bonds(wo)men as Muslim.[29] The first of these are the terms of the *ngwana*'s labour. In 1882, Griffith wrote that '[t]hose slaves who are willing are taught to repeat their devotions [to Islam], and if they continue faithful[ly] they obtain their freedom'.[30] Yet, most formerly enslaved people did not take up the option to become 'free'. Most instead chose to remain in a looser form of bondage with their former enslaver, such as in a form of clientage.[31] Among bondsmen, such labourers were usually boatmen, soldiers, proxy traders, or town governors, with agricultural work being reserved for the enslaved and women (both bonded and of 'freeborn' status).[32] Female 'former slaves' often worked in the domestic sphere, though they are less visible in the archive owing to European commentators' limited access to these zones. Second, new converts on the lakeshore are visible through their expression of certain cultural phenomena. Muslims spoke Swahili, preferred rice over other staples, wore imported cotton cloth (especially *merikani* and often in the style of a *kanzu*), and carried a gun.[33] Many also lived in square or rectangular *tembes* with *barazas*, and some claimed coastal origins despite being born in the interior.[34] Many non-Muslims shared these cultural forms, especially in terms of a widespread desire for imported cloths and

---

[27] RMCA ESA HA.01.017-7. Storms, 'Rapport sur un voyage dans la partie sud de Tanganyika', 1 Apr. 1884.

[28] See also: McDow, *Buying Time*, 93–7.

[29] A.G.M.Afr. C.16-73. Guillet to White Fathers, 20 Aug. 1881; A.G.M.Afr. Diaire de Kibanga, 16 Oct. 1888; CWM/LMS/06/02/014 Jones to Thompson, 23 Jan. 1889; CWM/LMS/06/02/015 Swann to Thompson, 13 Mar. 1890.

[30] CWM/LMS/06/02/007 Griffith to Thompson, 13 Mar. 1882.

[31] See: Chapter 6, but also: A.G.M.Afr. C.16-7. Journal du P. Deniaud, 14 Jan. 1880; Becker, *Vie en Afrique*, II, 45–6; Coulbois, *Dix années*, 64; Jacques and Storms, *Notes sur l'ethnographie*, 66–7.

[32] CWM/LMS/06/02/004 Hore to Mullens, 156 Apr. 1879; ZNA AA1-23 Hore to Kirk, 14 Apr. 1879.

[33] Bennett, *Arab versus European*, 10; Bimangu and Tshibangu, 'Contribution à l'histoire', 228; Iliffe, *A Modern History*, 78; Northrup, *Beyond the Bend*, 24; Page, 'Manyema hordes', 76–7; Roberts, *A Dance of Assassins*, 16; Rockel, 'Slavery and freedom', 88.

[34] For square houses, see: Chapter 1. For claims of coastal origins, see: RMCA ESA HA.01.017-7. Storms, 'Zanzibar', n.d.; Storms, 'Les wagoina', n.d.

guns and of speaking Swahili in caravans, but the coalescence of all these features within one person was synonymous with being Muslim and of *ngwana* status in much of the East African interior.[35] In this sense, conversion to Islam was part of a broader process of cultural and material exchange between coastal and interior populations.

The oral record further emphasises the importance of Islam in these exchanges. According to my informants in Ujiji, Islam appeared on the shores of Lake Tanganyika with the arrival of the first coastal traders.[36] Some reported additionally that a few people from Manyema were Muslim before they got to Ujiji (a reflection of coastal trader influence in Manyema itself), but that Islam was more entrenched in Ujiji at this time and that Ujiji was where most conversions of Manyema people took place.[37] Most Islamic learning occurred in the domestic sphere.[38] This was no doubt partly a symptom of there being no mosque constructed in Ujiji (or any other lakeshore region for that matter) until at least the mid-1880s, but likely later.[39] Informants emphasised a high degree of respect and closeness between coastal traders and Manyema, with marriage between male coastal traders and female Manyema often underpinning their relationships.[40] In using these terms, informants challenged prevailing conceptions of 'slavery' in popular Western discourse. Rather than treating those they held in bondage with brutality or coercion, they

---

[35] Abel, *Les Musulmans Noirs*, 9.

[36] Interview with Rashidi Hamisi bin Kasa, 12 Nov. 2013; Interview with Zuberi Shabani Aburula, 12 Nov. 2013.

[37] Interview with Rashidi Juma Hei al-Reith, 12 Nov. 2013; Interview with Selimani Kadudu Musa, 13 Nov. 2013; Interview with Zuberi Zindano Kalema, 13 Nov. 2013. See also: Northrup, *Beyond the Bend*, 24; Page, 'Manyema hordes', 74. If a West/North African case study is used as a precedent, it might be argued that some conversions may have taken place 'on the road' between Manyema and Ujiji as well. See: John Hunwick, 'The religious practices of black slaves in the Mediterranean Islamic world', in *Slavery on the Frontiers*, ed. Lovejoy, 150.

[38] Interview with Rashidi Hamisi bin Kasa, 12 Nov. 2013; Interview with Fatima Binti Mansour bin Nassour, 12 Nov. 2013.

[39] A.G.M.Afr. Augier to White Fathers, 16 Apr. 1879, *Chronique Trimestrielles*, 5 (Jan. 1880); CWM/LMS/06/02/006 Hutley, 'Mahommadanism in Central Africa: Its professors', Aug. 1881. Both these sources state categorically that there was no mosque in Ujiji at the time of writing. It is thought likely that missionaries would have reported on the construction of mosques in their vicinity at a later date, as their peers in other East African settings did. See also: Sperling, 'The coastal hinterland', 289.

[40] Interview with Rashidi Hamisi bin Kasa, 12 Nov. 2013; Interview with Branbati Ali Kiola and Isa Pama Kiola, 12 Nov. 2013; Interview with Fatima Binti Mansour bin Nassour, 12 Nov. 2013; Interview with Saidi Hamisi Kunga, 11 Nov. 2013; Interview with Selimani Kadudu Musa, 13 Nov. 2013; Interview with Hamisi Ali Juma al-Hey, 14 Nov. 2013. See also: Abel, *Les Musulmans Noirs*, 9.

argued that the coastal traders came in 'peace'.[41] In this context, Manyema populations did not simply convert to Islam because they were taught about it – rather, they converted of their own accord because of their perceptions of the coastal traders' 'character'.[42] For one informant, the whole region (including Uhehe, Unyamwezi, and Buganda) became Islamised through this process of respectful interaction between coastal traders and interior populations.[43] This is an overstatement of Islamic influence and it underestimates the violence associated with initial enslavement – especially in rural areas – but it does point to the importance of Islam in Ujiji's collective memory of the pre-colonial period.

Recognition of the oral record and scholarship from the wider IOW necessitates modifying some aspects of nineteenth-century East Africa's historiography and a rereading of the archive. First, the idea of semi- or part-Islamisation does not hold water for understanding the conversion of *ngwana* bondsmen. Islam was a key feature of the encounter between coastal traders and Manyema populations, not an unfinished or partially established concern. Second, informants stressed new converts' agency in the conversion process. This is opposed to the view that Islam had to be purposefully spread by traders or proselytisers. This perspective has also been explored in Becker's analysis of south-eastern German East Africa. In her study, agency was partially established through interior Africans acquiring knowledge of Islam and converting their peers.[44] Similar patterns may have existed around nineteenth-century Lake Tanganyika. One informant argued that the first Muslims in Rumonge were 'Congolese' – thus from Manyema – and they made efforts to convert their Rundi associates to Islam.[45] Additionally, nineteenth-century missionaries frequently lamented the influence of the coastal traders' followers, who they believed prevented them from converting others to Christianity.[46] In an extract that is characteristic of the missionaries' general attitude, D. Picton Jones of the LMS in Uguha wrote in 1884:

---

[41] Interview with Raphael Ntangibingura, 5 Nov. 2013; Interview with Rashidi Hamisi bin Kasa, 12 Nov. 2013; Interview with Rashidi Juma Hei al-Reith, 12 Nov. 2013.

[42] Interview with Saidi Hamisi Kunga, 11 Nov. 2013; Interview with Hamisi Ali Juma al-Hey, 14 Nov. 2013.

[43] Interview with Saidi Hamisi Kunga, 11 Nov. 2013.

[44] Becker, 'Commoners', 227–49.   [45] Interview with Daniel Rucintingo, 7 Nov. 2013.

[46] A.G.M.Afr. Randabel to White Fathers, 26 July 1883, *Chronique Trimestrielles*, 21–2 (Apr. 1884). CWM/LMS/06/02/007 Griffith to Thompson 13 Mar. 1882; CWM/LMS/06/02/010 Harris to Thompson, 15 Mar. 1885; CWM/LMS/06/02/012 Jones to Thompson, 14 Nov. 1887.

The introduction of the slave trade into a country is the introduction of a moral poison. ... It is a remarkable fact that these Zanzibar men have had far more influence over the natives than we have ever had – in many little things they imitate them, they follow their customs, adopt their ideas, imitate their dress, sing their songs, and it was with great difficulty I could get those of the Baguha [*sic*] on the station to speak their own language. I can only account for this by the fact that the Wangwana [*sic*] live amongst them in a simple manner like themselves, intermarry with them, and to some extent partake of their notions.[47]

Given the demographics of the coastal traders' labour recruitment at the time of writing, many of the 'Zanzibar men' or 'Wangwana' that Jones referred to were likely from Manyema and elsewhere in the interior. It is unlikely that missionaries were able distinguish people from the coast and the interior with the same cultural features, particularly given that many *ngwana* who originated in the interior claimed origins on East Africa's Indian Ocean littoral. Jones does not mention Islam explicitly in this cultural encounter. However, a critical approach to missionary under-standings of slavery and Islam coupled with an appreciation of the oral record indicates that it was an integral feature.[48]

Practising Islam on Lake Tanganyika's Nineteenth-century Shores

This analysis of Islamic practice on the shores of nineteenth-century Lake Tanganyika begins with a search for some of the orthodox tenets of Islam in the archive. These include circumcision, dietary restrictions, and adherence to the five pillars of Islam (declaration of the faith (*sha-hada*), prayer (*salah*), alms giving (*zakat*), fasting (*sawm*) and pilgrimage (*Hajj*)). The uneven response to these orthodox phenomena meant that academic Islamists may have doubted the extent of the new converts' faith if they ever came into contact with them. However, in the absence of such academics on Lake Tanganyika's shores, strict conformity was not required. This is in common with nineteenth-century Buganda, where lack of circumcision did not prevent conversion; with south-eastern German East Africa, where 'oral embroidering' in a mostly illiterate society replaced or heavily supplemented direct references to Islamic scripture; and with numerous other IOW regions where Islam has been adapted to pre-existing cultural contexts.[49] Islam had adaptive qualities

---

[47] CWM/LMS/06/02/009 Jones to Thompson, 2 Dec. 1884. See also: CWM/LMS/06/02/009 Jones to Thompson, 24 June 1884.

[48] Abel, *Les Musulmans Noirs*, 10–16.

[49] Oded, *Islam in Uganda*, 77–80; Becker, 'Commoners', 246; Prange, *Monsoon Islam*, 3; Ricklefs, 'Rediscovering Islam', 397–418.

on Lake Tanganyika's nineteenth-century shores – qualities that both new converts claiming *ngwana* status and coastal traders helped to shape. Furthermore, new converts augmented perceptions of their spiritual capabilities by interacting with ongoing spiritual and material frameworks centred on Lake Tanganyika's shores, but which were also influenced by perceptions and understandings of Islamic society on East Africa's Indian Ocean littoral. New converts' understandings of Islam were rooted in their comprehension of ostensibly coastal objects and beliefs in the context of their interactions with Lake Tanganyika's distinctive physical and cultural environment.

The clearest expressions of Islamic orthodoxy among new converts were circumcision and dietary restrictions. Circumcision appears to have been at the heart of the conversion process. According to Walter Hutley of the LMS, '[t]here were many of these slaves [of the coastal traders] circumcised, which they deem quite sufficient to convert a man from being an *mshenzi* [*sic*] or pagan into an *mgwana* [*sic*], which is the generalised term [in the interior] for Islamised native'.[50] From the point of circumcision onwards, the coastal traders' followers were known to eat only *halal* meat and to slaughter animals in the Islamic fashion.[51] The prominence of circumcision in this context offers a divergence from the Nyamwezi and Ganda, among whom it was rare.[52] The relative lack of circumcisions among Muslims in Buganda is likely attributable to pre-existing customs that 'abhorred any mutilation of the body'.[53] It is notable, then, that circumcision was customary among many people in the present-day eastern DRC, including among Manyema populations, before the arrival of Muslims.[54] This suggests a compatibility between pre-Islamic and Islamic customs that shaped the rites of conversion in the vicinity of Lake Tanganyika.[55] Furthermore, although David Livingstone wrote in his diary in 1866 that coastal traders sometimes

---

[50] CWM/LMS/06/02/006 Hutley, 'Mahommadanism in Central Africa: Its influence', Aug. 1881.

[51] Livingstone, *Last Journals*, 224; CWM/LMS/06/02/006 Hutley, 'Mahommadanism in Central Africa: Its influence', Aug. 1881; Jacques and Storms, *Notes sur l'ethnographie*, 66.

[52] Cameron, *Across Africa*, 116–17; Stanley, *Dark Continent*, I, 253 and II, 89, 157.

[53] Oded, *Islam in Uganda*, 77; Earle, *Colonial Buganda*, 147–8.

[54] Livingstone, *Last Journals*, 305; Stanley, *Dark Continent*, II, 89; A.G.M.Afr. Diaire de Massanze, 5 Sep. 1882; R. P. Colle, *Les Baluba*, Vol. I (Brussels: Institut Internationale de Bibliographie, 1913), 273–7.

[55] Similar patterns may have influenced the encounter between coastal Muslims and future Yao converts near to Lake Malawi's shores during this period. See: Augustine W. C. Msiska, 'The spread of Islam in Malawi and its impact on Yao rites of passage, 1870–1960', *The Society of Malawi Journal*, 48, 1 (1995), 73. For West/North Africa, John Hunwick argues that Muslim enslavers preferred those they enslaved to be

took their slaves (that is to say: bondsmen) to be circumcised at the coast, making this journey for this purpose was probably not universal, especially as the coastal traders' followings grew in size and they headed deeper into the interior during the 1870s and 1880s.[56]

Despite circumcision being a marker of conversion, declarations of faith (*shahada*: the first pillar of Islam) by new Muslim converts are largely absent in the archive. However, this is likely more a symptom of the archive's authorship than due to the absence of converts on Lake Tanganyika's shores. The absence of a mosque in the region meant that ceremonies marking circumcision and conversion took place in the domestic rather than the public sphere. European 'explorers' and missionaries were rarely welcomed into these zones. On the occasions when they were, it was usually for discussing the terms of their presence or their ongoing travel. Only on rare occasions were missionaries able to ascertain a process of conversion within a coastal trader's following. Griffith's aforementioned reference to enslaved people 'repeating their devotions' in a process that gave them opportunities for freedom is one of the few examples.[57] Additionally, in 1881, Hutley wrote of a 'slave-boy' from Manyema who 'taught himself to read and write'.[58] His coastal trader enslaver (or patron) then taught him more and allowed him to be circumcised and to convert to Islam.[59] In this process, the 'slave-boy' was seen to have transitioned from being a *shenzi* to an *ngwana*, at least in the context of the interior.[60] Although not referring to declarations of faith explicitly, these extracts point to an environment in which such declarations would have taken place.

The absence of discussion in European-authored writings about the coastal traders' domestic sphere means that women's conversions to Islam were even more hidden than those of men. As discussed in Chapters 2 and 6, women – whether enslaved, in a looser form of bondage, or free – were primarily domestic or agricultural workers. Missionaries tended to only comment on women's lives when women left these roles and entered the public sphere. On the lakeshore, this usually only occurred in cases of neglect on the coastal traders' part.

---

circumcised, even if they were not yet Muslim. See: Hunwick, 'The religious practices', 149, 151.

[56] Livingstone, *Last Journals*, 37.

[57] See earlier, in addition to: CWM/LMS/06/02/007 Griffith to Thompson, 13 Mar. 1882.

[58] CWM/LMS/065/02/006 Hutley, 'Mahommadanism in Central Africa: Its influence', Aug. 1881. See also: CWM/LMS/06/02/005 Hutley to Whitehouse, 12 Aug. 1880.

[59] CWM/LMS/06/02/006 Hutley, 'Mahommadanism in Central Africa: Its influence', Aug. 1881.

[60] See also: Glassman, *Feasts and Riot*, 117–20.

Thus, reading 'along the archival grain' gives the impression of a harsh and brutalised condition for all women on the lakeshore.[61] In reality, the lives of women in the domestic sphere likely varied depending on a range of factors. This assumption is supported by the oral record, in which women's role is remembered in terms of domesticity, Islamic study, and marriage rather than brutality.[62] Marriage was particularly important to coastal traders because they were exclusively male and because women from the coast did not enter the interior.[63] From a female perspective, and using Marcia Wright's *Strategies of Slaves* as a precedent, marriage to a coastal trader may have been welcomed, as it meant protection from the region's violence.[64] Conversion to Islam was likely expected in this context, and women may have gained 'free dependent' or another form of improved status upon giving birth to a child of their enslaver/patron's kin.[65] These examples and the collective memories of my informants from Ujiji suggest, therefore, that the experiences of brutalised women in Ujiji referred to in the archive were atypical. Women likely converted to Islam in a hidden, domestic arena as part of a process that incorporated them into coastal traders' households.[66]

There is evidence that some of the coastal traders' bonds(wo)men prayed (*salah*; the second pillar of Islam) and fasted (*sawm*; the fourth pillar) according to orthodox Islamic doctrine. Many European 'explorers' and missionaries were sceptical of interior people's ability to pray in the Islamic fashion. Both Livingstone and Hutley claimed that Islamic prayer was rare or non-existent among the Jiji and the coastal traders' followers.[67] However, Jérôme Becker of the AIA noted that the coastal traders' followers recited the *Fātihat al-kitāb* (the opening verse of the opening *surah* (chapter) of the Qu'ran) twice per day. They did so, he wrote, 'with faces turned in the direction of Mecca and hands crossed on the stomach or hanging [by their sides]. Then, they [rose] their arms to the heavens, pass[ed] their hands over their eyes and end[ed] by

---

[61] Hutley, *Central African Diaries*, 106; Médard, 'La traite et esclavage', 47.

[62] Interview with Fatima Binti Mansour bin Nassour, 12 Nov. 2013; Interview with Selimani Kadudu Musa, 13 Nov. 2013; Interview with Saidi Hamisi Kunga, 11 Nov. 2013.

[63] Interview with Rashidi Juma Hei al-Reith, 12 Nov. 2013; Interview with Selimani Kadudu Musa, 13 Nov. 2013.

[64] Wright, *Strategies of Slaves*, 26–8, 47–9.

[65] Wright, *Strategies of Slaves*, 37, 100; Lovejoy, *Transformations*, 14, 34; McDow, *Buying Time*, 152.

[66] For another case study that emphasizes the importance of the domestic sphere in Islamic history, see: Hunwick, 'The religious practices', 149–71.

[67] CWM/LMS/065/02/006 Hutley, 'Mahommadanism in Central Africa: Its influence', Aug. 1881; Livingstone, *Last Journals*, 223–4.

prostrating themselves, their elbows and forehead touching the ground'.[68] Hutley's and Livingstone's overlooking of such examples means that they could have been rare. However, they may also have simply not recognised interior Africans' prayer as 'Islamic'. Becker himself was sceptical of interior Africans' capacity to convert to Islam. He claimed that 'slaves' prayed because they were obliged to do so by coastal traders, and that they did not yet understand the act even if they 'wanted' to convert.[69] Such statements were rooted in highly racialised frameworks that were demeaning of Africans' mental capacities.[70] For at least some of the coastal traders' *ngwana* bonds(wo)men, prayer was likely a key act of their Islamic faith.

Further evidence for some newly converted bonds(wo)men's adherence to the second pillar of Islam comes from accounts of caravan journeys. Hutley noted that coastal traders prayed only three times per day while travelling.[71] This likely represented the customary practice of *jam'*, in which the second and third (*Zuhr* and *'Asr*) and the fourth and fifth (*Maghrib* and *'Isha*) prayers of the day are combined. How and if coastal traders' bonds(wo)men from the interior participated in prayers 'on the road' is not entirely clear from the sources. Tippu Tip mentioned in his autobiography that he prayed with his associates on journeys in interior regions, but neither the Swahili nor the translations make it clear who these associates included.[72] They could conceivably have just been coastal traders, even if, given Becker's account, this seems unlikely.[73] Also, the practising of *jam'* shows how the functioning of the caravan was affected by the Islamic prayer schedule and vice versa. As Rockel argues, caravans were sites of cultural exchange, and Islam was a feature of this broader process.[74] Crucially, populations from the interior were active agents in this cultural exchange. Thus, breaks in the journey to pray for coastal traders were likely interpreted by at least some newly converted bonds(wo)men as breaks to pray for them as well.

There is also evidence that some bonds(wo)men observed *Ramadān*, though Richard Burton was the only European 'explorer' to refer directly to interior populations of present-day Central Tanzania fasting.[75] Some primary sources referred to large-scale participation in festivals marking the beginning and end (*Eid*) of *Ramadān*, possibly by Muslims and

---

[68] Becker, *Vie en Afrique*, II, 310. [69] Becker, *Vie en Afrique*, II, 309.
[70] For a comparison with Buganda, see: Earle, *Colonial Buganda*, 144–5.
[71] CWM/LMS/065/02/006 Hutley, 'Mahommadanism in Central Africa: Its professors', Aug. 1881.
[72] Murjebi, *L'autobiographie*, 71, 118, 119. [73] Becker, *Vie en Afrique*, II, 309–10.
[74] Rockel, *Carriers of Culture*, 98. [75] Burton, *Lake Regions*, 503.

non-Muslims alike.[76] There was thus a consciousness of *Ramadān*'s importance, even if the meanings of the fast may not have been apparent to all festival participants. Also, both *Ramadān* and *Eid* had the capacity to affect the formation and travel of caravans. Livingstone noted that his travel was interrupted until *Eid* was over in Manyema in 1871, and Becker observed that a doctor who treated him in Tabora and then returned to the coast the day after *Ramadān* 'would benefit from the end of the fast'.[77] Becker did not make clear what these benefits were, but it is notable that the caravan in question was composed primarily of people from the interior.[78] This could imply that some porters of interior origin were more willing and available once their fast was over. Furthermore, 'explorer' and missionary references to Muslim bondsmen's demand for *halal* meat show the importance of diet in the latter's faith, which may have extended to further dietary restrictions during *Ramadān*.[79] Finally, many Ganda populations (including *kabaka* Mutesa I in 1867–75) observed *Ramadān* after the first conversions were made in the 1860s, as did some Nyamwezi chiefs in the early 1880s.[80] *Ramadān* was clearly important to both coastal traders and new converts in the chiefly classes; evidence suggests it may also have been important to at least some of the coastal traders' bonds(wo)men.

Overall, then, the evidence for the coastal traders' *ngwana* bondsmen practising some of the core aspects of Islamic orthodoxy is patchy. This is partly a symptom of the sources themselves, given that the Europeans who authored most of them failed to acknowledge Islam as important to people who they labelled as slaves. However, it is also a result of the uneven adherence to orthodox Islamic practices among new converts. Although there is evidence that some among them prayed and observed *Ramadān*, many likely did not. No evidence has been found that any *ngwana* bonds(wo)men adhered to the third (*zakat*; charity/alms giving) or fifth (the *Hajj*; pilgrimage to Mecca) pillars of Islam. Thus, by academic Islamist standards, the new converts' commitment to the faith was probably doubtful. Indeed, when *ngwana* bonds(wo)men visited the coast, they often found that their claims of being Muslim were dismissed

---

[76] Livingstone, *Last Journals*, 354; Becker, *Vie en Afrique*, II, 259; Murjebi, *L'autobiographie*, 118. See also: McCurdy, 'Transforming associations', 90, 257, 321.

[77] Becker, *Vie en Afrique*, II, 18; Livingstone, *Last Journals*, 354.

[78] Becker, *Vie en Afrique*, I, 463, and II, 18.

[79] Livingstone, *Last Journals*, 224; CWM/LMS/065/02/006 Hutley, 'Mahommadanism in Central Africa: Its influence', Aug. 1881; Jacques and Storms, *Notes sur l'ethnographie*, 66.

[80] Iliffe, *A Modern History*, 78–9; Oded, *Islam in Uganda*, 66–7; Pallaver, 'Muslim communities', 7.

by the coastal elites, although this was more a symptom of perceptions of their interior/*shenzi* origins and their status as bonds(wo)men than it was about the ways they practised Islam.[81] However, such standards were not set in the interior. As Oded argued, the decision of *kabaka* Mutesa I of Buganda to not be circumcised was 'tolerated' by coastal traders, and there is no evidence that they publicly refused to consider him a Muslim.[82] Oded's reasoning stemmed from the coastal traders' prioritisation of commerce over proselytisation.[83] A similar point could be made about the coastal traders' attitudes to their bonds(wo)men's conversion. The necessity of assimilating specialised, trustworthy, and 'respectable' labourers who could act as boatmen, soldiers, and proxy traders, as well as their needs to expand their kin among bondswomen, would have trumped any scruples they may have had about such people's lack of adherence to Islamic orthodoxy.

Further reasons for the coastal traders to respect the nature of their *ngwana* bonds(wo)men's conversion come from their own Islamic practices. This can partly be established by an examination of Islamic practice on East Africa's Indian Ocean littoral, which was heavily intertwined with beliefs in nature spirits, ritual healing, and spirit possession.[84] Islam on the East African coast and islands has had 'popular' and 'heterodox' elements since its arrival in the eighth century.[85] However, coastal traders made further adaptations to Islamic practice in the interior. For example, they did not construct a mosque in any part of present-day west-central Tanzania, Urundi, northern Zambia, or the eastern DRC.[86] This meant that the key piece of infrastructure was not in place for them to follow the third pillar of Islam. They instead used the *barazas* (verandas) of their *tembes* (houses) as the venue for their prayers, a practice which further illustrates that the domestic environment was key to Islamic practice on the shores of Lake Tanganyika.[87] Additionally, it is unlikely that many of the coastal traders went on the *Hajj*. Missionaries painted a picture of fixed residence in the interior for most coastal traders, with them only returning to the coast or Zanzibar once every

---

[81] Glassman, *Feasts and Riot*, 134.   [82] Oded, *Islam in Uganda*, 79.

[83] Oded, *Islam in Uganda*, 79.

[84] See for example: Chapter 3; Alpers, 'Ordinary household chores', 690; Brown, 'Bagamoyo', 79–80; Glassman, *Feasts and Riot*, 71, 77.

[85] Pouwels, 'The East African coast', 251–71.

[86] A.G.M.Afr. Augier to White Fathers, 16 Apr. 1879, *Chronique Trimestrielles*, 5 (Jan. 1880); CWM/LMS/065/02/006 Hutley, 'Mahommadanism in Central Africa: Its professors', Aug. 1881; Sperling, 'The coastal hinterland', 289.

[87] Vyncke, *Brieven van een vlaamschen*, II, 229.

five or six years to settle their debts.[88] In nineteenth-century East Africa, the *Hajj* appears to have been reserved for permanent residents of the coast and its islands.[89] Also, the leading member of Ujiji's coastal trader community in c.1875–85, Mwinyi Kheri, was illiterate.[90] Although some of his subordinates could read, this potentially shows a lack of knowledge of Islamic texts at the core of Ujiji's Muslim leadership. Coastal traders necessarily adapted their Islamic practices to interior contexts, and this led them further from Islamic orthodoxy.[91]

Given coastal traders' and *ngwana* bonds(wo)men's uneven adherence to some core Islamic practices, there is a need to question exactly how such people demonstrated their Islamic faith. The answers here lie in how they interacted with each other within the lakeshore environment and in their understandings of Islamic society on East Africa's coast and islands. In the latter region, Muslims lived in square or rectangular houses, ate rice as a staple, engaged with oceanic spirits, and wore imported cotton cloths. Thus, Muslims – coastal traders and new converts alike – sought to do likewise on Lake Tanganyika's shores as a demonstration of their Islamic faith and of their connections to coastal Islamic society. This, of course, did not mean an exact replication of cultural forms emanating from the Indian Ocean littoral. Rather, it meant their adaptation – for example, by using wattle and daub rather than stone to build houses; by repurposing *barazas* to be sites of prayer in addition to being sites of commercial and social exchange; by growing rice in one-season rather than two-season cycles; by interacting with lacustrine spirits in ways that were cogent with how coastal Muslims interacted with spirits in the Indian Ocean; and by reimagining *merikani* cloth as an item of prestige instead of as an item symbolising enslavement. Ownership of guns, as coastal traders and their followers demonstrated as they entered the interior, was also key. For many, 'being' or 'becoming' Muslim was partly about making cultural connections with East Africa's Indian Ocean littoral. New converts from the interior who claimed coastal origins as they also claimed *ngwana* status reinforced these connections.

At this point, it is worth re-emphasising bonds(wo)men's important role as new converts in this process. This is possibly clearest when discussing their role in interactions with spirits they believed inhabited Lake Tanganyika, discussed in depth in Chapter 3. By the late 1870s or

---

[88] CWM/LMS/065/02/006 Hutley, 'Mahommadanism in Central Africa: Its professors', Aug. 1881; McDow, *Buying Time*, 90–2.

[89] Becker, *Vie en Afrique*, II, 463. See also: Pouwels, 'The East African coast', 262.

[90] Bennett, 'Mwinyi Kheri', 151.   [91] See also: Abel, *Les Musulmans Noirs*, 37–8.

early 1880s, and according to missionary sources, it was people who referred to themselves as *ngwana*, not pre-existing lakeshore populations, who were the key actors who engaged with lacustrine spirits.[92] In referring to the spirits as *zimu*, in making offerings of imported global commodities, and in manning craft with *oculi* painted on them, they engaged with lacustrine spirits in ways that were cogent with how coastal Muslims engaged with spirits that they believed to inhabit the Indian Ocean. Many of the *ngwana* referred to by the missionaries in this context were, of course, the coastal traders' bondsmen. To illustrate the point, reporting on his visit to the lakeshore in 1876, Henry Morton Stanley wrote: 'The Arabs' slaves ... spread such reports of ... hobgoblins, fiery meteors, [and] terrible spirits, such as Kabogo, Katavi, Kateyé, Wanpembé, that the teeth of the Wanyamwezi [*sic*] and Wangwana [*sic*] chattered with fright'.[93] Here, those Stanley referred to as 'Wangwana' were free or emancipated men from East Africa's coast and islands who travelled with him inland; those he referred to as 'Arabs' slaves' were the coastal traders' bondsmen living on the lakeshore, who mostly came from Manyema. Like most of his contemporaries, he failed to comprehend the ways in which the coastal traders' bonds(wo)men navigated the conditions of their bondage and were able to claim 'freeborn' status with them; that is, most of those he described as slaves in this extract probably did not have 'slave status'. Nevertheless, this quotation and those addressed in Chapter 3 make the point clear: bondsmen, in taking a leading role in appeasing lacustrine spirits and in acculturating coastal influences to do so, were at the core of shaping Islamic belief and practice on Lake Tanganyika's shores.

Centring bonds(wo)men in this history of Islam allows for the creation of a rough timeline of Islamic conversion around Lake Tanganyika. Although the first Muslims to arrive on the lakeshore probably did so in the 1830s, significant numbers of conversions among interior populations probably did not take place until the 1860s, after coastal traders began settling in Ujiji. The first new converts were almost certainly of Manyema rather than Jiji origin. While the former were often enslaved by or bonded to the Muslim coastal traders from this time, the latter largely were not so at this stage, being confined instead to a different form of bondage to their respective *teko*.[94] It was only from the mid-1870s and especially during the 1880s that conversion by lakeshore populations became more widespread. This process coincided with the coastal

---

[92] A.G.M.Afr. Diaire de Massanze, 17 Oct. 1882; Léchaptois, *Aux rives du Tanganika*, 172; RMCA ESA HA.01.017-7. Storms, 'Resistance des marcheurs en caravan' n.d.
[93] Stanley, *Dark Continent*, II, 67.   [94] See: Chapter 6.

traders' commercial and military expansion around the lake and the consequential growth of several port towns, for which they were reliant on the labour of their *ngwana* bondsmen. These latter people were the primary actors who spread adapted versions of coastal cultural forms, including those related to architecture, diet, dress, language, and religion, to other lakeshore regions and populations. Their cultural influence and their residence in every lakeshore region during the 1880s show the geographically widespread nature of the Islamic faith at this time. Trade and religion linked peoples and networks across the entirety of the lake. For a brief moment towards the end of the nineteenth century, Lake Tanganyika appeared as an 'Islamic Sea', in common with much of the wider IOW over the *longue durée*.[95]

Conclusion

As in Chapter 6, this chapter shows that, with a combination of oral testimony and reference to frameworks established in studies of other regions of the IOW, a major contestation of the archive's trajectory is possible. The European-authored primary documents are particularly problematic for unpicking a history of Islam in nineteenth-century East Africa when they are used without the context of other primary and secondary sources. Nineteenth-century Europeans were largely uninterested in Islam, and they misunderstood the multiple ways it can be interpreted and practised, particularly by new converts. They also obscured the history of Islam through their preoccupations with documenting examples of slavery, which, if taken at face value, would disqualify most people that this chapter identifies as new converts from being Muslim according to Islamic law. However, read alongside the aforementioned sources, there is significant evidence for widespread Islamic influence on the shores of nineteenth-century Lake Tanganyika. In claiming to be *ngwana*, not only did the coastal traders' bonds(wo)men claim 'freeborn' status, they also claimed an Islamic identity. Furthermore, in the absence of many of the orthodox markers of Islamic faith in the interior, such as mosques and opportunities to go on the *Hajj*, they and their coastal trader patrons adopted distinctly local ways of practising Islam. In this context, they adapted coastal cultural forms and beliefs in nature spirits to the lakeshore environment.

---

[95] Islam continued to spread and take on new influences in lakeshore regions during the early colonial period, but, from around this time, Christianity became similarly influential. For more on the early colonial spread of Islam, see: Castryck, 'Living Islam', 263–98; Nimtz, *Islam and Politics*.

Conversion to Islam was an integral feature of the coastal traders' encounter with lakeshore and other interior populations, especially those that became the former's bonds(wo)men.

Thinking about the history of Islam in these terms suggests that there are more nineteenth-century East African histories of Islam to be written. Some of the patterns described here have wider applicability. Bonds(wo)men's desire to cease being considered slaves and to acquire 'respectability' and *ngwana* status encouraged conversion to Islam, whether on the shores of Lake Tanganyika or elsewhere in the interior of East Africa. Thus, in Buganda and among the Yao, where Islam is already known to have had an impact from East Africanist studies published in the 1960s and 1970s, a re-evaluation may be in order that might stress the needs and motivations of individual converts over the importance of political structures for enacting conversion. Additionally, in Manyema, closer analysis of the 'semi-Islamized' or 'partly-Islamicized' populations that Page and Northrup respectively identified might bring up interesting dynamics in which new converts integrated Islam into their pre-existing belief systems, a process which, according to the argument of this chapter, would demarcate them as 'fully fledged' rather than 'nominal' Muslims. Nevertheless, the Lake Tanganyika case study is likely to stand out somewhat against these other potential examples. The lacustrine environment lent itself to the adaptation of Islamic beliefs and practices emanating from East Africa's Indian Ocean littoral, owing to the compatibility between mutual beliefs in oceanic and lacustrine spirits. If trade across oceanic space was crucial to the spread of Islam in the wider IOW from the seventh century, it was also crucial to its spread around Lake Tanganyika in the nineteenth century.

It is also important to reiterate that bonds(wo)men's conversions to Islam were not universally recognised. As well as the Europeans on whose documents much of this book relies, people living in East Africa's Indian Ocean littoral regions contested the validity of bonds(wo)men's conversion to Islam. Given new converts' origins in the interior and their conditions of bondage, according to coastal custom they could not be regarded as 'freeborn' Muslims. They thus saw their conversions as heterodox or even blasphemous.[96] Their views in this context barred new converts' entry to certain mosques and important festivals on East Africa's coast and islands. Perhaps this pattern further encouraged new converts to look for other inspirations to develop their Islamic faith, such as through appeasing Lake Tanganyika's spirits. In any case, the extent to which

---

[96] Glassman, *Feasts and Riot*, 134.

coastal and island Muslims' views vis-à-vis new converts' faith (or, in their eyes, lack thereof) was a function of new converts' specific religious beliefs and practices was probably limited. Islam, as practised on the East African coast and islands in the nineteenth century, had several 'heterodox' elements. Indeed, beliefs in the need to appease oceanic spirits, especially on maritime voyages, have much more in common with approaches to nature spirits (by Muslims and non-Muslims alike) in the East African interior than they do with Islamic orthodoxy. Coastal populations' attitudes towards new converts, therefore, were shaped by a perceived need to enforce social distinctions between people from the Indian Ocean–facing littoral and from the interior. As might be expected, continued resistance to new converts' claims of Islamic identity and freeborn status bred a great deal of tension over time. This book now turns to how this tension turned into outright hostility through an analysis of riots in coastal towns in 1888.

Epilogue
The Littoral and the Lake

In August–September 1888, riots broke out in several towns on East Africa's Indian Ocean littoral, including in Tanga, Pangani, Saadani, and Bagamoyo. They coincided with the carnival of the Solar New Year, that year's *Eid al-Hajj* celebrations, and the end of the caravan season. The towns were thus full of festival goers, bonds(wo)men, and upcountry porters – 'free' and unfree; Muslim and non-Muslim. There were multiple layers that underpinned the riots. They occurred during a period of significant and dramatic change in coastal society. German colonial officials were at the time attempting to co-opt and rule through the sultan of Zanzibar's *liwalis* (governors) on the coast; old Swahili elites had been becoming increasingly marginalised socially, politically, and economically by Omani influence; and bonds(wo)men and upcountry porters were questioning the routes to *ngwana*-dom and 'respectability'. Most Omanis and some of the wealthiest Swahilis initially sided with the rioters, scared that they would lose their position under the new German regime. Later, their allegiances changed. Some took the side of the Zanzibar sultan and the Germans. Others, under the leadership of Abushiri bin Salim al-Harthi, a prominent Omani plantation owner in Pangani, sought to carve out an Omani-Swahili state on the East African coast. Although divergent in approach, both these allegiance changes were borne out of one core issue that both coastal Omanis and Swahilis faced: the riotous crowd was filled with people they regarded as *shenzi* – bonds(wo)men and people of interior origin. They were unable to harness them to their ends, and they were scared of what they might do to undermine their prominent position in coastal society.

The history of the 1888 riots has been well known to East Africanist historians since the publication of Jonathon Glassman's *Feasts and Riot* in 1994.[1] Glassman's core contribution was to contest older understandings of the riots that argued that they developed principally as a form of

---

[1] Glassman, *Feasts and Riot*.

'primary resistance' to the onset of European colonial rule.[2] Instead, he argued that the 'rebellious consciousness' of the rioters was 'forged in the context of struggles that pre-dated [the German] arrival'.[3] These struggles were, principally, the struggles of bonds(wo)men and others of interior origin who had acculturated to coastal cultural forms, but whose access to respectability and full personhood on the coast were denied by Swahili and Omani elites. Even if some ceased being referred to as *shenzi*, few, despite converting to Islam, leaving conditions of enslavement (*tumwa*), and acquiring their own followings, were considered by the coastal elites as freeborn Muslims (*ngwana*). They were barred entry from certain mosques and several festivals that marked the 'freeborn' from non-freeborn, including within the carnival of the Solar New Year and the celebrations that marked *Eid al-Hajj*. Only after the Germans sought to squash the riots and the Abushiri Rebellion did they take on a somewhat anti-colonial character. When they did eventually crush them, in 1889–90, the Germans destroyed the structures that underpinned Omani and Swahili elites' power – politically, economically, and socially. Former Swahili elites, their bonds(wo)men, and upcountry porters all consequentially became subjects of German colonial rule.[4]

Very little has been written on the coastal riots since the publication of *Feasts and Riot*, such is the book's seminal nature. The only major more recent contribution has been that of Steven Fabian, who analysed the history of the riots and the Abushiri Rebellion specifically in the context of Bagamoyo.[5] With this study, Fabian argued that the riots and rebellions of coastal towns in 1888–90 were heavily tied to place and that each town's experience of the riots had a distinctive local character. He did so by unpicking the interests of different groups within the riotous crowd in Bagamoyo and by contextualising their contribution through their various attachments to the town itself. This obviously implicated Swahilis and Omanis, but it also involved Indians and Baluchis from across the western IOW; Shomvi, Zaramo, and Nyamwezi from within and around Bagamoyo, as well as further inland; and even Catholic Spiritan missionaries, who had been resident on the edge of the town since 1868, and whose station acted as a place of refuge from rebel and German attack.

---

[2] 'Primary resistance' is usually defined as resistance to colonial rule as the first colonial rulers arrived. This is opposed to 'secondary resistance', which was resistance to colonial rule after it was established.

[3] Glassman, *Feasts and Riot*, 11.   [4] Glassman, *Feasts and Riot*.

[5] Fabian, *Making Identity*, 175–210. This was originally published as: Steven Fabian, 'Locating the local in the coastal rebellion of 1888–90', *Journal of Eastern African Studies*, 7, 3 (2013), 432–49.

The attachments that such peoples had to Bagamoyo, he argued, were different to those of similar and different origins in other coastal towns, and this indelibly shaped the nature of each respective town's riots. Fabian's points are well taken. The factors underpinning the riots took somewhat distinct forms in each town, even if there were prevailing themes that bound them together – as Glassman established. But there is another way to interpret the outbreak of the riots in 1888 as well. Rather than analysing the 'local', one can take a much more macro approach. Using this approach necessitates putting the riots' history in conversation with the history of places in East Africa's deep interior, especially Lake Tanganyika.

What follows here, then, is an attempt to place the history of Lake Tanganyika, as described in this book, in a wider context, linking it directly to dramatic changes on the East African coast in the late 1880s. Doing so builds on the conceptual foundation of the book, as described in the Introduction – that is, the idea of Lake Tanganyika representing a frontier region of the IOW. In the classic texts on frontiers, scholars sought to examine how encounters on the frontier affected the core regions from which these frontiers emerged. For example, Frederick Jackson Turner argued that conditions on the American frontier contributed to the creation of a distinctive political culture in colonial metropoles on the USA's eastern seaboard; and Igor Kopytoff argued that frontier societies in Africa prefigured metropoles, which then challenged the metropole from which the original frontier came.[6] In short, these analyses promote centring frontier regions in understandings of core regions. Building on these themes, Richard Reid argued that frontiers in the history of north-eastern Africa over the last 200 years 'have defined the very nature of [the region's] states and societies'.[7] The extent to which this argument can be extrapolated to the Great Lakes' relationship with the wider IOW may be limited. It is probably not reasonable to suggest that the IOW can be 'defined' by distant inland regions. Yet, in building broadly on this framework, these scholars' works suggest that conditions on the IOW's frontiers (its inland regions) are intrinsic to understandings of its core (its littoral).

Thinking about the riots in coastal towns through this framework necessitates attempting to understand the composition and motivations of the riotous crowds. The European-authored sources written in coastal towns, according to Glassman, do not provide definitive answers here.

---

[6] Turner, 'The significance of the frontier', 188–227; Kopytoff, 'Internal African frontier', 16.
[7] Reid, *Frontiers of Violence*, 20.

Europeans referred to the rioters using 'vague labels, such as "young men" or "barbarians"'.[8] In short, they referred to them as *shenzi*. In their wide view of who constituted the *shenzi*, this body of people included any bonds(wo)man in coastal society and any 'visitor' to the coast from the mainland. Most either had interior origins or were directly descended from at least one parent who came from the interior. Such heritage often barred people from *ngwana* status on the coast, even if long-term residents of the coast might not have been considered by elites as *shenzi* or *tumwa* (slaves) in the fullest senses of these terms – they might instead have been *twana* (vassals, clients) or *suria* (concubines).[9] Such distinctions were largely lost on European observers, however, who generally regarded all as *shenzi*. What is key here, though, is the spatial distinction. By referring to the rioters as 'barbarians', European observers were not just noting the lack of respect with which they were held among elite coastal society; they were also attaching to them origins in, and attachments to, the East African interior. The timing of the riots is also instructive, occurring as they did at the end of the caravan season. Coastal towns at this time were filled with people who had just arrived from the interior.

Tracing the spatial origins and labels of many in the riotous crowd allows historians to think about their motivations. Based on the analysis of this book, many among them would almost certainly have referred to themselves as *ngwana*, and they would have been respected as such in interior contexts, such as around Lake Tanganyika. They may have experienced being enslaved for a short period of their lives, but they would have left this condition and entered looser forms of bondage having gained their (former) enslaver's trust and taken on labour roles other than agricultural work, such as porterage, soldiery, and proxy trading. As part of this process, many would have converted to Islam, and they would have demonstrated their faith through adherence to some of Islam's five pillars and by appeasing nature spirits in ways they considered Islamic. Many would also have worn cotton cloths (especially *merikani*), seen rice as the crucial staple of their diets, lived in square or rectangular houses with *barazas*, and owned a gun. Again, these were demonstrations of their Islamic faith, but they were also demonstrations of their attachment to coastal trader patrons and to coastal culture more broadly. Around Lake Tanganyika and elsewhere in the interior, such demonstrations would have marked them out as wealthy or prestigious members of society. By contrast, their interior origins, their history of being enslaved and/or in bondage, and their wearing of *merikani* cloth

---

[8] Glassman, *Feasts and Riot*, 7.   [9] Deutsch, *Emancipation without Abolition*, 65–74.

would have marked them out as servile and thus of lowlier social status on East Africa's Indian Ocean littoral. Consequently, coastal populations rejected their claims of freeborn Muslim status.

The conclusion to draw from this, then, is that the rioters were not just contesting coastal social hierarchies – they were also asserting the validity of an identity loosely based on coastal cultural norms that was forged in the interior. Again, the timing and nature of the riots reinforces this point. The social politics that prevented people who were denied *ngwana* status at the coast from fully participating in the festivals marking the Solar New Year and *Eid al-Hajj* would have contrasted with social politics pertaining to Islamic festivals in the interior. In the interior, coastal traders, new converts to Islam, and possibly even non-Muslims participated in such festivities.[10] By rioting at the coast, therefore, they were attempting to build on more inclusive precedents related to Islamic festivals that had been established in parts of the interior. Furthermore, guns became important tools and symbols for the riotous crowd. Caravan workers fired them off as they reached coastal towns in 'noisy celebration' of the end of their long and arduous journeys.[11] Their usage thereafter was probably less about forming a formidable, armed force as it was about demonstrating solidarity across the crowd and its people's power and respectability. This was borne out of the associations between guns and prestige that formed in the interior.

Returning to the history of Lake Tanganyika specifically, it is possible to postulate on how encounters on the lakeshore shaped the nature of the riotous crowd. Of course, the sources do not permit a precise estimate of the proportion of people in the caravans that arrived at the coast in August 1888 who had come from, visited, or traversed Lake Tanganyika, either in the preceding caravan season or in previous years. But it is probable that most had encountered it at some stage, as, by this time, it was a crucial intermediary region between the 'El Dorado' of the ivory trade in Manyema and littoral regions of the IOW. Additionally, if some had not been to Lake Tanganyika, then they would certainly have been aware of it and of happenings across its shores. They would have known about its distinctive lacustrine environment, of the emporia that faced onto the lake and of the challenges faced by those who sought to cross it. These features gave the appearance of an ocean almost at the centre of the African continent. They represented an environment in which cultural forms could be negotiated and reimagined in ways that were cogent with and rooted in patterns that pervaded cultural life on

[10] See: Chapter 7, but also: Oded, *Islam in Uganda*, 66.
[11] Glassman, *Feasts and Riot*, 4.

East Africa's Indian Ocean littoral. By the 1880s, people who encountered lakeshore towns encountered an urban, Islamic, maritime, and mercantile way of life, just as they did on the coast and in Zanzibar. On the lakeshore, this way of life was not just accessible to people already called *ngwana*. The enslaved and other bonds(wo)men could aspire to this status through material, cultural, and religious exchanges over time. During the riots in coastal towns in 1888, the rioters sought to make this way of life accessible to them on East Africa's Indian Ocean littoral as well.[12]

---

[12] Of course, the riots did not resolve formerly enslaved people's struggles for status in littoral societies. Several works have examined these ongoing struggles in the context of colonial rule. Of particular note is: Fair, *Pastimes and Politics*, 64–109. In line with some of the themes of this book, on the pages cited, Fair shows how former slaves navigated their social status – and sought to enhance it – partly through their dress styles.

Glossary

Word	Language	Singular	Plural	Definition
ami	Ha	*umwami*	*abami*	Central chief in the Ha kingdoms
baraza	Swahili	–	–	Veranda or front-facing courtyard of a house
barsati	Swahili	–	–	Highly valuable Indian-made blue cotton cloth with a broad red stripe; later versions may have been manufactured in Britain before being died in Kutchchh or Gujarat
dagaa	Great Lakes	–	–	Small whitebait-like fish found in north-eastern Lake Tanganyika
dawa	Swahili	–	–	Medicine, including that which was used to appease spirits
debwani	Swahili	–	–	Highly valuable Omani-made cotton cloth with small blue and white checks
dhow	Swahili and Arabic	–	–	Sailing boat; ubiquitous in the western Indian Ocean
doti	Swahili	–	–	Measurement of cloth equivalent to about 3.7 metres
eene	Fipa	*mweene*	*aeene*	Central chief of Ufipa
fundi	Swahili	–	*mafundi*	Artisan; often in some form of bondage
frasilah	Swahili	–	–	Unit of weight; around 16 kilograms
fundo	Swahili	–	–	A bunch of strings of beads (usually ten strings)
ganga	Swahili	*mganga*	*waganga*	Religious specialist; could be Muslim or non-Muslim
jakazi	Swahili	*mjakazi*	*wajakazi*	Female domestic 'slave' or maidservant
jini	Swahili	*jini*	*majini*	Nature spirit (Arabic root)
kabaka	Luganda	–	–	King of Buganda
kaniki	Swahili	–	–	Blue-dyed cotton cloth manufactured in north-western India where it was known as cannequim

(*cont.*)

Word	Language	Singular	Plural	Definition
khete	Swahili	–		A string of beads
leza	Fipa		*amaleza*	Nature spirit
liwali	Swahili	–	*maliwali*	Governor
masaro	Swahili	–	–	Single unit of *sofi* beads
masika	Swahili	–	–	The long rainy season in East Africa; March–May
matunda	Swahili	–	–	Hamburg-made glass bead; ring-shaped; dark blue or near white; sometimes referred to as *mzizima*
mbugu	Great Lakes	–	–	Barkcloth
merikani	Swahili	–	–	Unbleached cotton sheeting manufactured in the USA, where it was known as calico
mtama	Swahili	–	–	Sorghum or millet
mvuli	Swahili	–	–	The short rainy season in East Africa; October–November
ngulu	Tabwa	–	–	Nature spirit
ngwana	Swahili	*muungwana*	*waungwana*	Gentleman; freeborn Muslim
oculi	Latin	–	–	'Eyes' painted on Indian Ocean *dhows*
pagazi	Swahili	*mpagazi*	*wapagazi*	Porter; usually free-waged and of interior East African origin; most commonly from Unyamwezi
samisami	Swahili	–	–	Venetian-made glass bead; red with a white centre; varying sizes
shenzi	Swahili	*mshenzi*	*washenzi*	Barbarian; usually denoting servile status and/or origins in the interior of East Africa
shinga	Ha	*ishinga*	*amashinga*	Nature spirit
sigo	Ha	*ikisigo*	*ibisigo*	Nature spirit
sofi	Swahili and Great Lakes	–	–	Venetian-made glass bead; varying colours; 8–13 millimetres in length; known in their place of manufacture as *cannetone*
suria	Swahili	–	*masuria*	Concubine
teko	Ha	*umuteko*	*abateko*	Earth priest; district chief; used in the kingdom of Uha (including Ujiji) and in parts of Urundi

(*cont.*)

Word	Language	Singular	Plural	Definition
tembe	Swahili and Great Lakes	–	–	A rectangular, flat-roofed house lived in by coastal traders and their associates
tumwa	Swahili	*mtumwa*	*watumwa*	Literally, 'one who is used or is sent'; usually translated as 'slave'; *tumwa* had the fewest rights of all bonds(wo)men
twana	Swahili	*mtwana*	*watwana*	Male domestic 'slave'; vassal
tware	Ha	*umutware*	*abatware*	Regional chief; regional representative of the *ami* in the Ha kingdoms
ugali	Swahili	–	–	A stiff porridge made from pounded *mtama* or, later, maize
utani	Swahili and Great Lakes	–	–	'Joking' relationships commonly found in East African caravans
ustaraabu	Swahili			To become or be like an Arab
zimu	Swahili and Great Lakes	*mzimu* (Swahili)	*mizimu* (Swahili)	Nature spirit (Bantu root)

Bibliography

Archives

Archivio Generale dei Missionari d'Africa (A.G.M.Afr.): White Fathers' Archive, Rome, Italy.

Church Missionary Society (CMS): Birmingham, UK.

Council for World Missions/London Missionary Society (CWM/LMS): London, UK.

Royal Museum for Central Africa Emile Storms Archive (RMCA ESA): Tervuren, Belgium.

Royal Museum of Central Africa Henry Morton Stanley Archive (RMCA HMSA): Tervuren, Belgium.

UK National Archives, Royal Geographical Society (NA RGS): London, UK.

Zanzibar National Archives (ZNA): Zanzibar Town, Zanzibar, Tanzania.

Interviews

Interview with Remy Ngirye, Kajaga (Bujumbura), 4 Nov. 2013.

Interview with Georges Sindarubaza, Kajaga (Bujumbura), 4 Nov. 2013.

Interview with Victoire Ndaruzinza, Kajaga (Bujumbura), 4 Nov. 2013.

Interview with Raphael Ntangibingura, Kajiji (Bujumbura) 5 Nov. 2013.

Interview with Simeon Sindimwo and Venant Baragasirika, Kajiji (Bujumbura), 5 Nov. 2013.

Interview with Silas Bujana, Kajiji (Bujumbura), 5 Nov. 2013.

Interview with Georges Ntigarika, Kizuka, 7 Nov. 2013.

Interview with Daniel Rucintingo, Rumonge, 7 Nov. 2013.

Interview with Saidi Hamisi Kunga, Ujiji, 11 Nov. 2013.

Interview with Rashidi Hamisi bin Kasa, Ujiji, 12 Nov. 2013.

Interview with Fatima Binti Mansour bin Nassour, Ujiji, 12 Nov. 2013.

Interview with Zuberi Shabani Aburula, Ujiji, 12 Nov. 2013.

Interview with Branbati Ali Kiola & Isa Pama Kiola, Ujiji, 12 Nov. 2013.

Interview with Rashidi Juma Hei al-Reith, Ujiji, 12 Nov. 2013.

Interview with Selimani Kadudu Musa, Simbo, 13 Nov. 2013.
Interview with Zuberi Zindano Kalema, Simbo, 13 Nov. 2013.
Interview with Musa Isa Rubinga, Gungu, 14 Nov. 2013.
Interview with Hamisi Feuse Kabwe Katanga, Gungu, 14 Nov. 2013.
Interview with Hamisi Ali Juma al-Hey, Ujiji, 14 Nov. 2013.

Published and Unpublished Sources

Abel, Armand. *Les Musulmans noirs du Maniema*. Brussels: Publications du centre pour l'étude des problèmes du monde musulman contemporain, 1960.
Abu-Lughod, Janet L. *Before European Hegemony: The world system A.D. 1250–1350*. Oxford: Oxford University Press, 1989.
Agius, Dionisius A., 'Decorative motifs on Arabian boats: Meaning and identity', in *Natural Resources and Cultural Connections*, eds. Starkey, Starkey, and Wilkinson: 101–10.
Akyeampong, Emmanuel Kwaku, Robert H. Bates, Nathan Nunn, and James A. Robinson, eds. *Africa's Development in Historical Perspective*. New York: Cambridge University Press, 2014.
Alam, Muzaffar and Sanjay Subrahmanyam. 'The Deccan frontier and Mughal expansion, ca.1600: Contemporary perspectives'. *Journal of the Economic and Social History of the Orient*, 47, 3 (2004): 357–89.
Alin, Simone R. and Andrew S. Cohen. 'Lake-level history of Lake Tanganyika, East Africa, for the past 2500 years based on ostracode-inferred water-depth reconstruction'. *Paleogeography, Paleoclimatology, Paleoecology*, 199, 102 (2003): 31–49.
Allen, James de Vere. 'Swahili culture and the nature of east coast settlement'. *International Journal of African Historical Studies*, 14, 2 (1981): 306–34.
     'Town and country in Swahili culture', in *Symposium Leo Frobenius: Perspectives of contemporary African studies*, Deutsche UNESCO-Kommission. Cologne: Pullach, 1974: 298–316.
Allen, Katherine Jean. 'Routes to deliverance: The development of social mobility among East African slave porters by way of missionary caravans, 1877–1906'. Unpublished MA dissertation, Clemson University, 2020.
Allman, Jean, ed. *Fashioning Africa: Power and the politics of dress*. Bloomington: Indian University Press, 2014.
Allman, Jean and John Parker. *Tongnaab: The history of a West African God*. Bloomington: Indiana University Press, 2005.
Alpers, Edward A. 'Debt, pawnship and slavery in nineteenth-century East Africa', in *Bonded Labour and Debt*, eds. Campbell and Stanziani: 31–44.
     The Indian Ocean in World History. Oxford: Oxford University Press, 2014.
     Ivory and Slaves in East Central Africa: Changing patterns of international trade to the later nineteenth century. Berkeley: University of California Press, 1975.
     'Muqdisho in the nineteenth century: A regional perspective'. *The Journal of African History*, 24, 4 (1983): 441–59.
     '"Ordinary household chores": Ritual and power in a 19th-century Swahili possession cult'. *The International Journal of African Historical Studies*, 17, 4 (1984): 677–702.

'Trade, state, and society among the Yao in the nineteenth century'. *The Journal of African History*, 10, 3 (1969): 405–20.

Alpers, Edward A. and Chhaya Goswami, eds. *Transregional Trade and Traders: Situating Gujarat in the Indian Ocean from early times to 1900*. New Delhi: Oxford University Press, 2019.

Anderson, David M. and Richard Rathbone. '*Urban Africa*: Histories in the making', in *Africa's Urban Past*, eds. Anderson and Rathbone: 1–18.

eds. *Africa's Urban Past*. Oxford: James Currey, 2000.

Arens, W., ed. *A Century of Change in Eastern Africa*. The Hague: Morton Publishers, 1976.

Armitage, David, Alison Bashford, and Sujit Sivasundaram, eds. *Oceanic Histories*. Cambridge: Cambridge University Press, 2017.

Austen, Ralph A. *African Economic History: Internal development and external dependency*. London: James Currey, 1987.

'Patterns of development in nineteenth-century East Africa'. *African Historical Studies*, 4, 3 (1971): 645–57.

Bang, Anne K. *Islamic Sufi Networks in the Western Indian Ocean (c. 1880–1940): Ripples of reform*. Leiden: Brill, 2014.

Sufis and Scholars of the Sea: Family networks in East Africa, 1860–1925. London: Routledge, 2003.

Bankoff, Greg and Joseph Christensen, eds. *Natural Hazards and Peoples in the Indian Ocean World: Bordering on danger*. New York: Palgrave, 2016.

Banshchikova, Anastasia. 'Historical memory of the 19th century Arab slave trade in the modern day Tanzania: Between family trauma and state-planted tolerance', in *The Omnipresent Past*, eds. Bondarenko and Butovskaya: 23–45.

Barber, Sarah and Corinna M. Peniston-Bird, eds. *History beyond the Text: A student's guide to approaching alternative sources*. Abingdon: Routledge, 2009.

Beachey, R. W. 'The arms trade in East Africa in the late nineteenth century'. *The Journal of African History*, 3, 3 (1962): 451–67.

'The East African ivory trade in the nineteenth century'. *The Journal of African History*, 8, 2 (1967): 269–90.

Becker, Felicitas. 'Commoners in the process of Islamization: Reassessing their role in light of evidence from southeastern Tanzania'. *Journal of Global History*, 3 (2008): 227–49.

Becker, Felicitas and Joel Cabrita. 'Introduction: Performing citizenship and enacting exclusion on Africa's Indian Ocean littoral'. *The Journal of African History*, 55, 2 (2014): 161–71.

Becker, Jérôme. *La Vie en Afrique ou trois ans dans l'Afrique Centrale*, 2 Vols. Paris: J. Lebègue & Co., 1887.

Bennett, Norman R. *Arab versus European: Diplomacy and war in nineteenth-century East Central Africa*. New York: Africana Pub. Co., 1986.

'Captain Storms in Tanganyika'. *Tanzania Notes and Records*, 54 (1960): 51–63.

Mirambo of Tanzania 1840?–1884. New York: Oxford University Press, 1971.

'Mwinyi Kheri' in *Leadership in Eastern Africa*, ed. Bennett: 139–64.
ed. *Leadership in Eastern Africa: Six political biographies*. Boston: Boston University Press, 1968.
Berge, Lars and Irma Taddia, eds. *Themes in Modern African History and Culture*. Padova: Libreria Universitaria, 2013.
Berman, Nina, Klaus Mühlhahn, and Patrice Nganang, eds. *German Colonialism Revisited: Africa, Asian, and oceanic experiences*. Ann Arbor: University of Michigan Press, 2014.
Bessems, Ilse, Dirk Verschuren, James M. Russell, Jozef Hus, Florias Mees, and Brian F. Cumming. 'Paleolimnological evidence for widespread late 18th century drought across equatorial East Africa'. *Paleogeography, Paleoclimatology, Paleoecology*, 259 (2008): 107–20.
Bhacker, M. Reda. *Trade and Empire in Muscat and Zanzibar: Roots of British domination*. London: Routledge, 1992.
Bhattacharyya, Debjani. *Empire and Ecology in the Bengal Delta: The making of Calcutta*. Cambridge: Cambridge University Press, 2018.
Bimangu, S. and Tshishiku Tshibangu. 'Contribution à l'histoire de l'implantation de l'islam au Zaïre'. *Paideuma*, 24 (1978): 225–30.
Bishara, Fahad Ahmad. *A Sea of Debt: Law and economic life in the western Indian Ocean, 1780–1950*. Cambridge: Cambridge University Press, 2017.
Blom, Philipp. *Nature's Mutiny: How the Little Ice Age of the long seventeenth century transformed the West and shaped the present*. New York: Liveright Publishing Corporation, 2019.
Bolser-Brown, Beverly. 'Muslim influence on trade and politics in the Lake Tanganyika region'. *African Historical Studies*, 4, 3 (1971): 617–29.
'Ujiji: The history of a lakeside town, c.1800–1914'. Unpublished PhD dissertation, Boston University, 1973.
Bolser-Brown, Beverly and Walter Brown. 'East African trade towns: A shared growth', in *A Century of Change in Eastern Africa*, ed. Arens: 183–200.
Bondarenko, Dmitri M. and Marina L. Butovskaya, eds. *The Omnipresent Past: Historical anthropology of Africa and African diaspora*. Moscow: LRC Publishing House, 2019.
Bose, Sugata and Ayesha Jalal, eds. *Oceanic Islam: Muslim universalism and European imperialism*. New Dehli: Bloomsbury, 2020.
Brady, C. T. *Commerce and Conquest in East Africa: With particular reference to the Salem trade with Zanzibar*. Salem: Essex Institute, 1950.
Brand, V. C., W. D. Cooley and Bernardino Freire F. A. de Castro. 'Notice of a caravan journey from the East to the West coast of Africa'. *Journal of the Royal Geographical Society*, 24 (1854): 266–71.
Braudel, Fernand. *The Mediterranean and the Mediterranean World in the Age of Philip II*, 3 Vols. Translated by Siân Reynolds. Berkeley: University of California Press, 1995.
Brauer, Ralph W. 'Boundaries and frontiers in medieval Muslim geography'. *Transactions of the American Philosophical Society*, 86, 6 (1995): 1–73.
Brode, Heinrich. *Tippoo Tib: The story of his career in Central Africa, narrated from his own accounts*. Translated by H. Havelock. London: Edward Arnold, 1907.

Brown, Walter. 'Bagamoyo: An historical introduction'. *Tanzania Notes and Records*, 71 (1970): 69–83.

'A pre-colonial history of Bagamoyo: Aspects of the growth of an East Africa coastal town'. Unpublished PhD dissertation, Boston University, 1971.

Bujra, Janet M. 'Women "entrepreneurs" of early Nairobi'. *Canadian Journal of African Studies*, 9, 2 (1975): 213–34.

Burke, Peter. *The French Historical Revolution: The Annales school*, 2nd edition. Cambridge: Polity, 2014.

Burton, Andrew. 'Urbanization in East Africa, circa 900–2010'. *Oxford Research Encyclopedia of African* History (2017). https://doi.org/10.1093/acrefore/9780190277734.013.31 (accessed 7 Dec. 2020).

'Urbanisation in Eastern Africa: An historical overview, c.1750–2000'. *Azania: Archaeological Research in Africa*, 36–7, 1 (2001): 1–28.

Burton, Richard F. *The Lake Regions of Central Africa: A picture of exploration*. New York: Harper & Brothers, 1860.

'Lake regions of Central Equatorial Africa, with notices of the Lunar Mountains and the sources of the White Nile: Being the results of an expedition undertaken under the patronage of Her Majesty's Government and the Royal Geographical Society of London, in the years 1857–1859'. *Journal of the Royal Geographical Society of London*, 29 (1859): 1–454.

Zanzibar: City, island, and coast, 2 Vols. London: Tinsley Brothers, 1872.

Burton, Richard F. and John Hanning Speke. 'Extracts from reports by Captains Burton and Speke, of the East Africa expedition, on their discovery of Lake Ujiji, &c, in Central Africa'. *Proceedings of the Royal Geographical Society*, 3, 3 (1858–9): 111–17.

Burton, Susan K. 'Issues on cross-cultural interviewing: Japanese women in England', in *The Oral History Reader*, eds. Perks and Thomson: 166–76.

Cameron, Verney Lovett. *Across Africa*. New York: Harper & Brothers, 1877.

'Livingstone east coast aid expedition'. *Proceedings of the Royal Geographical Society of London*, 18, 3 (1873–4): 281–3.

Campbell, Gwyn. 'Africa, the Indian Ocean World, and the "early modern": Historiographical conventions and problems'. *Journal of Indian Ocean World Studies*, 1, 1 (2017): 24–37.

Africa and the Indian Ocean World from Early Times to circa 1900. Cambridge: Cambridge University Press, 2019.

'Introduction: Bondage and the environment', in *Bondage and the Environment*, ed. Campbell: 1–32.

'Introduction: Slavery and other forms of unfree labour in the Indian Ocean world'. *Slavery and Abolition*, 24, 2 (2003): ix–xxxii.

ed. *Bondage and the Environment in the Indian Ocean World*. Cham: Palgrave Macmillan, 2018.

ed. *Early Exchange between Africa and the wider Indian Ocean World*. Cham: Palgrave Macmillan, 2016.

Campbell, Gwyn and Alessandro Stanziani, eds. *Bonded Labour and Debt in the Indian Ocean World*. London: Pickering and Chatto, 2013.

Caplan, Patricia. *African Voices, African Lives: Personal narratives from a Swahili village*. London: Routledge, 1997.

Choice and Constraint in a Swahili Community: Property, hierarchy and cognatic descent on the East African coast. Abingdon: Routledge, 2018.

'Life in Swahili villages', in *The Swahili World*, eds. Wynne-Jones and LaViolette: 577–88.

Casson, Lionel. *The Periplus Maris Erythraei: Text with introduction, translation, and commentary.* Princeton: Princeton University Press, 2012.

Castryck, Geert. 'Bordering the lake: Transcending spatial orders in Kigoma-Ujiji'. *International Journal of African Historical Studies*, 52, 1 (2019): 109–32.

'Indian Ocean Worlds', in *The Routledge Handbook of Transregional Studies*, ed. Middel: 102–9.

'Living Islam in colonial Bujumbura: The historical translocality of Muslim life between East and Central Africa'. *History in Africa*, 46 (2019): 263–98.

'"My slave sold all of Kigoma": Power relations, property rights and the historian's quest for understanding', in *Sources and Methods for African History and Culture*, eds. Castryck, Strickrodt, and Werthmann: 317–35.

Castryck, Geert, Achim Von Oppen, and Katharina Zöller. 'Introduction: Bridging histories of East and Central Africa'. *History in Africa*, 46 (2019): 1–22.

Castryck, Geert, Silke Strickrodt, and Katja Werthmann, eds. *Sources and Methods for African History and Culture: Essays in honour of Adam Jones.* Leipzig: Leipziger Universitätsverlag, 2016.

Chaiklin, Martha. 'Ivory in world history: Early modern trade in context', *History Compass*, 8, 6 (2010): 530–42.

'Surat and Bombay: Ivory and commercial networks in western India', in *The Dutch and English East India Companies*, eds. Clulow and Mostert: 101–24.

Chaiklin, Martha, Philip Gooding, and Gwyn Campbell, eds. *Animal Trade Histories in the Indian Ocean World.* Cham: Palgrave, 2020.

Chami, Felix. 'Graeco-Roman trade link and the Bantu migration theory'. *Anthropos*, 94 (1999): 205–15.

Chaudhuri, K. N. *Trade and Civilisation in the Indian Ocean: An economic history from the rise of Islam to 1750.* Cambridge: Cambridge University Press, 1985.

Chen, Jainhui, Jianbao Liu, Xiaojian Zhang, Shengqian Chen, Wei Huang, Jie Chen, Shengrui Zhang, Aifeng Zhou, and Fahu Chen. 'Unstable Little Ice Age climate revealed by high-resolution proxy records from northwestern China'. *Climate Dynamics*, 53 (2019): 1517–26.

Cherniwchan, Jevan and Juan Moreno-Cruz. 'Maize in precolonial Africa'. *Journal of Development Economics*, 136 (2019): 137–50.

Chrétien, Jean-Pierre. *L'Afrique des grands lacs: Deux milles ans d'histoire.* Paris: Flammarion, 2000.

'Le commerce du sel de l'Uvinza an XIXe siècle: De la cueillette au monopole capitaliste'. *Revue française d'histoire d'outre-mers*, 65, 240 (1978): 401–22.

L'Invention de l'Afrique des grands lacs: Une histoire du XXe siècle. Paris: Karthala, 2010.

Chubaka, Bishikwabo. 'Aux origines de la ville d'Uvira selon les explorateurs et les pionniers de la colonisation Belge au Zaire (1840–1914)'. *Civilisations*, 1 (1987): 83–126.

Clarence-Smith, William G. 'The expansion of cotton textile production in the western Indian Ocean, c.1500–c.1850', in *Reinterpreting Indian Ocean Worlds*, eds. Smith and Chaudhuri: 84–106.

Islam and the Abolition of Slavery. London: C. Hurst & Co, 1988.

'The textile industry in eastern Africa', in *Africa's Development in Historical Perspective*, eds. Akyeampong, Bates, Nunn, and Robinson: 264–94.

Clark, Andrew F. 'The challenges of cross-cultural oral history: Collecting and presenting Pulaar traditions on slavery from Bundu, Senegambia (West Africa)'. *The Oral History Review*, 20, 1–2 (1992): 1–21.

Clulow, Adam and Tristan Mostert, eds. *The Dutch and English East India Companies: Diplomacy, trade and violence in early modern Asia*. Amsterdam: Amsterdam University Press, 2018.

Cohen, Andrew S., Michael R. Talbot, Stanley M. Awramik, David L. Dettman, and Paul Abell. 'Lake level and paleoenvironmental history of Lake Tanganyika, Africa, as inferred from lake Holocene and modern stromatolites'. *Geological Society of America Bulletin*, 109, 4 (1997): 444–60.

Colle, R. P. *Les Baluba*, 2 Vols. Brussels: Institut Internationale de Bibliographie, 1913.

Collet, Dominik and Maximilian Schuh. *Famines during the 'Little Ice Age' (1300–1800): Socionatural entanglements in premodern societies*. Cham: Springer, 2018.

Connah, Graham. *African Civilizations: An archaeological perspective*, 3rd edition. Cambridge: Cambridge University Press, 2015.

Conway, Declan. 'Extreme rainfall events and lake level changes in East Africa: Recent events and historical precedents', in *The East African Great Lakes*, eds. Odada and Olago: 63–92.

Cooper, Frederick. *Plantation Slavery on the East Coast of Africa*. New Haven, CT: Yale University Press, 1977.

'The problem of slavery in African studies'. *The Journal of African Studies*, 20, 1 (1979): 103–25.

Coquery-Vidrovitch, Catherine. *Processus d'urbanisation en Afrique*, 2 Vols. Paris: L'Harmattan, 1988.

Coquery-Vidrovitch, Catherine and Paul E. Lovejoy, eds. *The Workers of African Trade*. Beverly Hills: Sage Publications, 1985.

Coulbois, François. *Dix années au Tanganyika*. Limoges: Pierre Dumont, 1901.

Coutu, Ashley N., Julia Lee-Thorp, Matthew J. Collins, and Paul J. Lane. 'Mapping the elephants of the 19th century East African ivory trade with a multi-isotope approach'. *PLoS ONE*, 11, 10 (2016): 1–23.

Creekmore, Andrew T. and Keven D. Fisher, eds. *Making Ancient Cities: Space and place in early urban societies*. Cambridge: Cambridge University Press, 2014.

Croucher, Sarah. 'Ujiji 2008'. https://scroucher.faculty.wesleyan.edu/research/ujiji-2008/ (accessed 14 Oct. 2020).

Crowther, Alison, Leilani Lucas, Richard Helm, Mark Horton, Ceri Shipton, Henry T. Wright, Sarah Walshaw, Matthew Pawlowicz, Chantal

Radimilahy, Katerina Douka, Llorenç Picornell-Gelabert, Dorian Q. Fuller, and Nicole L. Boivin. 'Ancient crops provide first archaeological signature of the westward Austronesian expansion'. *Proceedings of the National Academy of Sciences of the United States of America*, 113, 24 (2016): 6635–40.

Crul, Ruud C. M. *Limnology and Hydrology of Lakes Tanganyika and Malawi*. Paris: UNESCO Publishing, 1997.

Cunnison, Ian. 'Kazembe and the Portuguese 1898–1832'. *The Journal of African History*, 2, 1 (1961): 61–76.

Damodaran, Vinita, Rob Allan, Astrid E. J. Ogilvie, Gaston R. Demarée, Joëlle Gergis, Takehiko Mikami, Alan Mikhail, Sharon E. Nicholson, Stefan Norrgård, and James Hamilton, 'The 1780s: Global climate anomalies, floods, droughts, and famines', in *The Palgrave Handbook of Climate History*, eds. White, Pfister, and Mauelshagen: 517–50.

Davis, Mike. *Late Victorian Holocausts: El Niño famines and the making of the third world*. London: Verso, 2002.

De Datta, Surajit K. *Principles and Practices of Rice Cultivation*. New York: John Wiley & Sons, 1981.

Decker, Michelle. 'The "autobiography" of Tippu Tip'. *Interventions*, 17, 5 (2015): 744–58.

Declich, Francesca, ed. *Translocal Connections across the Indian Ocean: Swahili speaking networks on the move*. Leiden: Brill, 2018.

Depelchin, Jacques-Marie Francois. 'From pre-capitalism to imperialism: A history of social and economic relations in eastern Zaire (Uvira zone, c.1800–1965)'. Unpublished PhD dissertation, Stanford University, 1974.

Deutsch, Jan-Georg. *Emancipation without Abolition in German East Africa, c.1884–1914*. Athens, OH: Ohio University Press, 2006.

'Notes on the rise of slavery and social change in Unyamwezi', in *Slavery in the Great Lakes Region*, eds. Médard and Doyle: 76–110.

Donley-Reid, L. W. 'A structuring structure: The Swahili house', in *Domestic Architecture and the Use of Space*, ed. Kent: 114–26.

Eagleton, Catherine, Harcourt Fuller, and John Perkins, eds. *Money in Africa*. London: The British Museum, 2009.

Earle, Jonathon L. 'African intellectual history and historiography'. *Oxford Research Encyclopedia of African History* (2018). https://doi.org/10.1093/acrefore/9780190277734.013.305 (accessed 7 Dec. 2020).

Colonial Buganda and the End of Empire: Political thought and historical imagination in Africa. New York: Cambridge University Press, 2017.

El Hamel, Chouki. *Black Morocco: A history of slavery, race, and Islam*. Cambridge: Cambridge University Press, 2013.

Erdem, Y. Hakan. *Slavery in the Ottoman Empire and its Demise 1800–1909*. London: Palgrave Macmillan, 1996.

Fabian, Steven. 'East Africa's Gorée: Slave trade and slave tourism in Bagamoyo, Tanzania'. *Canadian Journal of African Studies*, 47, 1 (2013): 95–114.

'Locating the local in the coastal rebellion of 1888–90'. *Journal of Eastern African Studies*, 7, 3 (2013): 432–49.

Making Identity on the Swahili Coast: Urban identity, community, and belonging in Bagamoyo. Cambridge: Cambridge University Press, 2019.

'Wabagamoyo: Redefining identity in a Swahili town, 1860s–1960s'. Unpublished PhD dissertation, Dalhousie University, 2007.

Fair, Laura. 'Dressing up: Clothing and gender in post-abolition Zanzibar'. *The Journal of African History*, 39, 1 (1998): 63–94.

Pastimes and Politics: Culture, community, and identity in post-abolition urban Zanzibar. Athens, OH: Ohio University Press, 2001.

'Remaking fashion in the Paris of the Indian Ocean: Dress, performance and the cultural construction of a cosmopolitan Zanzibari identity', in *Fashioning Africa*, ed. Allman: 13–30.

Falola, Toyin and Christian Jennings, eds. *Sources and Methods in African History: Spoken, written, unearthed*. Rochester, NY: University of Rochester Press, 2003.

Farrant, Leda. *Tippu Tip and the East African Slave Trade*. London: Hamish Hamilton, 1975.

Fee, Sarah. '"Cloths with names": Luxury textile imports in eastern Africa, 1800–1885'. *Textile History*, 48, 1 (2017): 49–84.

'Filling hearts with joy: Handcrafted "Indian textiles" exports to central eastern Africa in the nineteenth century', in *Transregional Trade and Traders*, eds. Alpers and Goswami: 163–217.

Feierman, Stephen. *Peasant Intellectuals: Anthropology and history in Tanzania*. Madison: University of Wisconsin Press, 1990.

The Shambaa Kingdom: A history (Madison: University of Wisconsin Press, 1974).

Filippini, Nadia Maria. 'Un filo di perle da Venezia al mondo'. *La Ricerca Folklorica*, 34 (1996): 5–10.

Fisher, Alan W. 'Muscovy and the Black Sea slave trade'. *Canadian-American Slavic Studies*, 6, 4 (1972): 575–94.

Fleisher, Jeffrey and Adria LaViolette. 'Elusive wattle-and-daub: Finding the hidden majority in the archaeology of the Swahili'. *Azania: Archaeological Research in Africa*, 34, 1 (1999): 87–108.

Fleisher, Jeffrey, Paul Lane, Adria LaViolet, Mark Horton, Edward Pollard, Eréndira Quintana Morales, Thomas Vernet, Annalisa Christie, and Stephanie Wynne-Jones. 'When did the Swahili become maritime?' *American Anthropologist*, 117, 1 (2015): 100–15.

Fourchard, Laurent, Odile Georg, and Muriel Gomez-Perez, eds. *Lieux de sociabilité urbaine en Afrique*. Paris: L'Harmattan, 2009.

Frederick, Katharine. *Twilight of an Industry in East Africa: Textile manufacturing, 1830–1940*. Cham: Palgrave Macmillan, 2020.

Freitag, Ulrike and Achim Von Oppen. 'Introduction: "Translocality" – an approach to connection and transfer in area studies', in *Translocality*, eds. Freitag and Von Oppen: 1–21.

eds. *Translocality: The study of globalising processes from a southern perspective*. Leiden: Brill, 2010.

Fuentes, Marisa J. *Dispossessed Lives: Enslaved women, violence, and the archive*. Philadelphia: University of Pennsylvania Press, 2016.

Geertz, Clifford. *Islam Observed: Religious development in Morocco and Indonesia*. Chicago: University of Chicago Press, 1971.

Gergis, Joëlle L. and Anthony M. Fowler. 'A history of ENSO events since A.D. 1525: Implications for future climate change'. *Climatic Change*, 92 (2009): 343–87.

Gerhard, Dietrich. 'The frontier in comparative view'. *Comparative Studies in Society and History*, 1, 3 (1959): 205–29.

Gilbert, Erik. *Dhows and the Colonial Economy in Zanzibar, 1860–1970*. Athens, OH: Ohio University Press, 2004.

Giles, Linda. 'Spirit possession on the Swahili coast: Peripheral cults or primary texts?' Unpublished PhD dissertation, University of Texas at Austin, 1989.

Gillman, C. 'The hydrology of Lake Tanganyika', in *Tanganyika Territory Geological Survey Department*, 5 (1933): 1–25.

Giraud, Victor. *Les lacs de l'Afrique équatoriale*. Paris: Librarie Hachette, 1890.

Gissibl, Bernhard. *The Nature of German Imperialism: Conservation and the politics of wildlife in colonial East Africa*. New York: Berghahn Books, 2016.

Glassman, Jonathon. 'The bondsman's new clothes: The contradictory consciousness of slave resistance on the Swahili coast'. *The Journal of African History*, 32, 2 (1991): 277–312.

Feasts and Riot: Revelry, rebellion, and popular consciousness on the Swahili coast, 1856–1888. Portsmouth, NH: Heinemann, 1994.

Gleerup, Edvard. 'A journey across Tanganyika in 1886', ed. Norman R. Bennett. Translated by Per Hassing. *Tanzania Notes and Records*, 56 (1962): 129–47.

Good, Francis. 'Voice, ear, and text: Words, meaning, and transcription', in *The Oral History Reader*, eds. Perks and Thomson: 362–73.

Gooding, Philip. 'David Livingstone, UNESCO, and nation-building in 19th-century Scotland and 21st-century East and Central Africa'. *Journal of Indian Ocean World Studies*, 5, 2 (2021): 243–69.

'ENSO, IOD, drought and floods in equatorial East Africa, 1876–8', in *Droughts, Floods, and Global Climatic Anomalies*, ed. Gooding: 259–87.

'History, politics, and culture in Central Tanzania'. *Oxford Research Encyclopedia of African History* (2019). https://doi.org/10.1093/acrefore/9780190277734.013.674 (accessed 7 Dec. 2020).

'Islam in the interior of precolonial East Africa: Evidence from Lake Tanganyika'. *The Journal of African History*, 60, 2 (2019): 191–208.

'The ivory trade and political power in nineteenth-century East Africa', in *Animal Trade Histories*, eds. Chaiklin, Gooding, and Campbell: 247–75.

'Slavery, "respectability", and being "freeborn" on the shores of nineteenth-century Lake Tanganyika'. *Slavery and Abolition*, 40, 1 (2019): 147–67.

'Tsetse flies, ENSO, and murder: The Church Missionary Society's failed ox-cart experiment of 1876–78'. *Africa: Rivista semestrale di studi e ricerche*, 1, 2 (2019): 21–36.

ed. *Droughts, Floods, and Global Climatic Anomalies in the Indian Ocean World*. Cham: Palgrave, 2022.

Gordon, David M. 'Wearing cloth, wielding guns: Consumption, trade, and politics in the south central African interior during the nineteenth century', in *The Objects of Life*, eds. Ross, Hinfelaar, and Peša: 15–39.

Goswami, Chhaya. *The Call of the Sea: Kachchhi traders in Muscat and Zanzibar, c.1800–1880*. New Delhi: Orient Blackswan, 2011.
Globalization before Its Time: The Gujarati merchants from Kachchh. Delhi: Penguin, 2016.

Gratien, Christopher. 'The mountains are ours: Ecology and settlement in late Ottoman and early Republican Cilicia, 1856–1956'. Unpublished PhD dissertation, Georgetown University, 2015.

Gray, Richard and David Birmingham. 'Some political and economic consequences of trade in Central Africa in the pre-colonial period', in *Pre-colonial Trade*, eds. Gray and Birmingham: 1–23.
eds. *Pre-colonial Trade: Essays on trade in central and eastern Africa before 1900*. London: Oxford University Press, 1970.

Grewe, Bernd-Stefan and Karin Hofmeester, eds. *Luxury in Global Perspective: Objects and practices, 1600–2000*. New York: Cambridge University Press, 2016.

Grove, Richard H. 'The great El Niño of 1789–93 and its global consequences: Reconstructing an extreme climate event in world environmental history'. *The Medieval History Journal*, 10, 1–2 (2006): 75–98.

Grove, Richard H. and George Adamson. *El Niño in World History*. London: Palgrave Macmillan, 2018.

Gwassa, G. C. K. and J. F. Mbwiliza. 'Social production, symbolism and ritual in Buha: 1750–1900'. *Tanzania Notes and Records*, 79–80 (1976): 13–21.

Håkansson, N. Thomas. 'Criticizing resilience thinking: A political ecology analysis of droughts in nineteenth-century East Africa'. *Economic Anthropology*, 6, 1 (2019): 7–20.

Hall, Bruce S. *A History of Race in Muslim West Africa, 1600–1960*. Cambridge: Cambridge University Press, 2011.

Hamilton, Paula and James B. Gardner, eds. *The Oxford Handbook of Public History*. Oxford: Oxford University Press, 2017.

Hanson, Holly Elisabeth. *Landed Obligation: The practice of power in Buganda*. Portsmouth, NH: Heinemann, 2003.

Harding, J. R. 'Nineteenth-century trade beads in Tanganyika'. *Man*, 62 (1962): 104–6.

Hartwig, Gerald W. 'Demographic considerations in East Africa during the nineteenth century'. *International Journal of African Historical Studies*, 12, 4 (1979): 653–72.
'The Victoria Nyanza as a trade route in the nineteenth century'. *The Journal of African History*, 11, 4 (1970): 535–52.

Hastenrath, Stefan. 'Variations of East African climate during the past two centuries'. *Climatic Change*, 50 (2001): 209–17.

Hellie, Richard. *Slavery in Russia 1450–1725*. Chicago: University of Chicago Press, 1982.

Hillewaert, Sarah. 'Identity and belonging on the contemporary Swahili coast: The case of Lamu', in *The Swahili World*, eds. Wynne-Jones and LaViolette: 602–13.

Hillocks, Rory J. 'Cassava in Africa', in *Cassava*, eds. Hillocks, Thresh, and Bellotti: 41–54.

Hillocks, Rory J., J. M. Thresh, and A. Bellotti, eds. *Cassava: Biology, production and utilization*. Wallingford: CABI, 2002.

Hino, Shun'ya. 'Neighbourhood groups in African urban society: Social relations and consciousness of Swahili people of Ujiji, a small town of Tanzania, East Africa'. *Kyoto University African Studies*, 6 (1971): 1–30.

Hobsbawm, Eric and Terence Ranger, eds. *The Invention of Tradition*. New York: Cambridge University Press, 2012.

Holmes, C. F. 'Zanzibari influence at the southern end of Lake Victoria: The lake route'. *African Historical Studies*, 4, 3 (1971): 477–503.

Holsey, Bayo. 'Slavery tourism: Representing a difficult history in Ghana', in *The Oxford Handbook of Public History*, eds. Hamilton and Gardner: 479–91.

Hopkins, A. G. *An Economic History of West Africa*, 2nd edition. Abingdon: Routledge, 2020.

Hopper, Matthew S. 'Cyclones, drought, and slavery: Environment and enslavement in the western Indian Ocean, 1870s to 1920s', in *Natural Hazards and Peoples*, eds. Bankoff and Christensen: 255–82.

Horden, Peregrine and Nicholas Purcell. *The Corrupting Sea: A study in Mediterranean History*. Oxford: Oxford University Press, 2000.

Hore, Annie B. *To Lake Tanganyika in a Bath Chair*. London: Sampson Low, Marston, Searle & Rivington, 1886.

Hore, Edward C. 'An Arab friend in Central Africa'. *Chronicle of the London Missionary Society* (August 1891): 235–8.

'Lake Tanganyika'. *Proceedings of the Royal Geographical Society and Monthly Record of Geography*, 4, 1 (1882): 581–95.

'On the twelve tribes if Tanganyika'. *Proceedings of the Anthropological Institute of Great Britain and Ireland*, 12 (1883): 2–21.

Missionary to Tanganyika 1877–1888, ed. James B. Wolf. London: F. Cass, 1971.

Tanganyika: Eleven years in central Africa. London: Edward Stanford, 1892.

Horton, Mark. *Shanga: The archaeology of a Muslim trading community on the coast of East Africa*. London: British Institute in Eastern Africa, 1996.

'Swahili architecture, space and social structure', in *Architecture and Order*, eds. Pearson and Richards: 132–52.

Horton, Mark, Jeffrey Fleisher, and Stephanie Wynne-Jones. 'The mosques of Songo Mnara in their urban landscape'. *Journal of Islamic Archaeology*, 4, 2 (2017): 163–88.

Horton, Mark and John Middleton. *The Swahili: The social landscape of a mercantile society*. Oxford: Blackwell, 2000.

Hughes, Carl. and Ruben Post. 'A GIS approach to finding the metropolis of Rhapta', in *Early Exchange*, ed. Campbell: 135–55.

Hunwick, John. 'The religious practices of black slaves in the Mediterranean Islamic world', in *Slavery on the Frontiers*, ed. Lovejoy: 149–72.

Hutley, Walter. *The Central African Diaries of Walter Hutley, 1877–1881*, ed. James B. Wolf. Boston: African Studies Center, 1976.

Iliffe, John. *Honour in African History*. Cambridge: Cambridge University Press, 2005.

A Modern History of Tanganyika. Cambridge: Cambridge University Press, 1979.

Indian Ocean World Centre, 'Appraising risk, past and present: Interrogating historical data to enhance understanding of environmental crises in the Indian Ocean World'. www.appraisingrisk.com/about-us-2/ (accessed 10 June 2020).

Jacques, Victor and Emile Storms. *Notes sur l'ethnographie de la partie orientale de l'Afrique équatoriale.* Brussels: Académie Royale de Belgique, 1886.

Kagwa, Apolo. *The Customs of the Baganda*, ed. May Mandelbaum. Translated by Ernest B. Kalibala. New York: AMS Press, 1969.

Kamali, Bahareh, Karim C. Abbaspour, Anthony Lehmann, Bernhard Wehrli, and Hong Yang. 'Spatial assessment of maize physical drought vulnerability in sub-Saharan Africa: Linking drought exposure with crop failure'. *Environmental Research Letters*, 13, 7 (2018): 1–13.

Karklins, Karlis. 'Identifying beads used in the 19th-century central East Africa trade', *Beads*, 4, 49–50 (1992): 49–59.

Karrar, Adil Bashir, Hassan Ibrahim Mohamed, Haitham Ragab Elramlwai, and Atif Elsadig Idris. 'Rain fed sorghum (Sorghum bicolor L. Moench) crop growth yield forecasting model'. *Universal Journal of Agricultural Research*, 2, 5 (2014): 154–67.

Kelly, Alexandra Celia. *Consuming Ivory: Mercantile legacies of East Africa and New England.* Seattle: University of Washington Press, 2021.

Kenny, Michael G. 'The powers of Lake Victoria'. *Anthropos*, 72, 5–6 (1977): 717–33.

Kent, Susan, ed. *Domestic Architecture and the Use of Space: An interdisciplinary cross-cultural study.* Cambridge: Cambridge University Press, 1993.

Kimambo, Isaria N. and A. J. Temu, eds. *A History of Tanzania.* Nairobi: East African Publishing House, 1969.

Kjekshus, Helge. *Ecology Control and Economic Development in East African History: The case of Tanganyika 1850–1950*, 2nd edition. London: James Currey, 1996.

Koponen, Juhani. *Development for Exploitation: German colonial policies in mainland Tanzania, 1884–1914.* Hamburg: Lit Verlag, 1994.

People and Production in Late Precolonial Tanzania: History and structures. Helsinki: Finnish Society of Development Studies, 1988.

Kopytoff, Igor. 'The internal African frontier: The making of an African political culture', in *The African Frontier*, ed. Kopytoff: 3–87.

ed. *The African Frontier: The reproduction of traditional African societies.* Bloomington: Indiana University Press, 1987: 3–87.

Kopytoff, Igor and Suzanne Miers. 'African "slavery" as an institution of marginality', in *Slavery in Africa*, eds. Miers and Kopytoff: 3–77.

Kusimba, Chapurukha M. and Jonathan R. Walz. 'When did the Swahili become maritime? A reply to Fleisher et al. (2015), and to the resurgence of maritime myopia in the archaeology of the East African coast'. *American Anthropologist*, 120, 3 (2018): 429–43.

Kusimba, Chapurukha M. and Sibel B. Kusimba, eds. *East African Archaeology: Foragers, potters, smiths, and traders.* Philadelphia: University of Pennsylvania Press, 2010.

Kusimba, Chapurukha M., Sibel B. Kusimba, and Laure Dussubieux. 'Beyond the coastalscapes: Preindustrial social and political networks in East Africa'. *The African Archaeological Review*, 30, 4 (2013): 399–426.

Ladurie, Emmanuel Le Roy. *Times of Feast, Times of Famine: A history of climate since the year 1000*. Translated by Barbara Bray. Garden City, NY: Doubleday, 1971.

Laing, Stuart. *Tippu Tip: Ivory, slavery and discovery in the scramble for Africa*. Dar es Salaam: Mkuki na Nyota Publishers, 2019.

Larsen, Kjersti. *Where Humans and Spirits Meet: The politics of rituals and identified spirits in Zanzibar*. New York: Berghahn Books, 2008.

LaViolette, Adria and Stephanie Wynne-Jones. 'The Swahili world', in *The Swahili World*, eds. Wynne-Jones and LaViolette: 1–14.

Lechaptois, Mgr. *Aux rives du Tanganika: Étude ethnographique couronée par la Société de géographie de Paris*. Algiers: Missionaires d'Afrique, 1913.

Lehman, J. T., ed. *Environmental Change and Response in East African Lakes*. Dordrecht: Kluwer Academic Publishers, 1998.

Levtzion, Nehemia and Randall L. Pouwels, eds. *The History of Islam in Africa*. Athens, OH: Ohio University Press, 2000.

Lindström, Jean. *Muted Memories: Heritage making, Bagamoyo, and the East African caravan trade*. Oxford: Berghahn Books, 2019.

Livingstone, David. *The Last Journals of David Livingstone in Central Africa. From eighteen hundred and sixty-five to his death. Continued by a narrative of his last moments and sufferings, obtained from his faithful servants Chuma and Susi*, ed. Horace Waller. New York: Harper & Brothers, 1875.

'Letters of the Late Dr. Livingstone'. *Proceedings of the Royal Geographical Society of London*, 18, 3 (1873–4): 255–81.

Loffman, Reuben A. *Church, State, and Colonialism in Southeastern Congo, 1890–1962*. Cham: Palgrave Macmillan, 2019.

Loimeier, Roman. 'Africa south of the Sahara to the First World War', in *The New Cambridge History of Islam*, V, ed. Robinson: 269–98

'The baraza: A grass root institution in East Africa', in *Lieux de sociabilité urbaine*, eds. Fourchard, Georg, and Gomez-Perez: 171–90.

Lovejoy, Paul E. 'Slavery, the Bilād al-Sūdān and the frontiers of the African diaspora', in *Slavery on the Frontiers*, ed. Lovejoy: 1–30.

Transformations in Slavery: A history of slavery in Africa, 3rd edition. Cambridge: Cambridge University Press, 2011.

ed. *Slavery on the Frontiers of Islam*. Princeton: Markus Wiener Publishers, 2004.

Lydon, Ghislaine. *On Trans-Saharan Trails: Islamic law, trade networks, and cross-cultural exchange in nineteenth-century western Africa*. Cambridge: Cambridge University Press, 2009.

MacGaffey, Wyatt. 'Changing representations in Central African history'. *The Journal of African History*, 46, 2 (2005): 189–207.

Machado, Pedro. *Ocean of Trade: South Asian merchants, Africa and the Indian Ocean, 1750–1850*. Cambridge: Cambridge University Press, 2014.

Macola, Giacomo. *The Gun in Central Africa: A history of technology and politics*. Athens, OH: Ohio University Press, 2016. Kindle edition.

MacQueen, James. 'Notes on African geography'. *Journal of the Royal Geographical Society of London*, 15 (1845): 371–6.

Maddox, Gregory H. 'The church and Cigogo: Fr. Stephen Mlundi and Christianity in Central Tanzania', in *East African Expressions of Christianity*, eds. Spear and Kimambo: 150–66.

Maddox, Gregory H. and Ernest M. Kongola. *Practicing History in Central Tanzania: Writing, memory, and performance*. Porstmouth, NH: Heinemann, 2006.

Maddox, Gregory H., James L. Giblin, and Isaria N. Kimambo, eds. *Custodians of the Land: Ecology and culture in the history of Tanzania*. London: James Currey, 1996.

Malekandathil, Pius. 'Introduction,' in *The Indian Ocean*, ed. Malekandathil: 15–60.

ed. *The Indian Ocean in the Making of Early Modern India*. London: Routledge, 2017.

Manning, Patrick. 'Merchants, porters, and canoemen in the Bight of Benin: Links in the West African trade network', in *The Workers of African Trade*, eds. Coquery-Vidrovitch and Lovejoy: 51–74.

Slavery and African Life: Occidental, oriental and African slave trades. Melksham: Cambridge University Press, 1990.

Mapunda, Bertram B. B. 'Fipa iron technologies and the implied social history', in *East African Archaeology*, eds. Kusimba and Kusimba: 71–86.

Martin, B. G. *Muslim Brotherhoods in Nineteenth-Century Africa*. Cambridge: Cambridge University Press, 1976.

'Muslim politics and resistance to colonial rule: Shaykh Uways B. Muhammad Al-Barawi and the Qadiriya Brotherhood in East Africa'. *The Journal of African History*, 10, 3 (1969): 471–86.

Mbava, N., M. Mutema, R. Zengeni, H. Shimelis, and V. Chaplot. 'Factors affecting crop water use efficiency: A worldwide meta-analysis'. *Agricultural Water Management*, 228 (2020): 1–11.

McCann, James C. *Maize and Grace: Africa's encounter with a New World crop, 1500–2000*. Cambridge, MA: Harvard University Press, 2009.

McCaskie, T. C. 'Cultural encounters: Britain and Africa in the nineteenth century', in *The Oxford History of the British Empire*, III, ed. Porter: 665–90.

McCurdy, Sheryl. 'Fashioning sexuality: Desire, Manyema ethnicity, and the creation of the "kanga," "ca." 1880–1900'. *International Journal of African Historical Studies*, 39, 3 (2006): 441–69.

'Transforming associations: Fertility, therapy, and the Manyema diaspora in Urban Kigoma, Tanganyika, c.1850–1993'. Unpublished PhD dissertation, Columbia University, 2000.

McDougall, James. 'Frontiers, borderlands and Saharan/World history', in *Saharan Frontiers*, eds. McDougall and Scheele: 73–90.

McDougall, James and Judith Scheele, eds. *Saharan Frontiers: Space and mobility in northwest Africa*. Bloomington: Indian University Press, 2012.

McDow, Thomas F. 'Arabs and Africans: Commerce and kinship from Oman to the East African interior, c.1820–1900'. Unpublished PhD dissertation, Yale University, 2008.

Buying Time: Debt and mobility in the western Indian Ocean. Athens, OH: Ohio University Press, 2018.

McKim, Wayne. 'House types in Tanzania: A century of change'. *Journal of Cultural Geography*, 6, 1 (1985): 51–77.

McMahon, Elisabeth. *Slavery and Emancipation in Islamic East Africa: From honor to respectability*. Cambridge: Cambridge University Press, 2013.

McNeill, J. R. *The Mountains of the Mediterranean World: An environmental history*. Cambridge: Cambridge University Press, 1992.

McNeill, J. R. and Erin Stewart Mauldin, eds. *A Companion to Global Environmental History*. Chichester: Wiley Blackwell, 2015.

McPherson, Kenneth. *The Indian Ocean: A history of people and the sea*. New York: Oxford University Press, 1993.

McQuade, Joseph. *A Genealogy of Terrorism: Colonial law and the origins of an idea*. Cambridge: Cambridge University Press, 2020.

Médard, Henri. 'Introduction', in *Traites et Esclavages*, eds. Médard, Derat, Vernet, and Ballarin: 9–28.

'La peste et les missionnaires: Santé et syncrétisme medical au royaume du Buganda à la fin du XIXe siècle'. *Outre-mers*, 92, 346–7 (2005): 79–101.

Le royaume du Buganda au XIXe siècle: Mutations politiques et religieuses d'un ancient état d'Afrique de l'est. Paris: Karthala, 2007.

'La traite et l'esclavage en Afrique orientale et dans l'Océan Indien: Une historiographie éclatée', in *Traites et esclavages en Afrique orientale*, eds. Médard, Derat, Vernet, and Ballarin: 31–64.

Médard, Henri, Marie-Laure Derat, Thomas Vernet, and Marie-Pierre Ballarin, eds. *Traites et esclavages en Afrique orientale et dans l'Ocean Indien*. Paris: Karthala, 2013.

Médard, Henri and Shane Doyle, eds. *Slavery in the Great Lakes Region of East Africa*. Oxford: James Currey, 2006.

Meier, Prita. *Swahili Port Cities: The architecture of elsewhere*. Bloomington: Indiana University Press, 2016.

Meier, Prita and Allyson Purpura, eds. *World on the Horizon: Swahili arts across the Indian Ocean*. Champaign, IL: Krannert Art Museum and Kinkead Pavilion 2018.

Menon, Ramachandran. 'Zanzibar in the nineteenth century: Aspects of urban development an East African coast town'. Unpublished MA dissertation, UCLA, 1978.

Metcalf, Thomas. *Imperial Connections: India in the Indian Ocean arena, 1860–1920*. Berkeley: University of California Press, 2007.

Middel, Matthias, ed. *The Routledge Handbook of Transregional Studies*. New York: Routledge, 2019.

Middleton, John. *African Merchants of the Indian Ocean: Swahili of the East African coast*. Long Grove: Waveland Press, 2004.

Miers, Suzanne. 'Slavery: A question of definition'. *Slavery and Abolition*, 24, 2 (2003): 1–16.

Miers, Suzanne and Igor Kopytoff, eds. *Slavery in Africa: Historical and anthropological perspectives*. Madison: University of Wisconsin Press, 1977.

Miracle, Marvin P. 'The introduction and spread of maize in Africa'. *The Journal of African History*, 6, 1 (1965): 39–55.

Moloney, J. A. *With Captain Stairs to Katanga*. London: S. Low, Marston & Co., 1893.

Monson, Jamie. '*Maisha*: Life history and the history of livelihood along the TAZARA railway in Tanzania', in *Sources and Methods in African History*, eds. Falola and Jennings: 312–30.

Moyd, Michelle R. *Violent Intermediaries: African soldiers, conquest, and everyday colonialism in German East Africa*. Athens, OH: Ohio University Press, 2014.

Msiska, Augustine W. C. 'The spread of Islam in Malawi and its impact on Yao rites of passage, 1870–1960'. *The Society of Malawi Journal*, 48, 1 (1995): 49–86.

Mudimbe, V. Y. *The Invention of Africa: Gnosis, philosophy, and the order of knowledge*. Bloomington: Indiana University Press, 1988.

Mukherjee, Rila. 'Escape from terracentrism: Writing a water history'. *Indian Historical Review*, 41 (2014): 87–101.

Murjebi, Hamed bin Muhammed el-. *L'autobiographie de Hamed ben Mohammed el-Murjebi Tippo Tip (ca. 1840–1905)*. Translated by François Bontinck. Brussels: Académie Royale des Sciences d'Outre Mer, 1974.

Maisha ya Hamed bin Muhammed el Murjebi yaani Tippu Tip kwa maneno yake mwenyewe. Translated by W.H. Whitely. Dar es Salaam: East African Literature Bureau, 1974.

Murray, Alan V., ed. *The Clash of Cultures on the Medieval Baltic Frontier*. Farnham: Ashgate, 2009.

Musambachine, Mwelwa C. 'Nshimba (Simba) (c1820–1896) of Kilwa Island in the southwest corner of Lake Mweru, Zambia: A biography of an East African trader'. Unpublished paper. www.academia.edu/13153828/ Nshimba_Simba_c1820_1896_of_Kilwa_Island_in_the_Southwest_ Corner_of_Lake_Mweru_Zambia_A_Biography_of_an_East_African_ Trader (accessed 29 Apr. 2021).

Myers, Garth Andrew. 'Eurocentrism and African urbanization: The case of Zanzibar's other side'. *Antipode*, 26, 3 (1994): 195–215.

Verandahs of Power: Colonialism and space in urban Africa. Syracuse, NY: Syracuse University Press, 2003.

Nash, David J., Kathleen Pribyl, Georgina H. Endfield, Jørgen Klein, and George C. D. Adamson. 'Rainfall variability over Malawi during the late 19th century'. *International Journal of Climatology*, 38, S1 (2018): 629–42.

Newbury, David S. *Land beyond the Mists: Essays on identity and authority in precolonial Congo and Rwanda*. Athens, OH: Ohio University Press, 2009.

Nicholson, Sharon E. 'Climate and climatic variability of rainfall over eastern Africa'. *Reviews of Geophysics*, 55, 3 (2017): 595–635.

'Climatology: Methods'. *Oxford Research Encyclopedia of African History* (2017). https://doi.org/10.1093/acrefore/9780190277734.013.27 (accessed 7 Dec. 2020).

'Historical fluctuations of Lake Victoria and other lakes in the northern Rift Valley of East Africa', in *Environmental Change and Response in East African Lakes*, ed. Lehman: 7–35.

'Historical and modern fluctuations of Lakes Tanganyika and Rukwa and their relationship to rainfall variability'. *Climatic Change*, 41, 1 (1999): 53–71.

Nicholson, Sharon E., Chris Funk, and Andreas H. Fink. 'Rainfall over the African continent from the 19th through the 21st century'. *Global and Planetary Change*, 165 (2018): 114–27.

Nicholson, Sharon E. and Jeeyoung Kim. 'The relationship of the El-Niño Southern Oscillation to African rainfall'. *International Journal of Climatology*, 17 (1997): 117–35.

Nicholson, Sharon E. and Xungang Yin. 'Rainfall conditions in equatorial East Africa during the nineteenth century as inferred from the record of Lake Victoria'. *Climatic Change*, 48 (2001): 387–98.

Nicolini, Beatrice. 'Re-reading the role of Oman within its international trade relations from 16th to the 19th centuries', in *Regionalizing Oman*, ed. Wippel: 149–57.

Nielsen, R. L. 'Effects of flooding or ponding on corn prior to tasseling' (May 2019). www.kingcorn.org/news/timeless/PondingYoungCorn.html (accessed 10 July 2020).

Nimtz, August H. *Islam and Politics in East Africa: The Sufi order in Tanzania.* Minneapolis: University of Minnesota Press, 1980.

Northrup, David. *Beyond the Bend in the River: African labor in Eastern Zaire.* Athens, OH: Ohio University Center for African Studies, 1988.

Odada, Eric O. and Daniel O. Olago, eds. *The East African Great Lakes: Limnology, palaeolimnology, and biodiversity.* Boston, MA: Kluwer Academic Publishers, 2002.

Oded, Ayre. *Islam in Uganda: Islamization through a centralized state in pre-colonial Africa.* New York: J. Wiley & Sons, 1974.

Oliver, Paul, ed. *The Encyclopedia of Vernacular Architecture*, 3 Vols. Cambridge: Cambridge University Press, 1997.

Oliver, Roland. 'Discernible developments in the interior, c.1500–1840', in *History of East Africa*, I, eds. Oliver and Mathew: 169–211.

Oliver, Roland and Gervase Mathew, eds. *History of East Africa*, 3 Vols. Oxford: Clarendon Press, 1963.

Oliver, Roland and Neville Sanderson, eds. *The Cambridge History of Africa*, Vol 6, *From 1870 to 1905*. Cambridge: Cambridge University Press, 1985.

Page, Melvin E. 'The Manyema hordes of Tippu Tip: A case study in social stratification and the slave trade in eastern Africa'. *The International Journal of African Historical Studies*, 7, 1 (1974): 69–84.

Pallaver, Karin. 'Muslim communities, long-distance trade and wage labour along the central caravan road: Tanzania, 19th century'. *Storicamente*, 8 (2012): 1–10.

'New modes of production, urbanization and the development of Islam in nineteenth-century Tanzania', in *Themes in Modern African History*, eds. Berge and Taddia: 31–48.

'Nyamwezi participation in nineteenth-century East African long-distance trade: Some evidence from missionary sources'. *Africa: Rivista trimestrale di studi e documentazione dell'Istituto italiana per l'Africa e l'Oriente*, 6, 3 (2006): 513–31.

'"A recognised currency in beads" – Glass beads as money in nineteenth-century East Africa: The central caravan road', in *Money in Africa*, eds. Eagleton, Fuller, and Perkins: 20–9.

'A triangle: Spatial processes of urbanization and political power in 19th-century Tabora, Tanzania'. *Afriques: Débats, méthodes et terrains d'histoire*, 11 (2020): 1–32.

'From Venice to East Africa: History, uses, and meanings of glass beads', in *Luxury in Global Perspective*, eds. Grewe and Hofmeester: 192–217.

'What East Africans got for their ivory and slaves: The nature, working and circulation of commodity currencies in nineteenth-century East Africa', in *Currencies of the Indian Ocean World*, eds. Serels and Campbell: 71–92.

Patterson, Orlando. *Slavery and Social Death: A comparative study*. London: Harvard University Press, 1982.

Peacock, A. C. S., ed. *The Frontiers of the Ottoman World*. Oxford: Oxford University Press, 2009.

Peacock, A. C. S., Bruno de Nicola, and Sara Nur Yildiz, eds. *Islam and Christianity in Medieval* Anatolia. Burlington: Ashgate, 2015.

Pearson, Michael N. *The Indian Ocean*. London: Routledge, 2003.

'Littoral society: The case for the coast'. *The Great Circle*, 8, 1 (1985): 1–8.

'Littoral society: The concept and the problems'. *Journal of World History*, 17, 4 (2006): 353–73.

Port Cities and Intruders: The Swahili Coast, India, and Portugal in the early modern era. Baltimore, MD: Johns Hopkins University Press, 1998.

Pearson, Michael Parker and Colin Richards, eds. *Architecture and Order: Approaches to social space*. London: Routledge, 1997.

Pehlivan, Zozan. 'El Ninõ and the nomads: Global climate, local environment, and the crisis of pastoralism in late-Ottoman Kurdistan'. *Journal of the Economic and Social History of the Orient*, 63, 3 (2020): 316–56.

Peniston-Bird, Corinna M. 'Oral history: The sound of memory', in *History beyond the Text*, eds. Barber and Peniston-Bird: 105–21.

Perks, Robert and Alistair Thomson, eds. *The Oral History Reader*, 2nd edition. Abingdon: Routledge, 2006.

Pesek, Michael. 'Cued speeches: The emergence of *shauri* as colonial praxis in German East Africa, 1850–1903'. *History in Africa*, 33 (2006): 395–412.

'Ruga-ruga: The history of an African profession, 1820–1918', in *German Colonialism Revisited*, eds. Berman, Mühlhahn, and Nganang: 85–100.

Pollard, Edward John. 'The maritime landscape of Kilwa Kisiwani and its region, Tanzania, 11th to 15th century AD'. *Journal of Anthropological Archaeology*, 27, 3 (2008): 265–80.

Porter, Andrew, ed. *The Oxford History of the British Empire*, Vol. III, *The Nineteenth Century*. Oxford: Oxford University Press, 1999.

Pouwels, Randall L. 'The East African coast, c.750–1900', in *The History of Islam in Africa*, eds. Levtzion and Pouwels: 251–72.

Horn and Crescent: Cultural change and traditional Islam on the East African coast, 800–1900. Cambridge: Cambridge University Press, 1987.

Prange, Sebastian. *Monsoon Islam: Trade and faith on the medieval Malabar Coast*. New York: Cambridge University Press, 2018.

Preiser-Kapeller, Johannes. 'Liquid frontiers: A relational analysis of maritime Asia Minor as a religious contact zone in the thirteenth–fifteenth centuries', in *Islam and Christianity in Medieval Anatolia*, eds. Peacock, Nicola, and Yildiz: 86–109.

Prestholdt, Jeremy. *Domesticating the World: African consumerism and the genealogies of globalization*. Berkeley: University of California Press, 2008.

Ranger, Terence. 'The invention of tradition revisited: The case of colonial Africa', in *Legitimacy and the State*, eds. Ranger and Vaughan: 62–111.

Ranger, Terence and Isaria N. Kimambo, eds. *The Historical Study of African Religion*. Berkeley: University of California Press, 1972.

Ranger, Terence and Olufemi Vaughan, eds. *Legitimacy and the State in Twentieth-Century Africa: Essays in honour of A.H.M. Kirk-Greene*. Oxford: St Antony's/Macmillan Series, 1993.

Reefe, Thomas Q. *Rainbow and the Kings: A history of the Luba Empire to 1891*. Berkeley: University of California Press, 1981.

Reichard, Paul. *Deutsch-Ostafrika: Das land und seine bewohner*. Leipzig: O. Spammer, 1892.

Reid, Richard J. *Frontiers of Violence in North-East Africa: Genealogies of conflict since c.1800*. Oxford: Oxford University Press, 2011.

'The Ganda on Lake Victoria: A nineteenth-century East African imperialism'. *The Journal of African History*, 39, 3 (1998): 349–63.

'Mutesa and Mirambo: Thoughts on East African warfare and diplomacy in the nineteenth century'. *The International Journal of African Historical Studies*, 31, 1 (1998): 73–89.

'Past and presentism: The 'precolonial' and the foreshortening of African history'. *The Journal of African History*, 52, 2 (2011): 135–55.

Political Power in Pre-colonial Buganda: Economy, society and warfare in the nineteenth century. Oxford: James Currey, 2002.

War in Pre-colonial Eastern Africa: The patterns and meanings of state-level conflict in the nineteenth century. Athens OH, Ohio University Press, 2007.

Warfare in African History. Cambridge: Cambridge University Press, 2012.

'Warfare and urbanisation: The relationship between town and conflict in precolonial eastern Africa'. *Azania: Archaeological Research in Africa*, 36–7 (2001): 46–62.

Reid, Richard J. and Henri Médard. 'Merchants, missions and the remaking of the urban environment in Buganda, c.1840–90', in *Africa's Urban Past*, eds. Anderson and Rathbone: 98–108.

Richards, Sandra L. 'What is to be remembered? Tourism to Ghana's slave castle-dungeons'. *Theatre Journal*, 57, 4 (2005): 617–37.

Ricklefs, M. C. 'Rediscovering Islam in Javanese history'. *Studia Islamika*, 21, 3 (2014): 397–418.

Roberts, Allen F. *A Dance of Assassins: Performing early colonial hegemony in the Congo*. Bloomington: Indiana University Press, 2013.

'Fipa', in *The Encyclopedia of Vernacular Architecture*, III, ed. Oliver: 1976–7.

'"Fishers of men": Religion and political economy among colonized Tabwa', *Africa*, 54, 2 (1984): 49–70.

'Heroic beasts and beastly heroes: Principals of cosmology and chiefship among the lakeside Batabwa of Zaire'. Unpublished PhD dissertation, University of Chicago, 1981.

'Precolonial Tabwa textiles'. *Museum Anthropology*, 20, 1 (1996): 47–59.

'Tabwa', in *The Encyclopedia of Vernacular Architecture*, III, ed. Oliver: 2012.

Roberts, Andrew. 'The history of Abdullah ibn Suliman'. *African Social Research*, 4 (1967): 241–70.

A History of the Bemba: Political growth and change in northeastern Zambia before 1900. London: Longman, 1973.

'The Nyamwezi', in *Tanzania before 1900*, ed. Roberts: 117–50.

'Nyamwezi trade', in *Pre-colonial African Trade*, eds. Gray and Birmingham: 39–74.

'Political change in the nineteenth century', in *A History of Tanzania*, eds. Kimambo and Temu: 57–84.

ed. *Tanzania before 1900*. Nairobi: East African Publishing House, 1968.

Robinson, Francis, ed. *The New Cambridge History of Islam*, Vol. V, *The Islamic World in the Age of Western Dominance*. Cambridge: Cambridge University Press, 2011.

Rockel, Stephen J. 'Caravan porters of the *Nyika*: Labour, culture and society in nineteenth century Tanzania'. Unpublished PhD dissertation, University of Toronto, 1997.

Carriers of Culture: Labor on the road in nineteenth-century East Africa. Portsmouth, NH: Heinemann, 2006.

'Enterprising partners: Caravan women in nineteenth century Tanzania'. *Canadian Journal of African Historical Studies*, 34, 3 (2000): 748–78.

'Forgotten caravan towns in 19th century Tanzania: Mbwamaji and Mpwapwa'. *Azania: Archaeological Research in Africa*, 41, 1 (2006): 1–25.

'A forgotten drought and famine in East Africa, 1883–85', in *Droughts, Floods, and Global Climatic Anomalies*, ed. Gooding: 289–343.

'A nation of porters: The Nyamwezi and the labour market in nineteenth-century Tanzania'. *The Journal of African History*, 41, 2 (2000): 173–95.

'From shore to shore: People, places, and objects between the Swahili coast and Lake Tanganyika', in *World on the Horizon*, eds. Meier and Purpura: 71–88.

'Slavery and freedom in nineteenth century East Africa: The case of the Waungwana caravan porters'. *African Studies*, 68, 1 (2009): 87–109.

'The Tutsi and the Nyamwezi: Cattle, mobility, and the transformation of agro-pastoralisim in nineteenth-century western Tanzania'. *History in Africa*, 46 (2019): 231–61.

Roorda, Eric, ed. *The Ocean Reader: History, culture, politics*. Durham, NC: Duke University Press, 2020.

Ross, Robert, Marja Hinfelaar, and Iva Peša, eds. *The Objects of Life in Central Africa: The history of consumption and social change, 1840–1890*. Leiden: Brill, 2013.

Rossabi, Morris. 'Mongol Empire and its impact on Chinese porcelains', in *Early Global Interconnectivity*, ed. Schottenhammer: 251–9.

Rossi, Benedetta. 'Introduction: Rethinking slavery in West Africa', in *Reconfiguring Slavery*, ed. Rossi: 1–23.

ed. *Reconfiguring Slavery: West African trajectories*. Liverpool: Liverpool University Press, 2009.

Saini, Hargurdeep S. and Mark E. Westgate. 'Reproductive development in grain crops during drought'. *Advances in Agronomy*, 68 (1999): 60–96.

Schaller, Natalie, Thomas Griesser, Andreas Marc Fischer, Alexander Stickler, and Stefan Brönnimann. 'Climate effects of the 1883 Krakatoa eruption: Historical and present perspectives'. *Vierteljahrsschrift der Naturforschenden Gesellschaft in Zürich*, 154, 1–2 (2009): 31–40.

Scherer, J. H. 'The Ha of Tanganyika'. *Anthropos*, 54, 5–6 (1959): 892–3.

Schmidt, Peter R. and Stephen A. Mrozowski, eds. *The Death of Prehistory*. Oxford: Oxford University Press, 2013.

Schmitz, Robert and Cyrille van Overbergh. *Les Baholoholo*. Brussels: A. Dewit, 1912.

Schoenbrun, David L. 'Cattle herds and banana gardens: The historical geography of the western Great Lakes region, *ca* AD 800–1500'. *The African Archaeological* Review, 11 (1993): 39–72.

'Conjuring the modern in Africa: Durability and rupture in histories of public healing between the Great Lakes of East Africa'. *The American Historical Review*, 111, 5 (2006): 1403–39.

'Violence, marginality, scorn and honour: Language evidence of slavery to the eighteenth century', in *Slavery in the Great Lakes*, eds. Médard and Doyle: 38–75.

Schottenhammer, Angela, ed. *Early Global Interconnectivity across the Indian Ocean World*, Vol. II, *Exchange of ideas, religions, and technologies*. Cham: Palgrave Macmillan, 2019.

Serels, Steven. 'Food insecurity and political instability in the southern Red Sea region during the "Little Ice Age", 1650–1840', in *Famines during the 'Little Ice Age'*, eds. Collet and Schuh: 115–29.

Serels, Steven and Gwyn Campbell, eds. *Currencies of the Indian Ocean World*. Cham: Palgrave, 2019.

Shepherd, Gillian Marie. 'The Comorians in Kenya: The establishment and loss of an economic niche'. Unpublished PhD dissertation, London School of Economics, 1982.

Sheriff, Abdul. *Dhow Cultures of the Indian Ocean: Cosmopolitanism, commerce, and Islam*. London: Hurst, 2010.

'History of Zanzibar to 1890'. *Oxford Research Encyclopedia of African History* (2020). https://doi.org/10.1093/acrefore/9780190277734.013.669 (accessed 28 Nov. 2020).

Slaves, Spices and Ivory in Zanzibar: Integration of an East African commercial empire into the world economy, 1770–1873. Woodbridge: James Currey, 1987.

'The spatial dichotomy of Swahili towns: The case of Zanzibar in the nineteenth century'. *Azania: Archaeological Research in Africa*, 36–7, 1 (2001): 63–81.

'The Swahili in the African and Indian Ocean worlds to c.1500'. *Oxford Research Encyclopedia of African History* (2017). https://doi.org/10.1093/acrefore/9780190277734.013.152 (accessed 7 Dec. 2020).

Shorter, Aylward. 'Nyungu-ya-Mawe and the "Empire of the Ruga-Rugas"'. *The Journal of African History*, 9, 2 (1968): 235–59.

Simchile, Peter. *A History of the White Fathers in Western Tanzania: Their work in the Vicariate of Tanganyika with special emphasis on today's dioceses of Sumbawanga and Mpanda (1870–2002)*. Self-published, 2002.

Sinclair, Paul. 'Urbanism', in *The Swahili World*, eds. Wynne-Jones and LaViolette: 185–93.

Singh, Deepti, Richard Seager, Benjamin I. Cook, Mark Cane, Mingfang Ting, Edward Cook, and Mike Davis. 'Climate and the global famine of 1876–78'. *Journal of Climate*, 31, 23, (2018): 9445–67.

Sivasundaram, Sujit. 'The Indian Ocean', in *Oceanic Histories*, eds. Armitage, Bashford, and Sivasundaram: 31–61.

Sivasundaram, Sujit, Alison Bashford, and David Armitage. 'Introduction: Writing world oceanic histories', in *Oceanic Histories*, eds. Armitage, Bashford, and Sivasundaram: 1–28.

Smith, Alison. 'The southern section of the interior, 1840–84', in *History of East Africa*, I, eds. Oliver and Mathew: 253–96.

Smith, Stefan Halikowski and K. N. Chaudhuri, eds. *Reinterpreting Indian Ocean Worlds: Essays in honour of Kirti N. Chaudhuri*. Newcastle upon Tyne: Cambridge Scholars Pub., 2011.

Spear, Thomas. 'Toward the history of African Christianity', in *East African Expressions of Christianity*, eds. Spear and Kimambo: 3–24.

   Zwangendaba's Ngoni 1821–1890: A political and social history of a migration. Madison: African Studies Program, University of Wisconsin, 1972.

Spear, Thomas and Isaria N. Kimambo, eds. *East African Expressions of Christianity*. Oxford: James Currey, 1999.

Speke, John Hanning. 'Journal of a cruise on the Tanganyika Lake, Central Africa'. *Blackwood's Edinburgh Magazine*, 86 (1859): 339–57.

   Journal of the Discovery of the Source of the Nile. New York: Harper & Brothers, 1864.

   What Led to the Discovery of the Source of the Nile. Edinburgh: William Blackwood and Sons, 1864.

Sperling, David C. 'The coastal hinterland and the interior of East Africa', in *The History of Islam in Africa*, eds. Levtzion and Pouwels: 273–302.

Spinage, Clive A. *African Ecology: Benchmarks and historical perspectives*. New York: Springer, 2012.

St. John, Christopher. 'Kazembe and the Tanganyika-Nyasa corridor, 1800–1890', in *Pre-colonial African Trade*, eds. Gray and Birmingham: 202–27.

Stanley, Henry Morton. *How I Found Livingstone: Travels, adventures, and discoveries in central Africa including four months' residence with Dr. Livingstone*. London: Sampson Low, Marston & Company, 1872.

   Through the Dark Continent or the Sources of the Nile around the Great Lakes of Equatorial Africa and down the Livingstone River to the Atlantic Ocean, 2 Vols. London: Sampson Low, Marston, Searle & Irvington, 1878.

Starkey, Janet, Paul Starkey, and Tony Wilkinson, eds. *Natural Resources and Cultural Connections of the Red Sea*. Oxford: Archaeopress, 2007.

Steduto, Pasquale, Theodore C. Hsiao, Elias Fereres, and Dirk Raes. *Crop Yield Response to Water: FAO irrigation and drainage paper 66*. Rome: Food and Agriculture Organization of the United Nations, 2012.

Stoler, Ann Laura. *Along the Archival Grain: Epistemic anxieties and colonial common sense*. Princeton: Princeton University Press, 2009.

Subrahmanyam, Sanjay. 'Between eastern Africa and western India, 1500–1650: Slavery, commerce, and elite formation', *Comparative Studies in Society and History*, 61, 4 (2019): 805–34.

Sundqvist, H. S., K. Holmgren, J. Fohlmeister, Q. Zhang, M. Bar Matthews, C. Spötl, and H. Könich. 'Evidence of a large cooling between 1690 and 1740 AD in southern Africa'. *Scientific Reports*, 3, 1767 (2013): 1–6.

Suriano, Maria. 'Local ideas of fashion and translocal connections: A view from upcountry Tanganyika', in *Translocal Connections across the Indian Ocean*, ed. Declich: 163–89.

Sutton, J. E. G. and Andrew Roberts. 'Uvinza and its salt industry'. *Azania: Archaeological Research in Africa*, 3, 1 (1968): 45–86.

Swann, Alfred J. *Fighting the Slave-Hunters in Central Africa: A record of twenty-six years of travel and adventure round the Great Lakes and of the overthrow of Tip-tu-tib, Rumaliza, and other great slave-traders*. Philadelphia: J. B. Lippincott Company, 1910.

Thomson, Joseph. *To the Central African Lakes and Back: The narrative of the Royal Geographical Society's East Central African Expedition, 1878–80*, 2 Vols. London: Sampson Low, Marston, Searle, & Rivington, 1881.

Thornton, John. 'The slave trade in eighteenth century Angola: Effects on demographic structures'. *Canadian Journal of African Historical Studies*, 14, 3 (1980): 417–27.

Tosh, John and Sean Lang. *The Pursuit of History: Aims, methods and new directions in the study of modern history*, 4th edition. Edinburgh: Pearson Education, 2006.

Trimingham, J. Spencer. *Islam in East Africa*. Oxford: Clarendon Press, 1964.

Tripe, W. B. 'The death and replacement of a divine king in Uha'. *Man*, 39, 2 (1939): 22–5.

Trivier, E. *Mon voyage au continent noir: La 'Gironde' en Afrique*. Paris: Firmin-Didot & Cie, 1891.

Turner, Frederick Jackson. *The Significance of the Frontier in American History*. Madison: State Historical Society of Wisconsin, 1894.

Um, Nancy. *The Merchant Houses of Mocha: Trade and architecture in an Indian Ocean port*. Seattle: University of Washington Press, 2009.

Unomah, Alfred Chukwudi. 'Economic expansion and political change in Unyanyembe: (Ca.1840–1890)'. Unpublished PhD dissertation, University of Ibadan, 1972.

Van Asten, P. J. A., A. M. Fermont, and G. Taulya. 'Drought is a major yield loss factor for rainfed East African banana'. *Agricultural Water Management*, 98, 4 (2011): 541–52.

Van Zwanenberg, R. M. A. with Anne King. *An Economic History of Kenya and Uganda, 1800–1970*. London: Macmillan, 1975.

Vansina, Jan. 'Notes sur l'histoire du Burundi', *Aequatoria*, 24, 1 (1961): 1–10.
Paths in the Rainforests: Towards a history of political tradition in equatorial Africa. London: James Currey, 1990.

Verne, Julia. 'The ends of the Indian Ocean: Tracing coastlines in the Tanzanian "hinterland"'. *History in Africa*, 46 (2019): 359–83.

Living Translocality: Space, culture and economy in contemporary Swahili trade. Stuttgart: Franz Steiner Verlag, 2012.

Von Oppen, Achim. 'The making and unmaking of boundaries in the Islamic world: Introduction', *Die Welt des Islams*, New Series, 41, 3 (2001): 277–86.

Vyncke, Ameet. *Brieven van een vlaamschen missionaries in Midden-Afrika*, 3 Vols. Rousselare: J. de Meester, 1898.

Wagner, Michele. 'Environment, community and history: "Nature in mind", in nineteenth- and early twentieth-century Buha, western Tanzania', in *Custodians of the Land*, eds. Maddox, Giblin, and Kimambo: 175–99.

'Trade and commercial attitudes in Burundi before the nineteenth century'. *International Journal of African Historical Studies*, 26, 1 (1993): 149–66.

Walker, John Frederick. *Ivory's Ghosts: The white gold of history and the fate of elephants*. New York: Atlantic Monthly Press, 2009.

Walshaw, Sarah C. 'Converting to rice: Urbanization, Islamization and crops of Pemba Island, Tanzania, AD 700–1500'. *World Archaeology*, 42, 1 (2010): 137–54.

Walz, Jonathan. 'Early inland entanglement in the Swahili world', in *The Swahili World*, eds. Wynne-Jones and LaViolette: 388–402.

'Inland connectivity in ancient Tanzania'. *Islamic Africa*, 8 (2017): 217–17.

'Route to a regional past: An archaeology of the lower Pangani (Ruvu) Basin, Tanzania, 500–1900 C.E.'. Unpublished PhD dissertation, University of Florida, 2010.

'Routes to history: Archaeology and being articulate in eastern Africa', in *The Death of Prehistory*, eds. Schmidt and Mrozowski: 69–91.

Ware III, Rudolph T. *The Walking Qur'an: Islamic education, embodied knowledge, and history in West Africa*. Chapel Hill: University of North Carolina Press, 2014.

Watt, Nigel. *Burundi: The biography of a small African country*, 2nd edition. London: Hurst & Company, 2016.

White, Luise. *The Comforts of Home: Prostitution in colonial Nairobi*. Chicago: University of Chicago Press, 1990.

White, Sam. 'Climate change in global environmental history', in *A Companion to Global Environmental History*, eds. McNeill and Mauldin: 394–410.

A Cold Welcome: The Little Ice Age and Europe's encounter with North America. Cambridge, MA: Harvard University Press, 2018.

White, Sam, Christian Pfister, and Franz Mauelshagen, eds. *The Palgrave Handbook of Climate History*. London: Palgrave Macmillan, 2018.

Willis, Roy G. *The Fipa and Related Peoples of south-west Tanzania and north-east Zambia*. London: Routledge, 2017.

'The great mother and the god of the lake: Royal and priestly power in Ulungu'. *Zambia Journal of History*, 4 (1991): 21–30.

Some Spirits Heal, Others Only Dance: A journey into human selfhood in an African village. Oxford: Berg, 1999.

A State in the Making: Myth, history, and social transformation in pre-colonial Ufipa. Bloomington: Indiana University Press, 1981.

Wilson, Thomas H. 'Spatial analysis and settlement patterns on the East African coast', *Paideuma: Mitteilungen zur Kulturkunde*, 28 (1982): 201–19.

Wippel, S., ed. *Regionalizing Oman: Political, economic and social dynamics.* Dordrecht: Springer Science, 2013.

Wissmann, Hermann Von. *My Second Journey through Equatorial Africa from the Congo to the Zambesi in the Years 1886 and 1887.* Translated by Minna J. A. Bergmann. London: Chatton & Windus, 1891.

Woodward, Mark R. *Java, Indonesia and Islam.* Dordrecht: Springer, 2011.

Wright, Marcia. 'East Africa 1870–1905', in *The Cambridge History of Africa*, VI, eds. Oliver and Sanderson: 539–91.

Strategies of Slaves and Women: Life-stories from East/Central Africa. New York: Lilian Barber Press, 1993.

Wright, Marcia and Peter Lary. 'Swahili settlements in northern Zambia and Malawi'. *African Historical Studies*, 4, 3 (1971): 547–73.

Wynne-Jones, Stephanie. 'Lines of desire: Power and materiality along the Tanzania caravan route'. *Journal of World Prehistory*, 23, 4 (2010): 219–37.

A Material Culture: Consumption and materiality on the coast of precolonial East Africa. Oxford: Oxford University Press, 2016.

'The public life of the Swahili stonehouse, 14th-15th centuries AD'. *Journal of Anthropological Archaeology*, 32, 4 (2013): 759–73.

Wynne-Jones, Stephanie and Adria LaViolette, eds. *The Swahili World.* London: Routledge, 2017.

Wynne-Jones, Stephanie and Jeffrey Fleisher. 'Fifty years in the archaeology of the eastern African coast: A methodological history'. *Azania: Archaeological Research in Africa*, 50, 4 (2015): 519–41.

'Swahili urban spaces of the eastern African coast', in *Making Ancient Cities*, eds. Creekmore and Fisher: 111–44.

Wynne-Jones, Stephanie and Sarah Croucher. 'The central caravan route of Tanzania: A preliminary archaeological reconnaissance'. *Nyame Akuma*, 67 (2007): 91–5.

XiuQi, Fang, Xiao Lingbo, and Wei ZhuDeng. 'Social impacts of the climatic shift around the turn of the 19th century on the North China plain'. *Science China Earth Sciences*, 56 (2013): 1044–58.

Zöller, Katharina. 'Crossing multiple borders: "The Manyema" in colonial East Central Africa'. *History in Africa*, 46 (2019): 299–326.

Index

Printed in the USA
CPSIA information can be obtained
at www.ICGtesting.com
LVHW082324031223
765535LV00005B/108